PHILIPPIKA

Marburger altertumskundliche Abhandlungen 59

Herausgegeben von
Joachim Hengstl, Torsten Mattern,
Robert Rollinger, Kai Ruffing
und Orell Witthuhn

2013

Harrassowitz Verlag · Wiesbaden

Kauf, Konsum und Märkte

Wirtschaftswelten im Fokus – Von der römischen Antike bis zur Gegenwart

Herausgegeben von
Monika Frass

2013
Harrassowitz Verlag · Wiesbaden

Bibliografische Information der Deutschen Nationalbibliothek
Die Deutsche Nationalbibliothek verzeichnet diese Publikation in der Deutschen Nationalbibliografie; detaillierte bibliografische Daten sind im Internet über http://dnb.dnb.de abrufbar.

Bibliographic information published by the Deutsche Nationalbibliothek
The Deutsche Nationalbibliothek lists this publication in the Deutsche Nationalbibliografie; detailed bibliographic data are available in the internet at http://dnb.dnb.de.

Informationen zum Verlagsprogramm finden Sie unter
http://www.harrassowitz-verlag.de

Gedruckt auf alterungsbeständigem Papier.
Druck und Verarbeitung: ⊕ Hubert & Co., Göttingen
Printed in Germany

ISSN 1613-5628
ISBN 978-3-447-06864-2

Inhalt

Vorwort / Einleitung

Vorliegende Publikation basiert auf Vorträgen eines Symposiums zum Thema „Kauf – Konsum und Märkte" („Purchasing, Consumption and Markets"), das im Oktober 2011 in Salzburg vom Fachbereich Altertumswissenschaften veranstaltet wurde. Als Organisatorin dieser Tagung möchte ich mich für die spontane Bereitschaft der Teilnehmer, international ausgewählter Experten, bedanken, mit uns vor Ort aktuelle und traditionelle Wege der Forschung zu diesem auch tagespolitisch brisanten Sujet zu diskutieren. Im Sinne der Pluralität der rezenten wissenschaftlichen Positionen sollte sowohl das wirtschaftstheoretisch-modellhafte Verständnis von „Markt- (Wirtschaft)" und „Märkten" in der römischen Antike entsprechende Berücksichtigung finden, als auch die davon nicht zu trennende (Neu-) Interpretation der reichhaltigen Quellenbasis. Durch die zusätzliche Einbeziehung von Vortragenden aus der modernen Marktwirtschaft (mit Beiträgen zum Produkt-Marketing im regionalen und internationalen Wirtschaftsbereich) wurde zudem ein innovativer interdisziplinärer Austausch ermöglicht und damit die Relevanz dieser Thematik von heute bis zur Antike multiperspektivisch aufgezeigt. Eine Annährung an die mannigfaltigen Aspekte rund um das alltägliche „Marktgeschehen" der antiken Welt erfolgte in speziellen inhaltlichen Kategorien, welchen die mehr als 20 Vorträge zugeordnet waren: „die Bedeutung von Märkten in der modernen Konsumgesellschaft", „Konsum – Produktion – Vertrieb", „Kauf und Konsum in den römischen Provinzen", „die Bedeutung von Auktionen – von der Antike bis heute" und last but not least „Menschen – Märkte – Katastrophen".

Die Intention dieser interdisziplinären Tagung wird auch, wenngleich in bescheidenerem Umfang, in den vorliegenden publizierten Beiträgen deutlich: Neville Morley (Universität Bristol, GB) bietet ausgehend von modernen „Markt"-Theorien der komparativen Geschichte (z.B. Peter Bang), aber auch von Krisenszenarien diverser moderner „Märkte" einen kritischen Einblick in „überholte" (Primitivismus, Modernismus) und rezente wissenschaftliche Positionen und Wirtschaftstheorien (Neue Institutionen Ökonomie, Neoklassik, et al.). Durch Konzentration auf damit verbundene Kernfragen und -probleme, die sich, nicht zuletzt durch die Diskrepanz von idealen theoretischen Modellen, realen menschlichen Verhaltensweisen und der Unkenntnis antiker Bedingungen ergeben, werden auch Möglichkeiten und Grenzen für die weitere Erforschung des „Marktes" in der Antike hinterfragt, von dessen fundamentaler Bedeutung für die antike Wirtschaft der Autor überzeugt ist: „The nature and significance of ‚the market in classical antiquity' is a, if not the, fundamental issue for ancient economic history" (S. 103). Wenngleich der Beitrag von Neville Morley vor allem Einflüsse moderner Theorien in der Betrachtung antiker Wirtschaft aufzeigt, so verweist er auch auf die – keineswegs unumstrittene – Bedeutung antiker Wirtschaft für neuzeitliche Wirtschaftsmodelle: "However, the traffic between disciplines and between past and present is not always one-way; for all that much modern economics regards past experience as essentially irrelevant, it nevertheless rests on implicit historical claims such as a belief in an unchanging human nature, and that means that, at certain times, ancient economic history can contribute to contemporary debates" (S. 119). Entsprechender Thematik widmet sich der Neuzeit Historiker Christian Dirninger (Universität Salzburg, A), der gezielt „die Wirtschaftstheorie der Antike im Lichte der neuzeitlichen Marktwirtschaftslehre" analysiert. Auf der Basis einschlägiger Aussagen von Aristoteles, des „Ahnherrn der neuzeitlichen Wirtschaftsgeschichte" werden bezüglich des Marktverständnisses zwei inhaltliche Dimensionen (institutionell ordnungstechnisch und marktwirtschaftlich funktionell) erfasst, die untrennbar mit Fragen der Wirtschaftsethik und der Bedeutung marktwirtschaftliche Begrenzung verbunden sind.

Neben Einblicken in theorielastige neue und bekannte Wege der Forschung wird der Aussagewert spezifischer antiker Quellenkategorien – rechtshistorischer inschriftlicher Dokumente, Papyri und archäologischer Zeugnisse – für unser Leitthema durch drei weitere Beiträge verdeutlicht. Daniele Mattiangeli, dem Vertreter des Römischen Rechts (Universität Salzburg, A) gelingt es, anhand antiker Kaufverträge (Konsensualverträge), die Bedeutung des antiken Rechtsverständnisses, das sich auch in Form alltäglicher Vertragsabschlüsse äußert, bis in die heutige Zeit aufzuzeigen. Der Vergleich des antiken „Formulars" mit Beispielen moderner Kaufverträge lässt ein übereinstimmendes Grundschema erkennen, das durchaus den heutigen Anforderungen eines Kaufvertrages entspricht und in vielen Rechtsordnungen gültig wäre. Kauf und Ausgaben bilden auch die Basis des papyrologischen Beitrags von Dominic Rathbone (King's College London, GB). Zwei aus dem *grapheion* des Kronion gewählte Verzeichnisse von Ausgaben für diverse Produkte des alltäglichen Bedarfs (vorwiegend „privat") dienen dem Autor jedoch nicht nur zur Präsentation der genannten Waren, sondern auch zu weiterem innovativem Erkenntnisgewinn: Er versucht anhand numismatischer Details die Bedeutung der Monetarisierung im Leben der ländlichen Bevölkerung des römischen Reiches am Beispiel der „bürokratischen" Hinterlassenschaft von Kronion zu hinterfragen, eines vermutlich wohlhabenden Einwohners der römischen Provinz Ägyptens, aus Tebtunis im Fayyum, in den Jahren 45 und 46 n.Chr. Archäologische Zeugnisse, speziell Design von Transportgefäßen – Amphoren von hellenistischer Zeit bis zur Spätantike – stehen im Mittelpunkt der Untersuchung des amerikanischen Autorenkollektivs Nick Rauh/ Caroline Autret/ John Lund. Angeregt durch moderne marktspezifische Erkenntnisse zur Werbewirksamkeit von Verpackungsdesign und dessen Wirkung auf Verbraucher und das Konsumverhalten im Sinne der "sensation transference", versucht man hier hypothetisch und innovativ, eine „marktpsychologische" Erklärung für die im Laufe von Jahrhunderten unterschiedlichen Formen von Transportgefäßen zu finden: Aufwändiger gestaltete Produkte der hellenistischen Zeit werden als Ausdruck einer blühenden Wirtschaft interpretiert, während abgewandelte ästhetisch weniger ansprechende Gefäße der Spätantike mit gebotener Vorsicht auch als Ausdruck wirtschaftlicher Krisenzeiten gedeutet werden: "By applying modern principles of market advertising and packaging design to the study of ancient Mediterranean amphorae we have suggested that the well designed forms of the Hellenistic era functioned as advertising tools in an economy of abundance. The aesthetically inferior but ruggedized forms of the Late Roman era on the other hand appear better designed for use in an era of sustained conflict" (S. 166).

Althistorisch klassische Themen sind vor allem durch die Beiträge von Jesper Carlsen, Kai Ruffing und Ingomar Weiler vertreten. Mit der Rolle von Freigelassenen in der Produktion und im Vertrieb von Wein in der Zeit der Spätantike und in der Römischen Kaiserzeit beschäftigt sich der Althistoriker Jesper Carslen (Universität Aarhus, DK). Er gibt Einblick in die gestreuten überlieferten Tätigkeitsfelder im Zusammenhang mit dem Anbau und der „Vermarktung" von Wein und verweist auf die quellenbedingte Problematik des Nachweises von *liberti/libertini* im merkantilen Vertrieb. Kai Ruffing (Universität Marburg, D) widmet sich, in Anlehnung an Intentionen der Neuen Institutionenökonomik, der Funktion von Auktionen in der römischen Kaiserzeit und ihrem möglichen Beitrag zur Senkung von Transaktionskosten bei der Abwicklung von Geschäften. Als besonders charakteristisch wird dabei das Beispiel des Weinhandels von Ostia präsentiert und damit verbundene wirtschaftliche Kooperationen und soziale Netzwerke.

Mit dem Faktor Mensch und Markt beschäftigen sich zwei nachfolgende Untersuchungen aus unterschiedlichen zeitlichen und sachlichen Blickwinkeln. Der Mensch als Ware und somit als Kauf- und Verkaufsobjekt steht im Mittelpunkt der Untersuchung von Ingomar Weiler (Universität Graz, A). Menschenhandel und Sklaverei von der Antike bis heute werden dabei kritisch und historisch-komparativ hinterfragt. Aufgezeigt werden aber auch konkrete Verkaufs- und Kaufsszenarien auf antiken Märkten und damit verbundene Preis-Leistungskriterien, die Einblick in Angebot und Nachfrage im antiken Sklavenhandel ermöglichen.

In die Zeit des Mittelalters führt der Beitrag des Historikers Christian Rohr (Universität Basel, CH), der das Verhalten von Menschen in Zeiten von Naturkatastrophen beleuchtet. Der Fokus liegt, dem Kernthema entsprechend, auf Auswirkungen dieser elementaren Ereignisse (z.B. Hagel oder Tierplagen) auf das Kaufverhalten. Von Interesse sind auch bewusste menschliche Steuerungen in Krisenzeiten durch Verbote (z.B. Ausfuhrverbote notwendiger Ressourcen) bzw. Adaption in Risikokulturen zur Verringerung der Auswirkungen auf Angebot und Nachfrage.

Die moderne Wirtschaft wird repräsentiert durch den Beitrag „Trends im (Lebensmittel-) Handel. Gestern – Heute – Morgen" von Helmut Eymannsberger (Wirtschaftskammer Salzburg, A). Durch die Strukturierung der vier Grundfunktionen des Handels wird die Logistik dieses merkantilen Bereichs und ihre umfassende gesellschaftliche Vernetzung deutlich: 1. Distributive Funktion, 2. Ökonomische Funktion (Qualität der Ware, Preisbildung/ Vorfinanzierung-Kreditfunktion, 3. Kommunikative Funktion (Information, Beratung, Absatzförderung, Werbung etc.), 4. Servicefunktion (Recycling/Entsorgung, Anpassung an individuelle Kundenbedürfnisse). Als einem der wichtigsten Wirtschaftszweige der Volkswirtschaft wird dem Handel nicht zuletzt durch seine faszinierenden zeitspezifischen Facetten und fassbaren Konstanten eine besondere sozial-ökonomische Bedeutung, als Spiegel der Gesellschaft, zugeordnet.

Die Einbindung moderner aktiver Wirtschaftstreibender in den Kreis historischer Disziplinen sollte, wie nicht zuletzt der Beitrag von Helmut Eymannsberger dokumentiert, mehr sein als nur eine thematische Bereicherung des Vortragangebots. Der Einblick in aktuelles kaufmännisches Denken und marktorientierte Aktivitäten, wie Werbestrategien, Produktmarketing, Risikomanagement und Transaktionskosten ist durchaus dazu geeignet, wie auch Beiträge in dieser Publikation erkennen lassen (vgl. N. Rauh/C. Autret/J. Lund, K. Ruffing) – unter gegebener Vorsicht und unter Berücksichtigung der zeitspezifischen und kulturell unterschiedlichen Komponenten – durch adaptierte Fragestellungen aus der neuzeitlichen Ökonomie der aktuellen Geschichtsforschung neue Impulse zu verleihen. Die unmittelbare Begegnung von Historikern mit modernen Wirtschaftstreibenden verzeichnete zudem einen erfreulichen unmittelbaren Erfolg durch die Sensibilisierung von Unternehmensführungen für die Bedeutung der Geschichte ihrer eigenen Institutionen und ihr Interesse zu weiteren Kooperationen mit Historikern. Die Initiative zur Tagung „Kauf – Konsum und Märkte" in Salzburg und die Beschäftigung mit brandaktuellen wirtschaftlichen Szenarien scheint nicht zuletzt auch der Beschleunigung der fachspezifischen Auseinandersetzung mit modernen ökonomischen (Fehl-) Entwicklungen und potentiellen Lösungsmodellen in der (alt-) historischen Forschungs-Community förderlich gewesen zu sein, wie Neville Morley resümierend in seinem Beitrag vermerkt: "Given the amount of upheaval and controversy in the field of economics at present, in response to the global economic crisis and the perceived failure of the dominant theoretical paradigm, we would generally expect a reconsideration of assumptions in ancient economic history in about a decade or so; the focus of the Salzburg conference on the theme of markets and consumption was thus extremely opportune, a chance to reflect on recent intellectual developments and their implications for ancient history rather more promptly than usual" (S. 119).

Wenngleich im Rahmen dieser Tagung und der daraus hervorgegangenen Publikation wesentliche Aspekte zu „Kauf – Konsum und Märkten" präsentiert und diskutiert werden konnten, so bleiben immer noch viele Frage offen. So u.a. das in Abhandlungen zu Märkten der Antike bisher nur am Rande berücksichtigte Konsum- und Kaufverhalten von Individuen verschiedener sozialer Schichten bzw. von übergeordneten Gemeinschaften, ein faszinierendes vielfach noch unerschlossenes Forschungsgebiet, das mich selbst während meiner Habilitationstudien am Beispiel von bestimmten Immobilien, den sogenannten *horti Romani*, im kaiserzeitlichen Rom auch aus „marktpsychologischer" Sicht näher beschäftigt hat. Gerade hierin liegt meines Erachtens noch reichlich Forschungsdefizit und Bedarf an Aufarbeitung des gestreuten Quellenmaterials, sowohl im historisch/literarischen Textmaterial als auch in Zeugnissen der ergänzenden althistorischen Disziplinen wie vor allem Epigraphik und Papyrologie.

Für die eingereichten Beiträge, die einen weiteren Schritt bei der Erforschung dieser faszinierenden Thematik bilden, möchte ich mich bei allen Autoren herzlich bedanken, vor allem für die unkomplizierte zuverlässige Kooperation von ihrer Bereitschaft zur Teilnahme am Kongress bis zur Drucklegung ihres Beitrags. Mein Dank gilt auch allen weiteren Kongress-Vortragenden, die hier noch einmal namentlich genannt seien: Jean-Jacques Aubert (Universität Neuchâtel, CH), Peter Fibiger Bang (Universität Kopenhagen, DK), John Bodel (Brown Universität Rhode Island, USA), Elio Lo Cascio (Universität Rom/La Sapienza, I); Martin Engelmann (dm-Drogeriemarkt Österreich), Peter Mauritsch (Universität Graz, A), Johannes Nollé (Kommission für Alte Geschichte und Epigraphik – DAI, München, D), Marion Osztovits/Torsten Pedit (Stieglbrauerei Salzburg, A), Peter Scherrer (Universität Graz, A), Walter Sonnberger (Dorotheum Linz/Salzburg, A), Alexander Zeh (GfK Austria GmbH – Custom Research, Wien, A).

Mein Dank gilt auch den Sponsoren der Tagung „Kauf – Konsum und Märkte", den öffentlichen Förderungseinrichtungen, wie dem Bundesministerium für Forschung, der Stadt Salzburg (Magistrat – Kultur und Schule), dem Land Salzburg, der Universität Salzburg; weiters den geschätzten Salzburger Privatunternehmen, die, angeregt durch die Aktualität des Kongressthemas, diese cross-over Veranstaltung durch eigene inhaltliche Beiträge, aber auch finanzielle Unterstützung – durch die letztendlich auch vorliegende Publikation finanziert werden konnte – gefördert haben: DM-Drogeriemarkt Österreich; Kleider Bauer; Stiegl-Brauwelt; Vermögensberatung Robert Schmidauer.

Für die Realisierung der Drucklegung bedanke ich mich beim Verlag Harrassowitz, vor allem bei Herrn Jens Fetkenheuer, ebenso bei den Herausgebern der Reihe Philippika, besonders bei meinem Marburger Kollegen, Kai Ruffing. Für die freundschaftliche Bereitschaft zur Durchsicht der englischsprachigen Beiträge gilt meine Verbundenheit meinem erprobten Koautor gemeinsamer wissenschaftlicher Beiträge, Nigel Crowther (Ontario, Canada). Weiters möchte ich mich bei den verdienten Helferinnen vor Ort bedanken, ohne deren Einsatz die Realisierung des druckfertigen Bandes in der gebotenen Zeit und in der nunmehrigen ansprechenden Gestaltung nicht möglich gewesen wäre. Zum einen bei Sieglinde Fuger für die Hilfe bei den Korrekturarbeiten und last but not least bei Yvonne Wagner (Universität Salzburg/Universität Marburg), die die anspruchsvolle technische Layout-Gestaltung übernommen und in professioneller Weise umgesetzt hat, ohne dabei ihren unvergleichlichen Humor zu verlieren.

Salzburg im Februar 2013

Monika Frass

Freedmen and Wine Production in Roman Italy

Jesper Carlsen

The importance of agriculture in the Roman economy is a well-established fact, but it also raises a number of questions and issues heatedly debated in the recent decades. One important subject is the distribution and trade with agricultural products that has been crucial to the ongoing debate on economic integration in the Roman Empire.[1] This contribution has, however, a more narrow purpose, focussing on two different aspects of purchasing, consumption and markets in the Roman Empire. The point of departure will be a short presentation of the role of freedmen in Roman agriculture, but the paper will focus on the production and distribution of wine in Italy in the Late Republic and Early Empire in order to ask new questions about an important aspect of Roman economy.

Rural Freedmen in Roman Italy

Tacitus tells us in his description of Galba's attempts to make up the deficit after Nero's lavish spending that the new emperor hoped to recover nine-tenths of the 220 million sesterces Nero had used on gifts. But there was the problem that those of Nero's favourites who had been the recipients *had hardly one-tenth left, for they had wasted the money of others on the same extravagances as they had their own; the most greedy and depraved had neither lands nor capital* (non agri aut faenus), *but only what would minister to their vices.*[2] Tacitus does not give us the names of the beneficiaries, but other sources emphasize actors, gladiators and imperial freedmen among Nero's favourites.

Together with Cicero's famous passage in *De officiis* (1,150–151) on respectable trades and employments Tacitus' highly rhetorical paragraph has frequently been used by modern scholars to argue that the principal sources of the wealth of the Roman elite were land and money lending, and that there was a clear separation of commerce and agriculture in the Roman world. Previous research has therefore mostly focused on the importance of Roman freedmen in commerce and business making money for the elite or themselves, using Petronius' fabulously wealthy freedman character Trimalchio as a typical representative of a rich and independent *libertus*.[3] More recent research, however, has shown that *Satyricon* "sometimes faithfully reflects, sometimes comically distorts, contemporary Ro-

1 See Bang 2008 and Bowman-Wilson 2009 for overviews of the debates.

2 Tac.Hist.1,20: *At illis vix decumae super portiones erant, isdem erga aliena sumptibus quibus sua prodegerant, cum rapacissimo cuique ac perditissimo non agri aut faenus, sed sola instrumenta vitiorum manerent.*

3 Rostovtzeff 1957, 57: "a typical representative of this class is the wealthy retired business man of one of the South Italian cities, the freedman Trimalchio, whose portrait is so vividly drawn by Petronius."

man institutions and social realities."[4] According to his autobiographical account, Trimalchio built five ships and loaded them with wine *which was worth its weight in gold at the time*. When the ships were all wrecked and he lost thirty million sesterces in one day, Trimalchio built a larger ship with a cargo of wine, slaves, perfumes, bacon, and beans. He made ten million sesterces on one trip and invested the money in land and estates just as Cicero recommended.[5] But the remark of Trimalchio that *just now I want to join up all Sicily with properties of mine, so that if I take a fancy to go to Africa I shall travel through my own land* is an example of the novel's comical exaggerations.[6]

We have other – non-fictitious – examples of freedmen as landowners in Roman Italy. Cicero's own freedman, Tiro, bought a farm near Puteoli seven or eight years after his manumission as emerges from a letter written by the younger Cicero:

> *I am really delighted to hear that you have bought a property, and hope it turns out a successful investment ... Well, you are a landed proprietor! You must shed your town-bred ways – you are now a Roman squire,* rusticus romanus! *How amusing to picture the delightful sight of you now. I imagine you buying farm tackle, talking to the bailiff, hoarding pips at dessert in your jacket pockets.*[7]

According to Pliny the Elder, perhaps the wealthiest freedman of them all, C. Caecilius Isidorus, made a will in 8 BCE which reveals:

> *that in spite of heavy losses in the civil war he nevertheless left 4116 slaves, 3600 pairs of oxen, 257,000 head of other cattle, and 60 million sesterces in cash, and he gave instructions for 1,100,000 sesterces to be spent on his funeral.*[8]

In this case it has plausibly been suggested that most of this vast fortune was accumulated after Isidorus inherited from his wealthy master, who belonged to the noble *gens* Caecilii Metelli.[9] Further Pliny the Elder mentions in his *Natural History* not only three freedmen with notable success in viticulture, but also the industrious freedman C. Furius Chresimus. He was extremely unpopular among his neighbours because he got much larger returns from his rather small farm than they got from bigger estates. Chresimus was accused of magically increasing his

4 D'Arms 1981, 99.

5 Petr.Sat.76: *et tunc erat contra aurum.*

6 Petr.Sat. 48: *Nunc coniungere agellis Siciliam volo, ut cum Africam libverit ire, per meos fines navigem.*

7 Cic.Fam.16,21,7: *Emisse te praedium vehementer gaudeo feliciterque tibi rem istam evenire cupio ... Habes! Deponendae tibi sunt urbanitates; rusticus Romanus factus es. Quo modo ego mihi nunc ante oculos tuum iucundissimum conspectum propono! Videor enim videre ementem te rusticas res, cum vilico loquentem, in lacinia servantem ex mensa secunda semina.*

8 Plin.Nat.33,135: *quamvis multa bello civili perdidisset, tamen relinquere servorum 4116, iuga boum 3600, reliqui pecoris 257,000, in numerato 60 mill. HS, funerari se iussit 1,100,000 HS.*

9 Brunt 1975; Mouritsen 2011, 241–242.

revenues, but he was acquitted by a unanimous verdict, because he brought all his agricultural implements and slaves into court and declared:

> *These are my magic spells, citizens, and I am not able to exhibit to you or to produce in court my midnight labours and early risings and my sweat and toil.*[10]

Most freedmen involved in agriculture belonged to one of three groups: They were either landowners like the freedmen mentioned by Pliny the Elder or agents, often of their former masters. The third group was tenants, but Walter Scheidel has rightly pointed out that the sources for this group are very ambiguous: "In den literarischen Texten tauchen meines Wissens überhaupt keine Pächter auf, die eindeutig als ehemalige Unfreie zu identifizeren wären."[11] He questioned the few inscriptions mentioning manumitted *coloni*, of which one example is Q. Sertorius Antiochus from Trea in Picenum. His epitaph describes him as *colonus pauper fuit*,[12] but for my purpose it is not important whether Antiochus and the other manumitted *coloni* like L. Accasius Corinthus from Rome were tenants or peasants.[13] In both cases they were involved in agriculture.

I have elsewhere argued that, from the bailiff's point of view, manumission might, perhaps, be a rather unpleasant prospect – representing both a reward and some kind of dismissal. The future of a former *vilicus*, like that of many freedmen, might well depend on the size of his *peculium* and on his agricultural skills if he continued as a farmer on his own estate or as a tenant.[14] There exist only a few studies of the landed possessions of Roman freedmen, and Henrik Mouritsen has recently observed in his important book, "The Freedman in the Roman World (2011)," that "rural freedmen are very difficult to trace epigraphically, in stark contrast to the ubiquitous urban freedmen who put up thousands of inscriptions."[15]

Nero's notorious freedman, L. Domitius Phaon, is a rare exception. Christer Bruun's analysis has shown that Phaon owned at least three estates in different parts of Italy: one was the suburban villa between via Salaria and via Nomentana where Nero committed suicide. But Phaon also owned a *fundus* with a villa near Fundi in Campania, where he paid for a tomb reserved for former members of Domitia Lepida's household. Finally, Phaon owned also at least six *fundi* near Vol-

10 Plin.Nat.18,41–43: *Veneficia mea, Quirites, haec sunt, nec possum vobis ostendere aut in forum adducere lucubrationes meas vigiliasque et sudores.*

11 Scheidel 1993, 191.

12 CIL IX 5659: *Q. Sertorius Q(uinti) l(ibertus)/ Antiochus colonus/ pauper fuit aequo/ animo scibat moriun/dum sibi. Ex testamento/ Balbus Antiochi l(ibertus)/ Sertoria Q(uinti) l(iberta) Europa/ Nonia L(ucii) Asprenatis l(iberta)/ Helena Balbi soror./ In agr(o) p(edes) XVI in fro(nte) p(edes) XIIII.* de Neeve 1984, 195 n.12; Scheidel 1993, 193.

13 CIL VI 9273: *[L(ucius)] Accasius L(ucii) l(ibertus) Corinth[us]/ colonus fecit sibi et / Arriae Sabinae coniugi / suae et Arriae Hedone / matri posterisque suis.* Scheidel 1993, 193: „war zwar eindeutig Freigelassener, aber nicht notwendigerweise auch Pächter."

14 Carlsen 2010, 82; See also Roth 2010.

15 Mouritsen 2011, 198.

cei as attested by an inscription found at Caposele in Lucania where he appears as the benefactor of a *collegium* to Silvanus.[16]

Freedmen and the Wine Production in Roman Italy

The extensive epigraphical and archaeological material from Pompeii and the surrounding districts have provided the basis for several lists with names of villa-owners and wine-growers in this area, where wine production is mentioned several times by Pliny the Elder.[17] R.C. Carrington concluded in his "Studies in the Campanian 'Villae Rusticae'" (1931) that, "the ubiquitous freedman, who played a prominent part in the industrial life of the town, had already found his way into the country and had begun to take his place beside wealthy, aristocratic families, as landowner and farmer", and John Day identified thirteen private wine-producers as freedmen in his article on "Agriculture in the Life of Pompeii."[18] Most of these identifications are, however, either circumstantial or purely fictitious as pointed out by many scholars, including Willem Jongman: "the net result of all this scepticism is that we no longer possess information on the identity and social position of Pompeian wine-growers and villa owners. We may expect them to belong to the wealthier and perhaps also more respectable strata of Pompeian society, but we cannot demonstrate it."[19]

My point of departure for the discussion of freedmen and wine production will therefore be a re-examination of some rather well-known paragraphs in Book Fourteen of Pliny the Elder's Natural History. This book deals with wine-growing, and after discussing varieties of grapes and their use, Pliny presents the local Italian wines. He quotes Cato the Elder who in his De agri cultura recommends the Aminian grape on those parts of the estate estimated to be best for the wine.[20] Then Pliny continues with the statement that in our times, *in nostra aetate*, there have only been a few advances and examples of consummate skill in the wine production, but adds:

> *but it is all the more proper on that account not to omit them, so as also to make known the rewards of success, which in every department attract the greatest attention. Well, the greatest distinction was achieved by Acilius Sthenelus, a* plebe libertina, *by his intensive cultivation of a vineyard of not more than 60 iugera, in the region of Nomentana, which he sold for 400,000 sesterces. Also Vetulenus Aegialus, he too a* libertinus, *gained a great reputation in the district of Liternum in Campania, and a still greater reputation in public esteem on account of his*

16 Suet.Nero.48; CIL X 444 = ILS 3546; AE 1912, no. 219. Bruun 1989 and Gregory 1995, but see also Weaver 2005.

17 See Tchernia 1986, 332–335, for references.

18 Carrington 1931, 114; Day 1932, 177–179.

19 Jongman 1988, 128–131, but see also Andreau 1974, 224–241, and Łos 1992 on the Pompeian wine production.

20 Cat.Agr.6.4–7.2.

> *cultivating the estate which had been the place of exile of Africanus; but the greatest reputation, thanks to the activity of the same Sthenelus, attached to Remmius Palaemon, also famous for his treatise on grammar, who within the last twenty years bought a farm for 600,000 sesterces in the same region of Nomentana, at the turning off the main road ten miles from Rome.*[21]

Palaemon had his vineyards dug and trenched afresh under the supervision of his neighbour Acilius Sthenelus, but, according to Pliny, Remmius Palaemon *undertook the cultivation of this property not from any high motive but at first out of vanity, for which he was known to be so remarkable.*[22] He followed Cato's advice and sold within eight years the vintage, when the grapes were still hanging on the vine, for the sum of 400,000 sesterces.[23] Yet it is important to notice that Pliny considered the price that Remmius Palaemon paid for the property as low, and within hardly more than ten years he sold the vineyard to Seneca for four times what he had paid for it. Seneca, however, did not buy the vineyard for economic reasons, but because he wanted to be the owner of such a prestigious estate.[24]

These examples demonstrate that improvements in the labour-intensive viticulture could achieve a high level of profit, but Pliny is only talking of high-quality wine with an easy access to the market. Two of the three successful wine-growers owned suburban vineyards in the vicinity of Nomentum near Rome, while the third was located in Campania. An important question is the juridical status of the wine-growers. We know from Suetonius' short biography in his treatise On Grammarians and Rhetoricians that Q. Remmius Palaemon was a home-born slave. He first learned the weaver's trade, but got his education by accompanying his master's son to school. He was manumitted as an adult and became a teacher in Rome.[25]

Pliny the Elder is the only author who mentions the talented wine-grower Acilius Sthenelus, while Seneca in his essay on Scipio's villa says that Vetulenus Aegialus is its present owner and gives examples of his methods of cultivating olives and wine.[26] Pliny calls Acilius Sthenelus a *plebe libertina* and says that Vetulenus Aegialus was *perinde libertinus*. This terminology is important, but it has been translated in different ways. In his translation of Pliny in the Loeb Classical Libra-

21 Plin.Nat.14,47–49: *verum eo minus omittenda, ut noscantur etiam praemia, quae in omni re maxime spectantur. Summam ergo adeptus est gloriam Acilius Sthenelus e plebe libertina LX iugerum non amplius vineis excultis in Nomentano agro atque cccc nummum venundatis. Magna fama et Vetuleno Aegialo perinde libertino fuit in Campania rure Liternino, maiorque etiam favore hominum quoniam ipsum Africani colebat exilium; sed maxima, eiusdem Stheneli opera, Remmio Palaemoni, alias grammatica arte celebri, in hisce xx annis mercato rus DC nummum in eodem Nomentano decimi lapidis ab urbe deverticulo.* Duff 1928, 230; Los 1992, 711–712.

22 Plin.Nat.14,50: *Haec adgressus excolere non virtute animi sed vanitate primo, quae nota mire in illo fuit.*

23 Plin.Nat.14,50: *[...] the vintage, while still hanging on the trees was knocked down to a purchaser at a price of 400,000 sesterces (CCCC nummum emptori addicta pendente vindemia).*

24 Plin.Nat.14,51. Kolendo 1985, 182.

25 Suet.Gram.23. Kolendo 1994; Beagon 1992, 169–170.

26 Sen.Ep.86,14; 86,17–21; Hausik, RE 7.A.2, 1958, 1874, s.v. Vetulenus Aegialus.

ry H. Rackham describes Sthenelus as 'a plebeian, the son of a freedman', while J. André in the French Budé edition translated it as 'affranchi plébeien'. In his German Tusculum-translation R. König characterizes Acilius Sthenelus as 'aus dem Stande der Freigelassenen', while the Italian Einaudi-translation edited by G.B. Conte and G. Ranucci only says 'un liberto'.

It has sometimes been argued that sons of freedmen bore the label *libertini* until the second century BCE, but it has now been convincingly demonstrated that "the terms *libertus* and *libertinus* appear to have been used interchangeably, and only about people who had once been slaves."[27] Therefore there is no doubt that all the three successful wine-growers mentioned by Pliny the Elder were freedmen, and this is an important point. Some years ago Nicholas Purcell argued in an important article on "Wine and Wealth in Ancient Italy" (1985) that a change in the social position of vineyard owners can be traced during the Early Empire when interest in viticulture finally began in senatorial circles.[28] It is, however, doubtful and Cato's treatise with the careful treatment of the vines shows there was already senatorial interest in viticulture in the second century BCE, and it continued during the so-called 'Republican wine boom' in Central Italy. The best example is provided by the wine amphorae of the Dressel 1 type with the stamp SES found at Portus Cosanus, along the Tyrrhenian coast and in Gaul. Although some scholars have suggested that the stamps denote the producer of the amphorae, it is still more likely that both the wine and the amphorae were produced on the properties of the senatorial Sestius family in *Ager Cosanus* in the Late Republic.[29]

From the point of view of the producer the sale of the product was essential, and Roman law distinguished between two different kinds of wine-sellers. One was the wine-grower and the other defined in the Digest as *a merchant who regularly buys and sells wine.*[30] Direct sale from the farm is also mentioned by the agricultural writers. Cato the Censor gives us terms for the sale of grapes still hanging on the vine and the sale of wine in jars, *in doliis*, and in both cases storage is allowed until the first of October the following year.[31] Varro even says that *if the farm lies along a road and the site is convenient for travellers, a tavern might be built.*[32] He also stresses that profitable thought it might be, such an activity would form no part of agriculture, but it must have been close to a modern Italian "agriturismo" that often uses its own products in the kitchen and sells them too.

Purcell also argued in the same article that there was a change in the organization of the Italian wine trade during the Early Empire. The wine-growers were part of a complicated commercial network, which included long-distance, interregio-

27 Mouritsen 2011, 265, with references to e.g. Treggiari 1969.

28 Purcell 1985, 10–11.

29 Whittaker 1985, 52; Tchernia 1986, and *idem*, 2011, 356–363. Aubert 1994, 162–167.

30 Gaius.Dig.18.6.2: *mercator est, qui emere vina et vendere solet.* Paterson 1998, 153–155.

31 Cat.Agr.147–148.

32 Var.R.1,2,23: *si ager secundum viam et opportunus viatoribus locus, aedificandae tabernae devorsoriae.* Tchernia 2011, 19–26 contra Morel 2009, 69–70.

nal and regional trade. Both high and low quality wine were sometimes sold as a cash crop directly from the vineyard to intermediate traders before the harvest. This is indicated not only by Cato's contracts and Palaemon's anticipated sale of the grapes on the vines, but also by a letter of Pliny the Younger that implies that *negotiatores* attended to the grape harvest and to its processing into wine:

> *Other people visit their estates in order to recruit their purses; whilst I go to mine only to return much the poorer. I had sold my vintage to the merchants, who were eager to purchase it, encouraged by the price it then bore, and what it was probable it would rise to; however, they were disappointed in their expectations. To have made the same abatement to them all, would have been the easy, but not the equitable course.*[33]

A second method was the transportation of surpluses by the owner himself, and ships that were used for that purpose were part of the *instrumentum* of the farm.[34] Alternatively, the owners could make a contract with professional carriers, and once in the town the wine could be consumed by members of the *familia urbana* or sold to either middlemen or directly to the consumer through slaves and freedmen.

Pliny the Elder noted that there were few improvements in wine-growing, and Columella did much to promote intensive viticulture in his treatise De re rustica. His famous calculation of the return of a seven *iugera* vineyard is only one of his many arguments in favour of this crop being the most profitable.[35] He probably succeeded. Twenty years later viticulture was apparently in fashion, and, according to Suetonius, Domitian issued an edict forbidding anyone to plant any more vines in Italy and ordering half of the provincial vineyards to be cut down due to a scarcity of grain.[36] The measures were not carried out, but the famous edict together with the alimentary schemes and Pliny the Younger's letters on the problems with his tenants provides the basis for many modern scholars' positing of a first century agricultural crisis in Italy. They attributed the crisis to the competition with cheaper foodstuffs, especially wine and olive oil, imported from the overseas provinces.[37] Neville Morley is among those who have argued convincingly against this. The picture of a crisis has clearly been exaggerated, and "the result was a decline, not of Italian agriculture or Italian viticulture in general, but of a particularly intensive

33 Plin.Ep.8,2,1–2: *Alii in praedia sua proficiscuntur ut locupletiores revertantur, ego ut pauperior. Vendideram vindemias certatim negotiatoribus ementibus. Invitabat pretium, et quod tunc et quod fore videbatur. Spes fefellit. Erat expeditum omnibus remittere aequaliter, sed non satis aequum.* Rosafio1993, 73; Morley 1996, 161–163.

34 Dig. 33.7.12.1. de Ligt 1993, 164.

35 Col.RR. 3,3. Duncan-Jones 1982, 33–62, contra Carandini 1983. See also Marcone 1997, 142–143.

36 Suet.Dom.7,2.

37 See Patterson 1987 for an overview of this tradition most eloquent formulated by M.I. Rostovtzeff.

form of cultivation which had previously flourished under the exceptionally favourable market conditions offered by the growth of Rome."[38]

On the other hand, it is also true that occasionally the labour-intensive wine-growing was not profitable, as already indicated by Varro in Book One of his agricultural handbook:

> *As an argument against the vineyard, there are those who claim that the cost of upkeep swallows up the profits. In my opinion, it depends on the kind of vineyard, for there are several.*[39]

Wine Markets in Ostia and Rome

But let me return to the wine market and the supposed change in the distribution of wine in Italy in the late first century CE before concluding. We have only a few indications of the legal status of the so-called *vinarii*. An inscription from the small town of Ulubrae in *Regio* I lists sixteen members of a *collegium*, of which the fifteen were freedmen, while only one was freeborn. Four members also indicate their occupations, including the freedman L. Papius Phaselus who was a *mercator vinarius*.[40]

A handful of inscriptions from Ostia attest the existence of a *Forum Vinarium* with a temple and a *quadriga*. Despite several speculative identifications the forum has not been conclusively located, but it should be sought in Ostia and not in Portus.[41] In Ostia there were also at least two *collegia* of merchants concerned with the importation and sale of wine. Some of the wine sold in Ostia came from the Adriatic coast of Italy as recorded by the inscription mentioning a wine merchant who was also a shipper in the Adriatic. Unfortunately the surviving inscriptions mentioning the guilds of the Ostian wine dealers do not list the members of these two associations. We only know that the well-known Cn. Sentius Felix was also a patron of the *negotiatorum vinariorum ab urbe* and a member of a guild *ad quadrigam fori vinari*. L. Valerius Threptus was president of the builders' guild, treasurer of the traders in the wine market and president of the guild of the *genius* of the wine market. Despite his cognomen Sentius Felix proclaims his free descent for three generations. He became *duovir* and was patron of many guilds in Ostia in the late first and early second century CE. Valerius Threptus does not disclose his status, but a freedman with exactly the same name who died at the age of sixteen is known

38 Morley 1996, 142.

39 Var.R.1,8,1: *Contra vineam sunt qui putent sumptu fructum devorare. Refert, inquam, quod genus vineae sit, quod sunt multae species eius.*

40 CIL X 6493 = ILS 7483.

41 CIL XIV 376 = ILS 6147; CIL XIV 409 = ILS 6146; CIL XIV 430 = ILS 6168; AE 1940, no. 64; AE 1940, no. 65; AE 1955, no. 165; Meiggs 1973, 275–276, Hermansen 1982, 85. See now Coarelli 1996, 105–106, with references and the texts of the inscriptions.

in Rome. The Ostian Threptus had therefore been identified as a *libertus*, but the missing status indicators call for caution.[42]

In Rome a *Portus vinarius superior* on the bank of the Tiber is first attested in 68 CE and several wine depots are mentioned in inscriptions from the second century.[43] There is also evidence for a *Forum Vinarium* in Rome, but it is only known from inscriptions mentioning six manumitted slaves belonging to the same family and working as *argentarii* and *coactor de foro vinario*.[44] Such deposit bankers, brokers and moneylenders are also attested at *Portus vinarius*, and it seems that the wine passed from tradesman to tradesman on the wholesale market with the mediation of *argentarii* and *coactores*, who were freedmen, before it was delivered to the *taberna vinaria* or drink shops in the city. The surviving inscriptions mention only a few *negotiatores vinarii*. They are all devoid of status indicators, but their *cognomina* indicate that they were freeborn.[45]

According to Pliny the Elder, freedmen played an important role in the development of viticulture in the Early Empire. Successful agricultural freedmen are also attested in inscriptions, but the material dealing with their engagement in the distribution of wine in Italy is almost nonexistent. The few preserved names of the Ostian and Roman wine merchants and members of the associations of wine dealers do not include freedmen, but we find them acting as deposit bankers and moneylenders on markets specializing in wines. It is clear that a variety of market-related aspects and well-structured organisation of mercantile bodies existed in Italy during the Early Empire.

42 Mouritsen 2011, 260 n. 46.

43 Coarelli, LTUR IV (1999), 156, s.v. Portus Vinarius.

44 CIL VI 9181abc; CIL VI 9182. Andreau 1987, 142. F. Coarelli, LTUR II (1995), 360, s.v. Forum Vinarium. Palmer 1980, 224, thinks that the *Forum Vinarium* was located outside the customs boundary. Frayn 1993, 162.

45 CIL VI 712; CIL VI 9682; CIL IX 4680.

Bibliography

Andreau J., Les affaires de Monsieur Jucundus, Rome 1974.

Andreau J., La vie financière dans le monde romain. Les métiers de manieurs d'argent (IVe siècle av. J.-C.-IIIe siècle ap. J.-C.), Rome 1987.

Aubert J.-J., Business Managers in Ancient Rome. A Social and Economic Study of Institores, 200 B.C. – A.D. 250, Leiden 1994.

Bang P., The Roman Bazaar. A Comparative Study of Trade and Markets in a Tributary Empire, Cambridge 2008.

Beagon M., Roman Nature. The Thought of Pliny the Elder, Oxford 1992.

Bowman A. – Wilson A. (eds.), Quantifying the Roman Economy. Methods and Problems, Oxford 2009.

Brunt P.A., Two Great Roman Landowners, Latomus 34, 1975, 619–635.

Bruun Ch., The Name and Possessions of Nero's Freedman Phaon, Arctos 23, 1989, 41–53.

Carandini A., Columella's Vineyard and the Rationality of the Roman Economy, Opus 2, 1983, 177–204.

Carlsen J., Recruitment and Training of Roman Estate Managers in a comparative Perspective, in: Roth U. (ed.), By the Sweat of your Brow. Roman Slavery in its Socio-Economic Setting (BICS supplement 109), London 2010, 75–90.

Carrington R.C., Studies in the Campanian 'Villae Rusticae', JRS 20, 1931, 110-130.

Coarelli F., Il forum vinarium di Ostia: un'ipotesi di localizzazione, in: Gallina Zevi A. – Claridge A. (eds.), 'Roman Ostia' revisited, Rome 1996, 105–113.

D'Arms J.H., Commerce and Social Standing in Ancient Rome, Cambridge/MA 1981.

Day J., Agriculture in the Life of Pompeii, YClS 3, 1932, 165–208.

Duncan-Jones R., The Economy of the Roman Empire. Quantitative Studies, 2nd ed., Cambridge 1982.

Duff A.M., Freedmen in the Early Roman Empire, Oxford 1928.

Frayn J.M., Markets and Fairs in Roman Italy, Oxford 1993.

Gregory A.P., A Study in Survival. The Case of the Freedman L. Domitius Phaon, Athenaeum 83, 1995, 401–410.

Hermansen G., Ostia. Aspects of Roman City Life, Edmonton 1982.

Jongman W., The Economy and Society of Pompeii, Amsterdam 1988.

Kolendo J., Eléments courants et exceptionnels de la carrière d'un affranchi: le grammairien Q. Remmius Palémon, Index 13, 1985, 177–187.

Kolendo J., Praedia suburbana e loro redditività, in: Carlsen J. – Skydsgaard J.E. – Ørsted P. (eds.), Landuse in the Roman Empire (ARID supplementum 22), Rome 1994, 59–71.

Ligt L. de, Fairs and Markets in the Roman Empire, Amsterdam 1993.

Łos A., Les intérêts des affranchis dans l'agriculture italienne, MEFRA 104, 1992, 709–753.

Marcone A., Storia dell'agricoltura romana. Dal mondo arcaico all'età imperiale, Rome 1997.

Meiggs R., Roman Ostia, 2nd ed., Oxford 1973.
Morel J.-P., Entre agriculture et artisanat: regards croises sur l'économie de l'Italie tardo-républicaine, in: Carlsen J. – Lo Cascio E. (eds.), Agricoltura e scambi nell'Italia tardo-repubblicana (Pragmateiai 16), Bari 2009, 63–90.
Morley N., Metropolis and Hinterland. The City of Rome and the Italian Economy 200 B.C. – A.D. 200, Cambridge 1996.
Mouritsen H., The Freedman in the Roman World, Cambridge 2011.
Mrozek St., Wirtschaftliche Grundlagen des Aufstiegs der Freigelassenen im Römischen Reich, Chiron 5, 1975, 311–316.
Neeve P.W. de, Colonus, Amsterdam 1984.
Palmer R.E.A., Customs on Market Goods Imported into the City of Rome, in: D'Arms J.H. – Kopff E.C. (eds.), The Seaborne Commerce of Ancient Rome (MAAR 36), Rome 1980, 217–233.
Paterson J., Trade and Traders in the Roman World: Scale, Structure, and Organisation, in: Parkins H. – Smith C. (eds.), Trade, Traders and the Ancient City, London 1998, 149–167.
Patterson J., Crisis: What Crisis? Rural Change and Development in Imperial Appennine Italy, PBSR 55, 1987, 115–146.
Purcell N., Wine and Wealth in Ancient Italy, JRS 75, 1985, 1–19.
Rosafio P., Rural Labour Organization in Pliny the Younger, ARID 21, 1993, 67–79.
Rostovtzeff M.I., The Social and Economic History of the Roman Empire, 2nd ed. Oxford 1957.
Roth U., Peculium, Freedom, Citizenship: Golden Triangle or Vicious Circle? An Act in Two Parts, in: Roth U. (ed.), By the Sweat of your Brow. Roman Slavery in its Socio-Economic Setting (BICS supplement 109), London 2010, 91–120.
Scheidel W., Sklaven und Freigelassene als Pächter und ihre ökonomische Funktion in der römischen Landwirtschaft (Colonus-Studien III), in: Sancisi-Weerdenburg H. et al. (eds.), De agricultura in memoriam P.W. de Neeve, Amsterdam 1993, 182–196.
Tchernia, A., Le vin de l'Italie. Essai d'histoire économique d'après les amphores, Rome 1986.
Tchernia A., La vente du vin, in: Lo Cascio E. (ed.), Mercati permanenti e mercati periodici nel mondo romano (Pragmateiai 2), Bari 2000, 199–209 (reprinted in Tchernia 2011, 187–198).
Tchernia A., Les Romains et le commerce, Napoli 2011.
Treggiari S., Roman Freedmen during the Late Republic, Oxford 1969.
Weaver P., Phaon, Freedman of Nero, ZPE 151, 2005, 243–252.
Whittaker C.R., Trade and the Aristocracy in the Roman Empire, Opus 4, 1985, 49–75.

Die Wirtschaftstheorie der Antike im Lichte der neuzeitlichen Marktwirtschaftslehre

Christian Dirninger

Zwei inhaltliche Dimensionen bei Aristoteles

Die Beschäftigung mit der Geschichte der ökonomischen Theorie lässt in mehrfacher Weise Bezüge des neuzeitlichen europäischen Wirtschaftsdenkens zur antiken Wirtschaftstheorie deutlich werden. Im Sinne dessen sollen in diesem Beitrag einige derartige Bezüge hinsichtlich der modernen Marktwirtschaftslehre und der kritischen Auseinandersetzung mit dieser beleuchtet werden. Dabei konzentrieren sich die folgenden Ausführungen auf einige einschlägig relevant erscheinende argumentative Zusammenhänge in den wirtschaftstheoretischen Ausführungen bei Aristoteles, der in der ökonomischen „Dogmengeschichte" unbestritten als einer der Ahnherren der neuzeitlichen Wirtschaftstheorie gilt.[1]

Grundsätzlich lassen sich zwei inhaltliche Dimensionen der Bedeutung von Aristoteles für die neuzeitliche Marktwirtschaftslehre ausdifferenzieren: Zum einen eine ordnungstheoretische Dimension, die den Markt als Element bzw. institutionelle Kategorie der Wirtschafts- und Gesellschaftsordnung sieht. Damit sind eine Reihe grundlegender ordnungspolitischer Fragen, etwa jene der Eigentumsordnung oder jene der Rolle des Staates in Wirtschaft und Gesellschaft verbunden. Zum anderen eine hinsichtlich der konkreten Gestaltung von Marktbeziehungen funktionsbezogene Dimension. Diese betrifft die marktwirtschaftlichen Funktionsmechanismen und damit insbesondere die Verhaltensweisen der „Marktteilnehmer", aber auch die Marktregulierung, ebenso die Funktion des Geldes. In beiden Dimensionen sind die wirtschaftsethische Komponente sowie die Begrenzung marktwirtschaftlicher Erwerbstätigkeit von vorrangiger Bedeutung.

Zur ordnungstheoretischen Dimension

Diesbezüglich lässt sich in der längerfristigen dogmenhistorischen Perspektive zweimal ein verstärkter „Rückgriff" bzw. Bezug auf die aristotelische Wirtschaftstheorie verorten. Und zwar einmal in der Zeit der Herausbildung der modernen Marktwirtschaftslehre im Rahmen der Wirtschaftstheorie der Aufklärung, also des von Adam Smith begründeten „Klassischen Liberalismus" und ein zweites Mal in der Kritik am „Neoliberalismus" ab den 1990er Jahren.

Diese Kritik an den theoretischen Grundlagen und konkreten Auswirkungen neoliberalistischer Marktwirtschaftsverhältnisse drängt – in verstärktem Maße angesichts der jüngsten Wirtschaftskrisen – wieder nachdrücklich auf eine in gesellschaftlicher Hinsicht ethische bzw. moralische Sichtweise des Wirtschaftens,

1 Holub 2005, 139–168; Schefold 2004, 21–44; Söllner 2001, 3–6; Kolb 1997, 1–7.

speziell des Marktgeschehens. Dabei lassen sich einige relevante Bezüge zur aristotelischen Wirtschaftstheorie erkennen. Der ethisch-moralische Aspekt findet sich aber auch bei Adam Smith in dessen moralphilosophischer Kategorie der „moral sentiments" als Kontrollinstanz individueller Ethik im Marktgeschehen.[2] In der liberalen Klassik war es allerdings nicht die „Schockwirkung" von Wirtschaftskrisen, die dazu veranlasste, sondern die Einsicht, dass die Ordnung der Wirtschafts- bzw. Marktbeziehungen in der Gesellschaftstheorie der Aufklärung als ein wesentlicher Teil der Konzeption einer neuen, das ständisch-absolutistisch-etatistische System überwindenden, auf der Entscheidungsmacht des Individuums – hier eben des individuellen Marktverhaltens – basierenden Gesellschaftsordnung sein musste. In beiden Fällen – und darin liegt ein grundsätzlicher Bezug zur aristotelischen Wirtschaftslehre – geht es um eine ganzheitliche gesellschaftliche Sicht von Wirtschaft bzw. Marktgeschehen, also um eine gesellschaftliche bzw. soziale Relativierung des ökonomischen Prinzips.

Im groben Überblick kann davon ausgegangen werden, dass die neuzeitliche Marktwirtschaftslehre in ihrer weiteren Entwicklung ab dem späten 19. Jahrhundert bzw. im Übergang ins 20. Jahrhundert in zunehmendem Maße vom Theorem des vom rationalen Nutzenkalkül geleiteten „homo oeconomicus" bestimmt gewesen ist. Das fand etwa im „Methodenstreit" und in der Etablierung der Grenznutzen- bzw. Grenzkostenlehre („Österreichische Schule") in der ersten Hälfte sowie in der Forcierung der marktwirtschaftlichen Modelltheorie in der zweiten Hälfte des 20. Jahrhunderts seinen Niederschlag. Dieser „reinen" Marktlehre stellte John M. Keynes mit seiner „General Theory" in den 1930er Jahren (angesichts der damaligen großen Weltwirtschaftskrise) eine Theorie des antizyklischen staatlichen Interventionismus in die marktwirtschaftlichen Verhältnisse entgegen. Diese wurde nach dem Zweiten Weltkrieg bis in die 1970er Jahre hinein zum dominierenden Mainstream in der Theorie und in der wirtschaftspolitischen Praxis. In den 1980er Jahren verstärkte sich – u.a. angesichts steigender Staatsverschuldung – die Kritik am Keynesianismus und es kam im Rahmen der „konservativen Wende" (Thatcherismus, Reaganomics) zu einem Wandel im wirtschaftstheoretischen Mainstream in Richtung „Neoliberalismus", im Zuge dessen es – vor allem ausgehend von den USA („Havard-Ökonomie") – zu einer Renaissance der „reinen Marktwirtschaftslehre" und des „homo oeconomicus" gekommen ist. Dabei lieferten gerade auch die Nachfahren der „Österreichischen Schule" (insbesondere Friedrich A.v. Hayek) wesentliche, wenn auch selektiv aufgenommene und interpretierte theoretische Grundlagen. Ab den 1990er Jahren kam daran zunehmend Kritik, u.a. an „Marktfetischismus", „Marktgläubigkeit" und „Marktversagen" auf, die sich angesichts der sich häufenden Finanz- und Wirtschaftskrisen deutlich verstärkte und aktuell möglicherweise wieder in einen Wandel des wirtschaftstheoretischen bzw. wirtschaftspolitischen Mainstreams in Richtung von mehr staatlichem Interventionismus führt.

2 Recktenwald 1989, 135–143.

Im Rahmen dieser rezenten Kritik am „Neoliberalismus" lassen sich drei ordnungstheoretische Hauptstoßrichtungen erkennen. Erstens die Forderung nach mehr Regulierung der „Märkte" durch einen „starken" Staat im Sinne eines Primats der Politik gegenüber der Ökonomie. Zweitens die Forderung nach Ethik und Moral im Kapitalismus generell und speziell im Markt, was im Bereich der Theorie in einem zunehmenden Stellenwert der Wirtschaftsethik Ausdruck findet. Drittens die Forderung nach Stärkung regionaler Wirtschaftskreisläufe und damit regionaler Marktbeziehungen als eine wesentliche Dimension eines im Rahmen der Globalisierungskritik erstarkenden gesellschafts- und auch wirtschaftstheoretischen Regionalismus. Für das gegenständliche Thema sind v.a. die ersten beiden Stoßrichtungen relevant.

Im Zusammenhang mit der kritischen Auseinandersetzung mit dem „Neoliberalismus" ist es schon in den 1990er Jahren wieder zu einer verstärkten Beschäftigung mit der antiken Wirtschaftslehre, insbesondere jener von Aristoteles gekommen. So erschien im Juni 1993 im Rahmen einer in der Wochenzeitung „Die Zeit" veröffentlichten Serie „Zeit der Ökonomen" ein Artikel von Warnfried Dettling mit dem Titel „Wie modern ist die Antike?", worin der Autor die Bedeutung von Aristoteles für das moderne Wirtschaftsdenken thematisierte.[3] Dabei stützte er sich vor allem auf das damals soeben erschienene Buch von Peter Koslowski „Politik und Ökonomie bei Aristoteles".[4]

Von grundsätzlicher Relevanz erscheint dabei zunächst die bei Aristoteles vorgenommene theoretische Ausdifferenzierung des Ökonomischen als integriertes Teilsystem der Gesellschaft, das von der Politik zu gestalten ist. Also das Verständnis von Ökonomie als eine spezielle Sphäre des gesellschaftlichen bzw. des politischen Handelns. Und dabei wiederum die bei Aristoteles explizit formulierten ethischen bzw. moralischen Grundsätze der Gestaltung und Organisation von Ökonomie im Sinne einer „guten Gesellschaft". Davon ausgehend weist Dettling auf zwei für das moderne Wirtschaftsdenken wesentliche Punkte hin. Einerseits in historischer Perspektive auf die bei Aristoteles zu findende Grundlegung einer spezifischen Wissenschaft vom Wirtschaften und andererseits, hinsichtlich der aktuellen kritischen Auseinandersetzung mit einer Verabsolutierung der „Marktgesetze", auf deren von Aristoteles vorgenommene Einbindung in eine gesellschaftliche Moralphilosophie: „Aristoteles hat der Ökonomie den Namen gegeben (oikonomia) und sie als eigenständige Disziplin auf den Weg gebracht. Dabei hat er sie immer auch im umfassenden Sinne als Gesellschafts-, ja als ‚moralische' Wissenschaft verstanden. In seinem Denken hat der ‚Homo oeconomicus' den Homo politicus noch nicht verdrängt. Undogmatisch, aber moralisch engagiert, wie er war, könnte er einer Zeit Orientierung geben, die in Wissenschaft und Politik wieder auf der Suche nach Maßstäben jenseits der Ökonomie ist … Aristoteles könnte der modernen Ökonomie wieder den Horizont für gesellschaftliche und

3 Dettling 1993, 24.
4 Koslowski 1993.

auch für moralische Fragen öffnen. Damit würde sie an ihre besten Traditionen anknüpfen."[5] Mit diesen „besten Traditionen" meint Dettling explizit die Liberale Klassik. Denn: „Adam Smith wusste noch: dass Reichtum der Nationen ohne moralische Gefühle viel, aber nicht alles ist."[6]

Hinsichtlich der Institution „Markt" ist dabei wesentlich, dass dieser bei Aristoteles, wie die Wirtschaft in ihrer Gesamtheit, als Instrument bzw. Faktor der Gestaltung der Gesellschaft gesehen, ihr also eine „dienende" Funktion zugemessen wird. In diesem Sinne ist Wirtschaft und damit marktwirtschaftlicher Nutzen bzw. Erfolg nicht Selbstzweck, sondern ein auf ethisch-moralischen Grundsätzen basierender gesellschaftlicher Funktionsbereich. In dieser aristotelischen Tradition „spielt die Ökonomie", so Dettling weiter, „eine wichtige, aber nicht die wichtigste – und schon gar nicht die entscheidende Rolle. Sie hat eine dienende Funktion, sie leistet einen Beitrag zum Gelingen des Gemeinwesens, nicht mehr und nicht weniger."[7]

Und somit, so kann weiter gefolgert werden, sollte auch die Wirtschaftstheorie in ihrer Gesamtheit und die Marktwirtschaftslehre im Speziellen, nicht die Lehre von der Nutzen- und Gewinnoptimierung, sondern integrierter Teil einer Lehre zur Gestaltung einer, wie es Aristoteles nannte, „guten Gesellschaft" sein. Als solche wiederum kann sie gleichsam eine Richtlinie für die Politik und deren ordnungspolitisch gestaltende Funktion sein. Diesbezüglich macht Dettling auf einen aus Aristoteles heraus interpretierbaren hierarchischen Funktionszusammenhang aufmerksam, der in der Theorie die oberste Ebene und damit auch die primäre treibende Kraft der gesellschaftlichen Entwicklung sieht, die der Politik als gleichsam mittlerer Ebene Orientierung für die Gestaltung der ökonomischen Verhältnisse als unterste Ebene vorgibt. „In der Pyramide der Ziele und Zwecke ist die Ökonomie der Politik und die Politik der Theorie unter- und zugeordnet."[8]

Eine gewisse – wenn auch nur indirekte – Analogie ist hier zum System des Merkantilismus bzw. Kameralismus denkbar, wo ja auch die ökonomische Theorie gleichsam eine Anleitung für die Politik darstellte. Man denke nur an Jean-Baptiste Colbert, Philipp Wilhelm von Hörnigk oder Johann Heinrich Gottlob von Justi.[9] Eine zweite, ebenfalls indirekte Analogie zum System des Merkantilismus bzw. Kameralismus lässt sich dahingehend sehen, dass es Aristoteles um die Gestaltung einer im Prinzip ständischen Gesellschaft bzw. um ein „Elitensystem" geht. Insofern bietet Aristoteles keinen wirklichen Ansatzpunkt für die in der Moderne so zentrale Frage des Verhältnisses von Marktwirtschaft und Demokratie.

Ungeachtet dessen ist für die Entwicklung des modernen europäischen Wirtschaftsdenkens wesentlich, dass bei Aristoteles die Marktbeziehungen der zentrale Ansatzpunkt für die Verknüpfung von Wirtschaft und Gesellschaft sind und mit

5 Dettling 1993, 24.
6 Dettling 1993, 24.
7 Dettling 1993, 24.
8 Dettling 1993, 24.
9 Gömmel – Klump 1994; Dittrich 1974.

deren Gestaltung zwei wichtige ordnungspolitische Fragen verbunden werden. Nämlich die Frage der sozialen Gerechtigkeit und damit unmittelbar verbunden die Frage der Verteilung von Besitz und damit von Einkommen und Vermögen, also die Frage nach der Verteilungsgerechtigkeit als anzustrebendes Ergebnis der Marktverhältnisse.

Auf eine diesbezüglich dauerhafte Bedeutung von Aristoteles verweist Dettling ausgehend von den entsprechenden Diskursen der frühen 1990er Jahre, wenn er feststellt: „So sehr er also seiner Zeit verhaftet blieb, so war er doch auch einer der ersten und gründlichsten Theoretiker der sozialen Gerechtigkeit. Er hat die Begriffe geprägt (austeilende versus ausgleichende Gerechtigkeit), die richtigen Fragen gestellt und so das soziale Denken bis heute beeinflusst: Wo können soziale Ungleichheiten als gerecht, als Folge einer freien Gesellschaft und wo müssen sie als ungerecht, ja als gefährlich angesehen werden, da sie das Gemeinwesen zu sprengen drohen?“[10]

In der neuzeitlichen Wirtschafts- und Markttheorie wird die Existenz eines breiten Mittelstandes immer wieder als relevantes Kriterium einer gesellschaftlich stabilisierenden Verteilung des Volkseinkommens thematisiert. Dies entspricht in gewisser Weise dem in der aristotelischen Ethik postulierten „Prinzip der Mitte.“[11] Bei Aristoteles heißt es dazu: „In allen Staaten gibt es drei Teile, die sehr Reichen, die sehr Armen und die Mittleren. Wenn nun das Maß und die Mitte anerkanntermaßen das Beste sind, so ist auch in Bezug auf den Besitz der mittlere von allen der beste. Denn in solchen Verhältnissen gehorcht man am leichtesten der Vernunft.“[12]

Insofern liegt das entscheidende Kriterium der für eine „gute Gesellschaft“ erforderlichen „Verteilungsgerechtigkeit“ in der Gewährleistung einer „mittleren Besitzverteilung“.[13] Eine Erkenntnis, die gerade auch in den neuzeitlichen Diskursen über die Bedeutung der Einkommens- und Vermögensverteilung für die Ursachen und die sozialen und politischen Folgen der Krisen marktwirtschaftlicher Systeme wesentlich geworden ist. Dazu kann beispielsweise sowohl auf die „Kritik der politischen Ökonomie“ von Karl Marx als auch auf die gesellschaftstheoretischen Mittelstandskonzepte der „Historischen Schule der Nationalökonomie“ sowie auf die verteilungstheoretischen Ansätze bei John Stuart Mill im 19. Jahrhundert verwiesen werden, aber ebenso auch auf Analysen der jüngsten Wirtschaftskrisen, etwa von Harold James oder von Paul Krugman.[14]

Koslowksi fasst die entsprechende Argumentation bei Aristoteles folgendermaßen zusammen: „Denn das Gute ist die Mitte zwischen einem Zuviel und einem Zuwenig, das Gerechte ist das Angemessene und Proportionale. Die gute und gerechte Verfassung ist jene, die allen Gruppen und Bürgern nach Verdienst und Leistung das Gerechte zuteilt. Dies gilt auch für den Besitz ... Bei einer zu unglei-

10 Dettling 1993, 24.
11 Koslowski 1993, 47.
12 Zitiert bei Dettling 1993, 24.
13 Koslowski 1993, 47.
14 James 2001; Krugman 2009.

chen Besitzverteilung ist es nach Aristoteles unmöglich, zu einer mittleren und ausgeglichenen politischen Machtverteilung zu kommen."[15] Damit wird also in besonderem Maße die, auch in der Entwicklung des modernen Marktwirtschaftsdenkens, gerade in der aktuellen Diskussion wieder in den Vordergrund gerückte Frage nach dem Kriterium von „gerecht" bzw. „Gerechtigkeit" in der Ökonomie thematisiert.

Dabei ist allerdings einmal mehr zu beachten, dass diese Frage bei Aristoteles in Bezug auf eine prinzipiell ständische Gesellschaft abgehandelt wird und dass sich auf diese sein Begriff der „proportionalen Gerechtigkeit" bezieht, wenn er ausführt: „Denn das Proportionale ist die Mitte, und das Gerechte ist das Proportionale."[16] Bertram Schefold, einer der profundesten dogmenhistorischen Interpreten der aristotelischen Wirtschaftstheorie, erläutert dies: „Ausdrücklich geht es Aristoteles nicht um die Gleichheit, sondern um die Proportionalität, also das Angemessene.[...] Es geht Aristoteles also um die angemessene Berücksichtigung der Stellung, die die betroffene Person in der Gemeinschaft einnimmt.[...] Die Position muss mit dem jeweiligen Anteil am Verteilten in Beziehung gesetzt werden.[...] Eine Verteilung nach dem Prinzip der geometrischen Proportionalität lässt also jedem das im Rahmen der Gemeinschaft zustehende, jedem das „Seinige" zukommen. Es ist dies ein Konzept, welches ausdrücklich auf der Ungleichheit der Bürger der Gemeinschaft basiert. Die Ungleichheit der Verteilung von Reichtum und Ehre wird gleichsam zur Konsequenz der ungleichen Stellung der Bürger in der Gemeinschaft."[17]

Abseits des ständischen Konzeptes ist für das neuzeitliche Wirtschaftsdenken im Hinblick auf die marktwirtschaftlich zustande kommende bzw. wirtschaftspolitisch herzustellende Verteilungssituation die bei Aristoteles zu findende Ausdifferenzierung von zwei Formen der Gerechtigkeit relevant, nämlich der „verteilenden Gerechtigkeit" und der „ausgleichenden Gerechtigkeit". Bezeichnet „verteilende Gerechtigkeit" gleichsam den jeweils anzustrebenden Status einer gerechten Verteilung, so bezeichnet „ausgleichende Gerechtigkeit" im Grunde die auf das Ziel der verteilenden Gerechtigkeit ausgerichtete Regulierung und Steuerung der marktwirtschaftlichen Verhältnisse. In Schefolds Interpretation „geht es darum, die verschiedenen Beziehungen des täglichen Lebens, wie Verkauf, Darlehen, Nutznießung und Bürgschaft, aber auch Diebstahl, Ehebruch, Mord etc. zu regeln und Streitigkeiten zu schlichten. Ungerechte, aus Betrügereien etc. stammende Gewinne sollen beseitigt, erlittener Schaden soll ausgeglichen werden."[18]

Wird damit im Grunde Marktregulierung gesellschaftstheoretisch begründet, so wird darin zumindest im Ansatz auch eine theoretische Begründung für eine, die rein aus dem Markt resultierende „primäre" Einkommens- und Vermögensverteilung in eine durch normative und effektive (fiskalische) Maßnahmen in eine

15 Koslowski 1993, 47.
16 Zitiert bei Schefold 1989, 44.
17 Schefold 1989, 44–45.
18 Schefold 1989, 45.

„sekundäre" transferierende Umverteilungspolitik erkennbar. Dieser Zusammenhang stellt in der Entwicklung der neuzeitlichen Finanzwissenschaft in der später nach Richard A. Musgrave so bezeichneten Distributionsfunktion staatlicher Finanzpolitik als „Redistribution" eine wesentliche analytische Kategorie dar.[19]

Kann man hier zugleich auch eine theoretische Begründung für staatlichen Interventionismus und für die Herstellung von Verteilungsgerechtigkeit im marktwirtschaftlichen System durch staatliche Maßnahmen sehen, ergibt sich ein weiteres Mal auch eine indirekte Analogie zur sozioökonomischen Konzeption des „aufgeklärten Absolutismus", der in seiner „kameralistischen" Wirtschaftstheorie – bezogen auf eine ständische Gesellschaftsordnung bzw. mit dem Ziel von deren Stabilisierung – die Gestaltung einer „allgemeinen Glückseligkeit" als seine zentrale Aufgabe postulierte.[20] Diese Gestaltung erfolgte letztendlich – so ist es jedenfalls aus der kameralwissenschaftlichen Literatur des späten 18. und frühen 19. Jahrhunderts herauszulesen, aber auch in den konkreten Abläufen zu beobachten – durch einen hochgradigen normativen, regulativen sowie fiskalisch-effektiven Staatsinterventionismus in ein zunehmend kapitalistisch-marktwirtschaftlich funktionierendes territorialwirtschaftliches Wirtschaftsystem.[21]

Wiederum ungeachtet der Ausrichtung auf eine im Prinzip ständische Gesellschaftsordnung wesentlich für die Entwicklung des neuzeitlichen Wirtschaftsdenkens ist die sich bei Aristoteles aus der Frage der „gerechten Verteilung" des Besitzes ergebende zentrale Bedeutung der Eigentumsordnung im marktwirtschaftlichen System. Maßgeblich erscheint hierbei insbesondere die in seiner Auseinandersetzung mit Plato zum Tragen kommende Differenzierung von Gemeineigentum und Privateigentum. Koslowski kennzeichnet das platonische Prinzip des ausschließlichen, kein individuelles Privateigentum zulassenden Gemeineigentums folgendermaßen: „Für den einheitlichen Staat gibt es wie für den Einzelnen nur ein Eigentum, nämlich Gemeineigentum, das jeder Einzelne als sein ihn betreffendes Eigentum empfindet.[...] Plato glaubt nun zwischen den Individuen als Personen und ihren Rechtsansprüchen unterscheiden zu können. Der Bürger soll vom Staat zwar noch als dem seinen und vom staatlichen Gemeineigentum als seinem eigenen sprechen, den Anspruch auf konkretes, gegen andere Ansprüche durchsetzbares Eigentum aber aufgeben."[22] Und er verweist auch auf gewisse Parallelen zu Marx bzw. zur marxistischen Theorie: „Die Marx'sche Aufhebung des Privateigentums als Vindikation (Zurückgabe) des Eigentums durch seinen wirklichen Eigentümer, die Gattung Mensch, weist deutliche Parallelen zur platonischen Position auf. Der Kommunismus, der die Menschheit zum Eigentümer der gesellschaftlichen Produktion hypostasiert, hebt damit den Begriff des Eigentums ebenso auf, wie die platonische Politeia, in der alle dasselbe als ihres oder nicht-ihres

19 Musgrave 1959.

20 Matis 1981.

21 Diese Symbiose von Kameralismus und Kapitalismus wird sehr gut analysiert bei: Bauer – Matis 1988.

22 Koslowski 1993, 39.

bezeichnen. Hier wie dort wird das individuelle Subjekt als Träger eines Eigentumsanspruches aufgehoben und an Stelle des Individuums ein Abstraktum wie Gattung oder „Politeia" gesetzt."[23]

Dem gegenüber positioniert Aristoteles privates Eigentum als konstitutiven Faktor der Gesellschafts- und Wirtschaftsordnung. Grundsätzlich dadurch, dass er, wie Koslowski ausführt, die bei Plato insinuierte Möglichkeit der „Trennung von Individualität und Eigentum leugnet", da „das Eigene[...] unabdingbar zum Prozess der Individuation" gehöre.[24] Davon ausgehend sieht Aristoteles hinsichtlich der Wirtschafts- und Gesellschaftsordnung, so Bertram Schefold, einen „vom Privateigentum ausgehenden materiellen Anreiz" und verweist auf eine entsprechende Stelle in Aristoteles` „Politik", wo es heißt: „Wenn jeder für das Seine sorgt, werden keine Anklagen gegeneinander erhoben werden, und man wird mehr vorankommen, da jeder am Eigenen arbeitet"[25]

Dabei fühlt man sich an die bekannte Stelle im „Wohlstand der Nationen" von Adam Smith erinnert, wo es heißt: „Nicht vom Wohlwollen des Metzgers, Brauers oder Bäckers erwarten wir das was wir zum Essen brauchen, sondern davon, dass sie ihre eigenen Interessen wahrnehmen. Wir wenden uns nicht an ihre Menschen- sondern an ihre Eigenliebe."[26] In dieser argumentativen Parallele hinsichtlich der Bewirkung von gemeinschaftlichem Nutzen durch individuelles Nutzenstreben kommt wohl in besonders unmittelbarer Weise die Grundlegung eines wesentlichen ordnungstheoretischen Prinzips der neuzeitlichen Marktwirtschaftslehre bei Aristoteles exemplarisch zum Ausdruck.

Gleichermaßen ist dies der Fall bei der von Aristoteles, speziell hinsichtlich der Wirtschaftsordnung postulierten Erfordernis einer „gerechten" Eigentumsordnung, die Gemeineigentum und Privateigentum in funktioneller Weise spezifisch definiert und kombiniert. Koslowksi fasst entsprechende Aussagen in der „Politik" von Aristoteles zusammen: „Da die Bürger selbst wirtschaften, muss die Eigentumsfrage gerecht gelöst werden. Im Allgemeinen, so Aristoteles, gibt Gemeineigentum in besonderem Maße Anlass zu Streitigkeiten. [...] Privateigentum hingegen schafft klare Verhältnisse durch eindeutige Rechtsansprüche und reduziert dadurch Uneinigkeiten.[...] Die richtige Ordnung stellt einen Kompromiss zwischen Gemein- und Privateigentum dar. Jeder muss für das Seinige sorgen, damit keine Anklagen gegeneinander erhoben werden und Konflikte reduziert werden, weil jeder das erhält, was er für sich erarbeitet hat, weil Zurechnung von Aufwand und Ertrag eindeutig ist."[27]

Für die Nachwirkung der aristotelischen Theorie auf das neuzeitliche Wirtschaftsdenken von wesentlicher Bedeutung ist zweifelsohne, dass in dieser Differenzierung von Gemeineigentum und individuellem Eigentum auch Ansatzpunk-

23 Koslowski 1993, 39.

24 Koslowski 1993, 39.

25 Zitiert bei Schefold 1989, 36.

26 Smith 1978, 17.

27 Koslowski 1993, 40–41.

te für das Verständnis von „öffentlichem Gut“, als nicht dem privateigentümlichen Ausschließungsprinzip unterliegenden, in einem prinzipiell marktwirtschaftlichen System von einer „öffentlichen Hand“ bereitzustellenden Gütern und Leistungen stecken. Dieser Punkt erlangte in der neuzeitlichen Lehre von der öffentlichen Finanzwirtschaft, vom Kameralismus über Adam Smith (Wohlstand der Nationen, 5. Buch) bis hin zur Finanztheorie der 1970er Jahre[28], aber auch in der „neoliberalen“ Kritik am Keynesianismus wesentlichen Stellenwert und ist gerade auch in der rezenten Suche nach einer neuen Rolle des Staates im Lichte der Auswirkungen der Wirtschafskrise wieder in spezieller Weise relevant.

Ein weiterer, das neuzeitliche Wirtschaftsdenken in allen seinen Entwicklungsphasen seit der Frühen Neuzeit beschäftigender und bei Aristoteles in expliziter Weise im Rahmen seiner Eigentumstheorie thematisierter wesentlicher Punkt ist eine ethisch-moralisch begründete soziale Verpflichtung des Privateigentums in einer grundsätzlich marktwirtschaftlichen Gesellschaftsordnung. Dazu verweist Schefold auf eine Stelle in der „Politik“ die besagt: „Es ist also offenbar besser, dass der Besitz privat bleibt, aber durch die Benutzung gemeinsam wird“.[29] Und Koslowski fasst weitere diesbezügliche Aussagen bei Aristoteles dahingehend zusammen: „Den Ertrag des Besitzes aber wird der Tugendhafte großzügig und für die Gemeinschaft verwalten und gebrauchen.[...] Der Tugendhafte wird größte Freude darin finden, Fremden, Gästen oder Gefährten Freundlichkeiten oder Hilfe gewähren. Ohne privates Eigentum ist dies aber nicht möglich.[...] Besitz ist ein Mittel, diese Tugenden zu verwirklichen.“[30]

In gewissem Sinne wird hier eine karitative Ethik im marktwirtschaftlichen Kapitalismus angesprochen, die auch in der im Rahmen der Historischen Schule der Nationalökonomie entwickelten christlichen Soziallehre, den Konzepten der Bürgerlichen und der Betrieblichen Sozialpolitik im Rahmen des Verein für Socialpolitik („Kathedersozialismus“) eine wesentliche Rolle spielte, worin aber auch durchaus auffällige Bezüge zu den seit einigen Jahren im Mode gekommenen Corporate Social Responsibility-Konzepten zu sehen sind.[31] Die grundsätzliche Parallele liegt darin, dass nach Aristoteles Privateigentum nicht per se gerecht bzw. sozial ist, sondern dies nur durch eine spezifische marktwirtschaftliche Ethik zu bewirken sei. Darin dass ohne eine solche Wirtschaftsethik der Markt in Verbindung mit Privateigentum gesellschaftlich schädlichen Eigennutz erzeugen und befördern würde, liegt eine entscheidende Verbindung der ordnungstheoretischen Dimension mit der funktionsbezogenen Dimension der Bedeutung von Aristoteles für die neuzeitliche Marktwirtschaftslehre, auf die nun im Folgenden eingegangen wird.

28 Wittmann 1978.
29 Zitiert bei Schefold 1989, 37.
30 Koslowski 1993, 41.
31 Winkel 1977, 159–170; Wieser 2005.

Zur funktionsbezogenen Dimension

Ein grundsätzlicher allgemeiner Ansatzpunkt für die funktionsbezogenen Dimensionen der Bedeutung von Aristoteles für die neuzeitliche Marktwirtschaftslehre kann in der Bewertung des „Marktes“ als zentrale Institution bzw. Metapher der Auseinandersetzung und des Austausches und damit wohl letztlich auch des Kompromisses politischer Positionen hinsichtlich der Gestaltung der Rahmenbedingungen des wirtschaftlichen Marktsystems gesehen werden. Darauf verweist Warnfried Dettling in seinem oben zitierten Artikel in der Zeitschrift „Die Zeit“: „Der zentrale Freiheitsraum der Polis war der Marktplatz, die Agora, als Raum öffentlicher Rede und Gegenrede, auf dem die Menschen ihre ökonomischen Interessen austauschen.“[32]

Der spezifisch ökonomische Ansatzpunkt liegt in der bei Aristoteles vorgenommenen funktionalen Ableitung des „Marktes“ als Ort wirtschaftlicher Tauschbeziehungen aus der Arbeitsteilung der gesellschaftlichen Produktion von Gütern und Leistungen mit dem Ziel einer möglichst guten und möglichst autarken Versorgung der staatlichen Gemeinschaft. Für Aristoteles ist es „der Sinn des Staates“, so Koslowski, „die Ungleichheiten der Bürger für einander nützlich und fruchtbar zu machen. Indem die Bürger ihre sozialen und technischen Fähigkeiten arbeitsteilig in die staatliche Gemeinschaft einbringen, kann erst jener Austausch von Gütern stattfinden, der die Autarkie um des guten Lebens willen, das Telos des Staates, erst ermöglicht.“[33] Lässt man den Anspruch der Autarkie beiseite, dann ist hier ein weiterer wesentlicher Beziehungspunkt mit der Grundlegung der neuzeitlichen marktwirtschaftlichen Theorie zu sehen. So beginnt Adam Smith das erste Kapitel des „Wohlstand der Nationen“ mit dem Diktum: „Die Arbeitsteilung dürfte die produktiven Kräfte der Arbeit mehr als alles andere fördern und verbessern. Das gleiche gilt wohl für die Geschicklichkeit, Sachkenntnis und Erfahrung, mit der sie überall eingesetzt oder verrichtet wird.“[34] Allerdings ergibt sich hinsichtlich der Begründung der Arbeitsteilung insofern ein Unterschied als diese bei Aristoteles gleichsam im Sinne einer Optimierung der Versorgung innerhalb der staatlichen Gemeinschaft als Ursache bzw. Anlass für den Gütertausch am Markt erscheint, während sie Smith eigentlich als Folge eines grundsätzlichen gesellschaftlichen Tauschbedürfnisses erklärt, wenn er am Beginn des zweiten Kapitels schreibt: „Die Arbeitsteilung, die so viele Vorteile mit sich bringt, ist in ihrem Ursprung nicht etwa das Ergebnis menschlicher Erkenntnis, welche den allgemeinen Wohlstand, zu dem erstere führt, voraussieht und anstrebt. Sie entsteht vielmehr zwangsläufig, wenn auch langsam und schrittweise, aus einer natürlichen Neigung des Menschen, zu handeln und Dinge gegeneinander auszutauschen.“[35] Dass damit das Handeln am Markt gleichsam einer menschlichen Grunddisposi-

---

32 Dettling 1993, 24.
33 Koslowski 1993, 36.
34 Smith 1978, 9.
35 Smith 1978, 16.

tion zum Austausch, auch im wirtschaftlichen Bereich, entspringt, korrespondiert aber durchaus mit der von Aristoteles, wie oben angesprochen, dem Markt zugeschriebenen allgemeinen gesellschaftlichen Tauschfunktion.

In ökonomischer Hinsicht aber scheint der entscheidende Punkt zu sein, dass es bei Aristoteles um die möglichst optimale Deckung eines in der ständisch strukturierten Gesellschaft gegebenen Güter- und Leistungsbedarfes geht, während diese bei Smith und der ihm folgenden neuzeitlichen Markttheorie letztlich eine sekundäre Folgewirkung des Strebens nach Eigennutz bzw. Erwerbskraft (Kaufkraft) über die „Vermarktung" der eigenen Produktions- bzw. Arbeitsleistung ist. Dieses Streben nach Eigennutz bzw. Erwerbskraft (Kaufkraft) über den Markt bzw. dessen ethisch-moralische, aber auch normativ-regulative Kontrolle ist es aber, wo sich in der Herausbildung wesentlicher Kategorien der neuzeitlichen Wirtschaftstheorie direkte und indirekte Bezüge zur aristotelischen Wirtschaftslehre erkennen lassen. Jedenfalls dürfte das zumindest für vier theoretische Konstrukte gelten, die in der Entwicklung des neuzeitlichen europäischen Wirtschaftsdenkens generell und hinsichtlich der Gestaltung von Marktverhältnissen in spezieller Weise prägend wurden:

Erstens das „Bedarfsdeckungsprinzip" als wirtschaftliche Handlungsmaxime. Aus den Entwicklungsstufen-Theorien der Historischen Schule der Nationalökonomie heraus kommend, wurde dieses bei Werner Sombart als jenes Wirtschaftsprinzip theoretisch gefasst, das bis zur breiten Durchsetzung des kapitalistischen „Erwerbsprinzips" in der Frühen Neuzeit, gleichsam als Grundprinzip der „vorkapitalistischen" Wirtschaftsweise vorherrschend gewesen sei.[36] Interessant ist zu beobachten, dass das Bedarfsdeckungsprinzip, also die Deckung eines gesellschaftlichen Bedarfes als primäre ökonomische Handlungsmaxime im Rahmen der im Zuge der jüngsten Wachstums- und Neoliberalismuskritik entwickelten alternativen Wirtschaftsmodelle wieder an Bedeutung zu gewinnen scheint.[37]

Zweitens ein instrumentales Verständnis eines ethisch beschränkten bzw. kontrollierten marktwirtschaftlichen „Erwerbsprinzips" als Faktor zur Steigerung des allgemeinen Wohlstandes in einer sozial „gerechten" Gesellschaft. Auf derartige Bezüge zur aristotelischen Theorie bei Adam Smith, in der Historischen Schule der Nationalökonomie und der Bürgerlichen Sozialpolitik wurde bereits im vorigen Kapitel verwiesen. Diese Bezüge finden sich im Grunde aber auch in der Konzeption der „Sozialen Marktwirtschaft" der 1950er Jahre sowie in den aktuellen Bestrebungen zu deren Renaissance.

Drittens die theoretische Begründung von Geld im marktwirtschaftlichen System, sowohl hinsichtlich der Entstehung und Entfaltung von dessen drei „klassischen" Funktionen (Tauschmittel, Wertmaßstab, Wertaufbewahrungsmittel), als auch hinsichtlich der Gefahr einer Entkoppelung bzw. Verselbstständigung der Geldzirkulation von diesen dem realwirtschaftlichen Kreislauf dienenden Funkti-

36 Sombart 1987.

37 Felber 2010.

onen. Letzteres wird in der Geschichte des neuzeitlichen Wirtschaftsdenkens immer wieder in Zusammenhang mit Finanz- und Wirtschaftskrisen, so eben auch gegenwärtig, in besonderem Maße thematisiert.

Viertens schließlich das doppeldeutige Verständnis von „Staat" zum einen als Gesellschaft und zum anderen als institutioneller Akteur zu deren Gestaltung. Dies in spezifischer Weise dahingehend, dass der Staat Rahmenbedingungen für eine gesellschaftlich verträgliche Marktwirtschaft bzw. für ein sozial verträgliches individuelles marktwirtschaftliches Verhalten zu schaffen habe, aber auch hinsichtlich der für die konkreten marktwirtschaftlichen Ordnungen so zentrale Frage der „öffentlichen Güter". Das reicht von Adam Smith (5. Buch) bis zur aktuellen Diskussion über Regulierung der Güter-, Faktor- und Finanzmärkte und über die Bedeutung öffentlicher Güter in der gesellschaftlichen Infrastruktur und der Daseinsvorsorge.

Diese vier Bezüge lassen sich in einem spezifischen argumentativen Zusammenhang in der aristotelischen Wirtschafts- und Gesellschaftslehre verorten, der im Folgenden in knapper Form skizziert werden soll. Ausgangspunkt und Basis von Wirtschaft und Gesellschaft ist bei Aristoteles, als Subsystem der Polis, das „Haus" bzw. die „häusliche Gemeinschaft" (oikos) als elementarer Herrschafts- und Wirtschaftsverband in einer, wie Kowalski einmal mehr betont „herrschaftlich gegliederten politischen Gesellschaft im alteuropäischen Sinn".[38]

„Eigentliches Ziel der Hauswirtschaft" bei Aristoteles ist es, so Bertram Schefold, „die materielle Basis des ‚guten Lebens' des griechischen Bürgers bereitzustellen. Dazu gehört – innerhalb eines bestimmten Rahmens – materieller Wohlstand, der eine großzügige Lebensführung ermöglicht."[39] In dieser Zielsetzung der Bereitstellung der materiellen Basis des „guten Lebens" bei gleichzeitiger Ermöglichung eines materiellen Wohlstandes im Rahmen des Hauswirtschaftssystems liegen zum einen entscheidende Ansatzpunkte für die theoretische Begründung von Tauschwirtschaft über den Markt und zum anderen für die oben angesprochene in der neuzeitlichen Theorie, insbesondere in der „Historischen Schule der Nationalökonomie" entwickelte Differenzierung in das vorkapitalistische Bedarfsdeckungsprinzip und das kapitalistische Erwerbsprinzip.

Und zwar konkret in der bei Aristoteles vorgenommenen Differenzierung zwischen „Haushaltungskunst" und „Beschaffungskunst" bzw. „Erwerbskunst". Erstere im Sinne einer optimalen Verwendung der im Haushalt vorhandenen Ressourcen und damit der Absicherung der materiellen Lebensgrundlage bzw. des materiellen Wohlstandes der Hausgemeinschaft. Letztere im Sinne der Bereitstellung bzw. Herbeischaffung der entsprechenden Ressourcen. Schefold betont den komplementären Charakter der beiden „Künste" und den damit verknüpften Bezug zum „Tauschhandel" und damit zum „Markt", indem er festhält: „Eine naturgemäße Erwerbskunst ist auch Teil der Haushaltungskunst: nämlich jene, die die

38 Koslowski 1993, 50.
39 Schefold 1989, 36.

Beschaffung von Gütern zum Ziel hat, die zur Bedürfnisbefriedigung der Mitglieder des Hauses sowie zur Führung des ‚guten Lebens' des freien griechischen Bürgers gehören, auch wenn sie innerhalb des Hauses nicht hergestellt werden können. Der Erwerb solcher Güter durch Tauschhandel dient gleichsam der Erfüllung der ‚naturgemäßen Autonomie' des Hauses."[40] Meint die „naturgemäße Autonomie" des Hauses die Absicherung der materiellen Lebensgrundlage bzw. des materiellen Wohlstandes der Hausgemeinschaft als eigenständiges Basis-Element der Gesellschaft, wobei sich im Übrigen spezifische Bezüge zur frühneuzeitlichen „Hausväterliteratur" ergeben, so erscheint die Beschaffungs- bzw. Erwerbskunst als Ergänzung der Haushaltswirtschaft durch Güter, die notwendig sind, aber nicht selbst bereitgestellt werden können, im Wege des Tauschhandels über den „Markt". Dass hierbei das Bedarfsdeckungsprinzip zugrunde liegt, erläutert Schefold dahingehend: „Obwohl Sache und Begriff darüber hinausreichen, stellt man sich hier zweckmäßig ein Landgut vor, das sich weitgehend selbst versorgt, dessen Erzeugnisse teilweise am Markt verkauft werden und das sich für seinen Bedarf am Markt ergänzt. Es handelt sich hier um den Tausch von Gebrauchswerten, deren Bedarf begrenzt ist."[41]

Mit dem Begriff der „naturgemäßen" Erwerbskunst, womit im Grunde eine gesellschaftlich gerechte sowie auf den Bedarf der Hausgemeinschaft ausgerichtete und in diesem Sinne „natürliche" Tauschwirtschaft gemeint ist, lenkt Schefold die Aufmerksamkeit auf die für die Markttheorie entscheidende wirtschaftsethische Differenzierung bei Aristoteles. Nämlich jene zwischen positiv bewerteter „haushaltsgemäßer Erwerbskunst" und negativ bewerteter „Bereicherungskunst", der so genannten „Chrematistik." Ist unter „haushaltsgemäßer Erwerbskunst" die auf Deckung des gegebenen Bedarfes ausgerichtete, ergänzende und damit dienende Funktion des Tauschhandels und damit des Marktes bezeichnet, so bezeichnet die „Chrematistik" den Erwerb um des Erwerbes willen, also eine Form des Tauschhandels bzw. Marktes, dessen primäres Ziel nicht die Deckung eines gegebenen Bedarfes, sondern die Steigerung der individuellen Erwerbskraft ist. Im Grunde wird damit das kapitalistische Erwerbsprinzip gekennzeichnet, bei dem es letztlich um die Rendite von eingesetztem Kapital im Wege der Vermarktung von Gütern und Leistungen geht. In diesem Sinne wird bei Aristoteles, so Schefold, „Chrematistik als Grenzen sprengender Erwerb definiert. Ihr Ziel ist der Erwerb um des Erwerbes willen. Da es hier nicht mehr um die begrenzte Bedürfnisbefriedigung geht, lässt sich die Chrematistik durch allerhand Techniken wirkungsvoller machen; der Erwerb wird schrankenlos."[42] Dabei schlägt, so fasst Schefold die aristotelische Argumentation weiter zusammen, „Erwerb … durch Austausch allein nicht notwendig in Chrematistik um, solange unter dem Gesichtspunkt der Haushaltungskunst, welche die Grenzen kennt getauscht, d.h. erworben wird …

40 Schefold 1989, 37.
41 Schefold 1989, 37.
42 Schefold 1989, 38.

Ebenso ist die Tauschkunst natürlich, wenn dem Haushaltungsprinzip unterworfen, sonst aber tadelnswert."[43]

In der bei Aristoteles thematisierten Gefahr einer derartigen Entgrenzung der Tauschwirtschaft bzw. der „Märkte" können wiederum zwei wesentliche Bezüge zum neuzeitlichen Wirtschaftsdenken gesehen werden. Der erste Bezug liegt darin, dass ein entscheidendes Kriterium der ethisch-moralischen Kontrolle des Marktsystems in dessen Begrenzung auf eine gesellschaftlich wünschenswerte Bedarfsdeckung liegt und darüber hinausgehendes Erwerbsstreben negativ zu bewerten ist. Nicht zuletzt spiegelt sich dies in der rezenten Kapitalismuskritik häufig verwendeten Begrifflichkeit der „Gier" als entscheidende Ursache einer Systemkrise der Marktwirtschaft. Aristoteles sieht das maßgebliche institutionelle Potenzial dieser Entgrenzung in der Entwicklung des Handelssystems, indem sich die „Bereicherungskunst" im Übergang vom Kleinhandel zum überregionalen Großhandel entsprechend entfaltet.[44]

In engem Zusammenhang damit steht der zweite wesentliche Bezug der Problematisierung der marktwirtschaftlichen Entgrenzung bei Aristoteles zum neuzeitlichen Wirtschaftsdenken. Und zwar in der funktionalen Verknüpfung der Tausch- bzw. Marktwirtschaft mit der Geldwirtschaft. Damit dass Aristoteles sowohl die Entstehung der Geldwirtschaft, als auch die sich in dieser vollziehende Etablierung der Bereicherungskunst (Chrematistik) historisch erklärt, legt er gleichsam eine argumentative Basis für die einschlägigen stufentheoretischen neuzeitlichen Geldentstehungstheorien, nach denen zunehmende technische Probleme des Naturaltausches ein Tauschmedium und einen verbindlichen und beliebig teilbaren wirtschaftlichen Wertmaßstab, also Geld in diesen Funktionen, erforderlich machten.[45]

Darin, dass Geld damit aber auch Wertaufbewahrungsmittel und damit dessen Vermehrung (Reichtum) ein Ziel wirtschaftlichen Handelns wurde, liegt der Ansatzpunkt für die Etablierung einer darauf ausgerichteten „Bereicherungskunst" bzw. genuin geldwirtschaftlichen „Chrematistik". Bei dieser wird, so Aristoteles, die Vermehrung von Geld über den Handel zum Selbstzweck. Dies, indem „alle, die sich mit chrematistischem Erwerb befassen … ihr Geld ins Unbegrenzte" vermehren würden und auf diese Weise „die zweite Art der Erwerbskunst, die Bereicherungskunst" entstand, „anfangs wohl nur ganz einfach, später kunstmäßig auf Grund der Erfahrung, woher und wie man Güter vertauschen müsse, um den größten Gewinn zu erzielen."[46] Hierbei zielt seine Kritik speziell auf den Zwischenhandel, bei dem die Absicht der Gewinnerzielung aus dem Tauschhandel und das Anhäufen von Geld zum Selbstzweck würden.

Auf diese Weise kann in der Ablehnung der über die Bedarfsdeckung hinaus gehenden „Bereicherungskunst" ein zentrales Kriterium der marktwirtschaftli-

43 Schefold 1989, 39.
44 Vgl. Schefold 1989, 39.
45 North 2009.
46 Zitiert bei Schefold 1989, 39.

chen Ethik bzw. Moral gesehen werden, das in der neuzeitlichen Kritik am Prinzip der Gewinnmaximierung bzw. der gewinnorientierten Ausdehnung der Handelssysteme und des Geldsystems zum Tragen kommt. Im Sinne dessen liegt in der aristotelischen Forderung, dass die marktwirtschaftliche Erwerbskunst auf den für die Haushaltung erforderlichen Bedarf begrenzt werden muss, ein entscheidender Ansatzpunkt für die aus der fundamentalen Kapitalismuskritik resultierenden alternativen Wirtschaftsmodelle sowie für die Kritik am unbegrenzten Wachstum marktwirtschaftlicher Systeme.

In weiterer Konsequenz liegt in der argumentativen Verknüpfung der negativen Bewertung der Schaffung von Reichtum durch Handel („Schacher“) mit der Geldwirtschaft ein wesentlicher Bezug zu der auch in der neuzeitlichen Wirtschaftsentwicklung und Wirtschaftstheorie immer wieder relevanten Frage des Erwerbs im Geldsystem selbst durch Geldverleih und Zinsnahme. In diesem Zusammenhang ergeben sich hinsichtlich des Stellenwertes und der Funktion von Zins bzw. Zinsgewinn in der Marktwirtschaft Parallelen zu mittelalterlichen und neuzeitlichen Konzepten des Zinsverbotes, aber auch zu entsprechenden Positionen in der aktuellen Kapitalismuskritik. Dies im Speziellen darin, dass es nach Aristoteles eine „natürliche Rolle des Geldes“[47] als instrumentelles Medium im Marktgeschehen in der Vermittlung des Tausches gebe, dass aber der Handel von Geld selbst im Wege des Geldverleihs und die Einnahmenerzielung durch Zinsgewinn als „Wucher [...] der aus dem Geld selbst den Erwerb zieht“[48] und damit als eine spezifische Form der als unnatürlich abzulehnenden chrematistischen Erwerbskunst zu werten sei, die die prinzipiell dienende Funktion von Handel und Geldwirtschaft überschreite. „Denn das Geld“, so schreibt Aristoteles, „ist um des Tausches willen erfunden worden, durch den Zins vermehrt es sich aber durch sich selbst. Daher hat es auch seinen Namen: das Geborene ist gleicher Art wie das Gebärende, und durch den Zins entsteht Geld aus Geld. Diese Art des Gelderwerbs ist also am meisten gegen die Natur.“[49]

Als wichtiger Aspekt dabei erscheint, dass mit einem derartigen, wie es Schefold in seiner Interpretation von Aristoteles bezeichnet, „zielverkehrendem Verwenden“ von Geld[50] die in der Entwicklung neuzeitlicher Marktwirtschaftssysteme immer wieder auftretende Entkoppelung der Geldwirtschaft von der Realwirtschaft angesprochen wird, ein Phänomen, das insbesondere in Wirtschaftskrisen virulent wird. Im Sinne dessen erscheint es in der historischen Perspektive auch in spezifischer Weise interessant, dass Aristoteles seine Kritik an Geld als Geldkapital und am daraus folgenden Zinsgewinn möglicherweise auch in Auseinandersetzung mit einer Wirtschaftskrise entwickelt haben könnte. Jedenfalls sieht Koslowski in der Krise der griechischen Wirtschaft im ausgehenden 4. Jahrhundert ein Motiv für Aristoteles, die sich aus der Ausbreitung von Zwi-

47 Zitiert bei Schefold 1989, 40.
48 Zitiert bei Schefold 1989, 40.
49 Zitiert bei Schefold 1989, 40.
50 Schefold 1989, 42.

schenhandel, Geldverleih und Zinsgewinn ergebende „neue Wirtschaftsweise" abzulehnen.[51]

In dem Zusammenhang ist es wichtig zu beachten, dass Aristoteles hier explizit normativ argumentiert, indem er einen von der von ihm beobachtbaren Realität des Wirtschaftslebens, der so genannten „praktischen Erwerbskunst", abweichenden, aber anzustrebenden Idealzustand des „guten" bzw. „natürlichen" Lebens postuliert. Dass dies wiederum die Forderung impliziert, mittels Regulierungen zumindest eine Annäherung an diesen Idealzustand zu bewirken, begründet letztendlich die Funktion des Staates als die die marktwirtschaftlichen Verhältnisse regulierende Instanz. „Wir müssen schließen", meint Schelfold, „dass hier wie bei Platon die Institutionen des Staates und des Rechts diesem Ziel zu dienen haben."[52] Ziel-Kriterium dabei ist die Verhinderung einer von der Haushaltungskunst abweichenden chrematistischen Entwicklung von Handel und Geldwirtschaft und deren Gestaltung nach dem Prinzip des „gerechten Tausches". Was nun aber der „gerechte Tausch" ist, ist letztlich bei Aristoteles gleich wie in der neuzeitlichen Marktwirtschaft nur bedingt eine ökonomische, sondern viel mehr eine gesellschaftspolitische Frage und in Zusammenhang damit aber auch eine Frage der Positionierung von ethisch-moralischen Kategorien in der Marktwirtschaftslehre.

Indem das, wie angeführt, sowohl in der Etablierung der neuzeitlichen Marktwirtschaftslehre bei Adam Smith und deren weiterer Entwicklung im 19. und 20. Jahrhundert, sowie in besonderem Maße in den jüngsten kapitalismuskritischen Diskursen immer wieder eine wesentliche Rolle spielte und spielt, ist die Bedeutung der antiken Wirtschaftstheorie, insbesondere jener von Aristoteles, im Lichte der neuzeitlichen Marktwirtschaftslehre evident.

Dabei erscheint es aber wesentlich zu beachten, dass dem aristotelischen Wirtschaftsdenken letztendlich das „Bedarfsdeckungsprinzip" zugrunde liegt, während in der neuzeitlichen Markttheorie das „Erwerbsprinzip" bestimmend ist und das entscheidende Movens nicht die Deckung eines vorhandenen Bedarfes ist, sondern das individuelle Streben nach Gewinnmaximierung, aus dem sich durch die „invisible hand" ein gesamtgesellschaftlicher Nutzen ergibt.

Davon ausgehend ist abschließend festzustellen, dass die marktwirtschaftlichen Bezüge in der aristotelischen Gesellschaftstheorie nicht einfach gleichsam eine „Vorstufe" zur modernen neuzeitlichen Marktwirtschaftstheorie á la Adam Smith darstellen, sondern zum einen bestimmte Elemente enthalten, die in deren Entwicklung eingeflossen sind, zum anderen aber Ansatzpunkte für die Kritik am neuzeitlichen kapitalistischen Marktwirtschaftsverständnis bieten können, speziell in Bezug auf dessen ethisch-moralische „Disziplinierung".

51 Koslowski 1979, 60–83 (Hinweis bei: Schefold 1989, 40).

52 Schefold 1989, 44

Literatur

Bauer L. – Matis H., Geburt der Neuzeit. Vom Feudalsystem zur Marktgesellschaft, München 1988

Dettling W., Wie modern ist die Antike?, in: DIE ZEIT 11.6.1993, 24.

Dittrich E., Die deutschen und österreichischen Kameralisten, Darmstadt 1974.

Felber C., Gemeinwohlökonomie. Das Wirtschaftsmodell der Zukunft, Wien 2010.

Gömmel R. – Klump R., Merkantilisten und Physiokraten in Frankreich, Darmstadt 1994.

Holub H-W., Eine Einführung in die Geschichte des ökonomischen Denkens Bd. I, Wien 2005.

James H., Der Rückfall. Die neue Weltwirtschaftskrise, München/Zürich 2001.

Kolb G., Geschichte der Volkswirtschaftslehre. Dogmenhistorische Positionen des ökonomischen Denkens, München 1997.

Koslowksi P., Haus und Geld. Zur aristotelischen Unterscheidung von Politik, Ökonomik und Chrematistik, in: Philosophisches Jahrbuch, Vol. 86 (1979), 1. Halbb., 60 –83.

Koslowski P., Politik und Ökonomie bei Aristoteles. 3. durchges. u. erg. Auflage, Tübingen 1993.

Krugman P., The Return of Depression Economics and the Crisis of 2008, New York/ London 2009.

Matis H. (Hg.), Von der Glückseligkeit des Staates. Staat, Wirtschaft und Gesellschaft in Österreich im Zeitalter des Absolutismus, Berlin 1981.

Musgrave R., The Theory of Public Finance, New York 1959.

North M., Kleine Geschichte des Geldes. Vom Mittelalter bis heute, München 2009.

Recktenwald H.C., Adam Smith, in: Starbatty J. (Hg.), Klassiker des ökonomischen Denkens.Bd. 1, München 1989, 134–155.

Schefold B., Platon und Aristoteles, in: Starbatty J. (Hg.), Klassiker des ökonomischen Denkens. Bd. 1: Von Platon bis John Stuart Mill, München 1989, 19–55.

Schefold B., Beiträge zur ökonomischen Dogmengeschichte, Düsseldorf 2004.

Smith, A., Der Wohlstand der Nationen. Eine Untersuchung seiner Natur und seiner Ursachen. Aus dem Englischen übertragen und mit einer umfassenden Würdigung des Gesamtwerkes von Horst Claus Recktenwald, München 1978.

Söllner F., Die Geschichte des ökonomischen Denkens. 2. verb. Aufl., Berlin/Heidelberg/New York 2001.

Sombart W., Der moderne Kapitalismus (unveränderter Nachdruck der 2. neu gearbeiteten Auflage, München und Leipzig 1916), München 1987.

Wieser C., Corporate Social Responsibility – Ethik, Kosmetik oder Strategie? Über die Relevanz der sozialen Verantwortung in der strategischen Unternehmensführung, München 2005.

Winkel H., Die deutsche Nationalökonomie im 19.Jahrhundert, Darmstadt 1977.

Wittmann W., Öffentliche Finanzen. Einführung in die Finanzwissenschaft, Reinbeck bei Hamburg 1978.

Trends im (Lebensmittel-) Handel

Gestern – Heute – Morgen

Helmut Eymannsberger

Als Vorsitzender der „Franz Triendl Stiftung" für Wirtschafts- und Unternehmensgeschichte der Wirtschaftskammer Salzburg danke ich den Organisatoren, insbesondere Frau Prof. Frass, für die Initiative, diesen Kongress zu veranstalten.

Ich möchte aufgrund der Themenstellung einen Bogen aus der Vergangenheit in die Gegenwart bis in die Zukunft des Handels spannen.

„Kauf, Konsum und Märkte" waren seit dem „im 14. Jahrhundert einsetzenden wirtschaftlichen Aufschwung, der im 15. und 16. Jahrhundert seinen Höhepunkt erreichte und Salzburg in den Augen der Zeitgenossen zu einem wichtigen Handelsplatz machte",[1] auch in Salzburg wesentliche Faktoren einer langen „Handelskarriere" dieser Stadt.[2] Diese Handelstradition war in der Vergangenheit mit einigen deutlichen Brüchen versehen. Und doch konnte Salzburg in den letzten Jahrzehnten der Grenzlage zu Deutschland viele positive Seiten abgewinnen: Als Tor zum wichtigsten, österreichischen Haupthandelspartner Deutschland hat sich Salzburg vor Jahrzehnten bereits zum überdurchschnittlich aktiven Groß- und Einzelhandelsstandort mit Headquarter-Funktion entwickelt.[3] Unterstützt haben dabei sicher die Lagegunst mit sehr guten internationalen Verkehrsanbindungen mit dem größten Bundesländerflughafen Österreichs, Autobahnen und internationalen Eisenbahnverbindungen.

Was versteht man eigentlich unter „Handel"?

„Den" Handel, respektive „den" Lebensmittelhandel gibt es nicht! Der Handel war immer schon eine besonders lebendige, vielfältige und trendige Branche. Denken Sie etwa an „Spar" oder „Billa" – mit jeweils über 1.000 Filialen in Österreich und großteils standardisiertem Sortiment – und stellen diese einem jener Kramerläden (Greissler, Tante-Emma-Läden) gegenüber, von denen es auch in Salzburg noch einige gibt oder einem Kiosk oder Stand eines Marktfieranten, der Speck, Süßwasserfische oder Obst vertreibt. Betrachten Sie mit Ihren geistigen Auge alle

1 Dopsch 1983, 757.

2 Über Händler und Lebensmittelanbieter vor über 100 Jahren gibt einen Überblick über die Verhältnisse in der Stadt Salzburg: Gamsjäger 2008, 379 ff. Vgl. zur Entwicklung von ausgewählten Teilen des sogenannten Dienstleistungssektors (inkl. zumeist des gesamten Handels – in Stadt und Land Salzburg im 20. Jahrhundert mit statistischem Zahlenmaterial). Dirninger 1990, 183 ff. Einen Einblick in mehrere Facetten der Handelswelt in Salzburg gibt auch Hoffmann 1990, 152 ff.

3 Beispielsweise Porsche Austria als eines der größten Autohandelsunternehmen Europas, Mercedes-Pappas, BMW Austria oder die Spar Hauptzentrale, Lidl Austria (Lebensmittelhandel), dm Österreich.

hippen Läden in europäischen Großstädten, die auch ein paar Lebensmittel führen, daneben aber vielleicht CD's und Blumen und einen Fahrradverleih betreiben. Oder den Backwaren-Laden, der entweder zu einer kleinen Bäckerei gehört, dessen Chef sich als Bäcker und somit dem Gewerbe und nicht dem Handel zugehörig fühlt oder den Backwaren-Shop, in dem de facto industriell gefertigte Ware vertrieben wird. Oder eine Vertriebsabteilung eines Industrieunternehmens, das – bleiben wir in Salzburg – die im eigenen Unternehmen produzierten Ski in alle Welt „verkauft", alle Tätigkeiten eines Großhändlers ausübt und dennoch im wirtschaftsstatistischen Sinn definitionsgemäß kein Händler ist.

Um den Rahmen nicht zu sprengen, bleiben daher Handel im „weiteren" Sinn wie zum Beispiel der Ab-Hof-Verkauf, Drive-in-Stores, Duty-free-Shops, Factory-Outlets, der Handwerkshandel, der Personalkauf, die Werbetrends und Gehirnforschung (Werbung!), der Ladenbau, die Architektur u.v.a.m. ausgeklammert.

Viele Themen können daher nur kursorisch „angerissen" werden. Für eine weitere Vertiefung in die Handelswelt empfiehlt sich über diesen Beitrag hinaus die Lektüre handelswissenschaftlicher Literatur, von Fachzeitschriften oder Standardwerken der Handelsberatung oder die auch in Österreich erscheinenden Fachzeitschriften.[4]

Es ist eingangs höchst erforderlich Begriffsbestimmungen vorzunehmen: „Einzelhandel" – so Gablers Wirtschaftslexikon – bedeutet nicht, „einzeln handeln", sondern ist im Sinne einer sogenannten funktionalen Interpretation „der Absatz von Waren an den Letztverbraucher".[5] „Großhandel" heißt schon gar nicht, dass hier etwa nur große, schwere Waren gehandelt werden, sondern ist im Sinne der funktionalen Interpretation „der Absatz von Waren und sonstigen Leistungen an Wiederverkäufer, Weiterverarbeiter, gewerbliche Verwerter (inklusive Entsorger) oder Großverbraucher".[6]
Die Trends von gestern bilden im Ergebnis vereinfacht ausgedrückt den Status Quo von heute, außer es handelte sich in der Retrospektive dann doch nur um kurzfristige Modeerscheinungen.

Dieser Fachbeitrag aus der „modernen Handelswelt" versteht sich weder als Aufguss „boulevardesker Trendforschung",[7] die sich den Anschein „von Wissenschaftlichkeit"[8] gibt und sich mit „eigens erfundenen Methoden schmückt" noch

4 Zum Beispiel Beisheim O. (Hg.), Distribution im Aufbruch. Bestandsaufnahme und Perspektiven, München 1999 oder zahlreiche periodisch erscheinende Handelsjournale wie Key Account, Cash, Regal (etwa für den österreichischen Lebensmittelhandel), Österreichische Textilzeitung und viele andere Branchen- und Fachzeitschriften; www.ulricheggert.de/studien/index.php.; abgerufen am 26.10.2012.

5 http://wirtschaftslexikon.gabler.de/Definition/einzelhandel.html; abgerufen am 20.6.2011.

6 http://wirtschaftslexikon.gabler.de/Definition/grosshandel.html; abgerufen am 20.6.2011.

7 Rust „Zukunft und Forschung" des Zentrums für Zukunftsstudien Salzburg, 2009, 8.

8 Ebd.

als reine „Zukunftsforschung",[9] die sich ausschließlich den in der Gegenwart erzeugten und zu begründenden Zukunftsannahmen widmet.[10]

Dass allerdings alles, was in der Zukunft liegt, mit einem gewissen Maß an Unsicherheit behaftet ist, liegt in der Natur der Sache! Mit Konrad Paul Liessmann gesprochen: „Da die Zukunft in der Zukunft liegt, bleibt sie uns prinzipiell verschlossen".[11] Da mir dennoch eine „Zukunftsforschung",[12] die „nicht zukünftige Gegenwarten" , „sondern die Bilder, die wir uns heute von Ihnen machen"[13] oder anders ausgedrückt: „Was wir *gegenwärtig* unter Zukunft verstehen",[14] gerade in der Handelswelt doch zu unkonkret ist, deute ich den Begriff TREND in einen praxisbezogenen Sinn um: Unter HandelsTRENDS sind nach meiner Definition bereits (vereinzelt) sichtbare Maßnahmen zu verstehen, mit denen der Handel versuchsweise oder vereinzelt bereits in der Realität u.a. auf gesellschaftliche Entwicklungen reagiert, reagiert hat oder noch verstärkt reagieren wird. Dies steht im bewussten, teilweisen Gegensatz zu herkömmlichen Definitionen des Begriffs TREND, wie z.B. (über einen gewissen Zeitraum bereits zu beobachtende, statistisch erfassbare) Entwicklung(stendenz).[15]

Der leichteren Lesbarkeit wegen sind Trends (im hier gebrauchten Sinn) nachfolgend kursiv gesetzt. Allerdings wird der Kürze Tribut gezollt: Alle Globaltrends, die meisten Konsumtrends im herkömmlichen Sinn bleiben ausgeklammert bzw. werden stillschweigend vorausgesetzt. Alle Trends beziehen sich daher – wie gesagt – auf ganz konkrete Handlungen, Reaktionen und konkrete Maßnahmen vom Einzelnen bis zur Masse der Betriebe.

9 Grunwald „Zukunft und Forschung" des Zentrums für Zukunftsstudien Salzburg, 2009, 33.
10 Ebd.
11 Liessman K.P., 15.
12 Ebd., 26.
13 Ebd.
14 Ebd., 33.
15 www.duden.de/rechtschreibung/Trend; abgerufen am 10.9.2011.

1. Überlick über den österreichischen Handel (i.e.S.)

1.1 Die volkswirtschaftliche Bedeutung des Handels

- Anzahl der Unternehmen im Handel: 74.800
  - Entspricht 25% der Unternehmen in der marktorientierten Wirtschaft
  - 88% der Handelsunternehmen haben unter 10 Beschäftigte
- Anzahl der Unternehmen im Einzel- und Großhandel: 41.310
  - Zahl stationärer Geschäfte: 50.900
  - Verkaufsfläche stationärer Geschäfte: 16,0 Mio. m^2
  - Großhandel: 25.000 Unternehmen
- Überlebensquote im Handel: 65,6% nach 4 Jahren
  - Einzelhandel: 66,5%, Großhandel: 62,7%, Kfz-Bereich: 70,6%
- Handelsumsätze:
  - Einzel- und Großhandel in Österreich setzten im Jahr 2010 Waren im Wert von rund 220 Mrd. € um
- Mehr als 99,7% aller Handelsunternehmen in der EU sind Kleinst-, Klein- und Mittelunternehmen (KMU-2008)

Anmerkung: gerundete Werte: Datenbasis 2009, Neugründungen und Schließungen (2008), Umsatz (2010)

(Quelle: KMU Forschung Austria, Der österreichische Handel 2010, 13, eigene Bearbeitung)

Von rund 74.800 Handelsunternehmen in Österreich im Jahr 2009 zählten mehr als 50% zum Einzelhandel. Die beiden größten Branchen – nach der Anzahl der Unternehmen – waren und sind eindeutig der Einzelhandel mit Bekleidung sowie der Lebensmitteleinzelhandel.[16]

1.2 Die Bedeutung des Handels als Arbeitgeber

Die Entwicklung der Anzahl der Beschäftigten im österreichischen Handel verlief dynamisch, wie sich aus der Tabelle 1 im Anhang gut ablesen lässt: Zwischen 1995 und 2009 stieg die Zahl der MitarbeiterInnen im Einzelhandel von rd. 222.000 auf ca. 310.000. Im Großhandel und Kfz-Handel blieb sie dagegen im Wesentlichen gleich.

Rund 20% der MitarbeiterInnen des gesamten untersuchten Handels (i.e.S.) waren in jenen 20% der Unternehmen bis 9 ArbeitnehmerInnen tätig, in Großunternehmen mit mindestens 250 Beschäftigten rund 38% aller ArbeitnehmerInnen, obwohl nur 0,3% aller Handelsunternehmen zu dieser Größenkategorie zählen.

Im Lebensmitteleinzelhandel sind bei weitem die meisten MitarbeiterInnen im Einzelhandel beschäftigt, nämlich rund 89.500 (2009). Das entspricht einem An-

16 Vgl. Voithofer – Gittenberger, Wien 2010, 15, 17.

teil von 29%. Derzeit dürften an die 45% aller Beschäftigten im Einzelhandel Teilzeitbeschäftigte sein, das heißt weniger als 38,5 Stunden in der Woche arbeiten. 2008 waren es österreichweit rund 43%.

→ *Trend: Die Teilzeitbeschäftigung wird weiter leicht steigen*
In den letzten Jahrzehnten hat eine Entkoppelung der Geschäftsöffnungszeiten von der sogenannten wöchentlichen Normalarbeitszeit der Beschäftigten von 38,5 Stunden/Woche im arbeitsrechtlichen Sinn stattgefunden. Daher stieg m.E. der Anteil der Teilzeitbeschäftigten (inklusive der sogenannten geringfügig Beschäftigten) insbesondere an der Gesamtanzahl der MitarbeiterInnen im Einzelhandel kontinuierlich.

1.3 Anzahl der Geschäfte in Österreich – Konzentration im Einzelhandel

Wo können Frau und Herr Österreicher nun einkaufen?[17]

1. Im sogenannten stationären Einzelhandel, das sind im üblichen Sprachgebrauch die „Geschäfte" – waren dies Anfang 2010 – wie erwähnt – insgesamt rund 50.900.
2. Dabei zählten zum österreichischen „Einzel"handel (mit gewissen statistischen Unschärfen) rund 45.500 (ca. 89%) Geschäfte.
3. 3.500 (das sind etwa 7%) entfielen auf Ladengeschäfte von Herstellern.
4. 2.000 „Geschäfte" waren unter die Einkaufsmöglichkeiten von Großhändlern für Letztverbraucher einzureihen (beispielsweise Lagerhäuser).

→ *Trend: Investitition in die Qualität der Standorte*
Die große Expansionsphase der Filialisten der letzten Jahrzehnte dürfte wohl vorbei sein. Schon seit mehreren Jahren wird eher in die Qualität der Standorte investiert. Die durch Übernahmen und Verkäufe sich teilweise gegenseitig kannibalisierenden Niederlassungen wurden und werden im Wesentlichen sukzessive bereinigt, weniger gut gehende Filialen übersiedelt oder geschlossen.

Die Anzahl der Geschäfte im gesamten Einzelhandel hat sich österreichweit sukzessive verringert. Nach neuesten Daten hat sich die Gesamtzahl der österreichischen Geschäfte (nicht nur Einzelhandel) von 50.900 (2010 gegenüber 2011) noch einmal um 1,5% (das sind 800 Läden) auf 50.100 reduziert.

Im Gegensatz zur weit verbreiteten Meinung, vertritt die Administration des Landes Salzburg sinngemäß die Auffassung, es habe zwischen 1996 und 2008 keinen Rückgang an „Geschäften" im Bundesland Salzburg gegeben.[18] Da ein Hinweis auf die wirtschaftsstatische ÖNACE-Gliederung fehlt, dürfte darin die „Auflösung" liegen. Denn auch das Land Salzburg nimmt an, dass sich zwischen 1996

17 Vgl. Braumann – Terlinden – Will, Salzburg 2010, 7.
18 KMU Forschung Austria, 2006, 29 und Der österreichische Handel 2010, 21.

und 2008 die Verkaufsfläche im Bundesland Salzburg um 29% (!), das ist fast ein Drittel, erhöht und somit m.E. die Handelskonzentration voll durchgeschlagen hat.

1.4 Anzahl der Lebensmittelgeschäfte in Österreich

Laut *Regioplan*/Wien, verringerte sich in Österreich die Anzahl der Outlets, d.h. der Geschäfte und Filialen im Lebensmitteleinzelhandel im Zeitraum 2001 – 2009 von 6.410 auf 6.015. Diese werden von insgesamt 3.230 Unternehmen (Einzelhandel) betrieben. Somit waren 7,8% aller österreichischen EinzelhändlerInnen Lebensmittelhändler. Im Vergleich: zum Internet- oder Versandhandel (s.u.) zählten nicht ganz 1% aller Handelsunternehmen in Österreich.

→ *Trend: Die Mobilität beeinflusst das Einkaufsverhalten auch im Nahversorgungsbereich*
Die Anzahl der Lebensmittelgeschäfte generell ging und geht auch künftig zurück, sofern sich das Mobilitätsverhalten der Bevölkerung nicht gravierend verändert. Die Filialisierung nahm und nimmt auch weiter zu, jedoch mit geringerer Intensität als in der Vergangenheit.

1.5 Anzahl der Lebensmittelgeschäfte in Salzburg

Im Bundesland Salzburg waren 2010 unter anderem REWE mit 129 Outlets (davon 66 BILLAS), die Spar-Gruppe mit 116, die ZEV / MARKANT mit 48, Hofer mit 63 und Lidl mit 33 Niederlassungen bzw. somit mit insgesamt 632 Filialen vertreten.[19] Im Jahr 2000 dagegen entfielen auf Billa 73 Filialen, auf Spar 101, auf ZEV 75, auf Hofer 12 und auf Lidl 2. Daraus ist klar die Expansion der Diskonter ersichtlich.[20]

Der Anteil der Lebensmittelhändler[21] an der Gesamtzahl der Handelsunternehmen ist im Bundesland Salzburg etwas geringer als im Österreich-Durchschnitt. Dies hängt wohl mit dem teilweise touristisch an Besuchern und Touristen ausgelegten Handelsangebot in Salzburg und mit dem in unserem Bundesland somit überproportional vertretenen Textil- und Sportartikelhandel zusammen.

1.6 Filialisierung des Einzelhandels – ein Trend in der westlichen Welt

Der Unterschied in der Entwicklung zwischen filialisierten und nicht filialisierten Unternehmen führte in Österreich generell – wie erwähnt – und speziell auch im Lebensmittelhandel zu einem Konzentrationsprozess.[22] Dabei handelt es sich im Gegensatz etwa zur Selbstbedienung um keine ganz junge Erscheinung: Bereits

---

19 Regioplan Branchenreport 2010, 39.
20 Vgl. auch Kapitel 4.1., Regioplan, Einzelhandel im Bundesland Salzburg 2000, 15.
21 Gamsjäger 2008, 379 ff.
22 Vgl. Kapitel 3.4. und 3.5.

1866 wurde nämlich in Europa (Reims, Frankreich) die erste Ladenkette gegründet.[23]

2. Die Handelsstandorte gestern – heute – morgen: Vom Zentrum in die Peripherie (und wieder zurück?)

2.1 Selbstbedienung und Supermärkte – Einkaufszentren – Fachmärkte – Peripherie

→ *Trend: Selbstbedienung*
Das Eine (Selbstbedienung) ist ohne das Andere (Flächenbedarf) nicht denkbar... Wer bedingt was? Blenden wir ein wenig zurück, bevor wir uns dieser „Henne-Ei"-Thematik annähern: Sandgruber beziffert das „Geburtsjahr" der Selbstbedienung mit 1916.[24] In den USA entstanden 1930 auch die ersten Supermärkte eines Michael Cullen, der diese Geschäftsidee – auf dem Billigstverkaufspreis basierend – umsetzte.

In Österreich trat die Selbstbedienung 1950 ihren Siegeszug an und zwar in Linz. Sie setzte sich jedoch relativ langsam durch. Von rund 2.900 (Teil-) Selbstbedienungsgeschäften Anfang der 1960er Jahre im österreichischen Lebensmitteleinzelhandel (von insgesamt 24.000) erhöhte sich deren Anzahl gegen Ende dieser Dekade auf bereits ca. 5.400. Im Jahr 1972 stand dieser Wert bereits auf rund 6.800 (ca. 71% aller Geschäfte). Aufgrund des hohen Lohnkostenanteils in der Dienstleistungsbranche war es nicht verwunderlich, dass sich im Bereich des Lebensmittel-Vollsortiments die Selbstbedienung (außer je nach Firmenphilosophie im Feinkostbereich) mittlerweile praktisch lückenlos durchgesetzt hat.

Trend: „Grüne Wiese"
Mit den Supermärkten, die auf Selbstbedienung setzten, setzte der Trend der Verlagerung des Einzelhandels auf die sogenannte „Grüne Wiese" (=Peripherie) ein. Prägte der Einzelhandel gleichsam jahrhundertelang das Stadtleben der Neuzeit, zog es große Teile – insbesondere auch den großflächigen (Lebensmittel) Handel – an die Stadt- und Ortsränder.

Der Handels- und Wirtschaftspolitiker *Hans-Jörg Bauer* bezeichnete nach dem Zeitalter der „Industrierevolution" des 19. Jahrhunderts das darauffolgende Jahrhundert „als die Epoche der Revolution im Handel".[25]

Dies betrifft zum einen insbesondere neue Betriebstypen und zum anderen deren Lage. War das 19. Jahrhundert die Zeit der Spezialisierung, somit die „große

23 Sandgruber 2002, 50.
24 Sandgruber 2002, 50.
25 Vgl. Bauer 1982, 153.

Zeit der kleinen Kaufleute“[26] – man denke nur an Zuckerl-, Spirituosen-, Gemüse-, Milch- oder Kurzwarengeschäfte – revolutionierten Ende des 19. und in der ersten Hälfte des 20. Jahrhunderts Warenhäuser den innerstädtischen Handel in den großen Städten – auch auf dem europäischen Kontinent. Aus Konsumentensicht boten die Warenhäuser als m.E. erste Vorläufer der Einkaufszentren unserer Tage ein breites Warenangebot, eine durchgehende Preisauszeichnung, die Möglichkeit, Waren anzusehen, ohne sie kaufen zu müssen, allerdings anfänglich bei strikter Barzahlung mit Fixpreisen. (Interessanterweise ließen jedoch Wal-Mart, Target und Toys“R“US in den USA die Methode früherer [Dorf-] Krämer, nämlich als Kunde Waren zurücklegen bzw. „anschreiben“ lassen zu können – nunmehr gegen eine Anzahlung und eine fixe Gebühr – in der Zeit der Wirtschaftskrise 2009 wieder aufleben.)

Aus weiterer betriebswirtschaftlicher Sicht war dieser damals neue Geschäftstyp „Warenhaus“ von arbeitsteiliger Organisation mit einhergehender Rationalisierung, Marktbeobachtung mit systemisiertem Angebot, später dann doch durch mögliche Ratengeschäften als ergänzende Dienstleistung zur Barzahlung sowie zahlreiche jahreszeiten- und stichtagsabhängige Inszenierungen, Reklameaktivitäten rund um Weihnachten, Ostern, Muttertag, Valentinstag, etc. gekennzeichnet.

Diese neuen Warenwelten waren bereits ab Mitte des 19. Jahrhunderts entstanden: Bon Marché (in Frankreich) war der erste größere Händler in Europa mit dem neuen Rezept „Kleiner Aufschlag, aber großer Umsatz“, und auch damals schon mit einer Umsatzbeteiligung (!) der Angestellten.[27]

Vor dem ersten Weltkrieg spielte sich der Einzelhandel jedenfalls in der europäischen Innenstadt ab.

„Galerie Lafayettes“ in Paris oder aber die bekannten überdachten Einkaufsgalerien in Mailand, Genua, etc.[28] sind auch heute noch bekannte Namen wie auch das Kaufhaus Macy's in New York (NYC), Harrods in London oder beispielsweise Karstadt in Deutschland (gegründet 1891).

Die Verkaufsflächenentwicklung an der Peripherie (Grüne Wiese) verursachte städtebaulich gröbere Zäsuren, da in Folge viele Orts- und Stadtkerne von den Investitionen und Innovationen, somit auch den Handelsinnovationen, abgeschnitten waren. Die Gelder für Investitionen flossen an die Stadtränder. Dort war überdies das Grundstücksangebot größer und billiger. Die Verkehrswege (im Großen: etwa Autobahnen; im Kleinen: Kreuzungen, Unterführungen, etc.) prägten immer schon den Handel, so auch in den letzten Jahrzehnten.

Dies führt dazu, dass in den sogenannten Speckgürteln vieler europäischer, aber insbesondere auch österreichischer Städte oft ein Übergewicht an Verkaufsfläche im Vergleich zu den Innenstädten existiert. 33% aller von SABE-V unter-

26 Vgl. Sandgruber 2002, 42.
27 Vgl. Bauer 1982, 143.
28 Vgl. Bauer 1982, 143 ff; Sandgruber 2002, 42.

suchten Handelsstandort-Verkaufsflächen in Salzburg befanden sich 2005 im Orts- und Stadtkern, der Rest in sogenannten immobilienwirtschaftlichen D- und E-Lagen. (In den bayrischen Landeskreisen Berchtesgadener Land und Traunstein lag der Wert für den Bereich von Orts- und Stadtkernen erheblich höher [48% bzw. 49%].)

Diese Attraktivierung peripherer Handelsstandorte führte allerdings dazu, dass in innerstädtischen Arealen vielerorts sogenannte „trading-down"-Effekte einsetzen.[29] Eine „Faustregel": Nach dem Abzug oder „Einstellen" des Einzelhandels siedeln sich Wettcafés, später Shops für Erotikartikel o.Ä. an. Nach diesen offensichtlichen Anzeichen einer schleichenden negativen Entwicklung eines Areals wandelt sich auch das Bewohnermilieu, die Mieten sinken. Immobilienwirtschaftlich beginnt ein Teufelskreis. Einkommenskräftige BewohnerInnen verlassen den Straßenzug oder das Stadtviertel. Am Endpunkt kann die Devastierung ganzer Straßenzüge stehen.

In den USA gibt es bereits verschiedene Beispiele, wo man ganze Stadtviertel als sogenannte „businessimprovementdistricts" mit eigenen steuerrechtlichen und raumordnungsrechtlichen – diese Areale privilegierenden – Vorschriften gleichsam wieder neu entstehen lassen will. Hier seien ausnahmsweise wertende (und provokante) Fragen gestellt, ob Mitteleuropa denn solche von der Öffentlichkeit „subventionierten Raumordnungs- und Geschäftsmodelle" braucht?[30] Wäre es nicht bedeutend attraktiver, innerstädtische Areale mit Frequenz und einem Handelsbesatz aus Filialisten UND selbständigen Einzelhändlern zu formen? Dazu wäre allerdings ein ganz klares Bekenntnis der entscheidenden politischen Akteure PRO Ortskern bzw. Innenstadt und contra neue „Grüne Wiese"-Ansiedlungen notwendig! Dann würden auch wieder mehr Investitionen in den zentralen Lagen vorgenommen.

Auch wenn sich vielerorts innerstädtische Initiativen gebildet haben, die durchaus so manche Erfolge im Bereich des Stadt-/Standortmarketings (z.B. St. Johann im Pongau) zu verzeichnen haben, können diese generell das Überangebot an Verkaufsflächen in Österreich nicht egalisieren.

2.2 Verkaufsflächen und ihre Entwicklung in Österreich

Anfang 2010 waren in Österreich laut KMU Forschung Austria insgesamt rund 16 Mio. m^2 Verkaufsfläche (2011: 16,4 Mio. m^2) zu verzeichnen.[31] Die Verkaufsflä-

29 Eymannsberger 2001, 3 ff.

30 Das immer schon besonders fortschrittliche Salzburger Tourismusgesetz sieht Abgaben vor, mit denen auch „Stadtmarketingaktivitäten" (in Orts- und Stadtkernen) unterstützt werden. Die Pflicht zur Leistung von Abgaben besteht gemäß einem Verteilungsschlüssel nach der jeweiligen Nähe einer Branche zum Tourismus (Tourismusaffinität). Vgl. § 1 Abs. 4 des Salzburger Tourismusgesetzes 2003, LGBl. 43/2003 i.d.g.F.: Tourismusverbände mit obligatorischer Mitgliedschaft sind demnach gesetzlich verpflichtet, „die wirtschaftliche Infrastruktur" zu fördern (Ortsmarketing).

31 http://portal.wko.at/wk/format_detail.wk?angid=1&stid=634739&dstid=224 (4.10.2011).

che leerstehender Geschäfte („Flächenleerstände") ist dabei nicht berücksichtigt. Bereits 2005 gab es im Bundesland Salzburg – laut SABE-V-Untersuchung – bei einer Verkaufsfläche von insgesamt rund 1 Mio. m^2 weit über 80.000 m^2 an Leerständen.[32]

→ *Trend: Steigerung der Verkaufsfläche bei sinkender Zahl der Outlets*
Bei einer sinkenden Anzahl an Geschäften war und ist eine Zunahme an Verkaufsfläche zu verzeichnen. Somit verschwinden kleine Anbieter sukzessive vom Markt.[33] Die Zunahme der Verkaufsflächen wird weitergehen, aber wohl mit geringeren Zuwachsraten wie in der Vergangenheit.

2.3 Entwicklung der Einkaufs- und Fachmarktzentren

→ *Trend: Leichte Zunahme von Einkaufs- und Fachmarktzentren*
Auch wenn die in Österreich überaus hohen Wachstumsraten der letzten Jahrzehnte die Anzahl von Einkaufs- und Fachmarktzentren betreffend wohl nicht mehr anhalten werden, wird sich der Trend (insbesondere auch im Bereich von Erweiterungen) fortsetzen.[34]

Im Jahr 2009 entstanden in Österreich insgesamt 189 „künstlich geschaffene" größere Einkaufsagglomerationen. 112 davon entfielen auf „klassische" Einkaufszentren, ebenfalls überwiegend auf peripheren Arealen, 69 auf Fachmarktzentren, 2 auf Factory Outlets (zum Beispiel Wals bei Salzburg) und 5 auf Kaufhäuser.

2.4 Weitere Trends (Auswahl)

Die Strategien, mit denen der Handel auf Trends reagiert, können in drei Gruppen eingeteilt werden können. In eine Preis-Strategie, eine Convenience-Strategie und eine Erlebnis-Strategie.[35]

2.4.1 Lebensmittelhandel (Nahversorgung i.e.S.)

→ *Trend: Neue Formen der Nahversorgung*
In manchen Szenegegenden in europäischen Großstädten entstehen Läden, die Sortimente anbieten, die vordergründig nichts miteinander zu tun haben, ungewohnte Kombinationen wie ein ganz schmales Lebensmittelsortiment kombiniert mit Bildern oder Textilien, Blumen, Fahrradverleih sowie rezeptfreie Medikamente wurden bereits „gesichtet". Damit stellen diese Nahversorger ganz strikt auf die jeweilige Mitbewerbersituation und allfällig fehlende Sortimente ab.

32 Vgl. SABE-V 2005, 96.
33 Vgl. Der österreichische Handel 2010, 25.
34 Vgl. Der österreichische Handel 2010, 27.
35 In Anlehnung an Eggert in: Beisheim 1999, 1068 ff.

→ *Trend: Renaissance der Nahversorgung (versus weitere Zunahme der Mobilität)*
Zumindest beim wachsenden Bevölkerungsanteil der Senioren reduziert sich teilweise die Lust, nur mehr auf der grünen Wiese die Einkäufe erledigen zu können. Daraus könnten wieder mehr Geschäfte in Wohnortnähe resultieren, sowie kleinere Einkaufsformate. Für die 50+-Generation ist eine bessere Warenübersicht und bessere Warenzugänglichkeit wichtig. (Die Formate und deren betriebswirtschaftlich rentable Größe werden sich aber nach der betrieblichen Kostensituation auszurichten haben).

→ *Trend: Nach der Hyper-Welle ist Downsizing nun auch eine Option*
Zum Beispiel: Expressformate /„Kioskisierung“ / kundennahe, kleine Fachmarktkonzepte (RFID-Technologie [s.d.] in Kombination mit nur einem Angestellten im Laden). In den USA ist die Boom-Zeit der riesigen Mega-Malls und Mega-Shops wohl auch vorbei. Aufschwung zeigen in den Großstädten dagegen eher kleinere Supermarktkonzepte. Der US-Retailer „Target“ zum Beispiel baut kleine Läden aus. Die Zeitknappheit der Konsumenten und das junge, urbane Publikum könnten eine Renaissance der Nahversorgung einläuten.

→ *Trend „Convenience“*
Im Lebensmitteleinzelhandel ist „Mobile eating“ und „convenience (to go)“ angesagt. Das Motto lautet: „Schneller Snack“ statt selbst zubereitetes Essen und dennoch wird Frische, Bio etc. nicht vernachlässigt. Shops aus einer Mischung von Bäckerei, kleiner Gastronomie bis hin zur Café-Ecke treffen mit gesundem Fast Food den Zukunftsnerv.

→ *Trend: „Bio“ versus „Nicht-Bio“*
Als zusätzlicher Anbieter im Lebensmittelbereich haben sich in Österreich über Bio-Läden oder Bio-Supermärkte hinaus bereits mehrere Lebensmittelfilialisten, ja sogar Diskonter entschlossen, Bioware (teilweise auch „Fair-Trade“-Ware!) anzubieten. Auch dies unterstreicht die Modernität und Innovationskraft des österreichischen Lebensmittelhandels.

2.4.2 Im Handel allgemein

→ *Trend: Der Handel wird zum „Problemlöser“!*
Zusätzlich zum Warensortiment Dienstleistung anzubieten, ist in vollem Gange. Es entsteht eine ganze „Betreuungskette“: Ware bzw. Dienstleistung PLUS Service PLUS Beratung PLUS Information PLUS Nachbetreuung (After-Sales-Services). Der Handel wird überdies auch zum „Makler“ (Fertighäuser etc.).

→ *Trend: Mieten statt kaufen oder Nutzen statt besitzen*
Neue Geschäftsmodelle entstehen durch Konsumtrends: Vom Car-Sharing (Mobilität) über Babybekleidung[36] bis hin zu exklusiver Kleidung für singuläre außergewöhnliche Ereignisse, wie dies etwa Frack- oder Kostümverleih schon seit Jahrzehnten vormachen. Besonders der Autosektor beschäftigt sich bereits mit diesem Zukunftsmodell. Gerade in Großstädten und bei jüngeren KonsumentInnen stellt sich die Frage nach der Notwendigkeit des „Besitzes" eines PKW künftig immer weniger.

→ *Trend: Unmittelbare Produktion im Laden*
In den USA ist mittlerweile im Buchhandel eine sogenannte „Espresso Book Maschine" im Einsatz, die ein komplettes Buch in vier Minuten produziert. Dabei kann der Kunde aus vier Millionen Buchtiteln, die keinen Urheberrechtsschutz mehr genießen und die aus dem Internet heruntergeladen werden können, auswählen. Ein 200-Seiten Buch beläuft sich im Verkaufspreis auf rund 7 Euro. Wenn ein Fahrradkurier das druckfrische Werk auch noch heimbringt, scheinen „Amazon" und „Kindle" einen spannenden Mitbewerber bekommen zu haben.

→ *Trend: Umweltorientierte Öko-Läden*
Unternehmen agieren ganz bewusst (ganz plakativ natürlich) auch umweltbewusst: zum Beispiel bei Strom- und Heizenergieverbrauch oder mit energieoptimierten Beleuchtungssystemen oder wenn sie Solardächer installieren, die Dachfläche dafür vermieten etc.

→ *Trend: Produktpolitik stellt Zusatznutzen in den Vordergrund*
Stark im Kommen waren in den letzten Jahren **„**Wellness-Produkte", oder im Lebensmittelbereich Convenience–Produkte (s.o.), Funktional Food etc. Darunter versteht man Produktkategorien mit „Mehrwert", d.h. mit Zusatznutzen versehene Produkte.

→ *Trend: Zielgruppenspezifischere Geschäfte*
In den letzten Jahren entstanden auch noch mehr besonders zielgruppenorientierte Läden. In der Bekleidungsbranche (Frauen/Männer/Kinder) längst üblich, wurde auch der Sportartikelhandel von diesem Trend erfasst. Seniorenläden gab es bereits (vgl. 50+). Wer aber will wirklich „Senior" sein? Dennoch wird diese Entwicklung indirekt voranschreiten.[37] Weitere typische Erscheinungsformen sind Lebensmittelläden für die verschiedensten Ethnien.

---

36 www.thredup.com, abgerufen am 26.10.2011.

37 Einen weiteren guten Überblick – insbesondere zu den Herausforderungen des Handels im Bereich der 50+-Generation – bietet die Strategie–Studie von Eggert U., „Zukunft Handel – mit Kooperation und System, Innovation und Differenzierung"; vgl. auch www.ulricheggert.de, abgerufen am 16.10.2011. Vgl. ebenso: Eggert U., Handelsbericht 18, 2011 und Handelsbericht 22, 2011; sowie Eggert U. Handelsbericht 12, 2009.

→ *Trend: Zusatzleistungen (Ergänzungssortimente)*
„dm" etwa bietet in der Bundesrepublik Deutschland und Österreich mit ausländischen Versandapotheken diverse Arzneimittel an.

→ *Trend: „Guerilla-Shops" und „Temporary Stores" (Pop-up-Stores)*
Diese sind nur für einen begrenzten (!) Zeitraum (Wochen, Monate) eingerichtet und leben insbesondere von Mundpropaganda, Communities, sozialen Netzwerken etc.

→ *Der neueste Trend: „Handel goes Social-Media"*
Dies hat nur zum Teil mit Internet-Handel (s.d.) zu tun. Social Media ist fixer Bestandteil des Alltags vieler Konsumenten geworden. Denn die Grenzen sind zwischen Werbung, Service und Bestellung fließend. Dabei ist es nicht überraschend, dass etwa Amazon mittlerweile mit Facebook kooperiert.[38]

→ *Trend: Technologie und Handel: Von Bezahlsystemen bis zu elektronischen Preisetiketten am Regal u.a.m.*

„Plastic Money"
Die notwendigen Bezahl-(POS)-Terminals verbreiteten sich in Österreich Ende der 1990er Jahre bzw. Anfang der 2000er nicht nur bei den Filialisten, sondern auch im kleineren stationären Einzelhandel und werden sich sicher noch weiterentwickeln.

Verstärkt wird der Trend des bargeldlosen Bezahlens (damit ist nicht „Gratis Einkaufen" in Form von Ladendiebstahl, der im Handel bis zu 3% des Umsatzes ausmacht, gemeint!) durch das Nachrücken jüngerer KonsumentInnen und durch die verstärkte Nutzung der Online-Bestellmöglichkeiten, die vielfach nicht via Erlagschein, Nachnahme etc. abgewickelt werden, sondern zu einem Großteil via Kreditkartennummer. (Sicherheitsdiskussion hin oder her!)

Warum ist „Plastic Money" auch in Österreich weit verbreitet? Die Vorteile aus Kundensicht sind: Weniger Bargeld, „überraschende" Angebote können gekauft werden und aus Unternehmersicht ist eine Steigerung der Umsätze durch Spontankäufe (s.o.) möglich. Der bargeldlose Zahlungsverkehr verringert Bargeldmanipulation und Fehler beim Bargeldhandling oder beim Kassiervorgang.

Fazit ist dennoch: Bargeld ist weiterhin das beliebteste Zahlungsmittel der ÖsterreicherInnen.

„Mobile Payment" oder die „digitale Geldbörse"
Mobile Payment, das Bezahlen via Handy, ließ in der Vergangenheit noch etwas auf sich warten. Schon vor rund 10 Jahren etwa testeten in Wien Coca-Cola und der Netzbetreiber ONE die Bezahlung bei Getränkeautomaten (Titel: „SMS me for

38 Vgl. www.business.insider.com/facebook-e-commerce 2010-12; abgerufen am 25.7.2011.

a coke").[39] Einen Aufschwung bringt die Generation von Smartphones mit sich, die teilweise bereits mit einem sogenannten NFC (Near Field Communication)-Chip ausgerüstet sind. Die App-fähigen Smartphones verändern aber auch anderweitig den Einzelhandel. Die „Price Checker-App" von Amazon etwa stellt fest, wenn ein Konsument in einem Geschäft den Strichcode fotografiert, wie viel diese Ware bei Amazon oder einem anderen Anbieter auf seinem Marktplatz kostet. Dies wird wohl eine große Herausforderung für den stationären Einzelhandel.[40]

Weitere technische Neuerungen, die sich noch im Versuchsstadium befinden:

Self-scanning
Die Artikel werden – z.B. wie am Flughafen bei der Röntgenkontrolle des Handgepäcks – durch einen kleinen Tunnel gefahren und automatisch abgerechnet. Daher würde bei dieser Form des Self-Check-Out auch das sonst selbstständig vorzunehmende Strichcode-Scannen des Konsumenten entfallen.[41]

Elektronische Preisetiketten
Damit könnten ganz ungeahnte Pricing-Aktionen verwirklicht werden (z.B.: tageszeitabhängige Preise).

3. „Distanzhandel" – Internet-Handel[42]

Wir leben im zweiten Jahrzehnt des dritten Jahrtausends in einer Zeit, in der weltweit jeder 21-Jährige im Schnitt bereits geschätzte 250.000 Mails und SMS verschickt hat, 10.000 Stunden mobil telefoniert, 5.000 Stunden Videogames gespielt und tausende Stunden auf Social-Media-Seiten zugebracht hat.[43]

Auch die Handelswelt wird in einer Welt elektronischer Medien immer digitaler...

→ Trend: Der Versandhandel wächst
Der Distanzhandel konnte sich in dieser modernen Welt auch im klassischen Versandhandel etablieren. Hier besteht für die Zukunft wohl noch weiteres Wachstumspotential. Andererseits werden sogenannte „Multichannel-Retailer" (mit Geschäft und Versandschiene) aufgrund von Synergien ihrerseits wieder die reinen Online-Händler zu übertrumpfen versuchen.

39 Vgl. Beisheim – Maurer o.J., 53.
40 WISU-Magazin, Heft 1, 2012, 27 f.
41 Vgl. Trendletter Nr. 6, 2011, 6.
42 Die in diesem Kapitel verwendeten Daten entstammen einer sehr umfassenden Befragung der KMU-Forschung Austria mit einem Sample von 2.000 (!) Befragten, von denen 1.135 ÖsterreicherInnen über 15 Jahre Bestellungen im Distanzhandel vorzuweisen hatten.
43 Vgl. Zukunftsletter Nr. 3, 2010, 108.

Die wohl bemerkenswerteste Eigenschaft für den Distanzhandel via Internet ist der praktisch unendliche „Regalplatz". Und für den Einkauf brauchen die KonsumentInnen ihr Zuhause nicht zu verlassen.

Was versteht man nun unter Internet-Distanz-Versandhandel im Unterschied zum sogenannten stationären (ladengebundenen) Einzelhandel?

In den weiteren Ausführungen werden die gebräuchlichsten Definitionen verwendet, wobei einerseits jene aus Unternehmenssicht und andererseits aus Konsumentensicht zu unterscheiden sind:

Den Begriff „Distanzhandel" gibt es in der europäischen und nationalen Wirtschaftsstatistik nicht. In der österreichischen gültigen ÖNACE 2008 scheint dagegen der Terminus Versand- und Internet-Einzelhandel auf.[44] Dazu zählen in der Klasse 47.91 der Versand- oder Internet-Einzelhandel,[45] Teleshopping via Fernsehen, Hörfunk sowie Telefon und die über Internet laufenden gewerblichen Aktionen, die ebenfalls zum Einzelhandel zu zählen sind.[46] Jene Unternehmen jedoch, die gleichsam als Ergänzung einen Internet-Shop betreiben oder jene aus der Fahrzeugbranche sind hier somit nicht erfasst!

Im Katalog E des Instituts für Handelsforschung an der Universität Köln scheint dagegen eine Definition des „Distanzhandels" auf. Sie stellt im Wesentlichen auf die Merkmale Einzelhandel, gewerblicher Verkauf an LetztverbraucherInnen, unter Ausschluss von Kfz und touristischen Dienstleistungen ab.[47]

2009 waren in Österreich nach dieser ÖNACE Definition rund 300 (!) Unternehmen mit ca. 4.100 unselbstständig Beschäftigten im Distanzhandel tätig. Ihre Umsatzerlöse betrugen rund 1,2 Mrd. €. Diese 0,7% der im Einzelhandel tätigen Unternehmen erzielten 2,3% aller Umsätze im österreichischen Einzelhandel, somit rund 1,4% der gesamten Bruttowertschöpfung im Einzelhandel.[48] Weitere Branchendaten sind der Tabelle 2 im Anhang zu entnehmen.

Bis zum April 2010 haben sich rund ¾ aller ÖsterreicherInnen ab 15 Jahren selbst als KäuferIn auch im Distanzhandel bezeichnet. (Zum Vergleich: Im Zeitraum 12 Monate davor haben knapp 60% aller Befragten zumindest einmal etwas im Distanzhandel eingekauft.) Selbstverständlich haben dabei die jüngeren Generationen die Nase vorne. Etwa 80% der 15- bis 29-jährigen ÖsterreicherInnen haben überhaupt jemals im Distanzhandel bereits Waren bestellt, dagegen gut 60% der über 60-Jährigen.[49]

Beim Bestellvorgang dominiert das Internet. 1/3 der Bestellungen im Distanzhandel im Zeitraum Mai 2009 bis April 2010 wurden über dieses Medium abgewi-

44 www.statistik.at; abgerufen am 20.6.2011.
45 Somit nicht b2b (Abkürzung „businesstobusiness", was bedeutet: Internethandel zwischen Unternehmen).
46 Vgl. ÖNACE-Erklärung unter www.statistik.at
47 Vgl. Katalog E, 23, 61.
48 Vgl. Der österreichische Handel 2010, 136.
49 Vgl. Der österreichische Handel 2010, 138.

ckelt. Dies ist keinesfalls überraschend. Über die vielfältigen Gründe für den Online-Einkauf zu sprechen, hieße jedoch „Eulen nach Athen zu tragen".[50]

Dennoch: Trotz vielfältigster Internetportale, Produktinformationen der Hersteller im Internet, Suchmaschinen etc. hat der Versandhandelskatalog als Informationsmedium noch nicht ausgedient und dies nicht nur bei älteren KosumentInnen!

Interessanter Weise bestellen Frauen etwa gleich oft über das Internet wie über das Telefon. Bei Männern schlägt das Pendel klar in Richtung Internet aus. (39% zu 12%!)[51]

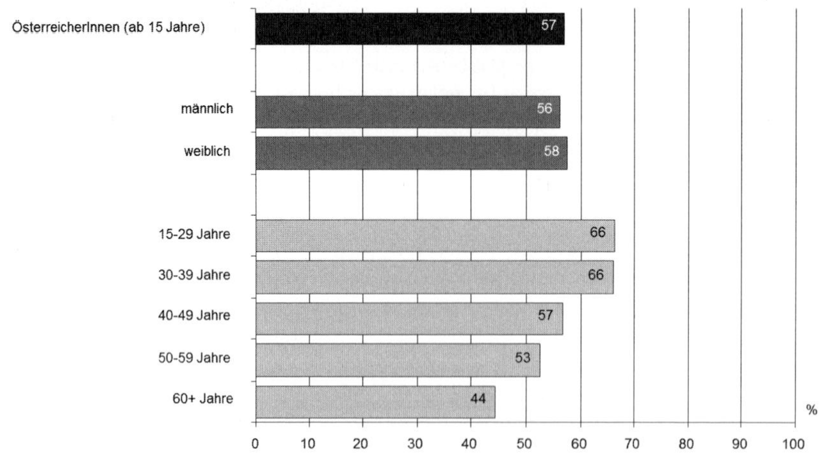

Grafik 1: Einkauf im Distanzhandel innerhalb von 12 Monaten (Mai 09 – April 10) Anteil der ÖsterreicherInnen (ab 15 Jahre) in %
(Quelle: Der österreichische Handel 2010, 139)

Insbesondere gehen Bekleidung und Textilien, Bücher, Elektro- und Elektronikgeräte über den virtuellen Ladentisch. Die umsatzstärkste Branche im Einzelhandel dagegen, der Lebensmitteleinzelhandel, steht aus verständlichen Gründen (Frische, etc.) – nicht im Vordergrund des Internet-Handels.

Im einjährigen (vorhin angeführten) Untersuchungszeitraum betrugen nach Angaben von Frau und Herr Österreicher die Umsätze im Distanzhandel etwa 5 Mrd. €. Dies entspräche ca. 9% aller einzelhandelsrelevanten Konsumausgaben in Österreich. Den Nettoumsatzerlösen des Distanzhandels in Österreich

50 Vgl. Beisheim – Maurer, 49.

51 Vgl. Der österreichische Handel 2010, 139.

gegenübergestellt,[52] bedeutet dies im Klartext, dass der größere Anteil des Volumens jedenfalls an ausländische Anbieter geht.[53]

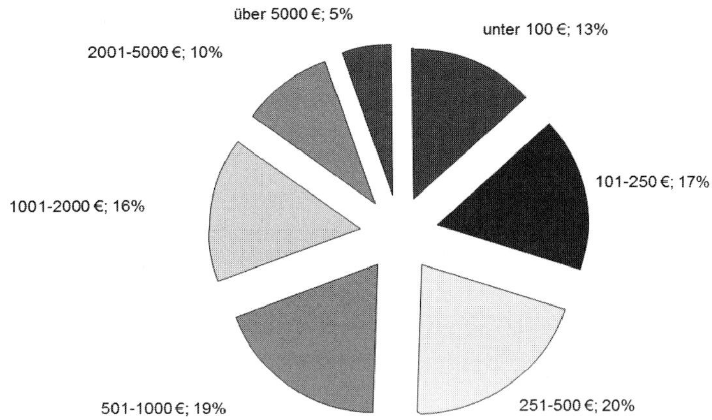

Grafik 2: Ausgaben im Distanzhandel (Mai 09 – April 10) – Anteil der KäuferInnen (ab 15 Jahre) nach Ausgabenkategorien in %, 2010 (Quelle: Der österreichische Handel 2010, 142)

Bei den durchschnittlichen Ausgaben der im Distanzhandel einkaufenden Konsumenten liegt wie bei den Bestellungen (s.o.) klar die Warengruppe Bekleidung, Textilien vor Bücher und Zeitschriften in Führung.

Wie wird der Einzelhandel auf den Aufschwung des Distanzhandels reagieren?

Gerade das Internet hat „die bereits in Vergessenheit geratene Formel: Handel als Marktplatz" wieder zum Leben erweckt. Das Internet hat den Handel nicht ersetzt, auch nicht verdrängt, sondern in vielerlei Hinsicht beflügelt.[54]

So sollen etwa Kunden zu „Fans" gemacht werden; es gilt „Erleben als Kontrast zum Alltag"; das Schaffen einer Community, die aus verschiedensten Gründen einen Laden aufsucht. Im unten abgebildeten Electronic-Shop in Manhattan, New York City, sind keine Preisangaben bei den ausgestellten Geräten angebracht, kaum Verkaufspersonal zu sehen, aber dafür jede Menge junger Menschen, die sich in diesem Laden aufhalten.

Zur Unterhaltung wird ganz allgemein immer mehr geboten: Showprogramme, Bühne, intelligente Events, Interaktionen, Treffpunkte, Kreativ-Workshops, Kunden-Wettbewerbe u.v.a.m. zur Verlängerung der Verweildauer am „Point of

52 Das heißt ohne 20% der von den Konsumenten noch zusätzlich zu bezahlenden Umsatzsteuer von rund 1,2 Mrd. €.

53 Vgl. Der österreichische Handel 2010, 142.

54 Wirtschaftskammer Wien (Hg.), 2003, 68.

Leisure". Die Bestellung der Ware kann dann durchaus von daheim aus über das Internet erfolgen.[55]

Abbildung 1: Electronic-Shop in Manhattan, New York (Copyright H. Eymannsberger, 2011).

3.1 Die Online-Welt verschmilzt mit der Offline-Handelswelt

→ *Trend: Stationärer Handel und Internethandel existieren auch künftig nebeneinander*

Läden des (stationären Handels) werden somit nicht aussterben, selbst wenn der Distanzhandel bis 2020 bis zu 20% des Umsatzkuchens auf sich vereinigen würde, weil: die Inszenierung zunehmen wird, die Kundenbindung auch hier verstärkt wird und der stationäre Handel die Vorteile des Netzes und des Ladens – wenn notwendig in adaptierter Form – anwenden wird.[56]

Die neue Grundregel wird wohl lauten: „Tu das eine und lass das andere nicht": Die Welt der Apps, Mobile-Couponing, selbstverständlich der Online-Shop (Store) selbst werden bei großen und auch vielen kleineren Händlern in ein Gesamtkonzept integriert (Multichanneling) bzw. die bestehenden Systeme weiter optimiert werden. Denn jene KundInnen, die auf all diesen Ebenen unterwegs sind, gehören zu den „lukrativsten", somit zur gehobenen Mittelschicht. („Genera-

55 Vgl. Zukunftsletter Nr. 8, 2010, 2.
56 Vgl. Trend Alert vom 22.6.2011, 1 f.

tion-Facebook-KundInnen") Im Vergleich konsumieren jene im Schnitt etwa bei Target, dem Filialisten, der in fünf US-Bundesstaaten Wal-Mart die Stirn bietet, 1.000 US $ / Jahr, die ausschließlichen FilialeinkäuferInnen 551 $ und die reinen Online-LebensmittelkundInnen dagegen nur 94 $.[57]

4. Globalisierung und Logistik

Der Handel war historisch sicher ein Treiber der Globalisierung, die durch die modernen Kommunikationsmittel, der sich der Handel selbstverständlich von Anfang an bedient hat, geradezu exponentiell beschleunigt wurde. Blenden wir kurz um einige tausend Jahre zurück.

Quer durch Europa wurden beispielsweise Rohstoffe wie Kupfer (u.a. aus Mitterberg, Gemeinde Mühlbach am Hochkönig im Salzburger Land) transportiert,[58] wie die bronzezeitliche Himmelscheibe von Nebra (Sachsen-Anhalt, BRD) belegt.[59] Will man überhaupt in die Steinzeit zurückgehen, wurde bereits mit Feuersteinen, Muscheln, Fellen etc. reger Tauschhandel betrieben.[60]

Bereits in frühen Kulturen wie Ägypten (Altes Reich) spielte der Handel eine bedeutende Rolle.[61]

Phöniker, Karthager, Griechen, Römer wiederum betrieben Handel quer über das Mittelmeer und auf dem Seeweg bis nach Britannien.[62]

Einige wenige Beispiele des Handels im Mittelalter seien nach einem großen zeitlichen Sprung herausgegriffen:

Mitteleuropäische, wie zum Beispiel Regensburger Kaufleute haben strategisch die Routen nach Nord und Süd und schließlich in den Osten erschlossen – von Kiew etwa bis Konstantinopel.[63] Von der Rolle Salzburgs im Mittelalter den Handel betreffend war bereits in der Einleitung die Rede. „Wir können der Kaufleute nimmer entbehren, denn sie führen aus einem Lande in das andere jenes; und darum sollen sie dies hinführen und jenes herführen, davon sollen sie mit Recht ihren Lohn haben", beschrieb der Franziskaner Pater Berthold von Regensburg in den Jahren um 1250 die Tätigkeit dieser Kaufleute.[64]

Stadt- und sozialgeschichtlich nicht hoch genug eingeschätzt werden kann der Stand der Kaufleute für die Entwicklung zahlloser europäischer Städte:

Bruckmüller bezeichnet den „überregionalen Kaufmann" sogar als neuen „Sozialtypus", mit dem im (Spät-)Mittelalter auch die städtische Autonomie überwie-

57 Quelle: Zukunftsletter Nr. 7/2011, 4 ff.
58 http://www.lda-lsa.de/himmelsscheibe_von_nebra/naturwissenschaftliche_untersuchungen/ abgerufen am 2.11.2011.
59 Ihr Gold wiederum stammte übrigens wie das Zinn für die verarbeitete Bronze aus Cornwall (GB).
60 Vgl. Bauer 1982, 15 f.
61 Ebd., 25, mit weiterführenden Beispielen, siehe Chuefhor.
62 Ebd., 28.
63 Vgl. Angerer 1993, 9.
64 Ebd., 43.

gend verbunden erscheint.[65] Was für ein gesellschaftlicher „Aufstieg", wenn man bedenkt, dass die Händler im 11. und 12. Jahrhundert noch „Staubfüße" genannt wurden, die Wertschöpfung des Handels angezweifelt und dieser noch zu den gesellschaftlichen Randgruppen gezählt worden war.[66]

So beeinflusste der Fernhandel nicht nur das konkret erhältliche Warenangebot in den Städten, sondern auch die wirtschaftliche und politische Entwicklung bis hin zur künstlerischen Vielfalt durch das Kennenlernen neuer Moden und Kunstgegenstände.

Es ist sicher angebracht, wenn man etwa von der Welthandelsorganisation (WTO)[67] in den Nachrichten liest oder hört, der Gefahren, Leistungen und Vermächtnisse der zuvor genannten Gruppe der Kauffahrer – oft als Unternehmer und Abenteurer – zugleich zu gedenken, die die Wegbereiter weltumspannender Kontakte und des globalisierten Handels mit entsprechender Logistik waren:

Bereits im Mittelalter ließen beispielsweise italienische Händler Waren durch Fuhrleute – mit Frachtbrief (!) – oder per Schiff mit Chartervertrag (!) transportieren. Der Wechsel war zu dieser Zeit bereits eingeführt, sodass keine großen Mengen an Bargeld mehr transportiert werden mussten. Der Abschluss von Versicherungen etwa im 14. Jahrhundert gegen „Meer, Menschen, Feuer" also Schiffuntergang, Kaperung oder auch Enteignung durch Landesherren sowie Banditen oder Krieg war weit verbreitet.[68]

Die „italienischen" Seerepubliken wie Venedig, Pisa, Amalfi etc. oder die „Hanse" im Norden prägten zum Teil jahrhundertelang den Fernhandel in ihren Einzugsgebieten. Von wirklichem „Welthandel" kann zu Recht jedenfalls ab 1571 gesprochen werden: In diesem Jahr landete erstmals eine spanische Galeone mit Schätzen aus Übersee in Spanien. Genau ein halbes Jahrhundert nach der ersten Weltumseglung Magellans kam es so zum Güteraustausch über Atlantik und Pazifik. Und die heutigen Dimensionen? Laut WTO tauschen 178 Staaten Waren und Dienstleistungen von rund 19 Billionen US-Dollar untereinander aus.[69]

Den später überregionalen grenzüberscheitenden Handel erleichterte natürlich die Einrichtung sogenannter „Freihandelszonen". Wenn auch nach heutigen Maßstäben – im Rahmen der sogenannten EU-Freiheiten wie dem Binnenmarkt[70] oder auch den WTO-Regeln – gemessen die Gründung des deutschen Zollvereins (1834) gleichsam ein kleinregionaler „Abklatsch" war, hatte dieser doch auch eine wirtschaftliche und politische Signalwirkung. Im 19. Jahrhundert wurde darüber hinaus schon die Gründung einer „Union du Midi" mit den daran zu beteiligenden Ländern Frankreich, Belgien, Schweiz und Spanien diskutiert.[71]

65 Bruckmüller 1985, 100.
66 Kaufer in: Beisheim 1999, 377.
67 Vgl. www.wto.org., abgerufen am 26.10.2011.
68 Origo 1985, 71, 121 ff.
69 Vgl. Stöllinger 2011, 639.
70 Vgl. http://europa.eu/pol/singl/index_de.htm, abgerufen am 26.10.2011.
71 Treue 1973, 485.

Österreich profitiert auch heute von der europäischen Freihandelszone. Aber immer weniger ist auch ÖsterreicherInnen bewusst, dass die so viele Arbeitsplätze im Inland sichernde Exportwirtschaft ohne den Beitritt Österreichs zur EU, ohne die Teilnahme am europäischen Binnenmarkt nie im gegebenen Ausmaß hätte reussieren können.

Nur den Spitzenleistungen der Logistiker bei Produzenten, Speditionen, Groß- und Einzelhändlern ist es zu verdanken, dass de facto die KonsumentInnen aus einem weltweit zur Verfügung stehenden Angebot tagtäglich wählen können. Nicht unter den Tisch gekehrt werden, sollen immer wieder geäußerte Meinungen, das Angebot des Handels gerade im Lebensmittelbereich sollte wieder „lokaler" ausgerichtet werden, was auch bereits zu den verschiedensten Kooperationsmodellen von regionalen Anbietern auch mit österreichischen Händlern/Filialisten geführt hat. Dennoch verlangen KonsumentInnen beispielsweise auch Erdbeeren im Winter, Tulpen im Jänner oder die mittlerweile so beliebte Ananas das ganze Jahr über. Dass nur mit einer ausgefeilten Logistik verderbliche Güter (mit entsprechender Kühlung etc.) transportiert werden können, versteht sich von selbst. Der Handel war immer schon unglaublich „modern" und in vielen Belangen der Wirtschaftswelt „Trendsetter", so auch bei der Logistik.

5. Vertikalisierung

→ *Trend: Vertikalisierung dringt weiter vor*
Der Produzent zieht dabei ein eigenes Ladennetz auf. Diese Entwicklung, die sich seit 10 Jahren verstärkt zeigt, ist ohne starke Markenbindung nicht denkbar. Im Textilsektor sind hier zum Beispiel H&M, Zara und Mango zu nennen. Marke und System verschmelzen hier und sind typische Beispiele für das sogenannte „Retailbrand(ing)". Aber auch weitere Franchisekonzepte (ein paar seit langem bekannte Namen: Palmers, Benetton, etc.) sind in den verschiedensten Bereichen (nicht nur im Handel) künftig denkbar.

6. Öffnungszeiten

→ *Trend: Seit Jahrzehnten verlängern sich die Öffnungszeiten der Geschäfte.*
Die verwaltungsrechtlichen Bestimmungen (Öffnungszeitenrecht)[72] wurden ab den 1980er Jahren sukzessive erweitert, obwohl in Meinungsumfragen die KonsumentInnen, sowie Unternehmer wie Arbeitnehmer die Öffnungszeiten jeweils als ausreichend empfunden hatten. Seit Jahren gibt das bundesrechtliche Regime den österreichischen Bundesländern für Tourismusorte eine differenzierte Ermächtigung zur Ausweitung vor, von der das Bundesland Salzburg immer kräftig Gebrauch gemacht hat.

72 Vgl. für Österreich Öffnungszeitengesetz 2003, BGBl. Nr. 48/2003 (in der Fassung BGBl. Nr. 62/2007).

Eine undifferenzierte plakative Betrachtung des Themas der Öffnungszeiten ist jedenfalls abzulehnen. Nicht nur MitarbeiterInnen-Anliegen nach gemeinsamer Freizeit mit Familie und Freunden, sondern auch Folgewirkungen bei der Kinderbetreuung, einer Beschleunigung des ohnedies rasch (s.o.) vor sich gehenden Strukturwandels bis hin zu fehlender Anbindung im öffentlichen Verkehr werden sowohl von der Wirtschaftskammerorganisation wie von der Arbeitnehmervertretung gegen eine weitere Verlängerung der Öffnungszeiten ins Treffen geführt.

Eine weitere Öffnungszeitenverlängerung würde m.E. die Handelslehrberufe für die Jugend eher noch unattraktiver machen. Eine qualitätsvolle Bedienung auf breiter Ebene mit gut ausgebildeten MitarbeiterInnen wäre für den Fachhandel dann noch schwieriger sicherzustellen.

Generell ist fest zu halten, dass die derzeit geltenden Bestimmungen über die Geschäftsöffnungszeiten auf Bundes- und Landesebene praxisorientiert und ausreichend sind. Wünsche nach einer Ausweitung, die mancherorts geäußert werden (wie z.B. in der Bundeshauptstadt Wien), könnten bei einer Inanspruchnahme des nach Bundesrecht zulässigen landesrechtlichen Rahmens in den meisten Fällen erheblich „abgefedert“ werden.

7. Literatur

7.1 Monographien

Angerer B., Menschen – Märkte – Mittelpunkte, IHK Regensburg (Hg.), Regensburg 1993.

Bauer H.L., 7.000 Jahre Handel. Eine Kulturgeschichte, Aarau 1982.

Beisheim E., Maurer R., Die Zukunft des Handels (o.J.).

Beisheim O. (Hg.), Distribution im Aufbruch. Bestandsaufnahme und Perspektiven, München 1999.

Braumann C. – Terlinden T. – Weissenböck P. – Will J., Die Entwicklung des Einzelhandels und der Nahversorgung im Land Salzburg, (Materialien zur Raumplanung des Landes Salzburg, Band 23), Salzburg 2011.

Bruckmüller E., Sozialgeschichte Österreichs, Wien – München 1985.

CIMA Österreich GmbH (Vgl. 36).

Dirninger C., Determinanten und Strukturmerkmale der Wirtschaftsentwicklung im 20. Jahrhundert, in: KaronaGmbh (Hg.), Chronik der Salzburger Wirtschaft, Band 2, Salzburg 1990, 183–233.

Dopsch H., Die wirtschaftliche Entwicklung, in: Dopsch H. – Spatzenegger H. (Hg.), Geschichte Salzburgs, Stadt und Land, Band I, 2, Salzburg 1983, 757–835.

Dopsch H. – Lipburger P.M., Die Entwicklung der Stadt Salzburg. Die rechtliche und soziale Entwicklung, in: Dopsch H. – Spatzenegger H. (Hg.), Geschichte Salzburgs. Stadt und Land. Band I, 2, Salzburg 1983, 675–746.

Eggert U., Der Handel im 21. Jahrhundert, in: Beisheim O., Distribution im Aufbruch. Bestandsaufnahme und Perspektiven, München 1999, 1063–1082.

Eggert U., Zukunft Handel – mit Kooperation und System, Innovation und Differenzierung, in: Handelsbericht 12, Dezember 2009.

Eymannsberger H., Verkaufsflächenanalyse der zentralen Orte im Bundesland Salzburg. (Unveröffentlichtes Manuskript zur Vorlage an die Arbeitsgruppe Handelsgroßbetriebe der Abteilung 7 des Amtes für Salzburger Landesregierung), Salzburg 2001.

Gamsjäger M., Produzenten – Händler – Konsumenten. Lebensmittelversorgung in der Stadt Salzburg um 1900 (Salzburg Archiv, Schriften des Vereins Freunde der Salzburger Geschichte, Band 33), Salzburg 2008, 379–416.

Grunwald A., Wovon ist die Zukunftsforschung eine Wissenschaft? in: Popp R. – Schüll E. (Hg.), Zukunftsforschung und Zukunftsgestaltung: Beiträge aus Wissenschaft und Praxis (Wissenschaftliche Schriftenreihe „Zukunft und Forschung“ des Zentrums für Zukunftsstudien Salzburg, Band 1), Berlin – Heidelberg 2009, 25–35.

Institut für Handelsforschung Köln, Katalog E. Definitionen zu Handel und Distribution, Köln 2005.

Kaufer E., Kirche und Kaufmann im europäischen Mittelalter, in: Beisheim O., Distribution im Aufbruch. Bestandsaufnahme und Perspektiven, München 1999, 373–389.

KMU Forschung Austria, Der österreichische Handel 2006.

Liessman K.P., Zukunft kommt (Bibliothek der Unruhe und des Bewahrens, Band 13), Graz – Wien – Köln 2007.
Öffnungszeitengesetz 2003, BGL Nr. 48/2003 (in der Fassung BGBl. Nr. 62/2007).
Origo I., Im Namen Gottes und des Geschäfts, München 1985.
Regioplan, Branchenreport im Lebensmittelhandel in Österreich 2010, Wien 2011.
Rust H., Verkaufte Zukunft. Strategien und Inhalte der kommerziellen „Trendforscher", in: Popp R. – Schüll E. (Hg.), Zukunftsforschung und Zukunftsgestaltung. Beiträge aus Wissenschaft und Praxis (Wissenschaftliche Schriftenreihe „Zukunft und Forschung" des Zentrums für Zukunftsstudien Salzburg, Band 1), Berlin – Heidelberg 2009.
SABE-V-Gesamtbericht der Salzburgisch-Bayerische Einzelhandels- und Verflechtungsbereichsuntersuchung 2005, erstellt für Euregio Salzburg-Berchtesgadener Land-Traunstein (kurz SABE-V 2005).
Salzburger Tourismusgesetz 2003, LGBl. 43/2003 i.d.g.F.
Sandgruber R., Handel und Wandel – eine Einführung, in: Wirtschaftskammer Oberösterreich (Hg.), Der Handel in Oberösterreich. Tradition und Zukunft, Linz 2002, 23–50.
Stöllinger R., Veränderungen im Welthandel. Chancen und Herausforderungen für Europa, in: Wirtschaftskammer Österreich (Hg.), Strukturwandel (Wirtschaftspolitische Blätter, Nr. 4/2011), 639–653.
Trend Alert, Innovations-Radar für Konsum, Handel und Dienstleistungen, Ausgabe vom 22.6.2011.
Treue W., Wirtschaftsgeschichte der Neuzeit, Band 1, Stuttgart 1973.
Voithofer P. – Gittenberger E., Der österreichische Handel 2006. Daten – Fakten – Analysen, KMU Forschung Austria (Hg.), Wien – Frankfurt 2007.
Voithofer P. – Gittenberger E., Der österreichische Handel 2010, Daten – Fakten – Analysen, KMU Forschung Austria (Hg.), Wien 2010. (auch abrufbar unter: http://portal.wko.at/wk/format_detail.wk?AngID=1&StID=319355&DstID=224.)

7.2 Fachpublikationen (periodisch)

Trendletter, Der Strategiebrief für zukunftsorientierte Unternehmer, Nr. 6/ 2011.
Zukunftsletter, Strategisches Wissen für Entscheidungen im Management und Marketing, Nr. 7/2011.
Zukunftsletter, Innovation Economy (Sondernummer 2010).
Zukunftsletter Nr. 3/ 2010, 108.
WISU-Magazin, Heft 1, 2012.

7.3 Internetquellen

www.business.insider.com/facebook-e-commerce 2010-12 (16.10.2011)
http://wirtschaftslexikon.gabler.de/Definition/einzelhandel.html (20.6.2011)
http://wirtschaftslexikon.gabler.de/Definition/grosshandel.html (20.6.2011)

www.duden.de/rechtschreibung/Trend (10.9.2011)
http://www.cdn.walmartstores.com/Sitel/AnnialReport/2010/PDF/WmT_2010AR_Final_pdf
www.statistik.at (20.6.2011)
www.ulricheggert.de, Handelsbericht 12, 2009 (16.10.2011)
www.ulricheggert.de, Handelsbericht 18,2011 (16.10.2011)
www.ulricheggert.de, Handelsbericht 22,2011 (16.10.2011)
www.ulricheggert.de/studien/index.php (26.10.2011)
http://portal.wko.at/wk/format_detail.wk?angid=1&stid=634739&dstid=224 (4.10.2011)
www.thredup.com (26.10.2011)
http://www.lda-lsa.de/himmelsscheibe_von_nebra/naturwissenschaftliche_untersuchungen/ (2.11.2011)
www.wto.org (26.10.2011)
http://europa.eu/pol/singl/index_de.htm (26.10.2011)

8. Anhang

Tabelle 1: Anzahl der unselbstständig Beschäftigten, 1995 – 2009, Einzel- (EH) und Großhandel (GH) sowie Kfz[73]

	1995*	1997	1998	1999	2000	2001	2002	2009
EH	220.125	221.878	235.129	234.145	236.659	239.515	236.931	307.527
GH	183.496	177.767	184.112	179.213	188.073	191.452	189.846	180.106
Kfz	68.700	67.424	71.162	69.694	72.266	72.796	73.124	68.270

*Im Jahr 1995 waren noch keine geringfügig Beschäftigten in der Statistik enthalten.
Gliederung nach ÖNACE
(Quelle: Statistik Austria, KMUForschung Austria, eigene Darstellung)

Tabelle 2: Unternehmen und unselbstständig Beschäftigte, Umsatzerlöse und Bruttowertschöpfung im Versand- und Internet-Einzelhandel[1], 2009

	2009[2]	Anteil am gesamten Einzelhandel
Unternehmen	302	0,7 %
Unselbstständig Beschäftigte	4.054	1,3 %
Durchschnittliche Unternehmensgröße[3]	13,4	
Umsatzerlöse in € Mio.	1.222	2,3 %
Bruttowertschöpfung zu Faktorkosten in € Mio.[4]	149 - 2008	1,4 %

1 Haupttätigkeitsschwerpunkt im Versand- und Internet-Einzelhandel nach ÖNACE 2008 (G 47.91)

2 Fortschreibung der KMU FORSCHUNG AUSTRIA

3 Unselbstständig Beschäftigte je Unternehmen

4 Daten von 2008

Anmerkung: Gliederung nach ÖNACE 2008

Quellen: KMU FORSCHUNG AUSTRIA, Statistik Austria

(Quelle: Der österreichische Handel 2010, 136)

73 Aufgrund der etwas veränderten ÖNACE-Zuordnung 2008 (gegenüber ÖNACE 2003) sind die Werte vor 2008 nicht direkt mit jenen ab 2008 vergleichbar, bieten aber zumindest einen guten Anhaltspunkt.

9. Abkürzungsverzeichnis

BRD: Bundesrepublik Deutschland
BGBl.: Bundesgesetzblatt
ca.: circa
d.h.: das heißt
d.Verf.: des Verfassers
ebd.: ebenda
EPU: Einpersonen-Unternehmen
etc.: et cetera
EU: Europäische Union
GB: Großbritannien
Hg.: Herausgeber
i.e.S.: im engeren Sinn
i.w.S.: im weiteren Sinn
Kfz: Kraftfahrzeug(e)
LEH: Lebensmitteleinzelhandel
m.E.: meines Erachtens
Mio: Million
Mrd: Milliarde
o.Ä.: oder Ähnliches
o.J.: ohne Jahresangabe
ÖNACE: Zuordnung aller Unternehmen zu einem Wirtschaftszweig gemäß der Wirtschaftstätigkeitenklassifikation
PKW: Personenkraftwagen
s.d.: siehe dort
s.o.: siehe oben
s.u.: siehe unten
SABE-V: Salzburgisch Bayerische Einzelhandels- und Verflechtungsbereichsuntersuchung 2005
u.a.:unter anderem
u.v.a.m.: und vieles andere mehr
vgl.: vergleiche
WTO: World Trade Organisation
z.B.: zum Beispiel

Menschen und Märkte

Peter Herz

Ich möchte mit einer auf den ersten Blick etwas provozierenden Aussage beginnen. Wirtschaftsgeschichte ist für mich deutlich mehr als die Frage nach Produktions- und Ertragszahlen, nach Kapitalrenditen und dem Bruttosozialprodukt. Natürlich sind diese Fragen wichtig, aber als Historiker sollten wir darüber niemals vergessen, dass im Mittelpunkt unseres Interesses vor allem der Mensch steht. Mit dem Menschen haben wir ein faszinierendes, aber auch ein höchst komplexes Untersuchungsobjekt vor uns. Und mit diesem Begriff der Komplexität lassen sich auch am besten die menschlichen Aktivitäten beschreiben, die sich auf das Generalthema unserer Tagung beziehen.

Für mich beschreibt ein Markt in erster Linie eine Situation, bei der höchst unterschiedliche Waren getauscht oder verkauft werden. Solche Märkte finden in der Regel an vorher festgelegten Lokalitäten statt, wobei es zunächst keinerlei Festlegung hinsichtlich des zeitlichen Rhythmus gibt, in dem ein solcher Markt stattfand. Dies bedeutet, wir können von einer ganzen Hierarchie von Märkten ausgehen, die als Wochenmarkt, als jahreszeitlich festgelegtem Markt oder auch als Jahresmarkt stattfinden können.[1] Dabei lassen sich gewisse Schwerpunkte im Frühjahr und im Herbst feststellen, wobei gerade die Herbsttermine in etwa den Endpunkt des durch Ackerbau charakterisierten Wirtschaftsjahres bezeichnen.

Eine Konzentration nur auf den Marktort im eigentlichen Sinne und die dort stattfindenden Transaktionen erscheint mir allerdings sehr vereinfachend, da dabei wesentliche Elemente der antiken Wirtschaftsgeschichte ausgeblendet werden.

Denn in meinen Augen steht und stand jeder Markt immer am Ende eines ihm vorgeschalteten wirtschaftlichen Prozesses, in dessen Verlauf die Produkte, die letztendlich auf diesem Markt angeboten wurden, hergestellt und transportiert wurden. Dabei macht es keinen grundsätzlichen Unterschied, ob es sich um einen lokalen, einen regionalen oder gar einen überregionalen Markt handelt, oder wie oft dieser Markt innerhalb eines bestimmten Zeitraumes abgehalten wurde. Das Marktgeschehen im eigentlichen Sinne, egal ob es ein Austausch von Waren oder eine Übergabe von Waren gegen Geld war, markiert dabei lediglich den Endpunkt.

Dieser vorgeschaltete Produktionsprozess kann recht kurz sein, d.h. man benötigt nur wenige Schritte, wenn es sich etwa um die Produktion von einfachen Lebensmitteln handelt. Bei vielen Produkten hingegen bedeutet das Angebot des Endproduktes auf dem Markt nur die letzte Etappe in einem vielstufigen Herstellungsprozess, in dem die notwendigen Rohstoffe gewonnen und verarbeitet wurden, aus denen schließlich das verkaufsfähige Endprodukt entstand.

Ich möchte dies an einem sicherlich sehr einfachen Textilprodukt verdeutlichen, das wertmäßig an das untere Ende der Produktion gehört: einer einfachen

1 de Ligt 1993.

Tunika, die aus Schafwolle hergestellt worden war. Bevor das marktfähige Produkt, also die Tunika, überhaupt als verkaufsfähiges Produkt in den Handel gebracht werden konnte, musste der Rohstoff Wolle einen sechsstufigen Produktionsprozess durchlaufen:[2]

1. Scheren der Schafe
2. Reinigen und Kämmen der Rohwolle
3. Spinnen der Rohwolle
4. Weben der Stoffbahnen
5. Nachbehandlung (Walken und Bleichen)
6. Weiterverarbeitung des fertigen Tuches zu Textilien

Sobald dieses Produkt aber eine höhere Qualität erlangen sollte, etwa durch Färben oder die Verzierung mit Borten, erhöhte sich die Zahl der vorgeschalteten Produktionsschritte deutlich.

Märkte existieren nicht unter Laborbedingungen, sondern die Existenz und auch das Funktionieren von Märkten und damit auch das Funktionieren der gesamten Wirtschaft wird durch eine ganze Reihe von Rahmenbedingungen vorbestimmt, die in ihrer Mehrzahl nicht vom Menschen kontrolliert werden konnten. Der Mensch hat keinerlei Einfluss auf die topographischen Voraussetzungen, also die Existenz von Bergen oder Flüssen, die Handelsoperationen ermöglichten oder behinderten. Er hatte auch keinerlei Einfluss auf die klimatischen Rahmenbedingungen, die Handelsoperationen bestimmten. Handelsoperationen, bei denen man sein Ziel mit einem Schiff über das offene Meer ansteuerte, waren den klimatischen Abläufen innerhalb eines Jahres unterworfen.

Kein vernünftiger Händler oder Kapitän verließ zwischen Mitte Oktober und Anfang März einen Hafen, um über das offene Meer zu fahren.[3] Und selbst dann, also in der günstigen Jahreszeit, war man weitgehend hilflos den Winden wie Bora, Mistral oder Meltemi ausgeliefert, die eine Fahrt behindern oder fast unmöglich machen konnten. Diese Einschränkungen galten selbst für die Zeiten des hochkaiserzeitlichen Klimaoptimums, wobei die Veränderungen, die durch die Klimaverschlechterung seit dem frühen 3. Jh. eintraten, noch nicht eingehend in ihren Auswirkungen auf den antiken Handelsverkehr evaluiert sind.

Der Mensch hatte auch keinerlei Einfluss auf die klimatischen Rahmenbedingungen seines Lebensraumes, die z.B. die Gewinnung bestimmter Naturprodukte wie Olivenöl bestimmten. Im Gegensatz zum Wein konnte Olivenöl, das für einen großen Teil der antiken Menschen ein Grundnahrungsmittel war, nur innerhalb eines begrenzten Streifens entlang der Küsten des Mittelmeergebietes kultiviert werden.[4] Da aber Olivenöl für Menschen, die in der Kultur der mediterranen Welt

2 Moeller 1976.

3 Rougé 1952, Rougé 1966, Udovitch 1978.

4 Vgl. die klassische Beschreibung des Mittelmeergebietes bei Braudel 1990 a.

verwurzelt waren, ein Produkt war, auf das man nicht gerne verzichtete, selbst wenn die Möglichkeit bestand, es durch andere Produkte zu ersetzen, wurde es damit fast zwangsläufig zu einem Handelsprodukt, das in den überregionalen Handel gebracht wurde. Der Historiker und Geograph Strabon vermerkt regelmäßig, wo Oliven angebaut werden können, da dies für ihn Indiz eines kultivierten Lebens ist.

Die hier skizzierten Rahmenbedingungen sind im Prinzip bis weit in die Neuzeit gültig gewesen. Erst dann hat die Entwicklung der modernen Verkehrstechnik die Rahmenbedingungen grundsätzlich geändert. Für diesen Bereich habe ich mich von den Untersuchungen von Fernand Braudel zum Mittelmeergebiet in der Zeit von Philipp von Spanien inspirieren lassen.[5] Solch ein Rückgriff erscheint mir durchaus legitim, denn die Grundstrukturen des 16. Jh. haben sich nicht grundlegend von denen der Antike unterschieden.

Welche Informationsmöglichkeiten haben wir, um zumindest ansatzweise eine Vorstellung von den Waren zu gewinnen, die zu den Märkten transportiert wurden? Die klassischen literarischen Quellen der Antike sind in der Regel, vorausgesetzt, dass sie solche Fragen überhaupt behandeln, sehr einseitig auf bestimmte Produkte oder Produktgruppen ausgerichtet und daher nicht besonders geeignet, um hier wirklich tragfähige Aufschlüsse zu geben. Dies verweist uns notgedrungen auf die Ergebnisse der Archäologie. So wertvoll aber diese Ergebnisse auch sein mögen, auch sie können uns nur ein sehr einseitiges Bild der Wirklichkeit vermitteln, dessen Analyse zudem noch sehr oft in den Kinderschuhen steckt.

Wir profitieren zunächst davon, dass Keramik zu den Werkstoffen gehört, die fast unverwüstlich sind, wofür die Massen an Amphoren ein beredtes Zeugnis ablegen. Ohne die intensive Erforschung der Amphoren wären z.B. substantielle Aussagen zum antiken Handel mit Wein, Olivenöl, *garum* usw. praktisch unmöglich. Damit fallen aber andere Warengruppen, die diesen Vorzug nicht besitzen, weil sie etwa vegetabilischer Natur waren oder für sie eine andere Verpackungsform verwendet wurde, nur zu oft durch unseren analytischen Rost.

Um zunächst bei den Lebensmitteln zu bleiben. Alle Lebensmittel, die nicht in Amphoren, sondern in Säcken, Kisten, Fässern, Schläuchen oder gar als sogenanntes Schüttgut transportiert wurden, lassen sich archäologisch nicht oder nur sehr schwer fassen. Lediglich bei den Fässern haben wir ansatzweise die Chance, ihren Einsatz zu dokumentieren.[6] Dies gilt z.B. für alle Arten von Getreide. Wenn wir die Zeugnisse ausklammern, die sich auf die Versorgung der Stadt Rom oder des römischen Militärs konzentrieren, so ist der dokumentarische Befund sehr einseitig, da z.B. die Inschriften vor allem Notsituationen oder Vorsorgemaßnahmen wie die städtischen Fonds zur Sicherung der Lebensmittelversorgung ansprechen, aber nicht den üblichen Handel.[7] Dies gilt auch für die anderen Arten von

5 Braudel 1990 b. Braudel 1990 a.
6 Marlière 2002 und zuletzt Tamerl 2010.
7 Grundsätzlich Erdkamp 2005, daneben auch Dierscherl 2000.

Lebensmitteln. Sollte man allerdings deswegen der Meinung sein, dass die Versorgung der größeren Städte sowieso vor allem aus dem Umland des jeweiligen Marktes stammte, so gibt es einige beunruhigende Nachrichten, die dieses Bild stören. So liefert die Inschrift OGIS 521 aus Abydos, die wir in die Zeit Justinians datieren können, die folgende Information.[8]

> „Die Transporteure von Öl, Gemüse und Salzfleisch zahlen den *classici*, die die Meerengen bewachen, sechs *folles* – die kilikischen Reeder (hingegen) zahlen den *classici*, die die Meerengen bewachen, (nur) drei *folles* – und wegen der Kontrolle ein *keration* und bei der Ausfuhr zwei *keratia*."

Offensichtlich wurde Gemüse aus größeren Entfernungen nach Konstantinopel transportiert, wobei leider zur Art des Gemüses nichts gesagt wird.[9] Immerhin wird damit gesichert, dass das Einzugsgebiet Konstantinopels bis weit in die Süd-west-Türkei reichte. Entscheidend war hier vor allem die Art des Transportmittels. Der Handel mit relativ einfachen Lebensmitteln war also durchaus möglich, was auch der Warenkorb des diokletianischen Preisediktes bestätigt.[10]

Ähnlich disparat sind auch die Nachrichten für Fleisch und Fleischprodukte.[11] Klammert man die staatliche Fleischversorgung Roms mit Lebendvieh aus Unteritalien aus, da dies eindeutig ein Sonderfall ist, so scheint man aus Transportgründen eher konserviertes Fleisch über größere Strecken auf den Markt gebracht zu haben. Also gesalzenes oder geräuchertes Fleisch. In welchem Umfang man Lebendvieh für den nicht staatlich dirigierten Handel auf den Markt brachte, muss unsicher bleiben. Immerhin wissen wir im Fall von Konstantinopel durch das Buch des Eparchen, dass bithynische, also kleinasiatische Schafe regelmäßig in die Stadt geliefert wurden.[12] Die Information, dass die Stadt auch mit lebenden Schweinen aus Kleinasien versorgt wurde, verdanken wir wie so oft einem reinen Zufall.

Als im 10. Jh. Erzbischof Leon von Syn(n)ada in Phrygien mit einer Fähre nach Konstantinopel übersetzen wollte, musste er sich das Schiff mit einer Herde bithynischer Schweine teilen, die ebenfalls auf dem Weg in die Stadt waren.[13] Offensichtlich störten die Tiere den heiligen Mann so sehr, dass er dieses später in einem Brief erwähnte. Die Schweine stammten wahrscheinlich aus den bewaldeten Bergregionen Bithyniens, die sich für eine Eichelmast anboten. Wenn wir hier auf die mittelalterlich-frühneuzeitlichen Zeugnisse zurückgreifen, so sichern sie, dass sowohl Schweine als auch Rinder über sehr große Strecken getrieben wurden. So wurden ungarische Rinder regelmäßig bis nach Frankfurt am Main geliefert, wäh-

8 Vgl. Herz 2011 b.

9 Zum Frischgemüse vgl. Koder 1993. Wichtig ist auch Grant 1997.

10 Giacchero 1974 cap. 1. 6.

11 Interessante Ansätze bei MacKinnon 2004.

12 Koder 1991, cap. 15,3

13 Vgl. Leo of Synada ep. 54 ed. Vinson 1985, 86–91.

rend im 14. Jh. der Kaiserhof in Prag Lebendschweine aus der Pfalz erhielt.[14] Eine Übertragung dieser Versorgungsstrukturen auf die antiken Verhältnisse ist momentan aus Mangel an einschlägigen Zeugnissen nur sehr bedingt möglich.

Obwohl wir davon ausgehen können, dass sich antike Menschen nicht in Dressel 20-Amphoren kleideten, sondern Textilien verwendeten, hat sich diese Erkenntnis nicht besonders auf die Intensität der entsprechenden Forschung ausgewirkt.

Während die Literatur zur Erforschung der Amphoren oder der in diesen Behältnissen transportierten Waren für den Nichtspezialisten kaum noch zu überschauen ist, sind die Forschungen zum antiken Handel mit Textilien oder Lederprodukten, aber auch den Grundstoffen, die zu ihrer Herstellung notwendig waren, lange Zeit relativ unterentwickelt geblieben.[15] Vom wissenschaftlichen Niveau des Mittelalters sind wir noch weit entfernt.[16]

Wenn man den diokletianischen Maximaltarif als Indikator nimmt, so scheint sich hier die Tendenz abzuzeichnen, dass man eher die Fertigprodukte als die Rohprodukte in den Handel brachte. Also weniger einen Handel mit Rohwolle oder gegerbten Lederhäuten, die erst später weiterverarbeitet wurden, sondern bereits die gebrauchsfähigen Endprodukte. Der archäologische Nachweis ist in beiden Fällen kaum zu führen.

Dies gilt auch für die Frage nach den in der Antike verwendeten Farb- und Gerbstoffen, die sich leider nur in Ausnahmefällen archäologisch nachweisen lassen. Bei den Gerbstoffen ist vor allem an Alaun zu denken, dessen antike Produktionsstätten fast alle im Osten des Reiches lagen.[17]

Im Falle der Farbstoffe, bei denen ich hier den echten Schneckenpurpur ausklammere, hat die Archäologie einige interessante Aufschlüsse geliefert.[18] Selbst die wenigen gefärbten Textilreste, die man im ariden Klima Ägyptens bergen konnte, sprechen für einen relativ hohen technischen Stand und zwar selbst bei einfachen Textilien und nicht nur bei dem Segment der Luxusprodukte.[19] Es gibt kaum ein Kleidungsstück, das nicht gefärbt war, wobei mehrfach gefärbte Kleidungsstücke überwiegen. Bei einem Teil der hier verwendeten Farbstoffe muss man von langen Handelswegen bis zum Endverbraucher ausgehen, denn einige Farbstoffe mussten über die Grenzen des Imperium Romanum importiert werden.

Zu diesen gehörten Brasil, Curcuma, Lac und *Indigofera tinctoria*, die teilweise aus Hinterindien oder China importiert werden mussten.[20] Die *Indigofera tinctoria* wurde im Mittelmeergebiet erst unter dem Einfluss der Araber einheimisch.

14 Exemplarisch Dalhede 1992; vgl. auch die Beiträge in Westermann 1979.
15 Eine Ausnahme stellt Ruffing 2007 dar.
16 Cardon 2000.
17 Herz 2012.
18 Zum Schneckenpurpur vgl. u.a. die Arbeiten von Steigerwald 1986. 1990 a. 1990 b, die durch die Beiträge in Alfaro 2005–2011 zu ergänzen sind.
19 Vgl. Herz 2012.
20 Vgl. Herz 2012.

Aber auch innerhalb des Imperiums dürfte ein reger Handel mit Farbstoffen existiert haben, die wie Kermes, Krapp und Safran aus dem Mittelmeerraum stammten.[21]

Für einen Teil dieser Rohstoffe scheint das Imperium Romanum sogar nur ein Transitland gewesen zu sein. So hat ein Zufallsfund aus dem Ort Brill im niedersächsischen Landkreis Wittmund, also jenseits der römischen Reichsgrenzen in Germanien, einen Klumpen Ägyptisch Blau gesichert.[22] Ägyptisch Blau ist ein mineralischer Farbstoff, der nicht in natürlicher Form vorkommt, sondern erst als Ergebnis einer Produktion anfällt. Dieser Farbstoff wurde u.a. für die Bemalung von Wänden verwendet und stammte wahrscheinlich aus einer Farbstoffproduktion im Mittelmeergebiet. Zumindest ist dank Vitruvius, '*De architectura*' (7.11.1) die Produktion des Vestorius aus Puteoli bekannt.[23] Man könnte sagen, dass wir hier einen kleinen Hinweis auf einen Handel fassen, der deutlich größere Dimensionen hatte.

Ich habe mit Absicht 'einfache Textilien' betont, denn eine genauere Analyse des Textilkapitels im diokletianischen Preisediktes liefert genügend Indizien, dass Textilien der mittleren und auch niedrigen Preiskategorie offensichtlich nicht nur lokal hergestellt und verkauft wurden, sondern offensichtlich auch im überregionalen Handel angeboten wurden.[24] Wenn man davon ausgeht, dass der diokletianische Maximaltarif einen Warenkorb beschreibt, der vor allem die Realität in der Asia Minor des frühen 4. Jh. abbildet, so ist es schon bemerkenswert, dass dort einfache Produkte vom Balkan, aus Afrika, aber auch aus dem nordgallischen Bereich aufgeführt werden. Zu den hier genannten Produktionsgebieten gehören Britannien, Gallien mit den regionalen Produktionsgebieten der Nervier und der Treverer, Raetien, Noricum, die Gebiete der Dardanii und der Bessi, sowie die Region von Poetovio im heutigen Slowenien.

Dieses Bild, dass in der Antike auch relativ einfache Textilien über größere Strecken verhandelt wurden, wird auch durch den Periplus Maris Erythraei bestätigt. In diesem Handbuch werden dem Händler für den arabischen Hafen von Muza die folgenden Textil-Produkte empfohlen.[25]

> "Handelswaren, für die es einen Markt bietet, sind: Purpurtücher, gute und gewöhnliche Qualität; arabische Kleidung mit Ärmeln, entweder ohne Verzierung oder mit der allgemeinen Verzierung oder mit Mustern oder mit Goldfäden durchzogen; --- Tücher [möglicherweise Leinen]; Mäntel [möglicherweise gefärbt]; Decken, in beschränkter Zahl, sowohl ohne Verzierung als auch mit der traditionellen einheimischen Verzierung; Gürtel mit verschiedenen Streifen [wahrscheinlich mit ineinandergehenden Farbabstufungen]".

21 Herz 2012.
22 Vgl. Lehmann 2002.
23 Jaschke 2010.
24 Giacchero 1974 cap. 19 sowie 26–27.
25 Casson 1989 cap. 24.

Dabei kann man nicht ausschließen, dass einige dieser Waren [„mit der traditionellen einheimischen Verzierung"] in Ägypten speziell für den arabischen Markt hergestellt wurden.

Dasselbe Problem der weitgehend archäologischen Nichtnachweisbarkeit gibt es auch für alle antiken Produkte, die aus Holz oder Leder hergestellt wurden. Auch hier liefert uns die literarische Tradition ein m.E. völlig abweichendes Bild der damaligen Realität. Bei dem berühmten Zitronenholz, das aus den Wäldern des nordafrikanischen Atlas stammte, gibt es genügend Hinweise, die einen regen Handel mit diesem absoluten Luxusprodukt bezeugen.[26]

So wird als Beweis für den immensen Reichtum des Philosophen Seneca berichtet, dass er fünfhundert Tische besessen habe, deren Tischplatten aus dem teuren Zitronenholz hergestellt worden waren.[27] Dabei dürfte es sich wohl um massives Zitronenholz und nicht um Furnier gehandelt haben. Dieses hochpreisige Luxusprodukt dominiert allerdings unverdient unser Bild des gesamten römerzeitlichen Holzhandels, da andere Holzsorten in der Regel kaum als Handelsprodukt erwähnt werden.[28] Nur gelegentlich werden bestimmte Holzsorten genannt, die etwa als hochwertiges Bauholz für Decken- oder Dachkonstruktionen verwendet wurden und die im Falle des augusteischen Rom aus den Südalpen herangeschafft wurden. Diese Baumstämme wurden aber von Plinius nur erwähnt, weil sie für das *Diribitorium* bestimmt waren und so gewaltige Dimensionen hatten, dass man sie für eine freitragende Decke mit 30 m Spannweite verwenden konnte.[29]

Von der Versorgung mit 'einfachen' Hölzern erfährt man in der Regel nur sehr wenig. Dieses Holz wurde aber in enormen Mengen für Gebrauchsmöbel, als Bauholz (für Baugerüste oder als Schalbretter) oder nur als Brennholz verwendet. Welch enormer Bedarf gerade im Bereich von Holz als Energielieferant existiert, wird deutlich, wenn man die wenigen belastbaren Verbrauchszahlen nimmt. Sie machen u.a. deutlich, dass in Rom ein enormer Bedarf an Brennholz bestand.[30]

So wird in einer Inschrift des 5. Jh. berichtet, dass man in Catania den Holzverbrauch der lokalen Thermen reduziert hatte und zwar von 32 *pensae* auf 18 *pensae* pro Tag.[31] Wenn wir die Mengenangaben *pensa* in moderne Werte umrechnen, dann handelte es sich um eine Reduktion des täglichen Holzverbrauchs von 4960 kg auf nur noch 2790 kg. Auf ein Jahr mit 365 Betriebstagen umgerechnet, wurde also der Brennholzverbrauch von 1785,6 t auf nur noch 1018,35 t reduziert. Leider wurde in dieser Quelle nicht gesagt, woher das Brennholz stammte und auf wel-

26 Zum Zitronenholz vgl. Kloft 1996.

27 Dio 61,10,3.

28 Herz 2011 c.

29 Plin. n.h. 16.200 ff.

30 Herz 2010.

31 Manganaro 1958, bes. 24 ff. zu der Inschrift IG XIV 455 = AE 1959, 26, die in einer gegenüber den IG deutlich verbesserten und erweiterten Form vorgelegt wird, vgl. Bull. épig. 1959, 541. An den Zahlenangaben ändert sich dadurch allerdings nichts.

chen Wegen die Gemeinde dieses Holz erwarb. Wir können daher nicht sagen, ob man es auf dem freien Markt bei Holzhändlern ankaufte oder ob es aus städtischen Wäldern stammte. Von diesen Kapazitäten ist natürlich nichts mehr archäologisch nachzuweisen. Wie sich der antike Normalbürger mit seinem Heizmaterial für Küche und Wohnung versorgte, wird nirgendwo wirklich thematisiert, obwohl hier sicherlich enorme Mengen umgeschlagen wurden.[32]

Dass es hier auch eine überregionale Versorgung mit Holz gab, lässt sich nur gelegentlich fassen. Spätantike Gesetzestexte ordnen an, dass die Getreideschiffe aus Nordafrika Brennholz für Rom mitbringen sollten.[33] Dieses Holz war vorher durch Sachsteuerabgaben der nordafrikanischen Bevölkerung aufgebracht worden. Dendrochronologische Untersuchungen, die Pauline van Rijn an Holzfunden aus den Niederlanden vorgenommen hat, sprechen dafür, dass dort auch Hölzer verwendet wurden, die nicht vom Niederrhein stammten.[34] Die naheliegendsten Versorgungsgebiete wären in diesem Fall die großen Waldgebiete vor allem am Oberrhein, die bis ins frühe 20. Jh. genutzt wurden. Das Holz wurde dann auf dem Rhein in Richtung Rheindelta geflößt. Dies dürfte eine Versorgungsart gewesen sein, die wir für praktisch alle Stromgebiete des Imperium Romanum, wenn wir einmal vom Nil absehen, vermuten dürfen. Dieser sicherlich enorm wichtige Sektor des Handels in der Antike wird allerdings von den antiken Quellen mit kaum einem Wort angesprochen.

Bei der Vorbereitung meines Beitrages habe ich bewusst die Grenzen der Antike sowie im zeitlichen als auch im geographischen Sinne überschritten und mich daher auch mit Forschungsergebnissen beschäftigt, die außerhalb des üblichen Spielfeldes eines Althistorikers liegen. Ich gehe dabei von der methodischen Prämisse aus, dass eine Veränderung der politischen Strukturen nicht zwangsläufig auch eine völlige Veränderung der wirtschaftlichen Strukturen mit sich bringt.

Es ist daher in meinen Augen durchaus legitim, die Frage zu stellen, in welchem Umfang Ergebnisse der mittelalterlichen Wirtschaftsgeschichte auf die Probleme der Antike übertragbar sind. Um dies an einem ausgewählten Beispiel zu illustrieren. Aus dem hohen Mittelalter ist ein System des überregionalen Textilhandels bekannt, das vor allem durch die Händler der italienischen Seestädte getragen wurde. Diese Kaufleute fungierten als Zwischenhändler zwischen den textilproduzierenden Städten in Flandern und Ostfrankreich und den damals unter dem Einfluss der Araber stehenden Handelsstädte entlang der Küste der Levante. Umgekehrt lieferten diese Zwischenhändler auch für die Textilherstellung wichtige Rohstoffe wie Alaun, aber auch ausgewählte Farbstoffe aus dem vorderen Orient, die dann in Richtung Norden wanderten.[35]

---

32 Herz 2010. Herz 2011 c.

33 CTh 13,5,1. Vgl. Callu 1980 zur Inschrift CIL VI 24609 = AE 1980,903. Jones 1964, 705 mit den Quellentexten auf den S. 1291–1292.

34 van Rijn 2011.

35 Herz 2011 a.

Die Textilregionen im nordgallischen Raum sind uns bereits durch die antiken Quellen hinreichend bekannt, wobei die Existenz von Händlern aus dem kleinasiatisch-syrischen Bereich vor allem für Lyon nachgewiesen ist. Besonders wichtig scheint dabei ein *negotiator laudacenarius* zu sein, also ein Händler mit Produkten aus Laodikeia am Lykos.[36] An diesem Beispiel sollte einmal modellhaft geprüft werden, ob dies ein reiner Zufall ist oder ob wir hier möglicherweise mit dem Fortbestehen von Strukturen rechnen müssen, die sich bereits in der Antike ausgebildet hatten.

Ich habe hier mit gewissen Bedenken den Begriff 'Modell' verwendet. Ich verstehe Modell ganz im Sinne von Karl Popper als ein intellektuelles Hilfsmittel, das es uns ermöglicht, unsere zunächst noch umherschweifenden Gedanken und Ideen in eine erste vorläufige Form zu bringen. Dabei sind diese Modelle keine mathematischen Lehrsätze oder theologischen Dogmen, die den Anspruch auf ewige Wahrheit erheben, sondern sie sollen uns in erster Linie helfen, unsere Gedanken zu fokussieren und dann kritisch zu überprüfen. Dabei ist eine Korrektur dieses Modells ebenso wie seine ständige Fortentwicklung und Verfeinerung vorgesehen.

Wenn ich unter diesen Prämissen meinen gegenwärtigen und sehr vorläufigen Erkenntnisstand zusammenfassen darf, so sollten wir davon ausgehen, dass der antike Wirtschaftsverkehr erstens wesentlich differenzierter war als wir es uns in der Regel vorstellen können und dass wir zweitens auch mit einem deutlich größeren Volumen an Gütern rechnen sollten, die über längere Strecken zu ihren Endverbrauchern geliefert wurden. Der überregionale Handel in der römischen Antike befasste sich also nicht nur mit Luxusgütern oder mit Waren, die im Auftrag des römischen Staates gehandelt oder transportiert wurden (also die typischen Güter der *annona*), sondern auch mit einer Vielzahl von anderen Waren.

Diese Diskrepanz zwischen dem anzunehmenden Volumen des Handels und seiner dokumentarischen Absicherung besteht auch auf dem Feld des Sklavenhandels.[37] Wir kennen natürlich die hinreichend bekannten Beispiele für die Versklavung großer Personengruppen,[38] doch die alltäglichen Formen des Sklavenhandels und auch seine mengenmäßigen Dimensionen verbleiben weitgehend im Dunkeln. Lediglich einige Papyri sichern diesen Handel als solchen, doch in diesen Zeugnissen wird in der Regel der Sklavenhandel zwischen Privatleuten dokumentiert.[39] Aus solchen Zeugnissen Hinweise auf berufsmäßige Sklavenhändler oder gar das Volumen des damaligen Sklavenhandels abzuleiten, dürfte sehr schwierig sein.

Welchen Beitrag können naturwissenschaftliche Analysen bei der Lösung unserer Fragen liefern? Zunächst dürfen wir feststellen, dass die naturwissenschaftliche Analyse von Amphoren uns eine zusätzliche Absicherung von Ergebnissen

36 Vgl. Material bei Herz 1985.
37 Harper 2011. Binsfeld 2008. Scheidel 2010.
38 Volkmann 1990.
39 Vgl. u.a. Ruffing, Drexhage 2008.

geliefert hat, die man bisher vor allem über die Typologie der Amphoren bzw. die Untersuchungen von Stempeln, Marken oder Aufschriften gewonnen hat.[40] Eine neue Dimension haben wir hingegen durch die Analyse von Inhaltsstoffen gewonnen, die z.B. sichern kann, welche Waren (Pharmazeutika, Salben, usw.) in bestimmten Behältern transportiert wurden.[41] Die Isotopenuntersuchung von Marmor und ausgewählten Metallen hat uns sowohl belastbare Informationen hinsichtlich des Ursprungs der Waren als auch der Handelswege geliefert.[42]

Besonders hilfreich war dies im Falle des römischen Bleiabbaus von Brilon im Sauerland, ganz in der Nähe des römischen Lagers von Rüthen-Kneblinghausen.[43] Mit Hilfe der Isotopenanalyse ließ sich eine Verbindung dieser Abbaustelle zu der Ladung eines Schiffswrackes herstellen, das man im Jahre 1997 vor der Küste Sardiniens an der Straße von Bonifacio gefunden hatte. 42 der insgesamt 72 Bleibarren, die man damals geborgen hat, trugen die Aufschrift *Augusti Caesaris (plumbum) Germanicum* = 'Germanisches Blei des Augustus Caesar'. Dies bedeutet, diese Bleibarren stammten aus einer Produktionsstätte, die direkt dem Kaiser gehörte. Auf einem weiteren Barren, der ein Gewicht von rund 240 römischen Pfund = ca. 78,6 kg hatte, fand sich eine Inschrift, die sich als *Pudentis (plumbum) Germanicum* = 'Germanisches Blei des Pudens' ergänzen ließ.

Unter methodischen Gesichtspunkten darf man feststellen, dass es bei dieser Fragestellung keinen Königsweg gibt, der alle Fragen umfassend beantworten könnte. Abhängig von den lokalen Umständen, aber auch den auf dem Markt gebrachten Produkten gibt es ganz unterschiedliche Wege, die zum gewünschten Ziel führen. Trotzdem einige Anmerkungen. Es lässt sich in der aktuellen Forschung ein gewisser Trend erkennen, sich auf die Erforschung einzelner Waren oder Warengruppen zu konzentrieren. Wer sich auf die Erforschung von Olivenöl- oder Wein-Amphoren spezialisiert hat, neigt in der Regel dazu, andere Warengruppen weitgehend unberücksichtigt zu lassen. Dies entspricht aber in vielen Bereichen nicht dem Bild, das uns die Archäologie für die Zusammensetzung von Schiffsladungen geliefert hat. Wenn man etwa die Warenströme untersuchen möchte, die aus dem Mittelmeergebiet über Lugdunum die römischen Siedlungen in Nordgallien und am Rhein erreichten, um dann zu einer Gesamtbewertung des römischen Handels zu gelangen, so sollte man möglichst eine generelle Untersuchung anstreben.

Da sich die technologischen Bedingungen zwischen der Spätantike und dem späten Mittelalter wenig oder überhaupt nicht veränderten, sollte man auch die Erkenntnisse, die uns für das Mittelalter vorliegen, im vollen Umfange nutzen und

40 Vgl. u.a. Laubenheimer, Schmitt 2009.

41 Exemplarisch Martlew 2004.

42 Vgl. zum Forschungsstand Jockey 2011, daneben auch Pollini, Herz, Polikreti, Maniatis 1998.

43 Hanel, Rothenhöfer 2005.

die antiken Bedingungen einmal systematisch vor diesem Hintergrund untersuchen. Dieser epochenübergreifende Ansatz gilt vor allem für die Erkenntnisse, die Leute wie Maurice Lombard für die islamische Welt und ihre Bedeutung bereitgestellt haben.[44]

44 Lombard 1992.

Literatur

Alfaro 2005–2011 = Alfaro C. et al. (Hg.), Purpurae Vestes I–III, València 2005/2008 u. Naples 2011.

Binsfeld 2008 = Binsfeld A., Menschenhandel – Frauenhandel, in: Heinen H. (Hg.), Menschenraub, Menschenhandel und Sklaverei in antiker und moderner Perspektive, Stuttgart 2008, 85–98.

Braudel 1990 a = Braudel F., Das Mittelmeer und die mediterrane Welt in der Epoche Philipps II., übersetzt von Osterwald G., dt. Ausgabe in 3 Bänden Frankfurt/Main 1990 (Paperback 1994).

Braudel 1990 b = Braudel F., Duby G., Aymard M., Die Welt des Mittelmeers. Zur Geschichte und Geographie kultureller Lebensformen, Frankfurt/Main 1990 (dt.).

Callu 1980 = Callu J.P., Pensa et follis sur un inscription d'Afrique, AntAfr 15, 1980, 273–283.

Cardon 2000 = Cardon D., La draperie au moyen âge. Essor d'une grande industrie européenne, Paris 2000.

Casson 1989 = Casson L., The Periplus Maris Erythraei. Text with introduction, translation, and commentary, Princeton/N.J. 1989.

Dalhede 1992 = Dalhede Ch., Zum europäischen Ochsenhandel: Das Beispiel Augsburg 1560 und 1578, St. Katharinen 1992.

de Ligt 1993 = de Ligt L., Fairs and markets in the Roman Empire. Economic and social aspects of the periodic trade in a preindustrial society, Amsterdam 1993.

Dierscherl 2000 = Dierscherl H.-C., Die Verteilung von kostenlosem Getreide in der Antike vom 5. Jh. v.Chr bis zum Ende des 3. Jh. n.Chr., MBAH 19, 2000, 1–33.

Erdkamp 2005 = Erdkamp P., The grain market in the Roman empire. A social, political and economic study, Cambridge 2005.

Giacchero 1974 = Giacchero M., Edictum Diocletiani et collegarum de pretiis rerum venalium in integrum fere restitutum e Latinis Graecisque fragmentis. I. Edictum, Genua 1974.

Goitein 1967 = Goitein Sh.D., A mediterranean society. The Jewish communities of the world as portrayed in the documents of the Cairo Geniza Vol. I. Economic foundations, Berkeley, Los Angeles, London 1967 (Paperback 1999).

Grant 1997 = Grant M., Dieting for an emperor. A translation of Books 1 and 4 of Oribasius' Medical Compilations with an introduction and commentary, Leiden – New York 1997.

Harper 2008 = Harper K., The Greek census inscriptions of late antiquity, JRS 98, 2008, 83–119.

Harper 2011 = Harper K., Slavery in the late Roman mediterranean, AD 275–425, Cambridge 2011.

Herz 1985 = Herz P., Parthicarius und Babyloniarius. Produktion und Handel feiner orientalischer Lederwaren, MBAH 4 II, 1985 (1986), 89–106.

Herz 2010 = Herz P., Das Problem der Energieversorgung in römischer Zeit, in: Appl T. – Köglmeier G. (Hg.), Regensburg, Bayern und das Reich. Festschrift für Peter Schmid zum 65. Geburtstag, Regensburg 2010, 27–42.

Herz 2011 a = Herz P., Färben und Gerben in der Vormoderne, in: Onken B. – Rohde D. (Hg.), In omnia historia curiosus. Studien zur Geschichte von der Antike bis zur Neuzeit. Festschrift Helmuth Schneider zum 65. Geburtstag, Wiesbaden 2011 (Philippika. Marburger altertumskundliche Abhandlungen 47), 141–158.

Herz 2011 b = Herz P., Freier Handel und staatliche Kontrolle in römischer Zeit, in: Herz P. – Schmid P. – Stoll P. (Hg.), Klima, Ökonomie und Politik. Neue Facetten der europäischen Geschichte, Berlin 2011 (Region im Umbruch 5), 11–31.

Herz 2011 c = Herz P., Überlegungen zur Holzwirtschaft in römischer Zeit, in: Scherrer P. (Hg.), Lignum. Holz in der Antike. Akten des interdisziplinären Symposiums „Holz in der Antike" (Graz, 5.–7. November 2009), Graz 2011 (Keryx 1), 153–165.

Herz 2012 = Herz P., Gerb- und Färbstoffe in der Antike, in: E. Olshausen – V. Sauer 2012, 175–191.

Jockey 2011 = Jockey Ph. (Hg.), Leukos Lithos. Marbres et autres roches de la Méditerranée antique, Études interdisciplinaires. Actes du VIII Colloque international de l'Association for the Study of Marble and other Stones used in antiquity (Asmosia) Aix-en-Provence 2006, Paris 2011.

Jones 1964 = Jones A.H.M., The Later Roman Empire. A social, economic and administrative survey, Oxford 1964 (2nd ed. Oxford 1973).

Karali – Megaloudi 2008 = Karali L. – Megaloudi F., Purple dyes in the environment and history of the Aegean. A short review, in: Alfaro C. – Karali L. (Hg.), Purpurae Vestes II. Vestidos, textiles y tintes. Estudios sobre la producción de bienes de consumo en la Antigüedad, València 2008, 181–193.

Kloft 1996 = Kloft H., Überlegungen zum Luxus in der frühen römischen Kaiserzeit, in: Strubbe J.H.M. – Tybout R.A. – Versnel H.S. (Hg.), ΕΝΕΡΓΕΙΑ. Studies in ancient history and epigraphy presented to H.W. Pleket, Amsterdam 1996, 113–134.

Koder 1991 = Koder J., Das Eparchenbuch Leons des Weisen. Einführung, Edition, Übersetzung und Indices, Wien 1991 (CFHB 33).

Koder 1993 = Koder J., Gemüse in Byzanz. Die Versorgung Konstantinopels mit Frischgemüse im Lichte der Geoponika, Wien 1993.

Laubenheimer – Schmitt 2009 = Laubenheimer F. – Schmitt A., Amphores vinaires de Narbonnaise. Production et grand commerce. Création d'une base de données géochimique des ateliers, Lyon 2009.

Lehmann 2002 = Lehmann Th.D., Verwendung von Ägyptisch Blau in Brill, Lkr. Wittmund, Niedersachsen, Germania 80, 2002, 615–621.

Lombard 1992 = Lombard M., Blütezeit des Islam. Eine Wirtschafts- und Kulturgeschichte 8.–11. Jahrhundert, Frankfurt/Main 1992 (dt.).

MacKinnon 2004 = MacKinnon M., Production and consumption of animals in Roman Italy. Integrating the zooarchaeological and textual evidence, Portsmouth/ Rhode Island 2004 (JRS Supplement 54).

Manganaro 1958 = Manganaro G., Iscrizioni latine e greche di Catania tardo-imperiale, Archivo storico per la Sicilia orientale [ASSO] 54, 1958, 1–30.

Marlière 2002 = Marlière É., L'outre et le tonneau dans l'Occident romain, Montagnac 2002.

Martlew 2004 = Martlew H., Minoan and Mycenaean technology as revealed through organic residue analysis, in: Bourriau J. – Philiipps J. (Hg.), Invention and innovation. The social context of technological change 2. Egypt, the Aegean and the Near East 1650–1150 BC, Oxford 2004, 121–148.

Matthews 1984 = Matthews J.F., The tax law of Palmyra. Evidence for economic history in a city of the Roman East, JRS 74, 1984, 157–180.

Moeller 1976 = Moeller W.O., The wool trade of ancient Pompeii, Leiden 1976.

Olshausen – Sauer 2012 = Olshausen E. – Sauer V. (Hg.), Die Schätze der Erde. Natürliche Ressourcen in der antiken Welt. Stuttgarter Kolloquium zur Historischen Geographie des Altertums 10, 2008, Stuttgart 2012 (Geographica Historica 28).

Pollini – Herz – Polikreti – Maniatis 1998 = Pollini J. – Herz N. – Polikreti K. – Maniatis Y., Parian lychnites and the Prima Porta statue. New scientific tests and the symbolic value of the marble, JRA 11, 1998, 275–284.

Rougé 1952 = Rougé J., La navigation hivernale dans l'empire romain, REA 54, 1952, 316–325.

Rougé 1966 = Rougé J., Recherches sur l'organisation du commerce maritime en méditerranée sous l'empire romain, Paris 1966.

Ruffing 2007 = Ruffing K., Textilien als Wirtschaftsgut in der römischen Kaiserzeit, in: Günther S. – Ruffing K. – Stoll O. (Hg.), Pragmata. Beiträge zur Wirtschaftsgeschichte der Antike in Gedenken an Harald Winkel, Wiesbaden 2007 (Philippika. Marburger altertumswissenschaftliche Abhandlungen 17), 41–53.

Ruffing 2012 = Ruffing K., Wirtschaft in der griechisch-römischen Antike, Darmstadt 2012.

Ruffing – Drexhage 2008 = Ruffing K. – Drexhage H.-J., Antike Sklavenpreise, in: Mauritsch P. – Petermandl W. – Rollinger R. – Ulf Ch. (Hg.), Antike Lebenswelten. Konstanz – Wandel – Wirkungsmacht. Festschrift für Ingomar Weiler zum 70. Geburtstag, Wiesbaden 2008 (Philippika 25), 321–351.

Scheidel 2010 = Scheidel W., The Roman slave supply, in: Bradley K. – Cartledge P. (Hg.), The Cambridge World History of Slavery. Vol. 1: The ancient mediterranean world, Cambridge 2010, 287–310.

Steigerwald 1986 = Steigerwald G., Die antike Purpurfärberei nach dem Bericht Plinius des Älteren in seiner 'Naturalis historia', Traditio 42, 1986, 1–57.

Steigerwald 1990 a = Steigerwald G., Das kaiserliche Purpurprivileg in spätrömischer und frühbyzantinischer Zeit, JbAC 33, 1990 [1991], 209–239.

Steigerwald 1990 b = Steigerwald G., Die Purpursorten im Preisedikt Diokletians vom Jahre 301, Byzantinische Forschungen 15, 1990, 219–276.

Tamerl 2010 = Tamerl I., Das Holzfaß in der römischen Antike, Innsbruck – Wien – Bozen 2010.

Udovitch 1978 = Udovitch A.L., Time, the sea and society. Duration of commercial voyages on the southern shores of the Mediterranean during the high Middle Ages, in: Settimane di studi del Centro italiano di Studi sull'Alto Medioevo 25, 1978, 503–546.

van Rijn 2011 = van Rijn P., Wood supply for the Roman army and reconstruction of the woodlands from c. AD 10–140 in the Lower Rhine delta of the Netherlands, in: Scherrer P. (Hg.), Lignum. Holz in der Antike. Akten des interdisziplinären Symposiums „Holz in der Antike" (Graz, 5.–7. November 2009), Graz 2011 (Keryx 1), 29–40.

Veropoulidoi – Andreou – Kotsakis 2008 = Veropoulidoi R. – Andreou S. – Kotsakis K., Small scale purple-dye production in the bronze age of Northern Greece: The evidence from the Thessaloniki toumba, in: Alfaro C. – Karali L. (Hg.), Purpurae Vestes II. Vestidos, textiles y tintes. Estudios sobre la producción de bienes de consumo en la Antigüedad, València 2008, 171–179.

Vinson 1985 = Vinson M.P., The correspondence of Leo, Metropolitan of Synada and Syncellus, Washington/D.C., 1985.

Westermann 1979 = Westermann E. (Hg.), Internationaler Ochsenhandel (1350–1750). Akten des "7th International Economic History Congress Edinburgh" 1978, Stuttgart 1979.

Der Kaufvertrag im römischen Recht*

Daniele Mattiangeli

Um das Thema des Kaufvertrages im römischen Recht zu behandeln, ist es notwendig, zuerst eine kurze Einführung zu den Konsensualverträgen zu geben und die verpflichtenden Versprechen zu erwähnen. Konsensualverträge sind eine Kategorie von Verträgen, denen auch der Kaufvertrag angehört.

Es gibt vier Arten von Konsensualverträgen oder *obligationes consensu contractae*[1], wie Gaius sie in den Institutionen (3,135) nennt:

- den Kaufvertrag *(emptio-venditio)*
- das Mandat *(mandatum)*
- den Mietvertrag *(locatio-conductio)*
- die Gesellschaft *(societas): „Consensu fiunt obligationes in emptionibus et venditionibus, locationibus conductionibus, societatibus, mandatis."*

Die Konsensualverträge hatten einen außergewöhnlichen Erfolg in der Geschichte und wurden von vielen verschiedenen modernen europäischen Rechtsordnungen (zum Beispiel der französischen, italienischen, deutschen, österreichischen und spanischen Rechtsordnung) übernommen.

In den **Konsensualverträgen** entsteht die Verpflichtung nur dank dem Konsens. Eine schriftliche oder mündliche Form ist nicht zwingend, um das Geschäft abzuschließen. Es ist nur notwendig, dass die Parteien eine Einigung treffen.[2] Es gibt in der Theorie keinen Bedarf eines materiellen Akts (wie zum Beispiel die Übergabe einer Sache in den Realverträgen) um die Wirkungen der gegenseitigen Verpflichtungen zu begründen.

Der **Kaufvertrag** ist der verpflichtende und gegenseitige Vertrag, der auf den Austausch der Ware (*merx*), zumeist einer Sache, gegen einen in Geld bestehenden Preis (*pretium)* gerichtet ist. Das ist die so genannte *emptio-venditio* der republikanischen, klassischen und spät-antiken Periode. In der frühen römischen Periode war wahrscheinlich der Kauf ein gegenseitiger und gleichzeitiger Tausch von Bargeld gegen eine Sache.[3]

Die *emptio-venditio* war in der Tat vielleicht der wichtigste und meist verwendete römische Vertrag aller Zeiten. Der Kaufvertrag kann, dank der zahlreichen Anwendungen im Bereich des Handelsverkehrs, als eine Art „Botschafter" der Vorteile der *Romanitas* in Europa angesehen werden.

---

* Für die wertvolle Unterstützung bei der Verfassung des Artikels danke ich J.M. Rainer. Diese Arbeit basiert in Teilen auf Mattiangeli 2009.

1 Betti 1960, 173–274.

2 Perozzi – Capogrossi Colognesi 2002, 32 f.

3 Kaser 2005, 203.

Der römische Kaufvertrag besitzt auch eine sehr lange und interessante „internationale“ Geschichte, dank seiner engen Verbindung mit dem *ius gentium*.

Aus diesen Gründen soll hier dieses Rechtsinstitut genauer untersucht und seine Vorteile aus einer historisch-vergleichenden Perspektive dargestellt werden.

Arangio-Ruiz, ein wichtiger Gelehrter auf diesem Gebiet, definiert dieses Rechtsgeschäft wie folgt: „Der Kauf ist jener Vertrag mit beidseitigem Konsens, wodurch die erste Partei (der Verkäufer) sich verpflichtet, der zweiten Partei (Käufer) Eigentum und ungestörten Genuss an einer Sache zu übertragen, während die zweite Partei sich verpflichtet, Besitz über eine bestimmte Summe Geld (Gegenwert) zu übertragen“.[4]

Aus dieser allgemeinen, jedoch genauen Definition kann man bereits die Grundmerkmale des Kaufvertrages der römischen Klassik erkennen: beidseitiger Konsens, klares Schuldverhältnis, Übertragung von Eigentum, Genuss an der besessenen Sache, die Verpflichtung des „*pretium*“ (Kaufpreis).

Diese Elemente sind in allen Arten des römischen Kaufvertrages, in jeder Epoche der juristischen römischen Entwicklung, vom Beginn bis zur Spätzeit zu finden.

Sehen wir uns also diese allgemeinen Grundmerkmale der Kaufverträge näher an:

Beim zweiseitigen Konsens wird das gegenseitige Schuldverhältnis zwischen Käufer und Verkäufer durch die unmittelbare Vereinbarung begründet. Die Quellen sind diesbezüglich alle unmissverständlich: sowohl Gaius (*Institutiones* III,136) wie auch Justinian *(Inst.* 3,22,1) fügen den Kaufvertrag in die Liste der vier auf Konsens basierenden Verträge ein. Beide weisen darauf hin, dass das Einvernehmen – aus dem das Schuldverhältnis entsteht – auf jede Art zum Ausdruck gebracht werden kann.[5]

Gaius besagt, dass „*neque verborum neque scripturae ulla proprietas*“ verlangt werden. Laut Justinian ist nicht einmal eine Datierung notwendig, um das Schuldverhältnis entstehen zu lassen. Gerade das dem römischen Geiste des *ius civile* widersprechende Fehlen der Formalitäten kann uns den Ursprung des Kaufvertrages im *ius gentium* erkennen lassen, was eigentlich auch deutlich von Gaius selbst bestätigt wird.[6]

Ein weiteres Hauptmerkmal ist der reine Schuldcharakter des Vertrages, eine Eigenschaft, die im Folgenden noch vertieft wird.

---

4 Arangio-Ruiz 1984, 337.

5 Siehe Gaius, *Institutiones* III,136: *Ideo autem istis modis consensu dicimus obligationes contrahi, quod neque uerborum neque scripturae ulla proprietas desideratur, sed sufficit eos, qui negotium gerunt, consensisse. unde inter absentes quoque talia negotia contrahuntur, ueluti per epistulam aut per internuntium, cum alioquin uerborum obligatio inter absentes fieri possit* und *Iustiniani Institutiones* 3,23: *de Emptione et venditione*, Anhang 4.

6 Siehe Gaius, *Institutiones* II,92–93, nach der Interpretation von Solazzi, und siehe ebenfalls Gaius, *Institutiones* III,154: *Item si cuius ex sociis bona publice aut priuatim uenierint, soluitur societas. sed ea quidem societas, de qua loquimur, id est, quae nudo consensu contrahitur, iuris gentium est; itaque inter omnes homines naturali ratione consistit.*

Der klassische Kauf ist kein Vertrag mit Realfolgen sondern ein Vertrag mit reinen obligatorischen Folgen.[7] Mit anderen Worten, die Vereinbarung unter den Parteien lässt lediglich die Verpflichtung (das Schuldverhältnis) für die Übertragung der Sache und die Verpflichtung der Preiszahlung entstehen.

Damit auch das Eigentum an der Sache (*merx*) oder an dem Zahlgeld übertragen werden kann, war eine weitere Handlung mit Realwirkung notwendig. Hierbei handelte es sich um die *mancipatio* für Sachen *res mancipi*, um die *traditio* für Sachen *res nec mancipi* und um die *in iure cessio* (die gerichtliche Abtretung eines Rechtes).

Die Trennung zwischen Real- und Schuldwirkung ist durchaus eine einzigartige Situation in der antiken Rechtsgeschichte, und ihr Ursprung ist umstritten und nicht sehr klar. Je mehr sich unsere Kenntnisse im historischen Rechtsvergleich vertiefen, umso mehr erscheint die gegenteilige Haltung Verbreitung gefunden zu haben, wonach ein Kauf ein reales Rechtsgeschäft ist, welches unmittelbar das Eigentum der Ware überträgt. Dies geschieht in den meisten modernen Rechtssystemen, ausgenommen in jenen deutscher Tradition.[8]

Diese besondere juristische Auffassung scheint also eine juristische Schöpfung der Römer zu sein.

Die Eigentumsübertragung scheint ebenfalls nicht aus dem alten *ius civile* entstanden zu sein, denn anlässlich der *mancipatio* war die Übergabe des Objektes gleichzeitig auch Eigentumsübertragung. Tatsache ist allerdings, dass im klassischen Kauf die Hauptverpflichtung (Leistung) des Verkäufers die Übergabe der Sache ist, nicht des Eigentums.[9]

Die Quellen diesbezüglich sind sehr deutlich, Paulus schreibt zum Beispiel in Bezug auf Verkäuferverpflichtungen, dass „*venditori sufficit ob evictionem se obligare possessionem tradere*"; ähnliches zum Thema wird auch von Celsus[10] gesagt.

Bezüglich der freien Nutzung bzw. dem Genuss an einem Vertragsobjekt, mit anderen Worten über die erste Form der Absicherung gegen Eviktion in der Ge-

7 Pugliese 1991, 558.

8 Arangio-Ruiz 1984, 337 f.

9 Pugliese 1991, 560.

10 Siehe Paulus, in D.19,4,1: *Sicut aliud est vendere, aliud emere, alius emptor, alius venditor, ita pretium aliud, aliud merx. at in permutatione discerni non potest, uter emptor vel uter venditor sit, multumque differunt praestationes. emptor enim, nisi nummos accipientis fecerit, tenetur ex vendito, venditori sufficit ob evictionem se obligare possessionem tradere et purgari dolo malo, itaque, si evicta res non sit, nihil debet: in permutatione vero si utrumque pretium est, utriusque rem fieri oportet, si merx, neutrius. sed cum debeat et res et pretium esse, non potest permutatio emptio venditio esse, quoniam non potest inveniri, quid eorum merx et quid pretium sit, nec ratio patitur, ut una eademque res et veneat et pretium sit emptionis.* und Celsus, in D.12,4,16: *Dedi tibi pecuniam, ut mihi stichum dares: utrum id contractus genus pro portione emptionis et venditionis est, an nulla hic alia obligatio est quam ob rem dati re non secuta? in quod proclivior sum: et ideo, si mortuus est stichus, repetere possum quod ideo tibi dedi, ut mihi stichum dares. finge alienum esse stichum, sed te tamen eum tradidisse: repetere a te pecuniam potero, quia hominem accipientis non feceris: et rursus, si tuus est stichus et pro evictione eius promittere non vis, non liberaberis, quo minus a te pecuniam repetere possim.*

schichte, finden wir eine berühmte Quelle in einem weiteren Text von Paulus. Dieser besagt, dass der Käufer gegen eine eventuell erfolgreiche *rei vindicatio* eines Dritten geschützt werden soll. Insbesondere: Unterliegt der Käufer einer *rei vindicatio* eines Dritten, muss ihm der Verkäufer eine Summe zurückzahlen, welche das Doppelte des erhaltenen „*pretium*" ist.

Komplex scheint auch hier die Herkunft einer solchen Absicherung: Ursprünglich, das heißt, im Kaufvertrag als schuldrechtliches Verhältnis bis etwa zum II. Jhdt. v. Chr., war sie entweder eine Folge der alten *mancipatio* als *obligatio auctoritatis*[11], oder der Verkäufer musste dafür ein weiteres Schuldverhältnis durch gesonderte *stipulatio* (zum Beispiel mit einer *stipulatio habere licere* oder einer *stipulatio duplae*) auf Ansuchen des Käufers eingehen.[12] Diese Art des Rechtsschutzes scheint dagegen aus der alten *mancipatio* im *ius Quiritium*[13] entstanden zu sein.

Darüber hinaus, wie auch Gaius bestätigt,[14] musste das *pretium* bestimmt bzw. zumindest objektiv bestimmbar sein. Nach der Proculianischen Schule musste es auch in *pecunia numerata* sein. Dagegen konnte sich die Theorie der Sabinianer, wonach jegliche Sache als *pretium* geleistet werden könnte, nicht behaupten.[15]

In justinianischer Zeit musste das *pretium* auch *iustum* sein, bzw. nicht weniger als die Hälfte des gerechten Wertes betragen. Um diesen Wert zu schätzen, konnte man auch das *arbitrium* eines Dritten zu Rate ziehen.

Diese Einstellung zum gerechten Preis ist interessant, da sich schon die Klassiker Gedanken machten, dass hinter einem Scheinkauf verbotene Schenkungen durchgeführt werden könnten. Ansonsten war es dem freien Ermessen der Parteien überlassen, sich über einen sie zufriedenstellenden Preis zu einigen.[16] Selbst Diokletian verlangt in seinem Edikt (vielleicht jedoch in der iustinianischen Epoche abgeändert), dass der Preis beim Immobilienverkehr nicht unter der „Hälfte des gerechten Wertes" liegen soll.[17]

11 Arangio-Ruiz 1984, 202 f.

12 Girard 1923, 65 f.; 106 f.

13 Arangio-Ruiz 1984, 342 f.

14 Gaius, *Institutiones* III,140: *Pretium autem certum esse debet. nam alioquin si ita inter nos conuenerit, ut quanti Titius rem aestimauerit, tanti sit empta, Labeo negauit ullam uim hoc negotium habere; cuius opinionem Cassius probat. Ofilius et eam emptionem et uenditionem esse putauit; cuius opinionem Proculus secutus est.*

15 Siehe Pugliese 1991, 559; wie auch Arangio-Ruiz 1984, 339.

16 Sehr interessant ist diesbezüglich Paulus in D.19,2,22,3: *Quemadmodum in emendo et vendendo naturaliter concessum est quod pluris sit minoris emere, quod minoris sit pluris vendere et ita invicem se circumscribere, ita in locationibus quoque et conductionibus iuris est.*

17 Siehe auch den *Codex Iustiniani* C. 4,44,8: *Si voluntate tua fundum tuum filius tuus venumdedit, dolus ex calliditate atque insidiis emptoris argui debet vel metus mortis vel cruciatus corporis imminens detegi, ne habeatur rata venditio. hoc enim solum, quod paulo minori pretio fundum venumdatum significas, ad rescindendam emptionem invalidum est. quod videlicet si contractus emptionis atque venditionis cogitasses substantiam et quod emptor viliori comparandi, venditor cariori distrahendi votum gerentes ad hunc contractum accedant vixque post multas contentiones, paulatim venditore de eo quod petierat detrahente, emptore autem huic quod obtulerat addente, ad certum con-*

Nachdem hier eine grundsätzliche Definition des Kaufes als Rechtsinstitut dargestellt wurde, versuchen wir nun seine Geschichte, beginnend mit der römischen Frühzeit, zu präsentieren.

Wie die verbreitete Rechtslehre besagt, und auch aus den wenigen, fragmentarischen Quellen aus der Zeit, soll die erste Form des römischen Kaufes aus der so genannten „*mancipatio*“ bzw. dem „*mancipium*“ entstanden sein. Genauer: Aus jener Form des Realvertrages, bei der ein gleichzeitiger „Tausch“ vom Objekt gegen einen Preis erfolgte. Die „*mancipatio*“ diente nur der (Eigentums-)Übertragung für jene Sachen, die als „*res mancipi*“ galten, d.h. einen bestimmten Wert hatten. Für die anderen Sachen, genannt „*res nec mancipi*“, existiert keine Quelle, aus der eine bestimmte Form der Übertragung überliefert wird, das heißt, sie wurden formlos übertragen.[18] Später dagegen, in der Klassik, weiß man, dass ihr Eigentum durch „*traditio*“ übertragen wurde.

Gaius[19] beschreibt die Abläufe der früheren „*mancipatio*“ sehr genau, weitere Informationen stammen aus den Schriften von Varrus und Festus[20]; weiters finden

---

*sentiant pretium, profecto perspiceres neque bonam fidem, quae emptionis atque v enditionis conventionem tuetur, pati neque ullam rationem concedere rescindi propter hoc consensu finitum contractum vel statim vel post pretii quantitatis disceptationem: nisi minus dimidia iusti pretii, quod fuerat tempore venditionis, datum est, electione iam emptori praestita servanda. * diocl. et maxim. aa. et cc. aureliae euodiae. * <a 293 d. k. dec. aa. conss.>*

18 Arangio-Ruiz 1978, 30 f.

19 Gaius, *Institutiones* I,119–122 *Est autem mancipatio, ut supra quoque diximus, imaginaria quaedam venditio: Quod et ipsum ius proprium civium Romanorum est; eaque res ita agitur: Adhibitis non minus quam quinque testibus civibus Romanis puberibus et praeterea alio eiusdem condicionis, qui libram aeneam teneat, qui appellatur libripens, is, qui mancipio accipit, rem tenens ita dicit: HUNC EGO HOMINEM EX IURE QUIRITIUM MEUM ESSE AIO ISQUE MIHI EMPTUS ESTO HOC AERE AENEAQUE LIBRA; deinde aere percutit libram idque aes dat ei, a quo mancipio accipit, quasi pretii loco. 120. Eo modo et serviles et liberae personae mancipantur; animalia quoque, quae mancipi sunt, quo in numero habentur boves, equi, muli, asini; item praedia tam urbana quam rustica, quae et ipsa mancipi sunt, qualia sunt Italica, eodem modo solent mancipari. 121. In eo solo praediorum mancipatio a ceterorum mancipatione differt, quod personae serviles et liberae, item animalia, quae mancipi sunt, nisi in praesentia sint, mancipari non possunt; adeo quidem, ut eum, qui mancipio accipit, adprehendere id ipsum, quod ei mancipio datur, necesse sit; unde etiam mancipatio dicitur, quia manu res capitur: Praedia vero absentia solent mancipari. 122. ldeo autem aes et libra adhibetur, quia olim aereis tantum nummis utebantur; et erant asses, dipundii, semisses, quadrantes, nec ullus aureus vel argenteus nummus in usu erat, sicut ex lege XII tabularum intellegere possumus; eorumque nummorum vis et potestas non in numero erat, sed in pondere; * asses librales erant, et dipondii * unde etiam dupondius dictus est, quasi duo pondo: Quod nomen adhuc in usu retinetur. Semisses quoque et quadrantes pro rata scilicet portione ad pondus examinati erant. Tunc igitur et qui dabat alicui pecuniam, non numerabat eam, sed appendebat; unde servi, quibus permittitur administratio pecuniae, dispensatores appellati sunt.*

20 Siehe Varrus, *De lingua latina* 5,163; unter: *rodus* S. 320: *Rodus, vel raudus significat rem rudem et inperfectam; nam saxum quoque raudus appellant poetae, ut Accius in Melanippo (438) : „constituit, cognovit, sensit, conlocat sese in locum celsum; hinc manibus rapere roudus saxeum grande (m) et grave(m)“; et in Chrysippo (262): „Neque quisquam a telis vacuus, sed uti cuique obviam fuerat, ferum alius# saxio rudem#.“ Vulgus quidem in usu habuit, non modo pro aere imperfecto, ut Lucilius, cum ait (1192) „plumbi pauxillum rodus linique matexam“: sed etiam signato, qui in manci-*

wir im Gesetz der 12 Tafeln mehrmals die Bezeichnung bzw. den Hinweis auf „*mancipium*“.

Beim Ritual der *mancipatio* treten Käufer und Verkäufer mit der Sache (wenn diese beweglich ist) und in Anwesenheit von weiteren fünf römischen volljährigen (*puberi*) Bürgern auf; dabei ist auch ein *libripens* (Waageträger) mit einer Waage (*libra*). Nun berührt der Käufer (dies ist der wesentliche Moment) mit einem Stäbchen (*radusculum*) die Sache und spricht folgende Formel aus: „*Aio hanc rem meam esse ex iure Quiritium, eaque mihi empta esto hoc aere*“. Gleichzeitig gibt er den bedungenen Gegenwert (*aes rude*) auf die Waage. Vom Verkäufer wird keine Erklärung verlangt.

Die *mancipatio* stammt also aus der Zeit, in der noch keine *pecunia numerata* verwendet wurde, sondern eben nur das *aes rude*, d.h. aus einer frühen Epoche. Aus den Quellen können wir also sagen, dass die *mancipatio* die erste Form des Kauf(-vertrages) der römischen Geschichte ist, ein Realvertrag mit unmittelbarer Rechtswirkung. Später sehen wir, wie in der Zeit von Gaius noch immer ein starrer Formalismus besteht, obwohl die *pecunia numerata* längst das *aes rude* ersetzt hatte: Die Anwendung des Stäbchens und der Waage ist noch verpflichtend, wenn auch nur mehr symbolisch.

Der Formalismus der Rechtsgeschäfte ist in der Tat eines der wesentlichen Merkmale der römischen Rechtskultur, vom Beginn bis in die klassische Zeit. Die Rechtsgeschäfte an sich änderten sich nach dem Bedarf und der Entwicklung der Zeit, aber die Gesten und die formellen Handlungen blieben als Konstante im früheren wie im klassischen römischen Rechtssystem bestehen. Erst ab der klassischen Zeit verzichtete man auf die tatsächliche Präsenz der Sache oder eines Symbols bei Eigentumsübertragung von Liegenschaften (noch im französischen Mittelalter nimmt man eine Handvoll Erde als Symbol dafür).

In der klassischen Zeit wird die *mancipatio* zum Rechtsgeschäft bezüglich *res mancipi* mit symbolischer Eigentumsübertragung über das Kaufobjekt, von Gaius selbst „*imaginaria venditio*“[21] genannt: *venditio*, weil noch formell die Aktion der Zahlung vorgespielt wird, obwohl die eigentliche Bezahlung außerhalb der Formalismen geschehen konnte; *imaginaria*, weil der Grund der Eigentumsübertragung auch ein anderer als der reine Kauf sein kann, und daher „abstrakt“, wie im heutigen Grundgedanken des deutschen Verfügungsgeschäftes.

Das wesentliche und auch ursprüngliche Element der alten *mancipatio* ist die gesprochene Erklärung des *mancipio accipiens*, des Käufers, über die Übernahme des Eigentums: „*Aio, hanc rem (homimem, bovem* oder was immer) *meam esse ex iure quiritium*“. Durch das aussagekräftige Verb *AIO*, stellt der *mancipio accipiens*

pando, cum dicitur: „rudusculo libram ferito“, asse tangitur libra. Cincius de verbis priscis sic ait: „Quemadmodum omnis fere materia non deformata rudis appellatur, sicut vestimentum rude, non perpolitum; sic aes infectum rudusculum. Apud aedem Apollinis aes conflatum iacuit, id ad rudus appellabant. In aestimatione censoria aes infectum rudus appellatur.“ Rudiari ab eodem dicuntur, qui saga nova poliunt. Hominem inperitum rudem dicimus.

21 Arangio-Ruiz 1984, 200 f.

fest, Eigentümer der Sache zu sein (*meam esse*) und nicht einfach sie erwerben zu wollen, fast als ob er eine *rei vindicatio* und nicht einen Kauf durchführen würde. Den Quellen nach ist diese Aussage des *mancipio accipiens* fast gleichlautend mit jener eines Klägers bei der *legis actio sacramento in rem.*[22]

An dieser Stelle soll die besonders enge Beziehung zwischen der *mancipatio* und der *rei vindicatio* betont werden, wenn auch einige Autoren auf die Ähnlichkeit mit der Handlung der *in iure cessio* hinweisen, da dieselbe Formel darin zu finden ist.[23]

Für die Entstehung der *mancipatio* findet man in der Lehre tatsächlich zwei Theorien:

Die erstere, die z.B. von Arangio-Ruiz vertreten wird, besagt, dass die *mancipatio* aus der *in iure cessio* abgeleitet wurde, und aus dieser ebenfalls der erste Formelsatz entstammt.[24]

Die zweite, deren Hauptvertreter Kaser und Betti sind, sieht die Entstehung der *mancipatio* auf der Basis der *rei vindicatio*, denn hier wird die Eigentumsübernahme durch Kauf mit einer kraftvollen Form bekleidet, welche für den römischen Geist der Frühzeit typisch war.

Bei genauerer Betrachtung wird es klar, dass die *mancipatio* nicht aus der *in iure cessio* entstanden sein kann (wie die erste Theorie besagt), denn diese Form war – schon wegen der Strukturierung – nur für eine Übertragung geeignet und nicht für zwei (Objekt und Preis), wie es in einem Kauf notwendig ist.

---

22 Zu diesem Thema, Gaius, *Institutiones* IV,16: *Si in rem agebatur, mobilia quidem et mouentia, quae modo in ius adferri adduciue possent, in iure uindicabantur ad hunc modum: qui uindicabat, festucam tenebat; deinde ipsam rem adprehendebat, uelut hominem, et ita dicebat: HVNC EGO HOMINEM EX IVRE QVIRITIVM MEVM ESSE AIO SECVNDVM SVAM CAVSAM; SICVT DIXI, ECCE TIBI, VINDICTAM INPOSVI, et simul homini festucam inponebat. aduersarius eadem similiter dicebat et faciebat. cum uterque uindicasset, praetor dicebat: MITTITE AMBO HOMINEM, illi mittebant. qui prior uindicauerat, ita alterum interrogabat: POSTVLO, ANNE DICAS, QVA EX CAVSA VINDICAVERIS? ille respondebat: IVS FECI, SICVT VINDICTAM INPOSVI. deinde qui prior uindicauerat, dicebat: QVANDO TV INIVRIA VINDICAVISTI, QVINGENTIS ASSIBVS SACRAMENTO TE PROVOCO; aduersarius quoque dicebat similiter: ET EGO TE; aut si res infra mille asses erat, quinquagenarium scilicet sacramentum nominabant. deinde eadem sequebantur, quae cum in personam ageretur. postea praetor secundum alterum eorum uindicias dicebat, id est interim aliquem possessorem constituebat, eumque iubebat praedes aduersario dare litis et uindiciarum, id est rei et fructuum; alios autem praedes ipse praetor ab utroque accipiebat sacramenti causa, quia id in publicum cedebat. festuca autem utebantur quasi hastae loco, signo quodam iusti dominii, quando iusto dominio ea maxime sua esse credebant, quae ex hostibus cepissent; unde in centumuiralibus iudiciis hasta proponitur.* Darüber hinaus wird das Problem ausführlich in Arangio-Ruiz 1978, 23 f. behandelt.

23 Siehe Gaius, *Institutiones*, II,24: *In iure cessio autem hoc modo fit: apud magistratum populi Romani uelut praetorem urbanum [aut praesides prouinciae] is, cui res in iure ceditur, rem tenens ita dicit: HVNC EGO HOMINEM EX IVRE QVIRITIVM MEVM ESSE AIO; deinde postquam hic uindicauerit, praetor interrogat eum, qui cedit, an contra uindicet; quo negante aut tacente tunc ei, qui uindicauerit, eam rem addicit; idque legis actio uocatur. hoc fieri potest etiam in prouinciis apud praesides earum.*

24 Arangio-Ruiz 1978, 24.

Viel glaubhafter ist dagegen die Verwandtschaft zwischen *mancipatio* und *rei vindicatio*. Die Eröffnungserklärung der *mancipatio* ist in der Tat identisch mit jener der *rei vindicatio*. Es scheint offensichtlich, dass die römischen Juristen beide Rechtsgeschäfte auf einer sehr starken Eigentumsaussage der Erklärenden basieren lassen wollten. Genau dieses Verhältnis wird wirkungsvoll von Betti vertreten.[25] Er stellt die *mancipatio* als außergerichtliche *vindicatio* dar. Kaser beschreibt die *mancipatio* als „formalen und öffentlichen Akt der Übernahme", gleich jenem der „*legis actio sacramento in rem*".[26] Zur weiteren Bekräftigung dieser Theorie behauptet Kaser, dass die *legis actio sacramento in rem* in den früheren Epochen lediglich für die *res mancipi*[27] möglich gewesen sei.

Es scheint allerdings eine weitere Kaser'sche Theorie sehr fraglich, wonach der *pretium* nichts anderes als eine Art „Lösegeld" sei, welches vom Übernehmer (*accipiens*) an den Geber (*dans*) bezahlt wird, um eine *contravindicatio* zu vermeiden.

Das stärkste Argument für eine Entstehung der *mancipatio* aus der *legis actio sacramento in rem* findet sich in den gleichlautenden Aussagen des *accipiens* und in der Anwendung des Verbs „*aio*". Der starke Wunsch nach einer kräftigen Handlung für die Übernahme einer Sache – welches vom Verb *aio* besonders deutlich ausgedrückt wird – entspricht der ursprünglichen Geisteshaltung der ersten Römer, Landwirte und Krieger. Dieses Verb findet man auch in den Texten von Cicero und Sallust in der Bedeutung von „mit besonderer Kraft etwas erklären, feststellen, behaupten".[28]

Nach dieser Darstellung über die früheren Entstehungsphasen der *mancipatio* als erste Form des Kaufes im römischen Recht, wird nun die Bedeutung dieser Art des Kaufes bzw. *mancipium* auf dem Hintergrund der Quellen, wie auch ihre Wandlung zu einem Konsensualvertrag *iuris gentium* untersucht.

Aus den *Institutiones* von Gaius (I 119–122, wie auch II 14 und 22) kann man sehen, dass der Anwendungsbereich der *mancipatio* sehr begrenzt war, da diese Prozedur nur bei *res mancipi* (d.h. Menschen, Lasttieren, Grundstücken am Land oder in der Stadt, bzw. *servitutes prediorum rusticorum*) möglich war; für alles Andere (*res nec mancipi*) bedarf eine Eigentumsübertragung der Form der *traditio*.[29]

Mehrere Autoren, darunter auch Kaser, behaupten, dass in früheren Epochen die *mancipatio* für alles verwendet wurde,[30] und dass der Unterschied zwischen *res mancipi* und *nec mancipi* erst später, in der republikanischen Zeit entstanden sei. Wir wollen auf diese theoretische Kontroverse nicht näher eingehen, sondern

25 Siehe Betti 1915, 321 f. In dieser Arbeit wird die Übereinstimmung der zwei Formulierungen bekräftigt, wie auch ihre durchaus ähnliche Etymologie, basierend auf dem gleichen Wortkern: *vindicare = vim + dicere*.

26 Kaser 1951, 175 f. Seine Theorie wird ausführlich formuliert in Kaser 1943, 107 f. wie auch 138 f.

27 Kaser 1951, 147 f.

28 Castiglione – Mariotti 1966, 67–68.

29 Siehe Gaius, *Institutiones* II,15–30.

30 Siehe Kaser 1943, 170, wo auch die zahlreichen Befürworter dieser Theorie erwähnt werden.

überlassen dies Gaius, der diesen Unterschied in seinem Beitrag über *res pretiosores* in den Institutionen darstellt (*Institutiones* I, 192).

Viel interessanter scheint es, die Kaufform für die *res nec mancipi* zu analysieren. Die *traditio* bestand in der tatsächlichen Übergabe einer Sache *nec mancipi*, mit der gleichzeitigen Absicht (*animus*), auch das Eigentum auf der Basis der *iusta causa* zu übertragen.[31] Es war das Rechtsgeschäft schlechthin für alles, was geringen Wert hatte, und behielt seine Merkmale durch alle römischen Epochen.

Darüber hinaus, wie auch Gaius[32] sagt, war der Akt *iuris gentium* und als solcher für alle Gesellschaftsschichten zugänglich, auch für „Nicht-Römer".

Sehr strittig ist allerdings sein kausales Wesen. In den Quellen[33] heißt es, dass eine *iusta causa traditionis* notwendig war, um *dominium* über *res nec mancipi* zu übertragen. Diese *causa* konnte verschiedener Art sein: *venditionis causa, solvendi causa*, usw. Diese zahlreiche Kausalität war scheinbar bereits in der Antike vorhanden, wobei sich dann langsam eine Abschwächung in der Klassik und Spätklassik abzeichnet, wie auch durch die Quellen bestätigt wird.[34]

Auf die Kausalität der *traditio* soll hier nicht weiter eingegangen werden, zumal die Lehre und die Quellen selbst strittig sind.

Zurück zum eigentlichen Kaufvertrag: der Handel und Umschlag der *res nec mancipi* unterlag – nach der vorherrschenden Lehre, darunter auch Kaser[35] – keiner besonderen Form. Es scheint in der Tat, dass seit frühester Zeit beim Kauf von *res nec mancipi* eine formlose doppelte *traditio* (vom Kaufobjekt und Kaufpreis) durchgeführt wurde, wobei beide Rechtsgeschäfte wechselseitig kausal waren.[36] Mit anderen Worten war das ein Realgeschäft gegen Bares, nach dem Prinzip der Vermögensumschichtung, ein Prinzip, das besonders in den hellenistischen Traditionen sehr geschätzt wurde und welches – meiner Meinung nach – das wesentliche Bindeglied zwischen dem römischen Kauf in der Antike und dem Konsensualvertrag in der Klassik darstellt. Leider gibt es keine Beschreibung oder Quelle bezüglich dieser Art des Erwerbs für *res nec mancipi*, nicht einmal in den *duodecim tabulae*; dies könnte allerdings als Bestätigung interpretiert werden, dass es

31 Pugliese 1991, 465 f.

32 Siehe Gaius, *Institutiones* III,60–178.

33 Siehe Ulpian in *Ulpiani epitomae* 19,7, wie auch Paulus in D.41,1,31.

34 Siehe Julianus in D.41,1,36: *Cum in corpus quidem quod traditur consentiamus, in causis vero dissentiamus, non animadverto, cur inefficax sit traditio, veluti si ego credam me ex testamento tibi obligatum esse, ut fundum tradam, tu existimes ex stipulatu tibi eum deberi. nam et si pecuniam numeratam tibi tradam donandi gratia, tu eam quasi creditam accipias, constat proprietatem ad te transire nec impedimento esse, quod circa causam dandi atque accipiendi dissenserimus.* Ulpian in D.12,1,18 vertritt eine andere Meinung: *Si ego pecuniam tibi quasi donaturus dedero, tu quasi mutuam accipias, iulianus scribit donationem non esse: sed an mutua sit, videndum. et puto nec mutuam esse magisque nummos accipientis non fieri, cum alia opinione acceperit. quare si eos consumpserit, licet condictione teneatur, tamen doli exceptione uti poterit, quia secundum voluntatem dantis nummi sunt consumpti.*

35 Siehe Kaser 1943, 195 f.; oder auch Wieacker 1950, 535 f.; und nicht zuletzt Arangio-Ruiz 1978, 40 f.

36 Arangio-Ruiz 1978, 40.

dafür keine bestimmte Formen gegeben hat, vielleicht weil man in der Antike dieser Art der Eigentumsübertragung keine Bedeutung zugemessen hatten.

Möglicherweise war diese Praxis beim Kauf von *res nec mancipi* als Usus von jedem seit eh und je durchgeführt und für selbstverständlich gehalten worden. Höchstwahrscheinlich wurde daher diese Prozedur als juridische Gewohnheit von Generation zu Generation übertragen und man sah keinen Bedarf seiner Niederschrift, zumal sie in Bezug auf Sachen von geringerem Wert angewendet wurde.

Sicher ist aber, dass der Kauf gegen Bares von *res nec mancipi* mittels doppelter *traditio* (Sache und Preis) zusammen und zugleich mit der *mancipatio* seit den frühesten römischen Epochen ein Rechtssystem bildeten, welches für die rechtlich-wirtschaftlichen Bedürfnisse der damaligen Gesellschaft ausreichend und zufriedenstellend war.[37] Weiters gibt es noch das von Gaius beschriebene, komplexere System des Konsensualvertrages mit schuldrechtlicher Wirkung, welches erst im II. Jhdt. v. Chr. mit der Einführung des *praetor peregrinus* entstehen soll.

Das Problem der *emptio-venditio* bzw. seiner Entwicklung kann aus einer anpassungsfähigen Perspektive betrachtet werden, um diesem Rechtsinstitut eine „Wandelfähigkeit" zuzusprechen. Diese Wandelfähigkeit erlaubt eine Anpassung an die sich stets ändernden historischen, wirtschaftlichen, sozialen und politischen Bedingungen und Umgebung.

Im Laufe der römischen Rechtsgeschichte gab es nicht eine einzige, lineare Evolution vom Kauf durch Barzahlung zum Konsensualvertrag mit schuldrechtlichen Folgen, sondern zwei in sich verwobene Entwicklungen, die in der späteren Kaiserzeit bis Justinian sogar in Konkurrenz standen. Einerseits finden wir den Ausgangspunkt in der *mancipatio* des *ius civile* und über die Etappen der *mancipationes emptionis causa* bis zu den *stipulationes* der justinianischen Epoche. Andererseits gibt es das *ius gentium* und die internationalen handelsrechtlichen Vereinbarungen, wobei auf der Basis des hellenistischen Vertrages mit *arrha* sich zuerst die wechselseitigen *stipulationes* (zur Zeit des *praetor peregrinus*), später das feierlich-formelle gleichzeitige Rechtsgeschäft (Kauf-Verkauf) entwickelten, um dann schlussendlich zu *emptio-venditio* zu gelangen, wie diese Transaktion von Gaius beschrieben wird.

Diese zwei Entwicklungslinien, obgleich sie in verschiedenen Umgebungen und aus verschiedenen Bedürfnissen entstanden, überkreuzen sich im Laufe der Zeit, beeinflussen sich gegenseitig, bis sie quasi in bestimmten Momenten sogar in gegenseitiger Konkurrenz innerhalb der römischen Rechtsentwicklung stehen.

Beide Entwicklungen sind stark von den wirtschaftlichen, politischen und sozialen Entwicklungen der römischen Gesellschaft beeinflusst, beide sind dadurch in ihrem Werdegang und in rechtsvergleichenden Perspektiven verbunden.

Um das gesamte Phänomen des Kaufvertrages und seiner Geschichte zu verstehen, wird hier die chronologische Entwicklung dieses Rechtsgeschäftes, von

37 Arangio-Ruiz 1978, 45.

seinen Anfängen als Tauschkauf gegen Bares bis zur schuldrechtlichen Konsensualerklärung kurz aufgezeigt.

Ein Datum hat einen fixen Platz in unserer Darstellung, und zwar das Jahr 241 v. Chr., d.h. die Entstehungsstunde der Fremdenprätoren (*praetor inter peregrinos* oder *praetor peregrinus*). Auf dieselbe Zeit ist ebenfalls die Anerkennung der Konsensualverträge zum Kaufzweck mit schuldrechtlicher Wirkung in Rahmen von „internationalen" Wirtschafts- und Handelsbeziehungen[38] zurückzuführen, d.h. ein Rechtsschutzmittel im Rahmen der rechtlichen Verhältnisse zwischen Römern und Fremden oder unter Fremden selbst.

Erst später, 150 v. Chr., wurde seine Anwendung auch auf Verhältnisse unter römischen Bürgern ausgeweitet, und zwar in einer Zeit als der Stadtprätor (*praetor urbanus*) die Anwendung des Verfahrens *per formulas* ebenfalls auf die Rechtsbeziehungen unter Römern ausweitete. Wahrscheinlich liegt die Zeit der offiziellen Anerkennung und Anwendung eines konsensualen Kaufvertrages im römischen Recht gerade in der Zeitspanne zwischen den zwei Daten, und nicht erst ab dem Jahr 150 v. Chr. wie von Arangio-Ruiz behauptet.[39] Seine Entstehung soll tatsächlich auf die Zeit zurückzuführen zu sein, in der die römischen Handelsbeziehungen sich rasch auf das ganze Mittelmeer ausweiteten dank der rasanten Entwicklung seiner militärischen und navalen Präsenz und auch dem Untergang von Carthago, das von Rom besiegt worden war.[40]

Zweifelsohne eine sehr dynamische Zeit, in der immer öfter Geschäfte mit weit entfernt angesiedelten Völkern zustande kamen, so dass ein unmittelbarer Kauf gegen bares Geld – wie bei der *mancipatio* – kaum mehr möglich war. Ein klassisches Beispiel dafür kann in dem regen Handel mit exotischen, wertvollen Gütern erahnt werden, die zwar sehr gefragt waren, aber erst nach monatelangen Transportwegen auf den römischen Märkten zu finden waren.

Geschäfte mit so weit entfernt angesiedelten Handelspartnern forderten eine effiziente Absicherung für beide Parteien, welche in der bindenden Willenserklärung (des Kaufens bzw. des Veräußerns) mit schuldrechtlicher Wirkung gesehen wurde. Beiden Parteien war damit auch noch eine gewisse vertragliche Freiheit gewährt, d.h. sie durften nach der Willenserklärung weitere konkretere Schritte innerhalb der Abmachung unternehmen, z.B. sich mit einer Anzahlung die versprochene Ware sichern, die nicht sofort lieferbar war.

Darüber hinaus waren beide Parteien sicher, auch wenn sie sich *pro futuro* verpflichteten, dass sie ihren Rechtsschutz vor den römischen Gerichten fordern konnten (bei entsprechendem Beweis der zustandegekommenen Vereinbarung[41]). Mit anderen Worten, ob römischer Bürger oder Fremder, alle Parteien durften sich auf ein römisches Gericht berufen, dank der anerkannten Rechtswirkung der Vereinbarung. Der Konsensualvertrag war also das ideale Rechtsinstrument für

38 Arangio-Ruiz 1978, 82 f.

39 Arangio-Ruiz 1978, 72–73.

40 Für eine historische Vertiefung des Themas siehe Talamanca 1979, 45 f.

41 Arangio-Ruiz 1978, 83.

diese „internationalen" Handelsbeziehungen, weil flexibel und in der Lage, den unterschiedlichen Bedürfnissen der Parteien gerecht zu werden. Diese Überlegungen allein sind – meines Erachtens – überzeugendes Indiz, um die Ursprünge aus dem volksnahen *ius gentium* zu belegen.

Der Vollständigkeit halber muss hier auch die Position von einigen Autoren[42] erwähnt werden, welche eine frühere Datierung des Konsensualvertrages wagen und ihn auf der Basis von Schriften von Cato und Plautus auf die Tradition des *ius civile* und auf eine Periode vor der Zeitspanne 242–150 v. Chr. zuschreiben. Im Endeffekt aber kehren auch diese Theorien auf die Jahresbegrenzung 241–150 v. Chr. zurück.

Alles in allem aber stellt sich diese „frühere" Datierung nicht als Problem dar, denn im Vergleich zur bereits angegebenen Zeitspanne (241–150 v. Chr.) bestätigt das nur, dass der Vertrag aus dem *ius gentium* allmählich in das römische System des *ius civile* eingedrungen ist, und zeitweise sogar parallel mit den *stipulationes* existierte. Meines Erachtens hat sich der Konsensualvertrag gerade während dieser 90 Jahre (zwischen 241 und 150 v. Chr.) in das *ius civile* graduell – beginnend mit der Anwendung des *ius gentium* durch den Fremdenprätor – eingegliedert.

Um diese Entwicklung zusammenzufassen, scheint es notwendig einen Überblick über die zeitlichen Anhaltspunkte für die weiteren Rechtsinstitute, die in Zusammenhang mit dem Kauf/Verkauf stehen, zu geben.

Zuerst die *mancipatio*, die die erste eigentliche Form des Kaufes im römischen Rechtssystem darstellt, deren Ursprung tief in der Urgeschichte der römischen Kultur liegt. Angeblich gab es diese Form bereits vor dem Zwölftafelrecht, daher sollte man als zeitlichen Anhaltspunkt die Periode mindestens um das 7. Jhdt. v. Chr. annehmen. Sicher existiert die Form des *mancipium* noch vor dem geprägten Geld, also in der Zeit des *aes rude*.[43] Das bedeutet, dass seine Geschichte mit der Geschichte Roms, d.h. bei der Gründung oder kurz danach, beginnt; jedenfalls muss Rom bereits eine stadtähnliche Siedlung gewesen sein, und nicht, wie z.B. von Perozzi behauptet, noch ländlichen Charakter gehabt haben.[44]

Die *traditio* scheint eine jüngere Schöpfung zu sein, und zwar aus der Zeit um das 4. Jhdt. v. Chr., obgleich einige Urformen der *traditio* – wenn auch ohne Formalismen und außerhalb des traditionellen Rechtssystems – sicherlich schon davor existierten.[45]

Der Ursprung der *sponsio*, der klassischen mündlichen Verpflichtungserklärung, ist ebenfalls sehr alt. Diese Form des Rechtsgeschäftes war ausschließlich den römischen Bürgern (die *Quirites*) gewährt, daher ist seine Entstehung in den früheren Epochen bzw. der Zeit des Zwölftafelrechts zu datieren (d.h. in etwa 6.

42 Darunter Longo 1937, 281 f.; Ferrini 1929, 63 f.; Scialoja 1907, 168 f.; Meylan 1950, 23 f., und Meylan 1936, 283; Bekker 1864, 416 f.; unter Angabe von verschiedenen Argumenten und Quellen.

43 Arangio-Ruiz 1984, 200.

44 Einen ausführlichen Überblick über die Theorien der *mancipatio* gibt Voci 1952, 27 f.

45 Arangio-Ruiz 1984, 203 f.

oder 5. Jhdt. v. Chr.). Einige Autoren, darunter Pugliese, halten die *sponsio* für die erste Form der schuldrechtlichen Verpflichtung des römischen Rechtes und sehen ihren Ursprung in den *mores*, also in einem sakralen und nicht rein rechtlichen Rahmen.[46]

Die *stipulatio* ist, von der Art her, dasselbe wie eine *sponsio*, sie war aber für die Fremden[47] (*peregrini*) gedacht, sie wurde also zu *obligatio iuris gentium*. Ihre Entstehung ist wahrscheinlich auf die Zeit der Einführung des *praetor peregrinus*[48] zurückzuführen. Ab dieser Zeit können alle anderen Formen der Stipulation entstanden sein, bzw. datiert werden – wie z.B. die bereits erwähnten gegenseitigen *stipulationes*.

Ein abschließendes praktisches Beispiel eines Vertrages soll die Aktualität und die Anpassungsfähigkeit des römischen Rechts zeigen. Auch heute sind viele Verträge des römischen Rechts noch aktuell geblieben und theoretisch könnte dasselbe Schema eines römischen Rechtsgeschäfts angewendet werden und wäre in den meisten europäischen Rechtsordnungen heute noch gültig.

Es mag seltsam anmuten, aber es ist eine Tatsache, dass in 2000 Jahren das Grundschema der meisten Verträge dasselbe wie bei den Römern geblieben ist. Die Gegenstände, die Parteien und die Gewährleistungsmerkmale haben sich sicherlich geändert, das Schema blieb jedoch gleich. Der Kaufvertrag stellt dafür das beste Beispiel dar. Als Musterbeispiel dieses allgemeinen Schemas des Kaufvertrages, das die Römer in einer langjährigen internationalen Handelserfahrung entwickeln konnten, wird hier ein Text aus dem II. Jhd. n. Chr., der in einem Goldbergwerk in Siebenbürgen im XIX. Jhd. gefunden wurde, dargestellt.

46 Siehe auch Pugliese 1991, 146 f. wie auch Gaius, *Institutiones* III,93; Festus: 441 und 440 (in der Lindsay-Ausgabe); Gellius, *Noctes Atticae* 4,4,2; Varrus, *De lingua latina* 6,69; Livius, *Ab urbe condita* 1,24.7. Die Theorie von Pugliese erweist sich als äußerst interessant: das lateinische Wort „*sponsio*" soll vom griechischen „*spendo*" in der Bedeutung von „Trankopfer bereiten, durchführen" stammen, und nicht aus dem lateinischen „*sponte*" – wie von Varrus behauptet – in der Bedeutung von „freiwillig, unaufgefordert". Diese griechische Interpretation von „*spendo*" würde die sakral-religiöse Herkunft der römischen *sponsio* auch besser erklären.

47 Für eine deutlichere Unterscheidung von *sponsio* und *stipulatio* siehe Gaius, *Institutiones* III,93 und 95: *Sed haec quidem uerborum obligatio DARI SPONDES? SPONDEO propria ciuium Romanorum est; ceterae uero iuris gentium sunt, itaque inter omnes homines, siue ciues Romanos siue peregrinos, ualent. et quamuis ad Graecam uocem expressae fuerint, uelut hoc modo „dØseis; dØsØ, homologeis; homologØ, pistei keleueis; pistei keleuØ, poi seis; poi sØ", etiam hae tamen inter ciues Romanos ualent, si modo Graeci sermonis intellectum habeant; et e contrario quamuis Latine enuntientur, tamen etiam inter peregrinos ualent, si modo Latini sermonis intellectum habeant. at illa uerborum obligatio DARI SPONDES? SPONDEO adeo propria ciuium Romanorum est, ut ne quidem in Graecum sermonem per interpretationem proprie transferri possit, quamuis dicatur a Graeca uoce figurata esse. 95. Unde dicitur uno casu hoc uerbo peregrinum quoque obligari posse, uelut si imperator noster principem alicuius peregrini populi de pace ita interroget: PACEM FVTVRAM SPONDES? uel ipse eodem modo interrogetur. quod nimium subtiliter dictum est, quia si quid aduersus pactionem fiat, non ex stipulatu agitur, sed iure belli res uindicatur.*

48 Gaius, *Institutiones* III,93: *DARI SPONDES? SPONDEO propria ciuium Romanorum est; ceterae uero iuris gentium sunt, itaque inter omnes homines, siue ciues Romanos siue peregrinos, ualent.*

Der Text ist der Nachweis[49] eines abgeschlossenen Kaufvertrages, mit dem eine Sklavin erworben wurde:

(Tabula cerata in Dacia reperta: J. Erdy in „*De tabulis ceratis in Dacia repertis cum quaestionibus de vetusta historia Magyarorum,* Pestini 1856, 4 f.; V. Arangio Ruiz, FIRA 3, *Negotia,* Firenze 1972, 287–288)

Cl(audius) Iulianus miles leg(ionis) XIII G(eminae) (centuria) Cl(audi) Mari emit mancipioque accepit mulierem nomine Theudotem, sive ea quo alio nomine est, n(atione) Creticam, apochatam pro uncis duabus, (denariis) quadrigentis viginti de Cl(audio) Phileto, f(fideiussore) a(ccepto) Alexandro Antipatri.
Eam Mulierem sanam traditam esse emptori s(upra) s(cripto), et si quis eam mulierem, q(ua) d(e) a (gitur), partemve quam quis ex ea… evicerit, qu(o) mi(nus) emptorem s(upra) s(criptum) eumve at quem ea res pertinebit uti frui habere possidereque recte liceat , tunc quantum id erit, quot ita ex ea… evictum ablatumve fuerit, sive quot ita licitum non erit, tantam pecuniam probam recte dari f(ide) r(ogavit) Cl. Iulianus m(i)l(es) s(upra) s(criptus), d(ari) f(ide) p(romisit) Cl. Philetus: id fide sua esse iussit Alexander Antipatri.
Inque ea(m) mulierem, quae s(upra) s(cripta) est, pretium eius (denarius) CCCCXX accepisse et habere se dixit Cl. Philetus a Claudio Iuliano mil(ite) s(upra) s(cripto)
Actum canab(is) leg(ionis) XIII G(eminae) IIII Nonas Octobres Bradua et Varo cos

In diesem Beispiel[50] ist gut ersichtlich, wie dieser alte Vertrag tatsächlich alle Erfordernisse eines modernen Kaufvertrages beinhaltet. Dasselbe Schema könnte als Formular im aktuellen Sinne für künftige Verträge genutzt werden.

Zu Beginn stehen die Namen der beiden Parteien (Claudius Iulianus, der Verkäufer, und Claudius Philetus, der Käufer), der Namen des Objektes des Kaufvertrages (die Ancilla Theudote) und sogar ein Bürge (… *fideiussore accepto* …) scheint auf, Alexandros Antipatros. Wir haben also die Parteien und das Objekt des Vertrages, in diesem Fall eine Sklavin, genau wie in einem modernen Kaufvertrag im technischen Sinn. Dazu besteht der Konsens über den Preis zwischen Claudius Iulianus und Claudius Philetus.

Der Käufer bestätigt sogar, dass er (*mancipioque accepit*) die Sklavin empfangen hat. Also rein auf Grund dieser Erfordernisse hätten wir auch einen für die heutige Zeit gültigen Kaufvertrag abgeschlossen.

49 In dieser Zeit (2. Jhdt. n. Chr.) war es üblich eine schriftliche Kopie des Kaufvertrages vor 7 Zeugen, die unterzeichneten, zu verfassen, als Beweis für den abgeschlossenen Kaufvertrag. Das schriftliche Dokument war aber nur ein Nachweis des Kaufes und nicht des Vertrages selbst und hatte keine dingliche Wirkung für die Eigentumsübertragung. Der Name dieser Art von Beweis ist *testatio*. Darüber siehe Kaser 1971, 231 f.

50 Für eine wissenschaftliche Untersuchung dieses alten Textes siehe Mattiangeli, 2010–2011, 307–323.

Der Vertrag beinhaltet auch eine Garantie gegen Mängel und Eviktion in Form einer Stipulatio (*eam mulierem sanam traditam esse ... partemve quam quis ex ea evicerit*) und eine Bestätigung des Verkäufers, die Bezahlung des Käufer erhalten zu haben (... *accepisse et habere se dixit* ...).

Dieser Kaufvertrag könnte heute, natürlich, dank Abschaffung der Sklaverei mit einem anderen Verkaufsgegenstand, in vielen Rechtsordnungen noch gültig sein und dingliche Wirkungen haben. Und dies nach fast 1900 Jahren.

Literatur

Monographien und Sammelwerke

Arangio-Ruiz V., Istituzioni di diritto romano, Napoli 1984.
Arangio-Ruiz V., La compravendita in diritto romano I, Napoli 1978.
Arangio-Ruiz V., FIRA 3, Negotia, Firenze 1972.
Betti E., Istituzioni di diritto romano, Padova 1960.
Castiglione L. - Mariotti S., Vocabolario della lingua latina, Torino 1966.
Erdy J., De tabulis ceratis in Dacia repertis cum quaestionibus de vetusta historia Magyarorum, Pestini 1856.
Ferrini C., Opere Bd. 2, Milano 1929.
Girard M.P.F., Melanges de droit Romain Bd. 2, Paris 1923.
Kaser M., Das römische Privatrecht, München 1971.
Kaser M., Eigentum und Besitz im älteren römischen Recht, Weimar 1943.
Kaser M., Römisches Privatrecht, München 2005.
Longo C., Corso di diritto romano, Milano 1937.
Meylan Ph., Periculum est emptoris, in: Meylan Ph. (Hg.), Vom Kauf nach schweizerischem Recht (Festschrift Theo Guhl), Zürich 1950, 9–40.
Mattiangeli D., Vorteile der Romanitas im Bereich des Vertragsrechts aus einer historisch vergleichenden Perspektive, Frankfurt 2009.
Perozzi S. - Capogrossi Colognesi L., Istituzioni di diritto romano, Buch 2, Roma 2002.
Pugliese G., Istituzioni di diritto romano, 3. Auflage, Torino 1991.
Scialoja V., Compravendita, Roma 1907.
Talamanca M., Lineamenti di storia del diritto romano, Milano 1979.
Voci P., Modi di acquisto della proprietà, Milano 1952.

Zeitschriften

Bekker E.I., Zeitschrift für Rechtsgeschichte 3, 1864, 416–445.
Betti E., La «vindicatio» romana primitiva, Filangieri 2, 1915, 321 f.
Kaser M., Neue Studien zum altrömischen Eigentum, ZRG 68, 1951, 131–190.
Mattiangeli D., La „Mancipatio emptionis causa“ delle tavolette transilvaniche, Seminarios Complutenses de derecho Romano, XXIII–XXIV, Madrid 2010–2011, 307–323.
Meylan F., La loi 23 Dig. 46,4 et la notion de bilatéralité du Contrat de Vente chez Labéon, Studi Riccobono 4, Palermo 1936, 273–312.
Wieacker F., Kommentar zu Kasers Eigentum und Besitz und Altrömisches Ius, ZRG 67, 1950, 529–537.

The Market in Classical Antiquity

Neville Morley

This paper seeks to offer a complement to the more detailed and empirical studies presented in this volume, by considering in general and theoretical terms the idea of „the market in classical antiquity" and the ways that ancient historians have discussed this topic. I focus on identifying the key questions and issues, the things that we need to think or worry about in approaching this aspect of the ancient world, rather than offering any substantive conclusions – apart from this one: the nature and significance of „the market in classical antiquity" is a, if not the, fundamental issue for ancient economic history. Our assumptions about the development of market exchange in classical antiquity have shaped both our ideas about what the ancient economy was like and our ideas about how we ought to study it, but we do not always think about those assumptions as much or as critically as we ought to.[1]

This is a theme with unavoidable contemporary overtones and parallels.[2] One of the most important political issues across the world today is the power of markets and of „the market" in the abstract, and the consequences of this power – for the fates of national economies and the well-being of their populations, for relations between states, for democratic engagement and accountability.[3] As most clearly exhibited in the ongoing Eurozone debt crisis (but equally present in the UK and US, not to mention many developing countries), there is a general feeling of helpnessness in the face of what is, after all, a human institution; not just individual helplessness (that is a long-standing phenomenon) but the helplessness of states and political elites, the sense that all decisions are subject to the impersonal judgement of „the market" and hence their power to act on behalf of their citizens is strictly limited. The market is taken for granted as a natural object, like the weather, so that they and we can only respond to the effects of its changing moods rather than do anything to control them. Despite this, it seems scarcely possible, above all since the collapse of Soviet Communism, to conceive of any alternative to the market as a means of organising modern society; it is widely seen as an expression of innate, unchanging human nature (the conventional reading of Adam Smith's assertions about the human propensity "to truck, barter and exchange one

1 I am extremely grateful to Monika Frass for organising the Salzburg conference and thus offering an incentive to think further about these issues; I have also benefitted enormously from conversations with Colin Elliott and Constantina Katsari.

2 Lindblom 2001 is an excellent introductory guide to the market system in the modern world, and the political and social issues surrounding it.

3 For a clear introduction to the Eurozone crisis, focusing on Greece, see Manolopoulos 2011; a more popular account of the 2008 crash in Lanchester 2010.

thing for another").[4] Concern about the dominance of the market and its consequences has been exacerbated in the last few decades by the triumph of a particular set of theories and conceptions in economic thought and policy-making that present the market as infallible and normative, the only rational way of organising any aspect of human society; where limits to market logic and market influence are identified, they must be swept away in the name of freedom and efficiency.[5] It is only in the aftermath of the 2008 crash that those economists who reject such 'zombie' theories have gained any sort of voice in the public sphere, and they remain firmly in the minority.

Emerging Consensus?

It may seem strange to suggest that this is a topic that has been largely absent from recent discussions in ancient economic history; after all, a crucial element of M.I. Finley's influential characterisation of the ancient economy as non-modern was the absence of any economic system that was a "conglomeration of interdependent markets" (in other words, the absence of anything that could be called a "market system" or "market economy"), while recent publications by Peter Temin, Paul Erdkamp and Peter Bang have all engaged with aspects of this theme.[6] However, the role of the market is a curiously muted theme in the would-be definitive Cambridge Economic History of Greco-Roman Antiquity, not mentioned at all in the introduction and discussed at length only in Frier & Kehoe's chapter on law and economic institutions; other chapters seem to contradict one another in their passing remarks on the significance of markets and exchange, without these disagreements being registered explicitly.[7] Douglass North's call for economic historians to focus on establishing the structure and performance of past economies, quoted by the editors of the volume as their guiding principle, seems to be interpreted by contributors solely as an injunction to focus on performance, as if the structure of ancient economies (and above all the significance of the market in co-ordinating and determining economic activity) can be taken for granted and/or has been adequately established by earlier studies.[8] This assumption is still more dominant in the ongoing publications of the Oxford Roman Economy Project, which strives to quantify different aspects of Roman economic activity by concentrating on such data sets (above all material evidence like amphorae and coins) as are large and coherent enough to be amenable to such analysis; questions of the structural framework within which this activity took place are left unexamined, as if they

4 Smith 1976, I.2.1–2.

5 Quiggen 2010 on zombie economics, especially the efficient markets hypothesis.

6 Finley 1973, 22–3; Temin 2001; Erdkamp 2005; Bang 2008.

7 Morris – Saller – Scheidel 2007; Frier – Kehoe 2007.

8 North 1981, 3, quoted in Morris – Saller – Scheidel 2007, 1–2.

are simply not important.[9] The idea that the role of the market in co-ordinating all economic activity can be taken for granted is of course the basic assumption of most modern economic theory, as Temin has noted, but the tradition of debate in ancient economic history makes it a curious a priori assumption in volumes drawing together contributors of quite different theoretical persuasions. It seems that ancient history has mirrored developments in economics and in western culture in general, especially since the collapse of the Soviet Union and the development of the Chinese experiment in economic (but not social or political) liberalism, in its increasing inability to question the dominance of the market as an institution, or to see it as anything other than a natural, near-universal phenomenon.

To some extent, this emerging consensus may be founded on a shared weariness with the polarised debates of the 1970s and 1980s, the feeling that any discussion of the ancient economy, whether of trade or industry or cities or slavery, would almost immediately fall into the ruts established by Finley and his opponents and interlocutors twenty or thirty years earlier.[10] The sense that the old primitivists v. modernisers debates had often asked the wrong questions and unhelpfully tended to gravitate to extreme positions, and the wish to move on and develop new interpretations, produced a certain degree of shared understanding and common purpose between historians of different persuasions.[11] Moreover, there was increasing agreement on a number of basic points that had previously been issues of dispute, all of which are closely connected to questions of the nature and significance of markets.

Firstly, ancient economic historians have largely accepted the arguments of Finley and Hopkins about the need to engage with the social sciences, against the anti-theoretical claims of old-fashioned positivists, and in particular they have adopted the position of Hopkins rather than Finley on the subject of economic theory.[12] That is to say, economic theory is not seen as an objective description of reality, such that it tells us how things must have been in the past (or, as Finley would argue, such that its use in ancient history assumes and asserts that antiquity must have been essentially identical to the modern world); rather, it is seen as offering abstract models of reality, that seek to identify and understand significant relationships between a limited number of variables through the deliberate simplification of a complex reality. The principle resembles the joke told about theoretical physicists, that they could develop a brilliant scheme for optimising production on a dairy farm provided one assumes that the farm consists of spherical cows in a

9 Bowman – Wilson 2009, 2011; for an example of the neglect of structural questions, see the contrasting views of whether 'the city' is a straightforward concept offered by Morley and Wilson in the 2011 volume.

10 General discussions in Hopkins 1983; Andreau 1995; Morley 2004, 33–50.

11 See for example the introductions to Cartledge – Cohen – Foxhall 2002 and Manning – Morris 2005, and various contributions to Bowman – Wilson 2009.

12 Exemplified by Hopkins 1980, contra Finley 1973. General discussion of the use of theory in ancient history in Morley 2004, 1–31.

vacuum. The fact that cows are not spherical and hence do not behave in a wholly regular and predictable manner does not, however, automatically mean that the model is useless; an idea of how particular variables would interact in an idealised situation offers a partial guide to how they will work in a messier, more complex reality. The same is true for economic theory; it makes unrealistic assumptions (for example, that all human agents share a single, predictable and quantifiable motivation, that information is universally available without cost, and so forth) in order to identify how the remaining variables, such as the relationship between supply, demand and price, would operate in an ideal situation. No market is actually frictionless, so the theory does not describe reality, but the insights of the model offer a starting point for interpreting economic activity and identifying its regularities and predictable aspects in a world that might otherwise appear wholly chaotic. The recognition that adopting economic theory does not commit them to a particular view of what antiquity was actually like has reassured many ancient historians that they can make use of it as a potentially useful tool.

Secondly, there is a general recognition of the existence of markets and market exchange in the ancient world, and their significance for the development of ancient society.[13] Throughout the classical period there was substantial exchange, based on money and market prices, between individuals who did not know one another, making use of institutions like coinage and the law to facilitate such anonymous exchange, locally, regionally and inter-regionally. The vast majority of the population, even supposedly self-sufficient peasant farmers and trade-despising senators, had some involvement in markets as both buyers and sellers. Different kinds of markets were found at the heart of ancient cities, and were a normal part of life in antiquity; ancient states depended on the market for many of their needs. The hard-line primitivist view that market exchange was always, in Karl Polanyi's terms, vastly inferior in scale and subordinate to reciprocity and redistribution, has long been abandoned, not least in the face of the evidence from archaeology and from legal texts.

Thirdly, there is a general recognition, even from the strongest modernisers, of the limitations of the development of market exchange in classical antiquity.[14] The slowness and expense of transport created significant costs in extra-local exchange, and above all affected transaction costs because of the expense of obtaining reliable information; markets were thus fragmented, inefficient and slow to clear. Economic behaviour remained fully embedded in society and dependent on social and political institutions, and market exchange never wholly dominated the ancient world (as, indeed, remains the case today). Redistribution (especially by the state) and reciprocity remained important means for the exchange of goods, and even Peter Temin, the strongest advocate of the existence of a fully-developed

13 General summary in Morley 2007 and relevant chapters in Scheidel – Morris – Saller 2007; specifically on concrete markets and their role, Ligt 1993.

14 Temin 2001, 179–81 accepts all the following limitations on market integration.

market economy in the Roman Empire, estimates that more than half of production must have been outside the market. The conventional „primitivist" insistence on the differences between ancient and modern and the limitations on ancient development have thus been substantially accepted.

Continuing Disagreements

On the face of it, these three points of agreement suggest an established post-Finley consensus, and to a significant degree this is true – but not entirely. The extent of agreement conceals some fundamental continuing disagreements, that may indeed be less visible because of the wish of many historians to avoid anything that looks too much like the old debates. There are, one might say, very different ways of being a post-Finley ancient economic historian. On the one hand, one may take for granted many of Finley's basic points about the essential differences between ancient and modern and the risks of anachronistic projection, while conceding that his understanding of economic theory was flawed and his account of antiquity often relentlessly negative. On the other hand, one may breathe a sigh of relief that we can now forget all about the sociological and anthropological nonsense and concentrate on understanding antiquity in properly economic, modern terms. The underlying conceptions of historical change (how far do we assume a universal human nature and universal principles of economic behaviour?) and the associated ideological commitments (is capitalism universal and eternal?) of these different accounts may remain poles apart.

The apparent post-Finley consensus has been reached from very different directions; it seems entirely possible that it is understood in quite different ways, and that historians beginning from this point will immediately head off in quite different directions. One might accept the consensus and argue, as Temin does, that the Roman Empire was a market economy with certain limits on its integration and the persistence of some non-market exchange and social values rather than pure instrumentalism – a description that equally applies to the modern economy, thus discounting the notion of fundamental differences between past and present in economic terms. Or one might argue, as Bang does, that the fragmentation and inefficiency of ancient markets, the dominance of the non-market sectors and the persistence of non-economic values and motivations serves to establish fundamental differences between past and present and hence the need for alternative models of interpretation besides neoclassical economic theory. These two accounts, falling at opposite ends of the current spectrum of opinion, have the advantage of stating their premises and conclusions explicitly, so that the differences between them are obvious; many recent accounts present their different interpretative frameworks and arguments less clearly, and may indeed not be wholly conscious of them. However, unless we face up to these divergent lines of interpretation underlying the new consensus, we can scarcely have a productive discussion of the nature, significance and performance of the market in antiquity.

How is it that we find ourselves in this position? There are in fact two different aspects to the way that the debate has developed, which have combined and reinforced one another. On the one hand, there is the persistence of issues which many historians thought, or hoped, had been resolved. Most obviously, there is the familiar problem that evidence can always be interpreted in different ways according to preconceived interpretative frameworks, rather than ever offering a conclusive test of those frameworks and their assumptions. Pure inductivism is always a hopeless illusion; we can only ever make sense of the data through a priori concepts and theories, but that means that we always find ourselves choosing between competing interpretations of the evidence on the basis of prior assumptions and subjective inclinations. Fragmentary price data from the ancient world can plausibly be interpreted as revealing market exchange and price formation through the market at a local level, but even where sufficient evidence from a specific locale and time period is available as in Egypt, such a conclusion still needs to be hedged with caveats.[15] The much less coherent data from across the empire can certainly be interpreted as showing the interconnection and interdependence of regional markets, if one is so disposed, but it is not remotely sufficient to establish this as a fact.[16] For another example, consider the classic passage of Gaius that is invariably mentioned in such discussions:

> The reason this action rests on the discretion of the judge is that we know how prices of things vary from one city to another, especially of wine, oil and grain. Even in the case of money, though it is supposed to have one and the same purchasing power everywhere, yet it can be quite easily raised and at low interest rates in some places, with difficulty and at steep interest in others.[17]

The passage is most interesting for what it reveals about ancient economic thought (in the loosest sense), but the confirmation that prices did vary across space as well as time (as we would have expected) is seized upon as evidence for the development of market exchange in antiquity. The problem is that this fact can equally well

15 Rathbone 1997 uses phrases like "as far as we can judge" and "on the whole". General discussion of ancient price formation in von Reden 2010, 125–40.

16 Rather – Temin 2001 resorts to a more impressionistic sketch intended to establish the ubiquity of market exchange and the fact that some markets at least were connected.

17 Dig.13.4.3.

be interpreted as evidence for a well-integrated and efficient market, with prices being formed according to the balance between empire-wide and local factors, and as evidence for a poorly-integrated market characterised by significant friction and asymmetric information, or even as evidence for the existence of isolated local and regional markets quite independent of one another.[18] The passage itself cannot decide between these different interpretations of its significance. This unavoidable dependence on prior interpretative frameworks is simply a fact of life; and the fact that the nature and development of the market is, as suggested earlier, a highly controversial and complex subject, today more than ever, means that debates over the best or most appropriate interpretative frameworks will continue. If this fact is not acknowledged, then it is likely that we will simply continue to echo unwittingly the frameworks of the earlier debates between primitivists and modernisers, since, whatever their limitations, they did capture the essential issues at stake.

Since these issues of evidence and interpretation are thoroughly familiar, it does seem curious that this continuing debate about the role of the market is apparently not noticed or acknowledged by many historians; it is as if they do not recognise the issues that actually divide them, or at any rate find them hard to articulate. One obvious reason is the use of the term „market" itself, which can refer to a number of related but quite different phenomena, of varying degrees of abstraction. Erdkamp, for example, offers three different meanings: a place where commercial exchange of goods takes place, the forces of supply and demand that govern the commercial distribution of goods, and the geographical area within which exchange operates.[19] Davies offers another three definitions: all activities and products generated by known consumption habits and effective demand; the varying values, attitudes and strategies of economic actors; and a price-setting marketplace in an institutional and sometimes physical sense.[20] Studies of concrete markets, like those of de Ligt and Frayn, are generally at pains to distinguish their subject matter from more abstract conceptions of „market" – in the latter case, on the curious grounds that there was no centralised control of either money or commocity markets in Rome.[21] All of these conceptions are valid and potentially significant, from the concrete marketplace where people buy and sell (the one instance where everyone agrees both about the meaning of the term and existence of the phenomenon in antiquity), via more abstract and controversial conceptions like „the grain market" or „the labour market" (with a distinction between relatively concrete manifestations at a local level, e.g. the grain market in Athens, and

18 The fact that over the last decade the same data on the performance of Eurozone economies have been interpreted as indicating both increasing convergence and continuing divergence between different countries (Manolopoulos 2011, 131–61) should be a warning against attempts at basing analysis on a single factor – but of course for ancient history we rarely have adequate data even for one single factor.

19 Erdkamp 2005, 1.

20 Davies 2007, 335.

21 Frayn 1993, 158.

hypothetical regional and inter-regional markets for different commodities), to the idea of "the market" as a general principle or co-ordinating force pervading the whole of society. The major problems with this situation, however, are the common failure to define clearly what kind of market is being discussed at any point, especially when talking about anything other than concrete markets, and the tendency to slippage between different meanings, so that establishing the possible existence of a more or less integrated grain market across the Mediterranean (or at any rate establishing the existence of mutual influence between, say, Rome and Egypt) becomes, without any explicit argument, a demonstration of the significance of the market economy as an organising principle of the Empire.

As well as problems with the definition of key concepts, there are certain persistent issues with the construction of arguments. The most significant, given its current dominance in debates, is the emphasis on economic performance rather than structure as the key focus for analysis, presented by the editors of the Cambridge Economic History volume as the way forward for ancient economic history. We can easily agree that there needs to be a constant dialogue between structure and performance, just as there needs to be a constant dialogue between evidence and interpretation, but in practice such a balance seems to be extremely difficult to maintain (and not only because of the issues with evidence noted above); most accounts tend to offer an account of one rather than the other. The difficulty of deducing performance from structure is familiar from earlier stages of the debate on the ancient economy; the obvious example is Finley's consumer city model, which rests on unwarranted assumptions about the economic consequences of a particular form of urbanism – it is no more the case that the presence of "consumer cities" necessarily inhibits economic growth and development than that the presence of cities, or special "producer cities", necessarily promotes it.[22] If comparative historical study shows anything, it is that apparently similar economic structures – a largely agrarian economy characterised by a high-pressure demographic regime and significant inequality, for example – can perform quite differently in different historical contexts in terms of productivity and other economic measures. On the other hand, the implicit argument that an economic performance superior to the pre-industrial norm could only have been achieved through the presence of a well-developed market system is equally fallacious and equally prone to questioning from comparative material. Such approaches offer mirror images of one another, both falling into the same modern/not-modern dichotomy: the absence of "modern" economic structures (such as cities based on trade and manufacturing) is assumed to indicate lower economic performance, while the identification of a superior performance is taken as evidence of the presence of "modern" structures, above all the all-powerful market system. The twin possibilities that the market is not the only generator of growth and that the market may not always generate growth are ignored.

22 Morley 1996, 14–20.

Finally, even among those historians who do define more explicitly what kinds of markets they are discussing and what theoretical assumptions are being made, there is sometimes an issue with different styles of argument leading them to talk past one another. Once again, the obvious examples of this tendency are Temin and Bang, whose approaches might be characterised as "there are markets, therefore" versus "there are markets, but". Temin takes the existence of concrete markets, and the apparent normality of market-orientated behaviour, as clear evidence that the Roman Empire was not dominated (in Polanyi's terms) by reciprocity or redistribution, nor by customary rather than instrumental behaviour; therefore, he argues, it must be considered a market economy, albeit one that was not fully integrated and has various inefficiencies. From this, he argues, it follows that the standard account offered by economic theory of markets and their influence and of human behaviour can be taken as valid for Rome, including the role of the market in promoting the efficient allocation of resources; this then raises important questions about how Rome operated and what that can tell us about the formation and preservation of markets in general. Bang, on the other hand, sets the existence of markets against the persistence of non-market behaviour and values and the dominant role of the state, not to mention the high costs of information, the fragmentation even of concrete markets and the innumerable other frictions that impeded market exchange; these are seen to undermine any hope that ancient markets or actors could have operated according to the assumptions of classical economic theory, which then raises important questions about how Rome operated and what this can tell us about the formation and preservation of pre-capitalist societies in general. It is not just that Temin takes a "glass half-full" and Bang a "glass half-empty" approach in their conception of the Roman Empire and its economic development; each is convinced that his approach adequately demolishes the argument of the other. Further, both seem to assume the same basic idea of "the market" and its role in society; but the one argues that it is valid for Rome (despite imperfections) and so its full implications must also apply, while the other argues that it is not properly applicable (because of the imperfections) and so an alternative model of the bazaar or the tributary economy is required instead. For each of them – less so, I think, for Bang – the idea that market systems as well as concrete markets can operate in very different ways and produce quite different outcomes does not appear to feature as a significant consideration.

Rethinking Ancient Market Systems

The main requirements for developing a proper understanding of the nature and significance of the market in classical antiquity are obvious: more careful and explicit definition of what is meant by the term "market" at any given point, simply to ensure that we are successfully communicating with one another, and a thorough examination of our conceptions about markets and their operation, to avoid importing questionable assumptions into our analysis. If we cease to take either the market or a particular conception of it for granted as a universal principle, this immediately opens up a wide range of important questions for research. For the remainder of this paper I want to look briefly at the different areas for investigation; in many cases work is already under way, but it is not yet fully integrated into a programme of research on the place of the market in classical antiquity – or, conceived more broadly, on the nature of the socio-economic web that co-ordinated ancient societies.

Microeconomics

This is the realm of individual economic behaviour and individual transactions. Given that cows are not spherical, so to speak, we need to explore the motivations, values and concepts that shaped the behaviour of ancient economic actors, rather than simply taking for granted the existence of the rational maximiser of utility found in simple economic models. Exploring these topics is not to fall back into primitivism or to assert that Greeks and Romans were irrational and alien and hence their behaviour must be opaque to any modern theory. On the contrary, those fields of modern economic theory that recognise that the rational maximiser is at best merely a convenient analytical fiction can offer fascinating insights into the ways that individuals make choices and develop strategies. Game theory, for example, offers a more subtle picture of the way that economic choices are made over time through a series of interactions rather than treating every exchange in isolation, emphasising the role of expectations and uncertainty; its predictions often (though by no means always) fit better with data gathered from empirical studies, even though it still assumes that individuals are rational maximisers.[23] Still within the standard neoclassical paradigm, there is the vital field of the economics of information, exploring how decision-making takes place under conditions of uncertainty: even small information costs can have large consequences, not least because information is not an ordinary commodity that can be inspected and evaluated before purchase. Markets, even modern markets, are inherently characterised by imperfect information, and shaped by the different ways that economic actors respond to this.[24] Most significant of all is the developing field of behavioural economics, emphasising the role of irrational "animal spirits" in the ways that economic actors evaluate situations and make decisions; human beings have a poor record in estimating risk accurately and dealing with uncertainty, let alone in predicting the future, while even among trained economists and financial professionals there is a tendency towards herd behaviour and other cognitive biases.[25] All of this means that markets cannot be considered rational or wholly predictable; but, while people may not be rational in purely instrumental terms, they may be seen as in some ways predictably unpredictable. All these themes need to be

23 On game theory, Rasmusen 2006.
24 For an excellent summary see Stiglitz 2000.
25 Akerlof – Shiller 2009.

considered in their specific historical context, rather than in abstract ahistorical manner still common to most economic analysis; above all we need to focus on the limits that ancient technology set on the availability and cost of information and on the ability of ancient actors to respond to different kinds of unexpected events, each of which would have affected their estimations of risk and thus their decision-making and responses to signals received from the market.[26]

However, economics does not have a monopoly on the analysis of economic behaviour; we also need to explore the contributions of sociology and anthropology towards understanding it as more than purely economic and instrumental, emphasising the role of values and beliefs in shaping behaviour.[27] There is clearly a need for a detailed study of "ancient economic thought", defined as broadly as possible: not just a search for the origins of abstract economic theory in Aristotle, in the traditional manner, but an examination of conceptions and attitudes, goals, ethics and so forth, seeking as far as possible to encompass the mass of the population as well as the dominant literate elite.[28] In particular, we need to explore the underlying (and often unstated) motivations for apparent oddities of ancient behaviour, the points when Greeks and Romans confound modern expectations. For example, why does there seem to be such a limited response to market incentives from peasant farmers even when they are receiving the right price signals? Is this a rational satisficing strategy in the face of an unpredictable environment, or an innate conservatism founded on certain traditional values? How do we account for the peculiarities of Roman laws on water distribution – the idea that everything should be done "as it was last year" in an environment where rainfall and water supplies were highly unpredictable – in rational economic terms, rather than seeing them as revealing ancient attitudes towards prediction and change and/or emphasising a key principle of social solidarity?

This is not only a study of the persistence of social and cultural values in economic behaviour, but also of the permeation of a market mentality into non-economic areas of society. We might note Graeber's argument, drawing on anthropological material, that reciprocity as commonly understood is already influenced by the logic of the market; we need to move beyond a simple dichotomy between market exchange and supposedly pre-market forms of interaction; to explore the dialectic, in different situations and contexts, between the market principle and other conceptions of human relationships. We might return, for example, to the old question of the relationship between slavery and economic development; not in the crude form that slavery meant no free labour so no development, but rather seeing slavery as an extreme instance of the application of the market principle to human relations and economic organisation, such that labour becomes just another commodity. This is of course something that more advanced capitalist econ-

26 A very preliminary discussion in Morley 2007, 29–34 and 91–2.

27 Graeber 2011. For an application of anthropological economics to archaic Rome, Viglietti 2011.

28 Compare Kehoe 1997 for one interpretation of what Roman legal sources reveal about economic conceptions and decision-making.

omies have, at least formally, rejected; rather than a simple contrast between limited market development in antiquity and a more thoroughly marketised capitalism, we might see instead a historical narrative in which the claims of non-instrumental, more "human" values have in recent centuries been reasserted over the pervasive influence of the market principle.

This is the realm of individual relationships and interactions between economic actors over time, and the ways that those individual interactions combined and influenced one another in aggregate, whether in actual markets and fairs (where we can look to studies such as von Reden on the agora and de Ligt on Roman periodic markets, and models such as Bang's bazaar) or in a more abstract manner (such as the way that numerous separate auctions, both of wine and of grapes on the vine, constituted "wine markets" in different areas of Roman Italy). In characterising such more-or-less concrete markets we need to estimate price volatility (from year to year and across the year), the availability of information and the levels of uncertainty and risk, as well as the social and cultural norms that influenced behaviour (for example, the extent to which an auction at the estate of a member of the elite brought the influence of the socio-political hierarchy to bear on apparently instrumental economic decisions, quite apart from the peculiar dynamics of the auction). This is also the realm of different social institutions which served both to shape and limit some forms of behaviour and to make other forms of behaviour possible (most obviously, anonymous market exchange); this can be understood solely in terms of the reduction of transaction costs (once again assuming that all individuals concerned are rational maximisers), but the study of organisational economics has emphasised the broader role of institutions in the generation of trust and confidence, the "animal spirits" necessary for market exchange to take place on any regular basis.[29]

Macroeconomics

The second level of study is to consider how concrete markets at a local level interacted and interconnected, to form regional and inter-regional market systems in the ancient world. There are obvious problems of evidence, but nevertheless we have at least to try to establish the boundaries of different systems and the extent to which they were integrated and interdependent; the study of the circulation of coinage, for all its uncertainties and limitations (for example, obviously prices in one market might be affected by those elsewhere without any transfer of coinage between them), offers the best hope for progress here.[30] Insofar as we can identify larger market systems, we then to characterise them. In part, this involves a focus on the same issues identified for local markets – price volatility, availability and cost of information, role of institutions and so forth – while keeping in mind that we cannot simply read off the macro from the micro. Even if concrete markets in

29 Compare Simon 1991, 26, on the limitations of New Institutional Economics in this regard.

30 von Reden 2010, 65–91; Katsari 2011.

antiquity were shown to have been well-integrated and efficient, that is no guarantee that the aggregation of such markets would be similar; the effects of scaling up, in a world in which travel and communication were slow and expensive, means the opposite is more likely to be the case. Ancient market systems are likely to have been "lumpy", with uneven geographical distribution of resources, power and connectedness, and unequal flows of goods and information between different nodes; that might not have made them less predictable, but it would certainly have reduced their overall efficiency in allocating resources. The costs of information, and the lengthy delays involved in establishing the reliability of information, imply that most economic actors would have adopted risk-averse approaches to decision-making, responding to well-established long-term trends (such as the growth of demand in major urban centres like Athens or Rome) but not to shorter-term price signals; in one respect this would have reduced market volatility – most people would have pursued similar strategies year on year, avoiding the risks incurred in modern markets through short-term herd behaviour, exuberance and crises of confidence – but it also reduced the ability of the system to respond promptly and effectively to any unexpected developments.

This is all part of the task of characterising ancient market systems, rather than assuming that there is a single model of a market economy that comes into existence once the level of market transactions and integration passes a certain threshold. Even in mainstream development economics, a distinction is made between developed market economies and emerging markets such as in post-Soviet Russia or Africa, with the latter characterised by massive market inefficiencies, weak institutions, the dominance of oligarchs, high levels of corruption and arbitrary prices, monopolistic behaviour and stark inequality – a list of characteristics that bears a striking resemblance to certain periods of antiquity. We need to identify the different kinds of organisation that make up the economic system (the term "enterprises" is regularly employed by modern analysts, but arguably that has unhelpful connotations of entrepreneurship), the extent to which such bodies are organised according to the market principle (normally, not very far, as in the modern firm) and the relative importance of market exchange and other kinds of interaction in relationships between these different bodies. It may be helpful to think of Herbert Simon's argument that a visiting Martian would not see the modern world in terms of a network of red lines of market exchange connecting green spots of firms, bureaucratic organisations and the like (the conventional idea of a market system), but rather large green areas organised on non-market principles interconnected by red lines of market exchange – and other kinds of relationships as well.[31] Simon argues that even the modern world is better described as an "organizational economy" than as a market economy, but even if we eschew this phrase, his analogy helps to emphasise the potential for variation even within systems where market exchange is well established as a normal form of interaction.

31 Simon 1991.

Discussion of these issues in ancient history has tended to focus on the role of the state, either assuming that its importance, and habitual pursuit of non-economic goals, would have inhibited the development of any market system, or insisting on the role of the state in the market as buyer, seller and regulator. Both these perspectives have considerable truth in them: on the one hand, the state undoubtedly depended on and encouraged market activity in the pursuit of its own goals, on the other hand the importance of the state meant that a substantial proportion of ancient resources were allocated and the activities of a substantial number of individuals were co-ordinated through non-market means, and that is equally significant. However, the inquiry needs to be widened, to consider the extent to which market exchanges and the market principle served to co-ordinate ancient societies in general – what, for example, might we deduce about the ancient economy from the fact that there is little trace of a market for ideas or other intellectual property? – and to identify the other types of organisation involved in the system and their relationships with one another and the state. Classical antiquity, even the Roman Empire, resembles not so much Simon's sketch of a developed market economy dominated by medium and large firms as his account of sub-Saharan Africa, with much smaller enterprises and fewer market exchanges between them, and numerous black dots of families close to self-sufficiency. This then raises questions of why antiquity remained so fragmented – is the continuing importance of households rather than firms as a basic mode of organisation simply a symptom of the limited development of the ancient market system and the persistence of older social values, or were there positive advantages in smaller units (and, a related issue, in dependent rather than hired labour) in this historical context? These preferences set limits on the extension of the market system through ancient societies; elites used and benefited from the market but also always feared it as an erosion of their traditional power, while states sought to control and limit it for political purposes.

Development and Crisis

The third key theme is the development and performance of these economic structures over time. There has been a clear tendency in past debates to focus on Rome, as a society where the market clearly plays a significant role and the market principle has become normal if not ubiquitous – it is far easier to represent classical Greece as a pre- or proto-market society – but that immediately raises the question of how and why this system emerged in earlier centuries. This needs to be explored in detail, rather than following Adam Smith's line in assuming that market exchange is simply a natural expression of universal human inclinations; one could equally argue that it's a highly artificial replacement for small-scale personal and social relationships. How does impersonal exchange develop in relation to the expansion of networks for the distribution of goods beyond the immediate locality, and in relation to new and more far-reaching forms of power and authority, as in David Tandy's arguments about the power of the market in archaic Greece?[32] How far should we interpret social relationships within the developing polis as a reflection of the growing influence of market exchange as a form of co-ordination and social interaction, or as a deliberate counter to it (the two are of course not mutually exclusive)?[33] At what date can we confidently speak of the emergence of genuine regional and inter-regional market systems, however limited and poorly articulated, and what is their relation to the emergence of regional and inter-regional systems of political power?

If (and this remains for the moment an extremely tentative suggestion) the market systems that had emerged by end of the Roman Republic are best characterised in terms of limited reach, fragmentary nature and many of the negative elements associated with modern emerging economies, what are the implications of this for our understanding of Roman history? It is widely agreed that the market is, at anything beyond a very simple and local level, more efficient than the alternatives as a means of allocating scarce resources as effectively as possible and hence generating investment, growth and development.[34] In the Roman market system, resources were certainly wasted as a result; compare Erdkamp's arguments on the way that the limitations of the market became a restriction on agricultural production strategies, resulting in high labour costs and low productivity, and we might conclude that the same applied to other economic actors.[35] The system was of course able, under normal conditions, to generate profits for many economic actors (most obviously the land-owning elite, but also at least some peasants and traders), above all through the incentives created by state expenditure; in the same way as the Roman state was able to co-ordinate certain activities across the empire through a mixture of coercion and alternative forms of co-ordination such as common elite values and personal relationships. It is not that co-ordination of activity over a large area is impossible without the market system, but it is liable to be less effective and efficient; and we may suspect that the Roman system worked because, as with the devolved style of Roman provincial administration, most co-ordination took place at the local level where the problems of slow and expensive communication and hence limited information were less intense.[36]

This also raises questions about the eventual deterioration and collapse of the Roman market system in late antiquity, and its consequences; the following sketch is, once again, extremely tentative and speculative. The market system operated, as individual actors did, within broad bands of bounded uncertainty, and according to custom and tradition as much as market signals. Within a predominantly agrarian economy, this bounded uncertainty related above all to variable harvests and

32 Tandy 1997.

33 Cf. von Reden 1995.

34 Cf. Spufford 2010 and the online seminar on the book, Farrell et al. 2012 (especially the contribution of Shalizi), on the limitations of planned economies.

35 Erdkamp 2005, 322–5.

36 On Roman devolved rule, Morley 2010, 38–69.

hence to variable levels of rent, tax and profit. These variations were, we may assume, generally within known parameters if considered over a number of years – rules of thumb about how often one should expect a bad year – and so many actors were able to adjust to more or less predictable uncertainties by adopting strategies of risk minimisation, as peasants for example pursued crop diversification and storage (those solely reliant on the market, like the majority of the urban population, were more exposed to risk and spillovers and less able to compensate).[37] We might imagine that other actors, including the political elite and those leading the state, operated with a similar sense of the likely range of variation in a normal year, and made decisions accordingly. In a relatively simple and stable society like the early Roman Principate, this was perfectly workable, and can explain why the system was able to tolerate significant wastage and inefficiency and still generate profits. However, we must consider what happens in such a system if the uncertainties become greater (whether through external shocks such as increased barbarian raids, or climate change producing greater volatility in harvest yields) and the past ceases to be a reliable guide to the future (for example, in the changing value of coinage). Traditional risk-avoidance strategies become less effective, profits become less secure, market prices become more volatile. One possible response is to reduce one's exposure to risk by, where possible, withdrawing from the market and/or concentrating activity at the local level – thereby reducing the scope and effectiveness of the market system still further. The costs of such a withdrawal were more manageable for Roman households than they would be today, not least because in many cases their involvement with the market was limited in the first place; for the Roman state, however, the attempt to shift from co-ordination partly through the market to co-ordination primarily through command and coercion, in the absence of sophisticated planning tools or reliable information, was ultimately doomed to failure. Under conditions of external stress, the more interconnected areas of the Roman system were the most vulnerable, precisely because they were larger, more complex and less able to respond rapidly and flexibly than local structures, while those making decisions were inevitably less well informed about all relevant circumstances. One key question is whether a more developed and extensive market system would have proved any more resilient.

Conclusion

Ancient history, insofar as it adopts a theoretically-informed approach at all, is almost always a consumer of other disciplines' theories. This borrowing often results in a partial understanding, based on a few key texts rather than a broad overview of current debates, and almost invariably involves a substantial time-lag in picking up on new ideas; ancient economic historians' turn to the New Institutional Economics in the late 1990s was merely catching up on developments in

37 On risk-avoidance and -management strategies, Garnsey 1988. For a modern comparison, Stiglitz 2002.

modern economic history in the early to mid 1980s.[38] Given the amount of upheaval and controversy in the field of economics at present, in response to the global economic crisis and the perceived failure of the dominant theoretical paradigm, we would generally expect a reconsideration of assumptions in ancient economic history in about a decade or so; the focus of the Salzburg conference on the theme of markets and consumption was thus extremely opportune, a chance to reflect on recent intellectual developments and their implications for ancient history rather more promptly than usual.

However, the traffic between disciplines and between past and present is not always one-way; for all that much modern economics regards past experience as essentially irrelevant, it nevertheless rests on implicit historical claims such as a belief in an unchanging human nature, and that means that, at certain times, ancient economic history can contribute to contemporary debates.[39] In the case of David Graeber's popular critique of conventional economic thought, Debt: the first 5,000 years (2011), a non-specialist has identified this possibility well before any ancient historians, taking the approach of contrasting ancient and modern. In ancient economic history, as in economic anthropology, debates about the structure of economic systems, the nature of human motivation and behaviour and the limits of the market system remained live issues, even as mainstream economics and much modern economic history reached a theoretical consensus based on neoclassical theory, rational maximisation and the efficient markets hypothesis. Sometimes being behind the times can be an advantage, and this continuing tradition of emphasis on the non-modern nature of classical antiquity has long offered a springboard for critiques of the assumptions of mainstream economics, questioning its universalising models of human behaviour by pointing to the existence of very different values and institutions in the past. Classical antiquity offers writers like Graeber, as it did to predecessors like Marx, the idea of an alternative to the present, a complex and sophisticated society that was free from capitalism.

It is curious that Graeber's book has little to say about Rome, besides discussion of its legal codes relating to slavery; perhaps the contrast with the present, as Rome appears as a society in which markets were relatively well-developed and the market principle was relatively important in co-ordinating activity, was insufficient for his purposes.[40] However, the less that the Roman example supports an absolute and polemical contrast between past and present, the more it offers the basis for a more subtle combination of comparison and contrast, for thinking through the nature and dynamics of markets. It is not so much that Rome now looks more modern than has generally been assumed, but that in the light of recent market failures the contemporary world looks less modern than neoclassical economic

38 Of course, economists' occasional use of ancient economic history tends to be even more dated.

39 Morley 2009 on antiquity's role in the economic debates of the late 18th and early 19th centuries.

40 It is interesting to note that another book seeking to critique conventional economics by taking a longer view, Sedlacek 2011, also ignores Rome; this may in part be a post-imperial matter of preferring to identify with the ancient Greeks rather than the Romans.

theory asserted and assumed. The market principle is never wholly pervasive, other forms of co-ordination always persist, and even among market economies there is significant variation – but there is also significant family resemblance between societies in which markets play an important role. The period of emergence of something that resembled a kind of market economy (indeed, arguably the first example of what would now be classified as an emerging economy), with the progressive (but never completed) co-ordination of society around the market principle, and just as importantly the collapse or reconfiguration of this system in the face of external shocks and internal conflicts, have the potential to be important examples for understanding our own situation – provided that ancient historians can seize the opportunity to rethink their old assumptions, clarify their arguments and engage fully in contemporary debates.

Bibliography

Akerlof G.A. – Shiller R.J., Animal Spirits: how human psychology drives the economy, and why it matters for global capitalism, Princeton 2009.
Andreau J., Vingt ans après l'Économie Antique de Moses I. Finley, Annales Histoires, Sciences Sociales 1995, 50, 947–60.
Bang P.F., The Roman Bazaar: a comparative study of trade and markets in a tributary empire, Cambridge 2008.
Bowman A. – Wilson A. (eds.), Quantifying the Roman Economy, Oxford 2009.
Bowman A. – Wilson A. (eds.), Settlement, Urbanization and Population, Oxford 2011.
Cartledge P. – Cohen E.E. – Foxhall L. (eds.), Money, Labour and Land: approaches to the economies of ancient Greece, London 2002.
Davies J.K., Classical Greece: production, in: Scheidel W. – Morris I. – Saller R. 2007, 333–61.
Erdkamp P., The Roman Grain Market, Cambridge 2005.
Farrell H. et al., Red Plenty Seminar, Crooked Timber 2012. (http://crookedtimber.org/category/red-plenty-seminar/)
Finley M.I., The Ancient Economy, Berekeley 1973.
Frayn J.M., Markets and Fairs in Roman Italy: their social and economic importance from the second century BC to the third century AD, Oxford 1993.
Frier B.W. – Kehoe D.P., Law and Economic Institutions, in: Scheidel W. – Morris I. – Saller R. 2007, 113–43.
Garnsey P., Famine and Food Supply in the Graeco-Roman World, Cambridge 1988.
Graeber D., Debt: the first 5,000 years, New York 2011.
Hopkins K., Taxes and Trade in the Roman Empire, JRS 70, 1980, 101–25.
Hopkins K., Introduction, in: Garnsey P. – Hopkins K. – Whittaker C.R. (eds.), Trade in the Ancient Economy, Cambridge 1983, ix–xxv.
Katsari C., The Roman Monetary System, Cambridge 2011.
Kehoe D.P., Investment, Profit and Tenancy: the jurists and the Roman economy, Ann Arbor 1997.
Lanchester J., Whoops! Why everyone owes everyone and no one can pay, London 2010.
Ligt L. de, Fairs and Markets in the Roman Empire, Amsterdam 1993.
Lindblom C.E., The Market System: what it is, how it works, and what to make of it, Yale 2001.
Manning J.G. – Morris I. (eds.), The Ancient Economy: evidence and models, Stanford 2005.
Manolopoulos J., Greece's "Odious" Debt: the looting of the Hellenic Republic by the Euro, the political elite and the investment community, London 2011.
Morley N., Metropolis and Hinterland: the city of Rome and the Italian economy, Cambridge 1996.

Morley N., Theories, Models and Concepts in Ancient History, London – New York 2004.
Morley N., Trade in Classical Antiquity, Cambridge 2007.
Morley N., The Roman Empire: roots of imperialism, London 2010.
Morris I. – Saller R. – Scheidel W., Introduction, in: Scheidel W. – Morris I. – Saller R. 2007, 1–12.
North D.C., Structure and Change in Economic History, New York – London 1981.
Quiggin J., Zombie Economics: how dead ideas still walk among us, Princeton 2010.
Rasmusen E., Games and Information: an introduction to game theory, 6th edn. Malden 2006.
Rathbone D., Prices and Price Formation in Roman Egypt, in: Andreau J. – Briant P. – Descat R. (eds.), Economie Antique. Prix et formation des prix dans les économies antiques, Saint-Bertrand-de-Comminges 1997, 183–244.
Scheidel W. – Morris I. – Saller R. (eds.), The Cambridge Economic History of the Greco-Roman World, Cambridge 2007.
Sedlacek T., Economics of Good and Evil, Oxford 2011.
Simon H.A., Organizations and markets, Journal of Economic Perspectives 5.2, 1991, 25–44.
Smith A., An Inquiry into the Nature and Causes of the Wealth of Nations, Campbell R.H. – Skinner A.S. (eds.), Oxford 1976.
Spufford F., Red Plenty: inside the fifties' Soviet dream, London 2010.
Stiglitz J.E., The Contribution of the Economics of Information to Twentieth Century Economics, The Quarterly Journal of Economics 115, 2000, 1441–78.
Stiglitz J.E., Globalization and its Discontents, New York 2002.
Tandy D.W., Warriors into Traders: the power of the market in early Greece, Berkeley 1997.
Temin P., A Market Economy in the Early Roman Empire, JRS 91, 2001, 169–81.
Viglietti C., Il Limite del Bisogno: antropologica economica di Roma arcaica, Bologna 2011.
von Reden S., Exchange in Ancient Greece, London 1995.
von Reden S., Money in Classical Antiquity, Cambridge 2010.

Village markets in Roman Egypt

The case of first-century AD Tebtunis

Dominic Rathbone

It has long been a matter of debate how far monetisation and a market economy penetrated the rural society of the Roman Empire that made up around 75% of its population.[1] In this paper I present and discuss some of the rare documentary evidence we have, which mostly comes from the papyri found in village-sites from the Arsinoite nome (Fayyum), Egypt, in particular two day-by-day accounts of expenditure made in AD 45-46 by Kronion son of Apion, who ran the local notarial office (*grapheion*) in the village of Tebtunis.

Tebtunis was one of the new Ptolemaic developments in the Fayyum, apparently expanding a previous settlement. Parts of it were excavated by English, German and Italian teams between 1900 and 1936, and new Italo-French excavations began in 1988. So we have some archaeological idea of the site, and also tens of thousands of documents on papyrus, most unpublished.[2] By the first century AD the site occupied some 50 ha (Pompeii has 67 ha) and, at a guess, had a total population of between 3,000 and 4,000. Although villages this large were not the norm in Roman Egypt, and were larger than many small cities in other provinces and even Italy, Tebtunis was officially a 'village' (*kômê*). It had some local state officials and a few state buildings, such as a state granary (maybe more than one) and a police-station for the 'desert-guards' (*erêmophulakes*); there were also several temples, of which the largest was the grand temple-complex of Soknebtunis. There were also privately run bath-houses, dining establishments, workshops and so on. It had no communal institutions of self-administration, although there were several self-regulating associations (see below). The local economy was primarily agricultural: Tebtunis was what we might now call an 'agro-town', but it was not just a peasant community. There were well-off families who had others work their land. Some people had incomes from state posts or concessions, such as Kronion himself and the numerous priests of the main temple. There were craftsmen of various types, some traders and others with specialist skills (see below). In short, Tebtunis was a modest rural community of a size and type which probably makes up many of the dots in the *Barrington Atlas of the Greek and Roman World*.

The *grapheion* archive of Kronion was excavated clandestinely, but is certainly from Tebtunis. Most of its 200 and more texts are now in the University of Michi-

1 Rowlandson 2001 argues for quite extensive monetisation in the villages of Ptolemaic to Roman Egypt but little discernible impact on economic behaviour.

2 Gallazzi 1989 summarises the older excavations. For an unsorted listing of papyri found at or referring to Tebtunis see w.trismegistos.org, PLACES, s.v. 'Tebtynis'. Daris 1986, 377–82 lists some of the references to public buildings and officials.

gan at Ann Arbor, and over three quarters have been published.[3] Almost every text in the archive is a record or product of the notarial business of Kronion, or of his father and predecessor Apion. The extant texts include over 140 draft contracts, three long day-by-day registers which summarise over 1,300 contracts and other documents drawn up in part of AD 41/2 and AD 45–46, and two day-by-day accounts of expenditure.[4] This study is based primarily on *P.Mich.* II 127, headed 'account of private expenses' (*logos dapanês idias*), which is a day-by-day record, in Kronion's hand, of his domestic spending, or at least some of it, over the first five months of AD 45/6, roughly September 45 to January 46.[5] I also use the similar purchases recorded in the other day-by-day account of expenditure, again in Kronion's hand, in *P.Mich.* II 123 recto.i, 124 recto.iii, and 123 verso, which covers the sixteen-month period from September 45 to December 46.[6] This longer account has no initial heading, but it has one internal rubric, 'common expenses (*koinê dapanê*) incurred in Phaophi (October)', which restarts the account after a totalling and division of costs for September between Kronion and Eutuchas, his then partner in running the *grapheion*.[7] I take the two accounts to be related: I think that Kronion noted all his day-by-day expenditure and then sorted it into what he claimed to be costs incurred in running the *grapheion*, such as, obviously, the monthly payment (*diagraphê*) towards the rent they had agreed to pay for the concession and purchases of papyrus and ink, for half of which his partner Eutuchas was liable, and his domestic expenses for which he alone was liable. Some

3 Details at: w.trismegistos.org, ARCHIVES, s.v. 'Kronion son of Apion head of the *grapheion* of Tebtunis'. Tebtunis has produced other archives with confusingly similar names, such as the Ptolemaic *grapheion* archive (I BC), and the archives of Kronion son of Cheos, Kronion and Isidora and Apollonios alias Lurius head of the *grapheion* (all II AD).

4 Husselman 1970 discusses the functioning of the *grapheion* as it can be reconstructed from its records. A general historical study of this archive is now being undertaken by Dr Micaela Langellotti at King's College London. The accounts have received almost no attention apart from the few, in part erroneous, notes by Harl 1996, 279–280, 460.

5 I convert the ancient dates to Julian equivalents. The civil year of Roman Egypt began on Thoth 1 (= 29 August in non-leap years), so in effect September was the first month. All Egyptian months had 30 days, except the last (Mesore = August) which had an additional 5 days (6 before leap years).

6 In what follows, I refer to these and other accounts from *P.Mich.* II just by their number and, if needed, side (e.g. 123 verso). There are no corrections recorded for 127. For 123 verso see *BL* III 107–8, X 122, XI 130, XII 119. I take the order of the parts of 123 recto.i to be a+c+b+d; I also identify and treat 124 recto.iii as the missing record (November) between 123 recto.i (September–October) and 123 verso.i (which I therefore assign to December). 128.ii.28–45 and i(a) are drafts of most of the entries in 123 verso.viii.34–ix.30. Two other published texts relate to Kronion's business expenditure, II 125.1–9 (some draft notes) and V 242 (lacunose summaries of receipts and expenses), but neither records any purchases of goods. Images and translations of these texts are available via the APIS data-base (http://www.columbia.edu/cu/lweb/projects/digital/apis/search/): under APIS Number enter 'Michigan' and the number given here in brackets: 127 (3031); 123 recto.i (3195), 124 recto.iii (3193), 123 verso (3217–31); 128.ii (3062) and i(a) (3059).

7 123 recto.i(b).25–(d).2; heading at (d).3. Cf. 123 recto.ix.15–24 for a similar totalling and division between Kronion and Eutuchas of income for December 45.

expenditure, especially on food and entertainment, was not clear-cut: in October 45, for instance, Kronion recorded the cost of wine for an official of the catoecic registry as a private expense, but a similar item in August 46 as a common expense.[8] Note that the common account was not, as Boak sometimes implies, a business account of allowable expenses, deductible from the rent for the concession; it was just Kronion's private record of costs he claimed Eutuchas should share.[9] Both accounts are rough syntheses of other records for Kronion's own use, and we do not know whether he thought them adequate as they were or wrote up neater final versions. This is particularly clear in the case of the common account which was drafted over several scraps of papyrus, some then stuck together, looks to be very incomplete for December 45 and July and October 46, and includes only four attempts at running totals for odd periods.[10] More detailed study of Kronion's accounting practices must be left to another occasion, although I will discuss below the question of monetary units and the use of cash.

Another area of obscurity, because of the archive's extremely narrow focus, is Kronion's background and business. His father Apion had held the concession to run the *grapheion* in Tebtunis and Kerkesoucha Orous from at least AD 7 to his death in 25/6. Kronion then held it until 52 or later; in AD 46–47, at least, he had a partner in the venture called Eutucheides, or more familiarly Eutuchas. Their duty was to register contracts and certain other documents drawn up in Tebtunis and some surrounding villages for forwarding to the nome registry, and they also seem to have provided a general scribal service. Boak calculated from Kronion's accounts that the costs of running the *grapheion* sometimes exceeded the income from scribal fees, and noted that Kronion and Eutuchas often borrowed money in order to make up their monthly payment (*diagraphê*) for the concession. Presumably, however, the *grapheion* was reasonably lucrative, or Kronion would not have continued to renew the concession each year. I can only surmise that the extant accounts do not cover some important income streams, such as fees for writing private documents, and I note that some of the loans were for a few days only, so apparently to raise enough silver tetradrachms for the *diagraphê*.[11] Regarding Kronion's family we happen to know that he had a son called Apion – familiarly Apis – after his grandfather (as was common), and that he had a house in Tebtunis

8 127.i.27; 123 verso.viii.27–8. Cf. 123 verso.vi.21 (4 June 46) where Kronion added to the common account one or more items 'from the private account' (*apo tou eteuou [l. idiou] logou*).

9 Boak, *P.Mich.* II pp. 5, 97. It seems that Eutuchas rarely paid any of the expenses; in 123 verso. viii.10–13 Kronion repaid Eutuchas 4 dr. which he had spent on wine two months previously.

10 See n.6 above and the editor's description of the papyrus (123), and note the earlier drafts of some items in 128.i–ii. Totals: see n. 49 below.

11 Boak, *P.Mich.* II (1933) pp. 4–5, 96, 102. Short-term loans: e.g. 123 verso.iv.9–22. We do not understand basic points, such as how the variable monthly *diagraphê* related to the fixed *phoros* (rent) which Kronion had bid for the concession, or whether the scribal fees included a charge for registration (if there was one). A re-examination of the accounts, along with comparative evidence from other attested notaries could clarify Kronion's finances, but that is another task for another time.

where, it is assumed, he ran the business, since there was no public office.[12] There is no evidence that Kronion owned or rented land, but it would be very odd if he had not. His recorded domestic purchases of agricultural products (see below) were not sufficient to support a family, and were probably to supplement his own supplies: for example he made no private purchases of wine in January, probably because his own vintage then became ready for drinking. Conversely, he clearly had at least one donkey for his trips to the city and other villages, but his private account records no purchases of fodder, and he once paid for wood to be cut and delivered but not for the wood itself.[13] This suggest to me that he was a landowner who sometimes sold produce rather than consume it, and that he kept separate agricultural records and accounts which have not survived.

The archive makes the scale of Kronion's shopping the best indicator to us of his wealth. His private account records a variable pattern of buying, including on his occasional visits to the 'city', that is the nome capital (*mêtropolis*) of Ptolemais Euergetis, also known as Arsinoe, and nearby villages. In September 45 he made purchases on 9 days, on about 17 days in November, about 15 in December, and 10 in January 46, that is an average of 13 every 30 days. His longest break from shopping was 5 days in September 45. However, the common account records purchases on other days which push up the overall totals; for instance in January 46 he made joint purchases on 17 days, and so, discounting overlaps, shopped on 20 separate days.[14] Also, many of his purchases involved eating out with friends (see below), and on some apparently blank dates it may have been their turn to pay. He was a pretty frequent shopper. He was also quite a big spender. In September 45 he spent 122 dr. 5 ob. on domestic items, mainly food, in October 54 dr. 5 ob., in November 44 dr. 1 ob., in December 92 dr. 4 ob., and in January 19 dr. 2 ob., an average of almost 67 dr. a month.[15] Food expenditure in the common account for the same period, which is lacunose and incomplete, amounted to at least 40 dr. in September, 20 dr. in October and about 20 dr. in January. The peaks of private expenditure in September and December, incidentally, were due to large purchases of wheat, barley, lentils and dates, presumably stocking up his household stores, and also of wool. In the later first to early second century AD, the nearest period with decent evidence, unskilled agricultural wages ranged between 3 and 6 obols a day, making a maximum monthly income of 30 drachmas.[16] That is less than half the average of Kronion's recorded domestic expenditure in September 45 to January 46. Despite the uncertainties about the profitability of the *grapheion* business and whether or

12 'Through Apis (my) son': 123 verso.v.28. 'In the house' (drinking beer): 123 verso.iii.6, 33, 36, 37.

13 See below on donkeys (n. 31) and the wood (n. 17).

14 The number of days is often uncertain because of lacunae in the margins of the accounts. Also, the common account seems incomplete for some months.

15 I ignore miscellaneous expenditure and convert obols into tetradrachms on a ratio of 24:1 (see below). Note that Boak's total for Phaophi (127 introd.) should be 65 dr. 5 ob.

16 Drexhage 1991, 413–415.

not he owned land, Kronion looks to have been one of the wealthier villagers of Tebtunis with a lifestyle several times above subsistence.

Turning to the purchases, I start with the few non-food items. On 10 December 45 Kronion paid 34 ob. for six donkey-loads of wood to be cut and transported, presumably firewood for his house.[17] He bought wool five times: 5 and 2 measures in September, 4 1/2 in November, 4 in December and an unknown quantity in January; related items in November included 'thread' (*stêmôn*), specified as 'for the completion of the mantle and tunics', and purple dye for 3 1/2 ob.[18] Kronion's household made at least some of their clothes. Food staples tended to be bought in relatively large quantities. In September and October 45 Kronion made eight purchases of wheat totalling just over 16 art. (say 620 litres, or 480 kg), almost enough to feed two adults for a year, but none in November to January; in November and December he instead bought over 3 art. of barley.[19] In three days in mid-September he also purchased over 3.5 art. of lentils.[20] On 3 December he bought around 11 art. of dates (430 litres), probably a year's supply, and paid for their transport.[21] Smaller items purchased over the five months include two jars of oil, turnips once, eggs twice, and once some very expensive fish, perhaps from the Mediterranean, costing 4 dr.[22] His most frequent small purchase, however, was cooked meat (*opson*, a kebab?), almost always accompanied by oil, probably vegetable (sesame?) oil; the meat and oil typically cost 2 plus 3 ob.[23] On three occasions, once when he was in Arsinoe, Kronion also bought vegetables, and at the end of October he made four purchases of loaves and pan-made breads (*klibanitai*), possibly for a party.[24] Presumably the meat and oil was normally for the main (evening?) meal of his household, which consumed its own bread and vegetables. To drink, Kronion once purchased beer, but he preferred wine: in September to December he bought, normally one at a time, a total of 13 amphorae (*keramia*) of wine, roughly 90 litres or a (modern) bottle a day.[25] He did not drink it all himself, for on several occasions the wine and other foodstuffs are said to have been purchased to host particular people, but he will have dined out himself and his aggregate wine consumption was probably fairly high.[26] Totalling the domestic ex-

17 127.ii.36–7. He paid nothing for the wood, probably because it came from trees on his land.

18 127.i.4, 18, ii.2–4, 21–4, 46, iii.15.

19 127.i.8, 12–17, 37–8, ii.1, 44.

20 127.i.9–11.

21 127.ii.29–31. The extra purchase of 3 metra of dates is curious; perhaps they were of special quality and hence expensive.

22 127.i.19 (oil), 43 (eggs), ii.15 (turnips), 32 (*selachia*, or *-ion?*), 41 (oil), 53 (eggs). The *selachion* was a cartilagenous fish, perhaps skate (usually *batis*): cf. Thompson 1947: 26–28, 270.

23 127 passim.

24 Vegetables: 127.ii.49, iii.13, 16. Bread:127.i.49–51.

25 Beer: 127.ii.9. Wine: 127 passim (ignoring i.19, which I take to be an uncancelled error in an entry really for a jar of oil).

26 127.i.14, 20, ii.50–3, iii.4; cf. ii.35, iii.8, 12: 'contributions' to hosting people, probably to do with parties organised by the association to which Kronion belonged (see below).

penditure recorded in this private account, the biggest item was wheat and barley at 124 dr.; other stores included 12 dr. of lentils, 29 dr. of dates, and 4 dr. for two jars of oil, making a total of 173 dr. on staples. Kronion also spent about 59 dr. on day-by-day items and 45.5 dr. on wine, making a grand total for foodstuffs of almost 280 dr. His only other significant expenditure was over 42 dr. on textiles.

The pattern of purchases of over the sixteen months covered by the common account is unsurprisingly somewhat different. The main foodstuff purchased was wine, a total of 36 *keramia* (c. 250 litres) for 130 dr. Most of the other items were small purchases of provisions to entertain visitors or for parties: cooked meat and oil, as in his private account, but far more beer, loaves and vegetables, mostly in various combinations, and fish of four types.[27] The spate of purchases of vegetables in mid-September 46 was perhaps for Kronion's household and should not have been included in this account.[28] Oil was also bought three or four times for the lamp of a scribe working overnight.[29] Occasional foodstuff purchases, mostly once only, included: sour wine, wheat, turnips, beet, cabbage and endive, garlic, gourds, dates, figs (three times), nuts, raw meat, eggs and sweetmeats for the children of an official.[30] Travel costs for officials and employees include some specified purchases of barley and fodder for animals, and the hiring of a donkey on three occasions.[31] Kronion also bought 28 rolls of papyrus and two part-rolls, and some ink and a pen.[32] As it happens, the archive of a contemporary of Kronion, Nemesion the collector of money taxes at Philadelphia, another large Fayyum village (on its eastern side), contains one account, apparently for AD 46/7, which records his receipts as he made his tax-collecting rounds, but also some of his expenses: five purchases of wine, four of dates, two each of raw meat, vegetables and fodder, and one each of wheat, beer, chickling, a skate and pan-breads(?), sweetmeats and papyrus and pens.[33]

In order to assess the evidence of Kronion's accounts for monetisation and market exchange, a word is needed on the monetary system of Roman Egypt in the AD 40s as it was evolving from late Ptolemaic practice. The following two paragraphs have proved the most difficult part of this paper to write. It took me a long

27 Wine, beer, meat, oil, beer, loaves, pan-breads, vegetables: 123 passim. Fish: one *latis* (Nile perch: Thompson 1947, 144–146), 123 verso.vii.19; one *phagros* (dogfish?: Thompson 1947, 274–275), 124 recto.iii.19; *korakinoi* (Nile tilapia; Thompson 1947, 123–125), 123 recto.i(d).9, 19, verso.vii.7, 22; *thrissai* (shad; Thompson 1947, 77–78), 123 recto.i(d).21, verso.ii.9, 13, 16, 24, v.10, 32, 33, 35, vi.38, xi.5, 7–8.

28 123 verso.ix.17, 19, 21, 26 (= 128.i(a).11, 13, 15, 20).

29 123 verso.ii.14, 23, viii.32(?), ix.29 (= 128.i(a).24).

30 123 verso.misc(a).3; xi.26–27; xi.11; ix.11 (= 128.i(a).6); ix.14, 23 (= 128.i(a).9, 17); ii.15, 34; vi.36, vii.26; recto i(d).5; verso.vii.7, 24, viii.9; vii.27; xi.18; vi.20, viii.29; v.21 (*tragêmatia*).

31 Fodder: 124 recto.iii.24, 123 verso.v.18, viii.2, 38 (= 128.ii.33), ix.34. Donkey hire (* denotes when Kronion was certainly away, using his own donkey): 123 verso.ii.29*, vii.18, ix.35*.

32 Boak, *P.Mich. II*, pp. 98–100.

33 *SB* XX 14575.18, 20, 21, 24, 30 (taking *batos* as a variant of *batis* [cf. n. 22 above] and perhaps reading *klibanitai*), 34, 36, 46, 48, 55–58, 61, 81, 87, 247, 528, 546–549.

time to realise that current views could not explain practice in Kronion's accounts because they conflate evidence from different periods in between which there had been significant changes and because they are primarily interested in explaining the surcharges imposed on payments to the state.[34] In particular I now believe that what they call the 'bronze standard', which used 'bronze' drachmas as well as obols, was a development of the later first century AD, because it was consequent on the minting of a copper drachma, called the *chalkinê* ('bronze one') in the papyri, which began under Nero, and it is first clearly attested in a set of estate accounts of AD 78/9.[35] Instead I try here to interpret Kronion's accounts against the background of the coins in circulation at that time. This approach is also novel in its focus on private transactions rather than public charges.

The basic coin was the Alexandrian silver tetradrachm, of which new Roman issues were only just beginning to replace the still circulating late Ptolemaic stock; in AD 42/3 there had also been a small output of silver didrachms and drachmas. In official accounts the drachma was always divided into the traditional six obols, and thus the tetradrachm had 24 obols. This was normal too in private calculations of interest on loans, and in totals in private accounts, and is what is called the 'silver standard'. From Augustus on sporadic minting had continued of four copper coins, sometimes marked 80, 40, 20 and 10 in descending order of size. The problem for us is that these copper coins appear to have had two alternative official face values, and in private dealings were sometimes reckoned at values between these two points. The numbers on the coins relate to the 'demotic bronze standard', a now otherwise purely notional relic of the earlier Ptolemaic bronze coinage, which officially had 300 'demotic' drachmas to the silver drachma.[36] Thus the copper coin sometimes marked 40 had a 7.5 ratio to the drachma, or 30 to the tetradrachm. The mostly unmarked copper versions, however, will have looked like Greek-style fractions of the drachma, with 24 expected to the tetradrachm; this must have been their primary face value, precisely because it was deemed to be self-evident, whereas the alternative demotic value needed marking. The nearest obol values to the ratios to the drachma of the marked demotic values are 2 obols, 1 obol, 1/2 obol and 1/4 obol; post factum confirmation is that when two new larger copper coins were minted under Nero, they were clearly 4 and 6 obol-coins because the biggest coin in the expanded series must be what texts call the *chalkinê*, 'bronze drachma'.

---

34 For details and background, despite the new suggestions here, see Rathbone 1997, 187–189, Maresch 1996, 110–133, West – Johnson 1944, 13–25, 43–64, and Gölitzer 2004 on the coins. I have benefited from discussion of the coins with Andrew Burnett.

35 AD 78/9 accounts: *P.Lond.* 131/131* recto (*SB* VIII 9699), on which see Johnson 1936, 177–207 (nos. 104–105), and Maresch 1996, 142–149.

36 The 450:1 ratio found in Oxyrhynchite texts probably represents 300 plus a half, the common 150% rate in contracts for penalties for default, which demotic drachmas were often used to express.

As we will see, the pricing of Kronion's purchases in AD 45–46 indirectly attests a 24:1 ratio between obol coins and the tetradrachm. However Kronion's accounts also show that the copper obols could be exchanged or reckoned at a discount against the tetradrachm at a ratio of 28:1 or 29:1, or rather that the tetradrachm was sometimes valued at a premium to the copper obols on these ratios. It would be misleading to talk of payments or reckoning on the 'bronze standard' because, apart from the notional demotic standard, there was no bronze drachma in existence at this time, and the copper coins, even though they could be discounted, had a primary face value on the silver standard of 24 obols to the tetradrachm. The 30:1 ratio implied by the figures for demotic drachmas marked on some copper coins is best taken as another discounted ratio, this one set by the state and never used, it seems, in private accounts. I note, finally, that written use of the demotic bronze standard is confined in the early Roman period to certain traditional Egyptian forms of contract, and there is no indication that reckoning in demotic drachmas underlies any of the everyday transactions recorded in Kronion's accounts.[37] Admittedly, the general picture remains very unclear and puzzling. We do not, for example, know whether the state in this period issued copper obols at 24 or 30 to the tetradrachm, or why it levied surcharges, normally called *prosdiagraphomena*, on some taxes.[38] We need more detailed studies of private accounts of different periods to examine, as I do here for Kronion's accounts, what they reveal about the practical workings of everyday small private monetary transactions.

It is helpful to start with *P.Mich.* II 123 recto.ii–xxii, a rough day-by-day record of Kronion's income from scribal fees (*grammatika*) for documents he had registered in the Egyptian year September 45 to August 46. It is fairly certain that all the payments had been made on the given date in cash, rather than being notional payments made on tick (credit), because when a fee had not been paid on the spot Kronion noted it as owing. In the 673 legible entries for the whole year, 44 payments (6.5%) were noted as owing in whole or part. Of these 24 have the rubric 'he owes the *grammatikon*' with no sum specified, 9 give the sum and add 'which he owes', and 11 give the sum and note the part of it which the client still owes. 25 entries (a generous 4%), incidentally, are marked 'favour' (*charis*), which means no

37 In Rathbone 1997, 204–205, I suggested that a few prices for two or three jars of wine which produce odd fractions when calculating price per jar imply background costing on the demotic standard, but they can be explained more simply as combinations of different prices or total prices with a discount. I cannot demonstrate that people were not reckoning on the demotic standard, just that it is not evident or necessary. Written use of it disappears completely in the later first century AD, probably a consequence of the emergence of a new 'bronze standard'.

38 On the *prosdiagraphomena* see Gara 1976, Maresch 1996, 120–127. Unsolved problems include that the *prosdiagraphomena*, supposedly surcharges on taxes assessed in Ptolemaic bronze drachmas, were in fact collected on payments in any medium, and that the fraction of 1/16 (6.25%) at which they were often, but not always, charged is curious. It is unclear why some copper coins were marked with values in demotic drachmas at a discount to their obol-value; the obvious answer is to mark the discount when they were used pay taxes still assessed in Ptolemaic bronze drachmas, but that is what the *prosdiagraphomena* are meant to have covered.

fee was charged.[39] The full fees noted as owing seem to be included in Kronion's monthly totals of income, and had presumably been paid off before Kronion totalled income for the month; Kronion recorded more delayed payments as new items on their day of receipt.[40]

At or towards the end of each month Kronion totalled the fees paid, which he usually recorded as a single sum in drachmas and obols. However, in the case of three or four months, he recorded first a total in obols which he converted into drachmas and obols, then another total in drachmas, and finally the overall total in drachmas and obols.[41] As Boak saw, in the first stage here Kronion was converting receipts in copper obols (on the bronze standard, as Boak put it) to the silver standard at the subsequently common ratio of 29 obols per tetradrachm (7.25 ob. per dr.), for which this still seems to be the earliest evidence. The details are presented in the following Table.[42]

Month and reference	**Receipts in obols**	**Converted into dr. / @ rate**	**Receipts in drachmas**	**Total receipts / (%age value of obol receipts)**
December 45 (part) 123 recto.viii.37	176 ob.	24 dr. 2 ob. @ 28.9 : 1	111 dr.	135 dr. 3 ob. (18 %)
February 46 123 recto.xii.34-35	390.5 ob.	52 dr. 13.5 ob. @ 28.8 : 1	94 dr.	146 dr. 13.5 ob. (36 %)

39 Unspecified sum: 123 recto.ii.31, iii.14, 23, 24, 37, 38, iv.17, v.3, vi.6, vii.5, 23, 29, 40, viii.32(?), x.8, 21, xi.7, 8, 30, xiii.11, xviii.13, xxi.31, xxii.17, 22. Whole fee owing: iii.29, iv.38, vi.9, xi.2(?), 40, xiii.42, xv.32, 40, xix.22. Part of fee owing: iv.7, v.14–15, vi.35, 41, viii.12, 39, ix.4, x.5, xv.12, xvii.44, xix.9. Favour: ii.32, 36, 37, iv.15, 25, 42, v.34, vi.4, 11, 21, vii.3, viii.7, 26, 33, xii.4, 18, xiii.17, xiv.8, 27, xv.4, 27, xvi.16, 19, xx.26, xxi.32.

40 Three entries in 123 recto record delayed payments: x.22, on 8 January 46 for a fee owing from 10 October 45 (v.3); x.31 on 16 January for a fee owing from September but not in Kronion's extant record; xix.42 on 24 July for a fee apparently from 21 July (xix.22).

41 It seems that Kronion had made the calculations on another piece of papyrus and then copied across the totals, occasionally including the intermediate total of payments in obols.

42 I have checked the figures against the online images. For March 46 (xiii.30), Boak's 24 dr. 20.5 ob. has been rightly corrected to 24 dr. 6.5 ob. (*BL* III 108), which gives the standard conversion ratio; but the total is certainly, and inexplicably, 145 dr. 20.5 ob. For June 46 Boak read '[Of those up to Pauni 2]7(?) 48 silver dr. 9.5 ob. and | [- - - - . .]6(?) [silver dr.] 27.5 ob., total for the whole up to | [Pauni 27] 172 silver dr. {dr.} (or 1 ob.?)'. He tried to interpret the figures as intermediate totals A + B = grand total C, but the sums do not work. The 'and' after 48 dr. 9.5 ob. suggests that it is the silver value of receipts in copper obols, to be followed by the total for receipts in drachmas, but the silver total must be a round number of drachmas, and cannot end in 27.5 ob. I think that the whole silver total is in the lacuna (the –6 is very uncertain) and that the 27.5 ob. is an exchange fee to be deducted (as at 123 recto.xi.14). Then the totals for the month can be reconstructed as: (copper receipts of 359.5 ob. converted @ 29 : 1) to 48 dr. 9.5 ob., plus [silver receipts of 127 dr.], minus (exchange fee) of 27.5 ob., gives total of 172 dr. This interpretation is plausible because it produces, as is required, a final total in a round number of drachmas.

Month and reference	**Receipts in obols**	**Converted into dr. / @ rate**	**Receipts in drach-mas**	**Total receipts / (%age value of obol receipts)**
March 46 123 recto.xiii.30	180.5 ob.	24 dr. 6.5 ob. @28.8 : 1	121 dr.	145 dr. 20.5 ob. (17 %)
perhaps June 46 123 recto.xvii.46-48	(not given?)	48 dr. 9.5 ob. —	[in lacu-na?]	172 dr. (29 %)

The intermediate and monthly totals of scribal fees in this account are often difficult to check because of the many lacunae, and sometimes look wrong, whether because Kronion had made mistakes or was including information from another account. However the record of fees for February 46 (Mecheir year 6) is almost complete and shows how Kronion reached his totals given in the Table above.[43] Of the 50 entries with legible payments, 36 (72%) record payments in obols, 12 (24%) in drachmas (twice specified as 'silver') and 2 in drachmas and obols; total legible receipts amount to 371.5 ob. and 80 dr., well within reach, allowing for the missing entries, of Kronion's totals of 390.5 ob. and 94 dr. The obol payments, which ranged from 2 to 27 obols, could all have been made in copper coins. Of the sixteen payments wholly or partly in drachmas, seven are of 4 dr., four of 8 dr. and one of 16 dr., all payable in tetradrachms, but three are of 2 dr. and one of 10 dr., which implies that some of the didrachm and drachma coins minted in 42/3 had percolated to Tebtunis.[44] This confirms that Kronion recorded fees in their actual medium of payment, whether silver or copper coins or both, and then totalled the obol payments separately, including the obols in mixed payments, for conversion to the silver standard.

In this sample of fifty fees paid in February 46, copper coins were, unsurprisingly used for 72% of the transactions worth a third of the total, and silver coins for 24% of the transactions worth two thirds of the total. Ideally the analysis should be extended to all the recorded *grammatika* for 45–46, but the pattern seems to imply that in setting his fees Kronion thought in terms of the silver standard, albeit here perhaps at a ratio of 28 obols to the tetradrachm, and priced jobs in steps to facilitate payment in the available coins. Of the 36 fees paid in obols only, 24 are of 7 to 14 obols, equivalent to one to two silver drachmas, and none exceed 27 obols. The

43 123 recto.xi.21–xii.33. Three lines are illegible (xi.46–48) and the sums in three entries are uncertain (xi.45, xii.1–2).

44 It is unlikely that payments of 2 dr. would have been made as a paper transfer through a bank, or by the client paying a tetradrachm and Kronion giving change in copper obols because 123 recto. xii.6 explicitly – and uniquely (which implies it was unusual) – records a transaction of this type as '8 dr. less 1 ob.'. Conceivably some payments were effected by barter, but I can find no purchase by Kronion from a named individual which corresponds to a fee due from them. In 123 verso. ix.26–27 Kronion's purchase of 16 dr. worth of wheat for a beer-brewer at Tristomos to cover the cost of beer is enigmatic, but perhaps was in effect a loan (cf. ix.24–25, 29, 32, 34).

next common level of fee was a round 4 dr., that is a silver tetradrachm, and most higher fees were also round multiples of tetradrachms. Presumably Kronion tried to round down or up fees in between 14 ob. and 4. dr. because they required too many copper obols or the rare silver didrachms or drachmas. He also tried to avoid payments in mixed units: most small fees were set and paid in copper obols, and higher ones in tetradrachms.

Kronion's decision to use the silver standard when setting and totalling his fees is understandable because the monthly rent to the state for his notarial concession was set and had to be paid in tetradrachms, and he had to split profits or losses with his partner Eutuchas, which was more easily done by totalling all common income and expenses on the silver standard than by keeping separate copper and silver accounts. It should, however, be noted that it was his choice to use the ratio of 29 copper obols to the tetradrachm (the closest ever used in private accounts to the official 30:1 ratio) for calculating his costs and totals, and perhaps the 28:1 ratio in pricing his obol fees. It would digress too far to discuss the details here, but it seems that in order to have sufficient silver coins for his monthly payment (*diagraphê*) towards the rent Kronion sometimes had to borrow tetradrachms from fellow villagers or buy tetradrachms from the local exchange-bank, for which he paid a fee in addition to whatever exchange ratio they used.[45] He may have chosen the high ratio of 29:1 in his totals to balance the costs to him of acquiring extra tetradrachms for the rent. Conversely, if he was able to spend the copper coins he had received, or exchange them for tetradrachms, at a more favourable ratio, that would have been to his slight financial advantage. We do not know how much exchanging copper coins for tetradrachms or the loans cost, but we can examine Kronion's accounts of expenditure for clues about how he and those who sold to him valued their goods and services.

On the analogy of his account of income from notarial fees, we would expect Kronion's day-by-day accounts of private expenditure for September 45 to January 46 and of common expenditure from September 45 to December 46 both to record payments as he had actually made them in silver or copper coins.[46] One supporting indication is that all the 115 payments with legible amounts in the private account are recorded as made in drachmas only (30%) or obols only (70%). So too of the 326 payments in the common account 95 (29%) were made in drachmas, 223 (68%) in obols and a mere 8 (2%) in a mixture of drachmas and obols.[47] Furthermore, almost all the drachma payments in both accounts are multiples of 4 dr. payable in tetradrachms. The payments in drachmas in the common account make

45 Cf. nn. 11 and 42 above.

46 That payments were made on the stated date is confirmed by 123 verso.viii.10–13 where a joint purchase of wine made by Eutuchas on 14 June 46 was not recorded until 9 August, the day when Kronion reimbursed him.

47 At least one of these, 123 verso.v.25, combines two separate payments, 8 dr. for papyrus and 1 ob. for ink.

up a striking 92% by value of all payments.[48] That is because the common account includes 34 large payments towards the rent of the concession, to repay loans and so on. When those are stripped out, payments in drachmas alone make up 21% of the (remaining) total payments in number, and all drachma payments comprise of 71% of the total by value.

Kronion will have needed to total common expenditure periodically on the silver standard so he could set it against income to calculate the share of profits or losses with his partner Eutuchas. His extant common account has only four internal totals (there are none in the private account), and because of lost entries or arithmetic errors we cannot discern the ratio at which he converted obol expenditure onto the silver standard.[49] I suspect it was 24 obols to the tetradrachm because, as we will see shortly, most petty sellers set their prices on this ratio. It may seem odd to us that Kronion converted fees he received in copper onto the silver standard at a 29:1 ratio but apparently priced those fees using a 28:1 ratio, and perhaps converted his petty expenditure in copper at a 24:1 ratio. However, this was presumably second nature to him, and if pressed he would have said that it gave him a fair idea of how his business was really doing, and that it was a reasonably effective way of protecting his own position while also satisfying his partner Eutuchas, who in theory lost out slightly by the 29:1 conversion of receipts, in an economy which used silver and copper coins with a variable relationship between them. There was, after all, no income tax authority to impose a universal accounting policy.

Analysis of the sums spent in obols takes us further. Of the 81 obol payments in Kronion's private account, 53 (65%) were of 1 to 6 ob.; two series are also discernible, one of 3 – 6 – 18 ob., the other of 5 – 10 – 20 ob., but no 7–based pattern.[50] Of the 230 obol payments in the common account, 177 (77%) were of 0.5 to 6 ob., and the same two series appear, although the first series has more points, both 1.5 – 3 – 4.5 – 6 and 2 – 4 – 6 ob., and again there is no 7–based pattern; also striking here is the clear modal payment, with 41 cases (18%), of 1 ob.[51] The 5 – 10 – 20 obol series is mostly for combined payments such as cooked meat with oil (often 3

48 I here convert copper payments to the silver standard using the 24:1 ratio (obols to tetradrachm). Using 29:1 would marginally increase the figure to 93%.

49 123 recto.i(b).25–26 (September 45) – Kronion's total seems less than the items in i(b).1–24; 124 recto.iii.25 (October–November) – many lacunose items; 123 verso.ii.35, copied to the account of fee income at 123 recto.xi.16 (January 46) – two missing items are enough to prevent choosing between 29:1 or 24:1; 123 verso.xvii.[24] (mid-June) – total restored by the editor from the entries so not testable.

50 Obol sums x number of payments: 1 ob. x 4, 2 x 7, 3 x 19, 3.5 x 1, 4 x 4, 5 x 10, 6 x 8, and 10 ob. x 7, 18 x 3, 20 x 2; also one payment each of 7, 8, 9, 12, 16, 17, 19, 19.5, 22, 34, 36 and 42 ob., and two of 14 ob.

51 Obols x payments: 0.5 ob. x 2, 1 x 41, 1.5 x 17, 2 x 25, 2.5 x 4, 3 x 24, 3.5 x 6, 4 x 21, 4.5 x 6, 5 x 12, 5.5 x 1, 6 x 18, and 10 ob. x 9, 18 x 4, 20 x 3; also one payment each of 9, 10.5, 15, 19, 22, 23, 24.5, 28, 36, 50 and 52 ob., two each 12, 13, 17 and 21 ob., three of 7, 9.5 and 14 ob., four of 16 and 18, and five of 8 ob.

+ 2 ob.) or 'travel expenses'. The other series is more significant, and implies that petty retailers at Tebtunis were pricing their goods in copper coins at their primary face value of 6 obols to the drachma, and the two common fraction systems of the drachma, 1/4 – 1/2 – 3/4 and 1/3 – 2/3. Before examining pricing in more detail, I note an important difference here from the pattern of Kronion's notarial fees. Kronion set or accepted few fees in obols for more than 14 ob. and none for over 27 ob.; for higher fees it seems he demanded tetradrachms. When spending, however, he made payments of up to 42 ob. (private account) or 52 ob. (common account), and payments of 6.5 ob. and above made up 70% by value of his private and 62% of his common aggregate payments in obols.

Although the obol was divided into eight chalkoi, and a half-obol and a dichalkon coin had been minted (and a chalkos coin was briefly added under Nero), in Tebtunis the general starting price for goods was one obol: for a pen, a pot of ink, a loaf of bread, a portion of vegetables or specifically cabbage, garlic and gourds, a basket of figs, a local fish, a kebab, some eggs, a jar of beer (Kronion's only two purchases at 0.5 ob. were of 'halves' of beer), vinegar, some vegetable oil for dinner.[52] Higher sums were were needed for rations of fodder, bags of turnips, larger or rarer fish, a basket of figs, oil for the office lamp, once some purple dye, and various of the one-obol items in larger quantities or in combinations, and also for hiring donkeys and – which are not well represented in these accounts – wages for casual labour. Goods in large quantities, however, or by nature more expensive, were almost always sold and bought for silver coins, and were usually priced by varying the (loose) quantity sold per tetradrachm: thus wheat was sold in amounts varying from 1/2 to 11/12 of an artaba (40 litres) per tetradrachm, barley at 1 and 1 1/5 artabas, lentils at from 1 to 1 1/3 artabas, dates at 1 1/2 artabas, and wool at from 2 to 2 1/2 'measures' per tetradrachm. This traditional method of pricing, used for instance in the Achaemenid to Hellenistic-period astronomical tablets of Babylonia, was often used to cope with an absence of small denominations, but at Tebtunis was apparently used to avoid payments which mixed tetradrachms and copper obols.[53] Wine is the only significant good which was priced and sold either in drachmas (13 cases) or obols (18 cases) or even both (2 cases) for the simple reason that its quality was particularly variable and its measure for sale, the clay amphora, was inflexible. The attested wine prices range from 14 to 24 ob. per jar, with 3 and 6 dr. as the most common prices (9 and 6 cases), neither suited to payment in tetradrachms. Seven times Kronion paid 18 ob. per jar, clearly intended as the copper equivalent for the price of 3 dr. which he paid in silver twice. Turnips too were purchased once for 6 ob. and once for 12 ob., clearly meant as 1 and 2 dr. (it seems a tetradrachm's worth of turnips would have been too much of a good thing), although sellers of vegetables (*lachanos*) in quantity regularly received, and

52 There is not space here to publish my full analysis of prices, which will follow elsewhere. Meanwhile for wheat and wine prices see Rathbone 1997, 217 and 224.

53 Its use seems to have faded in Roman Egypt by the later first century, I suspect because private credit arrangements had in the meantime become widespread.

had presumably insisted on, payment of one silver drachma. New rolls of papyrus were all, or almost all, sold for silver; the few payments in obols were probably for recycled rolls or scraps.[54]

A clear link between coin use and economic status emerges. The government, its officials and agents (like Kronion) and wealthier individuals in a private capacity (Kronion again) operated primarily on the silver standard. They used it to price their charges, for which there was little or no competition (Kronion had paid for the notarial concession), and exacted a premium (28:1 to 30:1) on payments to them in copper obols. The poor, when selling their labour or goods in small quantities, used the copper coins at face value, and had to accept payment on the 24:1 ratio. The monetised economy of Roman Egypt, if we include taxation, sales of property and so on, was almost entirely a silver-standard economy, using the Alexandrian tetradrachm. Indeed it seems there was little overlap between transactions in tetradrachms and transactions in copper coins; the copper obols did not in practice function as small change for the silver coins, but as a separate and somewhat marginal system. Combining the results of my analysis of Kronion's fees and his private and common expenditure (with official items stripped out) the consistent picture is that, at the everyday local level, copper coins were used for some 70–80% of transactions in number which made up around 20–30% (from 17% to 36%) of all transactions by value, while silver coins were used for 20–30% of transactions in number and around 70–80% by value. If we make a guesstimate for Roman Egypt as a whole, including tax payments, official salaries, purchases of property, and so on, it is clear that a minute percentage by value, probably well under 1%, of monetised transactions will have been effected in copper coins. It is rare in the ancient world to be able to document and quantify coin use so precisely (I compare Pompeii in my conclusions below), and while the low importance of copper coins by value is not unexpected, the scale of their overall economic insignificance is a surprise. The impact of copper coins, however, should not be underestimated. Even if they were not minted regularly or in great quantity, they probably had a high velocity of circulation. Men like Kronion were keener to spend than to receive them; for everyone copper coins were best used for petty purchases, rather than saved to buy higher-cost items – including tetradrachms, which were the medium for storage of wealth. Without copper coins villagers would have had to barter, or trade and work on credit, with associated risks of dependency. The copper coins sufficed to monetise the rural economy from the bottom up, and gave even the poor an entrance to, and some independence within, the monetised economy.

Returning to the nature of the market in Tebtunis in the AD 40s, Kronion's accounts of expenditure show that the more expensive goods and those bought in quantity were subject to fluctuations in price which imply the operation of a free

54 Papyrus prices are listed by Boak, *P.Mich.* II p. 98. Note that in two payments the odd obol was the price of the ink also purchased.

local market. The only fixed price is the 4 dr. charged for a new roll of papyrus, whose sale may have been a state-controlled concession. One drachma was often charged for vegetables, but probably the quantity varied in a rough way Kronion did not bother to record. The price of wool varied between 1.6 and 2 dr. per 'measure'. Across six days in September 45 lentils bought from the same family (see below) cost 3 then 4 then 3.08 dr. per artaba. The price of wheat rose dramatically from 4.36 dr. per artaba on 7 September 45 to 5.71 dr. on 21 September, and then 8 dr. from 24 September into December. Other evidence suggests that the inundation that autumn, whose level was just then becoming apparent, was weak, indicating a poor harvest in summer 46, to which these price rises were a rational response. Wine cost around 2.5 dr. a jar in September 45, around 3 dr. from October 45 to January 46, and had risen to 6 dr. by August 46, the month of the vintage, which seems to mirror the expected seasonal pattern of supply; on 1 September 46 old wine was still selling at 6 dr. a jar, but new wine (fizzy grape juice?) at 3 dr. It would help if we had other contemporary archives with similar data to compare, but we have only a few prices from Nemesion's account of AD 46/7 from the east side of the Fayyum. For what it is worth, he bought wine apparently at prices, again in both drachmas and obols, ranging from 8 ob. (perhaps an error) or 3 2/3 dr. to 7 dr. a jar, wheat once at 6 dr. an artaba, a skate for 3 dr. (Kronion once paid 4 dr.), and vegetables and beer for dinner for 4 ob. (against Kronion's 2 to 3.5 ob.).[55] Allowing for the uncertain quantities and different year, this suggests that the Tebtunis prices represent the operation of at least a regional market.

Kronion's accounts also reveal something about who sold goods, and where, in Tebtunis. In general a wide variety of craftsmen and specialist traders are attested in the Fayyum villages of the first and second centuries AD.[56] Here, however, we can try to resist the ancient historian's vice of lumping together evidence from different places and times. Unfortunately Kronion's account of common expenditure only names the people through whom he purchased papyrus; his private account too does not name the sellers of the takeaway foodstuffs he frequently bought, but most sellers of more valuable goods are named.[57] Before looking at the named sellers, I start with the takeaway foodstuffs, for which Kronion's meticulous noting of purchases as of separate or combined items permits some interesting observations. There seems to have been a choice of stalls selling prepared meals or snacks based on combinations of cooked meat, local fish, loaves and pan-baked breads, a variety of vegetables (mostly just called 'vegetables'), oil as relish and beer. Beer-shops and stands selling cooked meat and fish were all separate, but

55 *SB* XX 14576.18, 55, 247, 546–547, 549 (wine); 34 (wheat); 30 (skate); 48 (dinner).

56 Ruffing 2008, Teil 1, 313–357, lists those attested at Ptolemais Euergetis, the nome capital, and the villages of Soknopaiou Nesos and Philadelphia.

57 A name in the dative could represent the seller or the person for whom Kronion bought the item. Most, whether at the start or in the middle of the entry, clearly denote the seller. The few probable exceptions include the payments of wine in 127.i.8 and 27 presumably 'for' rather than 'to' officials whom Kronion was entertaining.

sold the other items as well; there were probably other sellers of bread, vegetables and oil. Wine, it seems, was only sold in jars, and hence not from these stalls.

The picture for the named sellers is mixed. Kronion once bought wheat from the (anonymous) grain-dealers at the granaries, his only village purchase recorded as from a specialist dealer, and once from Onnophris the granary-guard; but Onnophris was a friend, and the other sellers included an Aphrodisios twice and Marsisouchos a priest.[58] The *grapheion* archive as a whole attests by title specialist grain-dealers, vegetable-sellers, salt-sellers, wool-sellers, and beer-brewers and beer-shops in Tebtunis, but Kronion did not have cause to give the profession of the sellers he named in his accounts.[59] His five purchases of wool, for instance, were from different people, but two probably, including Orsenouphis son of Tabas, and maybe all five, were textile workers.[60] Curiously only two sellers of wine are named, a man from a neighbouring village and Tenesrois daughter of Apias, the only identifiable woman seller in Kronion's accounts.[61] Pehaps the other sellers were not named because they were regular wine-dealers. Sometimes Kronion seems to have used friends or people with whom he had other dealings as intermediaries. He purchased his expensive skate from Orsenouphis the cloth-beater, and a jar of oil 'through' Tabas, another cloth-beater, who are probably to be linked to the Orsenouphis son of Tabas who sold wool to Kronion.[62] On 11, 13 and 16 September 45 Kronion bought an artaba plus of lentils each from Chrates, Eutuchos son of Takolleeinis and Eutuchos son of Chrates: other references suggest the three all belonged to the same wealthy family, and had other business with Kronion.[63] New papyrus rolls, incidentally, were bought in Ptolemais Euergetis, as Boak noted, often through intermediaries who had other cause to visit the *mêtropolis*; one entry specifies 'through Eutuchas to go to the merchant (*emporos*)', probably a state concessionaire.[64] Detailed prosopographical work is difficult because many names were very common, but would probably confirm that Kronion dealt with a mixture of specialised traders and individuals making casual sales, some but not all on a regular basis.

As to where selling and buying took place in Tebtunis, the only direct evidence is that the specialist grain-sellers operated at the granaries. There is no documen-

58 Grain-dealers and Onnophris: 127.i.13–16; Aphrodisios: 127.i.14, 17; Marsisouchos: 127.i.8.

59 *Sitokapêloi*: 127.i.15. *Lachanopôlai*: 123 recto.xxi.3, verso.vi.28. *Halopôlai*: 123 recto.vii.27, xxi.40, xxii.27; 128.iii.10, *P.Mich.* V 240.31, 245. *Eriopôlai*:123 recto.vi.25, 124 recto.ii.15. *Zutopoioi*: 123 recto.i(d).8, xv.14, verso. xi.27 (at Tristomos?); *zutopôleia*: 123 verso.ii(a).4, vi.21, *P.Mich.* V 322b (temple concession), 326.62.

60 Orsenouphis son of Belphis: 127.ii.2, 4 (labour charge). Orsenouphis son of Tabas: 127.ii.11. Papontos son of Marames: 127.i.18. Pnesis: 127.ii.46. Kronion son of Belles: 127.iii.15; cf. *P.Mich.* V 247.9, a Kronion son of Pabelles in an association (of textile workers?).

61 Posis from Theogonis: 127.i.21; Tenesrois (possibly Kronion's sister?): 127.ii.42.

62 127.ii.32 (fish), ii.41 (oil).

63 Purchases: 127.i.9–11. Other references include 123 recto.viii.40; 127.iii.3; *P.Mich.* V 343. The two Eutuchoi may have been half-brothers.

64 See above. Merchant: 123 verso.iii.23.

tary or archaeological evidence for an agora or colonnaded streets at Tebtunis. Craftsmen needed workshops, but probably many of them and most dealers ran their businesses from their homes.[65] Much selling apparently took place on and around the broad processional ways (*dromoi*) which extended from most temples, especially the recently expanded *dromos* of the temple of Soknebtunis, and even inside the temple compounds. The *insula* immediately west of the north end of the main *dromos* was identified by its excavators as a large covered market fronted by four lock-up shops, built in the second century AD (long after Kronion's day), but the identification is questionable; to the east just beyond the *dromos* was a fullery.[66] At least one beer-shop was a temple concession. Six times in the common account Kronion specifies that he bought wine or beer on the *dromos*, once even 'inside the gates'.[67] Three times in September and October 45 he and friends bought wine and partied in the *komastêrion tês anabaseôs*, a building used to prepare religious processions, and on 8 February 46 they partied in the shrine of Zeus-Serapis and on 24 May in the shrine of Nemesis (risking hangovers?).[68] These parties may have been connected with religious festivals, but temples and their avenues seem to have been the economic as well as the social and cultural centres of Egyptian villages and, to some extent, towns.[69]

One final point concerns dining, or drinking. Several times a month Kronion entertained friends apparently at home, and presumably he dined out reciprocally. A particularly grand party on 31 July 46 to host the visiting sales-tax official (*enkukliakos*) is implied by Kronion's purchase, on the common account, of a Nile perch, 19 bolti (tilapia), eggs, oil, 13 loaves, a drachma's worth of figs, gourds, nuts and three jars of wine.[70] It is clear these parties were sometimes organised by a group, almost certainly the association (*sunodos*) of the god, or of Harpokrates, to which Kronion apparently belonged.[71] In the Roman period these associations, a long-standing tradition, seem to have increased in number and become more job-specific. A visible sign of their success is the several new dining-rooms (*deipnêtê-*

65 *P.Mich.* V 245 reveals that all gypsum supplies had to be deposited in the house of the member of the salt-sellers' association who held the sub-monopoly for gypsum.

66 Gallazzi 1989, 187–188, with *CdE* 9, 1934, 269; 10, 1935, 281–282. I suspect the supposed 'khan' may instead have been the headquarters of some group of officials. Karanis, the best excavated Fayyum village, has no obvious market-buildings or rows of shops.

67 123 recto.i(d).4–5, 18–19, verso.vi.22, 33–34 (with viii.10–13), xi.26, misc(c).5.

68 *Komastêrion*: 123 recto.i(a).20–21, i(c).4–5, i(d).11–13. Diserapieion: 123 verso.iii.7. Nemesieion: 123 verso.vi.14.

69 Compare the major market at the Serapeum in Oxyrhynchus (*SB* XVI 12695, *P.Köln* V 611) and, although they are much later, the *topos*/'pitch'- reservations of merchants inscribed next to the shrine entrance of the north temple at Karanis (*I.Fay.* I 95 and 96, pl. 73).

70 123 verso.vii.19–30 (the last item is uncertainly read).

71 127.i.20, ii.13, 33: payments of 4 dr., 10 ob. and 4 dr. to Patron the annual president of the association of the god; 127.i.30: purchase of two jars of wine for the association of Harpokrates.

ria) built along the *dromoi* of Tebtunis.[72] In the *grapheion* archive itself, the following associations are attested: of the priests, of the farmers of crown land, of the exempt of the imperial estate (or the farmers of Germanicus), of the shepherds, of the sheep-and-donkey-feeders, of the builders, of the weavers, of the cloth-beaters, of the wool-sellers, of the salt-sellers, of Harpokrates (or of the god) – perhaps for people with unique or rare jobs like Kronion, and some others whose titles are not given or missing. Many adult males must have belonged to one or another association. The associations provided regular business for Kronion: every year they renewed and registered their rules of association with a list of current members, and they dealt collectively with others through written contracts and other documents. The role of such associations in the Roman world, or rather in its cities where the evidence is richest, has been much discussed: reacting against the old idea that they were like mediaeval guilds, recent scholarship has put the stress on their social and religious roles.[73] The Tebtunis evidence shows that associations could be numerous in villages too, and that their role was economic as well as social. The weavers of Tebtunis, for instance, dealt collectively with an inspector (*epistates*) overseeing their craft; the animal-feeders made two contracts with the imperial tenants, one over access to water; the imperial tenants bound themselves to lend 100 dr. to rescue a member from seizure for debt; the association of salt-sellers specified the division of village-markets between them, a minimum price they would all charge and a cap to the amount they would sell to independent dealers.[74] These associations, with the partial exception of the salt-sellers, did not hold monopolies, but they probably had a considerable impact on patterns of economic behaviour by enhancing their members' confidence as independent economic actors.

All in all Kronion's accounts reveal a complex and vibrant market for everyday transactions in Tebtunis in the AD 40s. It is not a complete picture: we must await the results of Dr Langellotti's project to analyse the numerous bigger transactions attested in the copies and summaries of the contracts Kronion registered, including purchases of property of all types, dowries, loans, work agreements and so on. Nevertheless, at this petty level Tebtunis already fits better with a free market model than, say, a 'bazaar' economy. Friendships and associations facilitated dealings, as they always do, but as an occasional modifier to a dominant pattern of spot transactions. The associations, whose presidents were annually elected, were not hierarchic or clientilist organisations; they supported, rather than constrained, the economic activities of individuals. The state did provide significant security, not least in the obligatory registration of all contracts to the benefit of the weaker

72 Boak 1937 discusses the rules of three associations in *P.Mich.* V 243–245 and the Egyptian tradition behind them. See Bastianini – Gallazzi 1991 for an inscription attributing a dining-room to the *sunodos* of Doruphoros (probably a later title of the imperial tenants).

73 Carrié 2002 summarises the trend, and argues against it.

74 Weavers: 123 recto.iii.41, cf. xxi.31. Animal-feeders: 123 recto.iii.40, viii.26. Imperial tenants: *P.Mich.* V 244. Salt-sellers: *P.Mich.* V 245.

party. Crucial economic information, such as the probable harvest yield next summer, was known to all from the inundation, and the constant traffic between Tebtunis and other villages and the *mêtropolis* helps explain the apparent regional consistency of prices. Wider economic integration is harder to investigate (pottery imports would be worth checking), but it was around this time that the wealthier Fayyum inhabitants began to have Roman-style veristic portraits inserted in their mummies, with women sporting the latest imperial look in hairstyle and jewellery.

If Roman Egypt did have one peculiarity, it would seem to be its closed coinage system. However, I think that the implications of Kronion's accounts for monetisation and the working of a bimetallic system have a general importance for the Roman empire. To recap the main points, the silver and copper coinages functioned as separate systems with a limited variable exchange ratio; some 70–80% in number of petty everyday transactions, but 20–30% in value, were effected in copper coins, but in the economy as a whole, allowing for big transactions, silver coins must have accounted for around 99% of all transactions by value. For comparison elsewhere we can only use coin finds, and we have only one snapshot specific to a place and time, that of Pompeii in August AD 79. As analysed by Duncan-Jones, gold, silver and bronze coins make up 2%, 31% and 67% of the recorded Pompeian finds in number, but 61%, 32% and 7% by aggregate face value.[75] Direct comparison is impossible, because the Tebtunis figures are a sample of petty transactions (coins and velocity) while the Pompeii finds (just coins) include savings (especially the gold coins, which Tebtunis did not have). However, even if we assume that bronze coins were minted in greater quantities in Italy and the west than in the eastern provinces, unless we also assume that Pompeians saved in bronze and shopped with large bags of bronze, there is patently a mismatch. The impression given by numismatic catalogues and studies is that copper coins were relatively rare in Egypt, say less than a third of circulating issues.[76] Either this is very wrong, or bronze coins are drastically over-represented in the recorded Pompeian finds; for the latter possibility one simple explanation may be that the many successful fugitives took most of the silver and gold coins in circulation with them. Whatever the case, the Tebtunis figures provide a unique template for testing the plausibility of conclusions about circulation and monetisation from casual coin finds in the Roman empire. As regards bimetallism, in Italy and the west the bronze coins had a set official ratio to the principal silver coin (16 asses per denarius, and there were 25 denarii to the aureus), so maybe in the west copper and silver coins were used together and there was no premium for buying denarii with asses (as distinct from any exchange fee); if so, this will have been a minor transaction cost advantage. In the eastern provinces, however, most bronze coinage was local civic (copper) issues, for which documented Egyptian practice can provide a more directly appli-

75 Duncan-Jones 2003.

76 It is mostly an impression, with the exception of the statistical analysis by Christiansen 1988, I 96–98, 107, of the (low) output of copper coins under Nero; cf. the statement of Gölitzer 2004, 124 that 'relatively numerous' copper coins marked 80 and 40 were minted under Kleopatra VII.

cable model of behaviour. The existence of varying exchange ratios here too has long been noted, as in the Hadrianic(?) edict which allowed the exchange-bankers of Pergamum to buy denarii for a premium of one as (standing for the local copper coinage?) but sell them for a premium of two asses (13%), presumably with the normal exchange fee on top.[77] Scarcity of evidence and the lack of context has made such evidence difficult to interpret. This Tebtunis study shows that it would be worth re-examining the eastern evidence systematically in the context of a new investigation of monetary behaviour attested in the papyri.[78] We need to start with Egypt in order to clarify changes over time which produced different models of behaviour. By the late first century AD, for example, there was a wider range of copper coins and a 'bronze standard' now existed, with its own bronze drachma (the *chalkinê*); by the third century only one copper coin, the bronze drachma, was occasionally minted, private credit arrangements were widespread and everyone used a single monetary system with seven obols to the drachma. Comparable changes in other eastern provinces are to be expected.

77 *OGIS* II 484, = Oliver, *Greek Constitutions* 84.

78 As Gara 1976, 110–132, tried to do.

Bibliography

Bastianini G. – Gallazzi C., Un'iscrizione inedita di Tebtynis e la *synodos* di Dorypho-rus, ZPE 89, 1991, 44–46.

Boak A.E.R., The organization of gilds in Greco-Roman Egypt, TAPhA 68, 1937, 212–220.

Carrié J.-M., Les associations professionelles à l'époque tardive: entre *munus* et convivialité, in: Carrié J.-M. – Lizzi Testa R. (eds.), "Humana sapit": études d'antiquité tardive offertes à Lellia Cracco Ruggini, Turnhout 2002, 309–332.

Christiansen E., The Roman Coins of Alexandria. Quantitative Studies, Aarhus 1988.

Daris S. (ed.), Dizionario dei nomi geografici e topografici dell'Egitto greco-romano, IV.4, Milan 1986.

Drexhage H.-J., Preise, Mieten/Pachten, Kosten und Löhne im römischen Ägypten bis zum Regierungsantritt Diokletians, St. Katharinen 1991.

Duncan-Jones R.P., Roman coin circulation and the cities of Vesuvius, in: Lo Cascio E. (ed.), Credito e moneta nel mondo romano, Bari 2003, 161–180.

Gallazzi C., Fouilles anciennes et nouvelles sur le site de Tebtynis, BIFAO 89, 1989, 179–191.

Gara A., Prosdiagraphomena e circolazione monetaria, Milan 1976.

Gölitzer, E., Entstehung und Entwicklung des alexandrinischen Münzwesens von 30 v. Chr. bis zum Ende der julisch-claudischen Dynastie, Berlin 2004.

Harl K.W., Coinage in the Roman Economy, 300 B.C. to A.D. 700, Baltimore 1996.

Husselman E., Procedures of the record office at Tebtunis in the first century A.D., in: Samuel D.H. (ed.), Proceedings of the Twelfth International Congress of Papyrology, Toronto 1970, 223–238.

Johnson A.C., Roman Egypt to the Reign of Diocletian (Frank T. [ed.], Economic Survey of Ancient Rome, vol. II), Baltimore 1936.

Maresch K., Bronze und Silber. Papyrologische Beiträge zur Geschichte der Währung im ptolemäischen und römischen Ägypten bis zum 2. Jahrhundert n. Chr. (Papyrologica Coloniensia 25), Cologne 1996.

Rathbone D.W., Prices and price-formation in Roman Egypt, in: Andreau J. – Briant P. – Descat R. (eds.), Economie antique. Prix et formation des prix dans les économies antiques, St-Bertrand-de-Comminges 1997, 183–244.

Rowlandson J., Money use among the peasantry of Ptolemaic and Roman Egypt, in: Meadows A. – Shipton K., Money and its Uses in the Ancient Greek World, Oxford 2001, 145–155.

Ruffing K., Die berufliche Spezialisierung in Handel und Handwerk. Untersuchungen zu ihrer Entwicklung und zu ihren Bedingungen in der römischen Kaiserzeit im östlichen Mittelmeerraum auf der Grundlage griechischer Inschriften und Papyri (Pharos 24), Rahden 2008.

Thompson H.W., A Glossary of Greek Fishes, London 1947.

Wallace S.L., Taxation in Egypt from Augustus to Diocletian, Princeton 1938.

West L.C. – Johnson A.C., Currency in Roman and Byzantine Egypt, Princeton 1944.

Amphora Design and Marketing in Antiquity

Nicholas Rauh – Caroline Autret – John Lund

1. Introduction

Along with ancient shipwrecks, transport amphorae represent the most tangible artifact of ancient maritime commerce. Identified use-chronologies have enabled scholars to determine not only the production origins of transshipped amphorae (even if we are less certain of the commodities themselves), but also their distribution patterns, and the approximate volume of trade.

The main aim of the paper is to investigate whether there was a connection between the design of ancient transport amphorae and their marketing from the Hellenistic era through to Late Antiquity. The long time frame was chosen in order to enable us to distinguish differences (if any) in this through time.

The source material for this study is primarily the amphorae themselves and the contexts in which they are found. These are generally useful enough, despite the lack of scholarly agreement about several basic issues, and modern marketing theory may likewise provide helpful clues. Still, the material remains cannot make up for the total absence of written sources on the subject which might have provided an insight into the underlying thought-processes. For these reasons whatever conclusions to emerge from this study necessarily remain preliminary.

Our study will range through a number of related issues beginning with a review of the functional purposes of ancient transport amphorae. We then will examine "case studies" of widely circulating amphorae from the Hellenistic (323–27 BC) and the Late Roman (ca. 300–700 AD) eras. During the course of this discussion we will consider potential insights furnished by marketing researchers regarding the function of packaging and packaging design in modern advertising.

2. The purpose of transport amphorae

Ancient transport amphorae had at least three specific purposes. They were designed to carry quantities of agricultural products, primarily but not exclusively wine, oil, and by the Roman era *garum*. Their contents need not always to have been liquid in form, but the general tendency to convey liquid commodities helps to explain the tall necks and narrow mouths of Greco-Roman transport amphorae. These could be sealed using cloth, wax, and string, or otherwise by plugged with corkwood and clay.[1]

In general a transport amphora was a container designed to be handled, that is, lifted, tipped and poured, by one or two persons.[2] It was often given two handles at

1 See for instance Thomas – Tomber 2006.

2 For Greek amphorae, cf. Koehler 1986, and for the Roman period Lund 2011.

the top to enable lifting and hefting, and a toe-like point at the base to facilitate tipping and pouring (in some instances the toe resembles a third handle *per se*). The form was designed for a specific task, namely, to be filled with a significant volume of contents, sealed to avoid spillage, raised and lowered into cargo ships, transported across the seas, unladed, placed in storage, retrieved, opened, and poured all by one or two workers, if need be. It is important to recognize that function must also have influenced the design. Thick strong handles seem essential to the task of raising and lowering. To withstand the pressure and weight of stacking as high as six layers deep in cargo holds, forms grew progressively taller and narrower by the end of the Hellenistic era.

Implicit in this description is the fact that the transport amphora was a form of "cargo container," designed to be stacked in the holds of ships and shipped to distant markets across the Mediterranean. The fact that they were so easily stored in the holds of ships undoubtedly influenced their morphology. Certainly it was more important that they fit snugly in ship's holds than it was that they stood upright on their own. The transport amphora was otherwise a relatively ungainly form, because it always had to be leaned against something or set in specially designed ring stands. As a container it was likewise inefficient because a high percentage of its total weight when filled was borne by the vessel itself. Nonetheless, the presence of transport amphorae throughout the Greco-Roman archaeological landscape confirms the extent to which the inhabitants of the ancient Mediterranean depended on amphorae for maritime trade, and it does so in a manner unmatched by other archaeological remains. Iconographic evidence shows that amphorae were also distributed over land, but the involved quantities were no doubt far smaller than those of sea-borne transport. Moreover, having fulfilled their primary objective, amphorae were reused as containers for a wide variety of purposes.[3]

Having explained these essential features to the form of the transport amphora itself, we must probe deeper to understand the apparent need for uniformity within amphora types. From early Iron Age examples of the Near East through those of the early Roman Empire, the forms of certain widely transported forms remained remarkably uniform over dozens if not scores of years. When combined with data obtained from excavated archaeological contexts, changes in amphora morphology enable amphora specialists to recognize and to date patterns of seriation for specific forms. Initially we are justified in asking why uniformity should have mattered at all, let alone why it should have mattered to the degree that it obviously did.

To make this argument we will focus on test cases from two eras, the late Hellenistic (200–100 BC) and the Late Roman (ca. 300–700 AD) eras. Particularly from the perspective of amphora morphology the forms of these two eras exhibit

3 Peña 2007; Lawall – Lund (eds.) 2011.

the most contrasting design techniques, thus indicating that the conditions determining amphora design in these two eras were significantly different.

3. Case Study of Standardization: Hellenistic Era Transport Amphorae

To illustrate the tendency toward uniformity within amphora typologies, we will examine four widely circulating Aegean amphorae produced during the Hellenistic era, the Rhodian, the Chian, the Koan, and the Knidian. All four examples were manufactured by craftsmen working at leading commercial states at the height of the Hellenistic era, at a time, that is, when the uniformity of amphora typologies possibly reached its apex.

Rhodian Amphorae (*c.* 85cm tall; 24 litres volume) exhibited widely imitated design features, including tall cylindrical necks, narrow rolled rims, sharply pitched handles, rounded shoulder, tapered bodies, and peg toes (IMAGE 1).[4] As the federated state of Rhodes acquired overseas territory, it extended its production activities to neighboring islands and the opposite mainland, imposing its standards on the design of amphorae produced by neighboring polities such as Knidos and Kos in turn. Because of the multiple production areas, the fabric of Rhodian amphorae tends to vary. Over the course of a century the design of the Rhodian jar was altered repeatedly to arrive at a recognizably "standardized" form. In the early 2nd century BC each handle was stamped prior to firing, with one stamp bearing the name or symbol of a Rhodian magistrate.[5] The most commonly encountered fabric is hard, fine buff-red clay, frequently with a cream surface slip.

Chian amphorae (*c.* 95cm; volume *c.* 20 litres) represent a sustained history of wine production, documented as early as the 6th century BC as the most expensive wine of the Aegean (IMAGE 2). By the Hellenistic era Chian amphorae exhibit a tall, slender, and uniquely designed biconical form. The jar's cylindrical neck is nearly as tall as the lower body is long, and its equally long rolled handles extend from high on the neck to the shoulder. The shoulder is sharply angular with the body then turning sharply inward, tapering to a long 'needle-like' toe at the base. The fabric was fine, hard and darkly red. The form and fabric are so distinctive that Chian remains are relatively easy to distinguish.[6] The amphorae were stamped at an irregular rate, possibly one per so many jars simply to designate the owner or producer of a given batch of jars that was about to be fired along with other batches in a given kiln. In any event, the form was distinctive, so much so that it was exhi-

4 Grace 1979, figs. 22–25; Grace 1934, 214–240; Grace – Savvatianou-Petropoulakou 1970, 289–317; Alpözen *et al.* 1995, 92; Doğer 1992, 87–90; Finkielsztejn 2001, 46–51; Monachov 2006.

5 During the peak period of production these stamps were dated by the month: Grace 1934, 199. Grace argues that the date applied primarily to the stamp itself or its die, which was then a license, valid for a limited period, permitting a manufacturer to sell goods in return for a payment to the government which he in turn collected by raising the price of his commodity to cover the amount. See Finkielsztejn 2001.

6 For an overview of the Chian amphorae, see Demestica 2011, 41–44.

bited as an "emblem" on silver coins produced by state officials of the island "polity" itself (IMAGE 3). [7]

Koan amphorae (*c.* 80cm tall; 45 litres volume; IMAGE 4) resemble Rhodian amphorae in their narrow rolled rims and cylindrical necks.[8] However, their shoulders tend to be broader and their bodies longer. Typically Koan amphorae exhibit an offset ridge that separates the neck from the flaring line of the form's broad shoulder. The body remains fairly broad, curving inward toward the base to form a short thickened toe fashioned with a small projecting basal knob to absorb shock. The fabric is relatively coarse and ranges from tan to red to brown, frequently displaying a pale green surface wash that presumably results from 'seawater slipping'. The unique Koan bifidal handles, small, closely set, double-rolls of clay sharply pitched in imitation of the Rhodian handle, are the most salient features of all Koan amphorae. The bifidal handles remained a characteristic trait of imitative Koan (Koan styled or pseudo-Koan) amphorae throughout the Mediterranean during the early Roman Empire. Like Chian jars, Koan jars were irregularly stamped, possibly one jar per batch as suggested, and some of the later stamps appear in Latin, indicating gradual acquisition of the island's wine production by Italians.[9] Like Chian jars, however, Koan amphora stamps employed "emblems" such as the crab and the club (of Herakles?) that appear as well on Koan coins and thus bore likely municipal significance.[10]

Like Koan jars Knidian amphorae (*c.* 90cm tall; 39 litres capacity) tend to resemble the Rhodian model in many respects,[11] but they display a characteristic, finely molded "ring toe", or ring of clay just above the pointed tip of the toe. Like the Chian jar the clay has a hard, relatively fine red fabric. Stamped handles bearing the names of Knidian magistrates occur during the 2nd century BC, when Knidos was influenced, if not politically dominated by Rhodes.[12] Many stamps also bear emblems such as the bucranion (IMAGE 5), the ship's prow, or the trident, which like the other emblems we have discussed possibly bore municipal

7 The Chian seal of the sphinx likewise appears on both coins and amphora stamps: Grace 1979, figs. 48–49; Zemer 1977, 37, no. 31; Doğer 1992, 86, type 6. Alpözen *et al.* 1995, 82–5; Lawall 2004, 247 note 18. For Chian luxury wines, see as well Salviat 1986, 160 f.; Tchernia 1986, 33, 64, 100–4.

8 Grace – Savvatianou-Petropoulakou 1970, 363–4; Grace 1979, figs. 6–60; Alpözen et al. 1995, 97; Doğer 1992, 95; Zemer 1977, 43, no. 35 is a late 3rd /early 2nd century version.

9 Finds at Delos suggest as little as 5% of Koan jars were stamped: Empereur 1982, 233; Sherwin White 1978, 240; Höghammar 1993, 35.

10 Grace 1979, no. 59; see further Γιαννικουρή *et al.* 2011.

11 For example, the handle is arched but not pitched. See Grace 1934, 240–275; Grace – Savvatianou-Petropoulakou 1970, 317–353; Doğer 1992, 91–5; Alpözen *et al.* 1995, 86–91 and Koehler 2004.

12 Knidian nomenclature is not as well recorded as Rhodian, and a period of stamps naming *phrourarchoi* has generated considerable disagreement among scholars. See Grace – Savvatianou-Petropoulakou 1970, 318; Fraser & Bean 1954, 93–4.

significance. However, Knidian amphora stamping became intermittent about the time that Knidos seceded from Rhodian hegemony in 166 BC.[13]

Generally speaking, the Rhodian, Chian, Koan and Knidan amphorae had fairly standardized forms in the first part of the Hellenistic period (broad jars, widest at the shoulder). However, the jars of the late 2nd – early 1st centuries BC were slimmer and more streamlined. This change in morphology has been interpreted by Virginia Grace, for example, as evidence that amphora producers adapted from the volumetric standards of early Hellenistic Rhodes to those in use at Delos during the "second" period of Athenian domination (146–86 BC), when the importance of the Athenian (and Roman) emporium at that island increased.[14] Another possible reason for this change concerns the already mentioned point that the jars were being loaded and stacked into increasingly larger cargo vessels and that the more slender forms facilitated denser "packing" in some manner. The fact that these changes, for whatever reason, occurred contemporaneously across typologies suggests at the very least that universal adaptations like this did not occur by chance, nor were they made for aesthetic reasons alone.

Other attributes reveal additional common traits among Hellenistic era typologies, including uniformity of container capacities, and a common use of amphora stamps and *tituli picti*. Uniformity in amphora forms or more specifically the uniformity of container capacity probably helped merchants and officials to identify the volume (or quantity) of a given commodity being shipped in a given jar for commercial and / or fiscal purposes. Recent experiments have indicated that while the volumes of specific amphora types are not exactly uniform, their capacities were close enough to demonstrate that genuine and sustained efforts to achieve uniformity were made within each type[15] Consistency in volume capacity is probably the chief explanation for the standardization of amphora types. Since the contents of any given jar were not intended to be opened or sampled until time of use (especially jars filled with perishable commodities such as wine, oil, or *garum*), a merchant could remain justifiably anxious about the quantity (volume) of a given commodity being borne by a specific form until such time as the jar's contents could be opened and measured. *Sekomata*, or large hollowed-out stone measuring devices that survive at Delos (IMAGE 6), demonstrate the way this was probably facilitated. The contents of a given jar would be emptied into a long trough-like basin of officially sanctioned measurement. Potential purchasers could then sample the product to judge its worth and calculate to a reasonable degree the amount of the commodity that was contained in the jar. Based on the number of jars available for purchase in the vendor's consignment (jars either stored on ship or at

13 Frequently encountered Knidian stamped emblems include the *bucranion*, or facing head of a bull, the *caduceus*, the trident, the ivy leaf, the ship's prow, the anchor, the double axe, and the club of Herakles.

14 Grace 1949, 183 n. 35; Grace 1965: 10; Sherwin White 1978: 236–41; Höghammar 1993, 35; cf. Rauh 2000. This point has never been demonstrated by volume studies however.

15 See Matheson – Wallace 1981 and Wallace 2004.

a nearby warehouse), interested merchants could then tender bids to purchase the shipment in an auction format.[16]

Accordingly, uniformity in amphora morphology was probably intended first and foremost as a means of guaranteeing uniform volumes of the commodities being exchanged. The standardization of amphora forms accelerated the pace of commerce in a circulating commodity and made it more convenient and more reliable. As noted earlier, the evolution of Hellenistic Aegean amphora forms from those with broad shoulders and squat bodies of the early 3rd century BC, to the taller, more slender forms of the late 2nd century BC has been pointed to as evidence of a widespread shift in volumetric standards from those used at Rhodes to those at Delos (146–86 BC). As noted earlier, it may equally have resulted from the need to withstand the weight of increased stacking in cargo packing. Regardless of the precise reason, the fact that all forms were turned by hand and constructed in sections by individual artisans working simultaneously at one or more kiln production centers needs to be emphasized. Insofar as internationally traded jars were concerned, numerous kiln sites were typically active in the production of a given form.[17] Naturally, "uniformity" remained an approximate achievement in the production of these jars, with considerable variation in the measured volume capacities of the forms in question.[18] In view of the hand-produced character of these jars, the degree of uniformity that existed within any given form seems remarkable, nonetheless. This, in turn, reinforces the argument that the design of these containers was intended as much for commercial purposes as it was for storage or for the conveying goods to market.

In addition, as we have noted, during the 3rd and 2nd centuries BC Hellenistic Greek amphorae in particular displayed a heavy usage of amphora stamps, particularly stamps applied by municipal magistrates (IMAGE 7). We cannot be sure that stamps fulfilled the same role everywhere, but the application of such names suggests that amphora stamping fulfilled some important role – probably in municipal fiscal policy.[19] The rationale behind the stamping of Rhodian amphorae is a thorny issue,[20] but stamps such as those set on the jars by magistrates at Rhodes and Knidos presumably indicate that prior to packing and shipping the "producer" of the amphora was required to show proof that he had paid the necessary fees and taxes for the commodity in question. A magistrate or his "agent" presumably applied his stamp to a "batch" of jars to verify that this was so. The fact that stamping occurred prior to firing demonstrates that the procedures required to obtain a shipment of surplus agricultural goods for export purposes were potentially elabo-

16 This obviously assumes that the process was conducted in a wholesale manner, as indicated by the discovery of the *sekomata* in warehouses in the Delian harbor.

17 More than twenty kiln sites for Rhodian amphorae have been identified on the island of Rhodes itself (Rauh 2003, 71).

18 See sources in note 16 above.

19 Garlan 2000, 154–156; Muller 2011, 191.

20 Cf. Garlan 2000, 153–72; Lawall 2005, 194–96; Garlan 2006, and Finkielsztejn 2006.

rate. We cannot be sure about the modalities involved,[21] but a possible hypothesis suggests that the "entrepreneur" who assumed this task, presumably a merchant, first had to obtain the rights to a given vintage (assuming that the merchant himself was not the proprietor); he then had to order the production of the necessary number of amphorae to bottle and ship the vintage. He then had to pay the required fees and taxes to export the vintage as well as obtain proof of payment by having the local magistrate charged with this responsibility (or one of his agents) apply his stamp to the unfinished transport jars. Again, all this had to be accomplished prior to the firing of his "batch" of amphorae, let alone to the "bottling", lading, and shipment of the cargo itself. The stamps of municipal magistrates thus demonstrate a remarkable degree of integration between commercial and municipal activities.

Stamps representing non-magistrates likewise occur frequently on the jars: in most instances the names and symbols that survive presumably identified the artisans who manufactured the jars (and who applied their stamp to indicate which of the jars about to be fired in a given kiln belonged to their batches as opposed to others). Most stamps found on jars manufactured in Hellenistic or Late Republican Italy, for example, appear to bear the names of slave and freed-person artisans who were directly engaged in production. However, other names, particularly those found in Rhodian amphora stamps, indicate the activity of freeborn entrepreneurs alternately identified as the proprietor of the amphora production center, the vintner of the wine itself (who may have been the proprietor of the vineyard, the kiln site, and the merchant vessel), or the merchant who purchased and bottled the wine intended for export.[22] Analysis of Dressel 1 amphorae stamps produced by the Sestius family at Cosa reveal, meanwhile, the names and "signet marks" of numerous artisans engaged in their production, as well as those of additional professionals engaged in the bottling process.[23] For example, the names of freeborn entrepreneurs, such as C. Statius shown in IMAGE 8, occur on stamped clay lids used to seal amphorae once they were filled. Much like Rhodian stamps these quite possibly belonged to the merchants who purchased the vintage for export purposes, and thus distinguishes their activity from that of the persons stamped on the amphorae themselves. Although Italian amphorae of the Republican era were not stamped as consistently as their Rhodian or Knidian counterparts[24], Italian marketers probably relied more extensively on *tituli picti*, or graffiti-like labels etched on the jars, to indicate various phenomena such as ownership, the payment

21 Lawall 2011, 38–40 for a broad discussion.

22 For Rhodes see Finkielsztejn 2001, 34; Badoud – Dana forthcoming and Palaczyk forthcoming.

23 For the stamps, see in particular Benoit 1961, 42 f.; for an example of the interrelationships between stamped jars and lids, D'Arms 1981, 46–71.

24 And therefore possibly reflect production procedures such as "batching" more than they do fiscal policies.

of taxes and fees, the date of the vintage (IMAGE 9), or the labeling of contents.[25] Much like the methodical amphora stamping of Hellenistic Aegean transport amphorae, in other words, the numerous marks employed by the Sestius firm and the heavy reliance on *tituli picti* elsewhere in Italy offer yet another example of the complexity of the operations that undoubtedly transpired in the production, storage, shipment, and marketing of surplus agricultural commodities in the wider Mediterranean during the Hellenistic / Roman Republican era. By the Late Roman period, however, very few transport amphorae were stamped.[26]

Given the degree to which the surviving remains of transport amphorae demonstrate the implementation of methodical production procedures, the effort required to produce jars of consistently uniform appearance and volume – and to do so at multiple production centers sometimes located at considerable distance from one another – appears to have been painstaking. The central role played by the transport amphorae in the marketplace caused them to be viewed as recognized units of measurement and to be used as such by municipal authorities in ancient Mediterranean polities (Moore 2010, 103). The question remains their likely role in advertising. It has long been suspected, for example, that the uniformity of shapes and volumes within amphora typologies served to advertise the jar's contents to consumers in overseas markets, in other words, that the unique design of internationally traded amphorae served as symbols or "visual cues" for their contents.[27] It is fair to ask therefore to what degree the uniform production of transport amphorae reflected ancient advertising practices known as today as "branding."[28]

4. Evidence of Branding as a Marketing Strategy in the Hellenistic Transport Amphorae

Market branding represents a recent development of the past two centuries. As commercial networks became more distant and merchandising more impersonal manufacturers worked to devise ways to distinguish their product from those of

25 See, for example, Lang 1976; Rodríguez Almeida 1985; Rodríguez Almeida 1989; Zevi 1966; Tchernia 1986, 322–341; Will 2001b; Moore 2010, 102–3. Since *tituli picti* tend not to survive well in the archaeological record, our awareness of their use is limited. Names of families ranked in the Roman senatorial aristocracy (such as the Sestii) appear on amphora stamps with increasing frequency during the last century of the Republic. These stamps seem to indicate that members of leading Roman families in Italy engaged in large scale commerce in agricultural produce for export purposes: Will 1979; Will 2001a; D'Arms 1981, 48–71; Tchernia 1986, 116–118.193.

26 See however, Diamanti 2010 and 2012.

27 See Lawall 2004, 248–249; Moore 2010, 101; either the shape was dictated by popular aesthetics or it indicated that the jar bore Koan type wine (the contents dictates shape theory). See Moore 2010, n. 65, for additional references.

28 Sacharow 1982, 118. According to the Encyclopedia Britannica a trademark is defined as, "Any word, name, symbol, device, or any combination of these adopted and used by a manufacturer or merchant to identify his goods and distinguish them from those of others. It is a brand name used on goods moving in the channels of trade."

their competitors.[29] They increasingly focused on package design as the means to achieve this end. In one respect, modern package design represents a transition from pre-industrial commercial practices that operated at the level of "provisions merchants" to that of an anonymous, long distance market.[30] In another respect, uniform packaging represented the emergence of an "economy of abundance". In other words, modern marketing specialists increasingly focused on the role of packaging as a visual cue to distinguish a given product from an array of competitors.

As a modern form of advertising, product branding requires not only the deliberate invention of an advertising strategy on the part of the vendor but also a deliberately induced recognition of the uniqueness of the vendor's product in the eye of the consumer. Louis Cheskin, a pioneer in consumer motivation research during the 1950s, noted (1959, 41) that "decision making in a marketing program is frequently and crucially in the area of communication, in finding an effective means of persuading potential consumers to buy the particular product or brand".[31] Advertising specialists identify five principal components to "brand development": the product, the package, the price, the advertising strategy, and the creation of a consumer relationship.[32] A "branded" product naturally has to exhibit quality to earn its initial reputation, while the price has to reflect the product's worth in a reasonable manner. An advertising strategy helps to publicize the product's significance and availability as well as to sustain its reputation in the public mind. Once the consumer acquires sufficient confidence and faith in (if not dependence on) a product to purchase it repeatedly, he develops an anonymous relationship with that product that becomes ingrained in his consciousness for a potentially long period of time.

All marketing specialists agree that the package ranks second only to the product itself in advertising importance. The package contributes to the marketing success of a product in two ways: in its ability to sell the product and its ability to contain the product for a satisfactory shelf-life. The most effective package is one that successfully functions as a symbol for the product it contains. The package is supposed to communicate the significance of the product and to motivate the consumer to purchase it. As Cheskin (1959, 56) observed, "It represents the product. It is a visual image of the product, it is the symbol. The consumer does not judge the product, he judges the package. The package tells the shopper whether the product is of high quality, whether it is the kind of product he wants or does not

29 Sacharow 1982, 1. Trademarks were used as early as 1780s but the Smith Brothers actually pioneered the concept in 1866.

30 Calver 2004, 6, in "provision marketing" consumers would purchase quantities of a given commodity such as salt or sugar measured out and poured into sacks or nondescript containers by a general store merchant.

31 Kahn – Deng 2009, 259. Marketing researchers study the role of packaging in the formation of consumer inferences and how these inferences can affect consumption behavior and judgment.

32 Cheskin 1959, 56; Sacharow 1982, 118. Encyclopedia Britannica defines a trademark as "any word, name, symbol, device, or any combination of these adopted and used by a manufacturer or merchant to identify his goods and distinguish them from those of others."

want". The explanation for this assertion, an assertion universally recognized by marketing specialists,[33] lies in a consumer reaction identified by Cheskin (1959, 73) as "sensation transference". Sensation transference is the tendency of the consumer to associate the quality of a product with the attractiveness of its packaging. Marketing specialists believe that consumers initially react to the image of the product when they know very little about the product itself.[34] In an anonymous marketplace in which competing products are displayed, a consumer's decision to purchase one product or brand versus another is often determined by the package. "If the label symbolizes high quality, consumers assume that the product is of high quality. If the label (design or color) symbolizes low quality, consumers transfer the "low quality" effect of the label to the product itself (Cheskin 1959, 73)". Determining the reasons why consumers find some packaging designs attractive and others unattractive lies at the heart of "motivation research".

Modern motivation research applies methods derived from sociology, psychology, optics, and art design to investigate the power of visual cues. Researchers typically study the reactions of hundreds of subjects to the design of a product's packaging. They not only query consumers' reasons for selecting one packaging design over another, but they also investigate the subliminal reasons for the consumer's preference by studying subjects' eye movements and the tendency of a subject's eye to linger over certain areas of the package as opposed to others (and for how long). More recently, marketing researchers have added analysis of neural activation, the tendency of certain areas of the brain to react or "light up" when exposed to particularly pleasing stimuli displayed in the packaging.[35] By focusing on the subliminal determinants of visual aesthetics they identify the manner in which the human eye translates visual input (visual cues) into information that it believes to be veridical (Greenleaf – Raghubir 2008; Raghubir 2009).

As a result specialists have learned that the human eye is naturally attracted to specific colors, shapes, sizes, and designs in a product's packaging. Small details

33 Calver 2004, 44: "The packaging becomes a manifestation of the brand itself and because a brand is more than just the product itself the packaging becomes a compound of consumer' perceptions, memories, and feelings. In effect, a brand becomes a compound of tangible and intangible values, the latter being formed in the consumers' minds." Cf. Sacharow 1985, 102.

34 Sacharow 1982, 112, motivational researchers believe that the average consumer sees the package only as a representation of the product at the point of sale. The consumer is not conscious of the fact that he or she is influenced by the package, or that he or she transfers the sensation, the imagery, or the color to the product. Cheskin uses the term sensation transference to denote the transfer of a consumer's feelings from the package to the product. Motivational research testing has demonstrated that consumers also associate certain patterns, colors, names, symbols in a negative manner, something researchers refer to as "element isolation" (Sacharow 1982, 113).

35 Raghubir 2008, 207, eye-tracking is used as a mechanism to examine the level and focus of attention, and functional magnetic resonance imaging (fMRI) brain scans to assess the level and areas of neural activation. According to Kahn – Deng 2009, 265, studies of ocular dominance suggest that visual input from the dominant eye affects the process of visual information. Research indicates that 65% of the population is right-eye dominant, 32% left-eye dominant, and 3% ambiocular.

such as the type, shape, and placement of an icon, the character, size, and placement of the font labeling, or the background color of the label all furnish significant visual cues to the consumer, stimuli capable of communicating subliminal messages of "quality" or "attractiveness".[36] As Cheskin observed (1959, 73), "consciously we assign no importance to symbols, but unconsciously we are deeply affected by them. The psychological powers of basic shapes, images, and colors are difficult for most people to comprehend fully, because these powers operate in the realm of the subconscious". Modern advertising specialists believe that consumers are unknowingly stimulated by aesthetic qualities of packaging to make purchasing decisions. Product marketers carefully craft visual cues in their packaging to attract the eye of the consumer and to distinguish their product from competitors in an "economy of abundance".[37]

Armed with this information the question remains whether it is possible to identify similar strains of purposefully crafted design features in ancient transport amphorae, that is, features that impart visual aesthetics capable of inducing "sensation transference" to the product. We need briefly to revisit the design features of Hellenistic transport amphorae to determine whether we can identify likely sources of aesthetically attractive qualities to the amphorae in question, including the treatment of such packaging features as shape, color, and labeling.

Insofar as amphora morphology is concerned, recent analysis of sensation transference has concentrated on several types of visual cues related to package shape (Raghubir 2009, 206). These include forms crafted for their geometry (including complexity, curvature, and congruence), completeness, color, tone, texture, strength, size, light, and valence. Geometry or the shape of the package seems particularly relevant to the issue of amphora design. To be "uniform" Greenleaf and Raghubir (2008) classify geometric properties according to four characteristics: their complexity (including their dimensionality, form, regularity, and clutter), their curvature (including their circularity, angularity, and convergence), their congruence (including their symmetry, stability, and centrality), and their completeness (amount of information and the synthesis of this information). One such cue, congruity, encompasses the extent to which a shape is rotationally sym-

36 The use of color has been shown to play a significant role in labeling. Cheskin's laboratory in California was known as the Color Research Institute. Blue has been found to be the most popular color, except for packaging of meat where consumers prefer the color red: Cheskin 1959, 121. Package designers experimenting with larger details such as the size and shape of the package have determined that rectangular and oval shapes with a length to width ratio of 1:1.618 (referred to as "phi") are more appealing: Greenleaf – Raghubir 2008, 115.

37 Invariably the subjects are presented with three or more package designs each bearing precisely the same product and are asked to determine which product is superior. Unaware that they are sampling the same product in each package, most subjects will identify one product as superior to the others based entirely on their reaction to the packaging design. Cheskin's most compelling example is that of dog food labels, since none of the human subjects were actually asked to sample the product. Test subjects, nonetheless, insisted on the superior quality of one labeled example over the others based entirely on their reaction to the design of package.

metric (e.g., a square or a circle) versus asymmetric (e.g., rectangles or ovals with a length-width ratio of 1:1.618 or phi). Symmetry has been shown to affect consumers' attitudes toward two-dimensional products. While one can hardly envision a "survey" of (ancient) consumer responses to the aesthetic qualities of Hellenistic amphora forms, the very fact that we began this paper with the assertion that Hellenistic amphora forms seem more "attractive" than Late Roman forms presupposes a response emitted from aesthetic biases on our part. These biases most likely result from subliminal attraction to the relative success of the symmetry, the curving surfaces, the convergence of lines, the visible center lines, the lack of sharp edges and angles, as well as to the congruence and completeness of design visible in these forms.[38] If placed in a line against the less distinctive regionally and locally circulating amphorae of the Hellenistic era, the internationally traded forms would most likely have stood out for their well crafted forms. It is, therefore, possible to argue that by crafting aesthetically pleasing shipping packages for their products, the designers of these jars engaged intuitively in "sensation transference". Moreover, anecdotal evidence indicates that ancient consumers understood and appreciated the value of aesthetic quality in amphora design. Pliny the Elder (*N.H.* 35.161), recorded, for example, a public competition that occurred during his lifetime at Erythrae to determine the most attractive amphora: the Koan jar won first place with an Italian jar finishing second.[39] This raises the likelihood that the manufacturers of ancient transport amphorae relied intuitively on aesthetic principles of "complexity, congruence, convergence, and completeness" when crafting their forms.[40]

To be certain, not all parallels with modern packaging design are relevant. Differences in technology, packaging materials, and cultural preferences make comparisons difficult from the perspective of color, for example, particularly since the color of most amphorae was determined by the minerals in the clay and beyond the control of the designers. If we pause to reconsider some of the other physical characteristics of Hellenistic transport amphorae, however, certain features raise the potential of having served "double roles" for the purposes of marketing. For example, the combination of magisterial stamps and the uniform design of Hellenistic amphora types become relevant. As noted earlier, these features most probably fulfilled important roles in fiscal management and measurement for purposes

38 Not everyone will agree with our assessment. Cheskin 1959, 224 argued that any time 75% or more of consumer test subjects agree on the design of a given package, this was a successful design.

39 *Erythris in templo hodieque ostenduntur amphorae duae propter tenuitatem consecratae discipuli magistrique certamine, uter tenuiorem humum duceret. Cois ea laus maxima, Hadrianis firmitas, nonnullis circa hoc severitatis quoque exemplis*; cf. Moore 2010, 95.

40 In another example, a passage in Book 11 (784c) of *Athenaios' Deipnosophistai* was until recently thought to imply that the sculptor Lysippos designed a model transport amphora for the Macedonian king, Cassander. Mark Lawall (2004) recently argued, however, that the context of the passage indicates that the vessel in question was a celebratory cup for the king. Be that as it may, the text suggests that "industrial design" was already an issue in Antiquity.

of exchange. However, they may also have served to reassure consumers in a maritime economy of anonymous markets of the genuineness of the product in question, more specifically, famous wines originating from Chios, Kos, Rhodes, or Knidos. Conceivably, the stamp of a Rhodian magistrate possessed the added value of furnishing an imprimatur or official form of guarantee for the "genuineness" of the commodity for sale as expressed by the design of the jar. Unlike *tituli picti*, moreover, the stamps of urban magistrates could not be counterfeited, and in this small but significant manner the very presence of stamps possibly elevated the status of a municipally "branded" commodity by distinguishing it from its competitors. If so, then in at least some instances it is possible to argue that notions of product "branding" existed in the Hellenistic era.[41]

In addition, the very fact that political emblems such as the Rhodian "rose",the Knidian "prow", or the Koan "club" appeared in the amphora stamps, not to mention the fact that the Chian amphora itself was employed as an "emblem" on Chian municipal coinage, demonstrates that municipal authorities in the Hellenistic Aegean made a conscious and deliberate effort to associate the products being conveyed in these jars with the commercial success of their respective polities. In order for the symbol of a transport jar to become identified with the activity of a given community, the design of the jar by necessity had to be universally recognized as the product of that polity and no other. This commercial and municipal interplay of iconography logically implies, therefore, that the Hellenistic Greek municipal authorities (and their citizens) were fully aware of the marketing success of their commodities as reflected by the shape of their transport jars, that they were proud of this success, and that they attempted to draw further attention to it. Short of textual evidence for ancient trademark or copyright laws, the necessary requirements for the ancient practice of what modern marketers refer to as "geographical branding" would appear to have been achieved (Pike 2011, 11).

Neither of these arguments adequately explain certain unique design qualities of internationally traded Hellenistic amphorae, such as the pitched (and later "horned") handles of the Rhodian jar, the double rolled (bifidal) handles of the Koan jar, the "ring toe" of the Knidian jar, or the uniquely biconic body of the Chian jar. Unlike other aspects of amphora uniformity among these types there is nothing particularly "functional" about the turn of one handle versus another or

41 The existence of ancient "branding" has been successfully argued recently by Gary Reger (2005, 2010 [2011]) with respect to the ancient perfume trade. While staple goods such as wine and olive oil were hardly analogous to ancient perfumes, it is worth noting that modern marketing designers believe that perfume bottles with long slender necks generate a sensation transference of "luxury" and "expensiveness" (Sutnar 1953, C6; Kahn – Deng 2009, 254; Greenleaf – Raghubir 2008, 135). Since we know that the Hellenistic Chian wine was extremely expensive, it is fair to ask whether or not the tall neck and uniquely elongated form of this jar stimulated a similar sense of heightened value.

the ring at the base of a Knidian amphora.[42] In lieu of functional explanations, therefore, it is possible to argue that these small design features, sustained in amphora morphology over centuries, served as unique and successfully crafted visual cues that enabled these forms to surpass their competitors when displayed in an "economy of abundance." The abundance of competing commodities generated by the expansion of overseas commerce in the Hellenistic world needs always to be borne in mind. Many nondescript jars (and their commodities) circulated locally and regionally; however, a small number are known to have circulated throughout the Mediterranean due to their widespread distribution and recognized sense of worth. Through "sensation transference" the ancient consumer readily identified and came to develop long-standing relationships with these products due in part to the attraction of their uniform, aesthetically pleasing packages. Much like the internationally recognized profile of the modern Coca Cola bottle,[43] the unique yet uniform shapes of ancient transport amphorae rendered their contents instantly recognizable to Mediterranean consumers.

5. From Advertising to Ruggedizing: the Late Roman Transition in Amphora Design

We have used the examples of Hellenistic jars to make our case for the importance of amphora design and uniformity in ancient market advertising largely because the jars of this period represent a procedural "high point" in this regard. During the Roman era the inherent logic governing the design amphorae was complicated by the expansion of agricultural and amphora production across the Mediterranean and perhaps by a gradual decline in notions of local identity.[44] Generally speaking, an exponentially greater number of forms were distributed across the Mediterranean during the Early Roman era. Whereas, in the Late Hellenistic Era perhaps 10–12 forms enjoyed international patterns of distribution, in the Early Roman era (as the celebrated Dressel chart published in volume XV of the *CIL* [1899, Table 2, fig. 4] makes clear) this number rose to 40 and beyond. To this day the production origins of several widely distributed jars of the Roman and Late Roman era remain unidentified.

Assuming that the high number of forms is indicative of the scale of production and volume of trade in commodities conveyed by amphorae, then it stands to reason that these rose dramatically at this time. In general, Roman-era forms be-

42 Were the double-rolled handle of the Koan and pseudo-Koan jars known to be functionally more effective than a solid one, one suspects that it would have been more universally adapted with less effective handles becoming abandoned.

43 The classic profile of the glass Coca Cola bottle (believed to imitate the curving profile of the human female) still functions as a trademarked advertising icon even though it has largely gone out of use with the advent of metal packaging. Its recent reintroduction with plastic bottles represents a form of modern archaizing.

44 For this process, see Wallace-Hadrill 2008.

came less distinctive and uniformity declined.[45] This having been said, several examples demonstrate that the prevailing "logic" governing amphora design persisted: unique forms such as the Dressel 20 olive oil jar produced in Spain were familiar throughout the Mediterranean,[46] within typologies amphora volumes remained highly uniform. In addition analysis done on stamps and *tituli dipinti* recorded on the Dressel 20 amphora has demonstrated the important role played by that jar in the logistical apparatus of the alimenta at Rome.[47] The fact that remains of Dressel 20 oil jars from Spain are found as far removed as Egypt or that the "horned handled" Rhodian amphorae are found as far removed as Britain demonstrate the potential reach of Roman maritime commerce at this time. As is well known, imitations of amphora design features such as the Koan bifidal handle (from Spain to Egypt) or the Rhodian "horned handle" (from Crete to Phoenicia) became so widespread in this era that they render the identification of production origins for various circulating jars (let alone the significance of these forms of imitation) an imposing challenge.[48] In short, the confusion arising from the welter of amphora forms produced during the Roman era appears to reflect the vibrancy and robust strength of the Roman economy itself. At the same time the broad array of Roman-era amphorae appears to reflect a shift away from the more tightly controlled fiscal economies of Hellenistic Greek poleis to a more open Mediterranean-wide commercial economy in Roman times. Widespread imitation of amphora features may also reflect an inability of Hellenistic era "brand" marketers to protect their niche in an era of widespread export production.[49]

All this seemingly changed around the time of the Roman "Barracks Emperors," the period of military chaos marked by a rapid succession of twenty-four emperors in a fifty-year span (238–285 AD) as well as by the top-down reorganization of Roman provincial administration that attained its height during the reign of the Emperor Diocletian (284–305 AD).[50] From this time onward, amphora forms grew increasingly amorphous. The number of internationally traded forms diminishes to less than twenty. In general, jars grew smaller, and their body surfaces became heavily "profiled", with relief variously described as wheel-ridging, corrugation, finger grooves, bands, or combing. Irregularities in design and dimensions appear to have multiplied. This is adequately illustrated by a briefly exa-

45 Particularly when one considers the wide array of forms produced in North Africa, the many forms of the African Grande and Tripolitanian amphorae, for example.

46 Rodriguez Almeida 1984, 1989; Will 1983.

47 Rodriguez Almeida 1984, 1989.

48 Moore 2010; for horned handled amphorae, see Riley 1979, 147–149, ERA 3.

49 Rauh 2004; Lawall – Van Alfen 2010.

50 By this time the existing provinces were divided into into smaller, more compact and easily controllable units, each of which was administered by members of a vastly expanded military bureaucracy. The more localized provinces were in turn grouped into twelve dioceses, each headed by a *vicarius*. The diocese themselves were grouped into four vast prefectures, each one ruled by a praetorian prefect. The largest diocese, Oriens, included sixteen provinces, and the smallest, Britannia, comprised only four provinces.

mination of four Late Roman amphora types: The LRA 1 (Yassi Ada), the LRA 7 Carrot, The Samian Cistern, and the Palestinian Bag Amphora.

6. Case Study Two: The Late Roman amphora "package"[51]

The LRA 1 – Yassi Ada amphora, so called for the shipwreck where the first identified forms were recovered, was the most widely distributed form of the Late Roman era, with a use chronology extending from the 5th to the 7th centuries AD.[52] Using an example excavated at Kelenderis as the standard of the type (IMAGE 10), this squarish form is of medium height (50cm) with thickened rim (typically with a low flange visible below the lip) and a short cylindrical neck that flares out slightly to the shoulder. The shoulder is narrow and round and the body is long, broadest at the top. The waist displays a characteristic "cinch" just below midriff. The form bulges out below the cinch to a rounded base with a basal knob. The entire form is wheel-ridged with grooves that spiral down the form to become wide bands toward mid-section before narrowing again. The bowing handles are thick, irregularly fashioned, and characterized by a deep, hastily worked slice. The fabric and size of this type vary widely. In fact, van Alfen (1996) attempts to classify it according to eleven different forms. Rauh and Dillon (2009) attempted to classify LRA 1 amphorae at the Anamur Archaeological Museum according to four distinct fabrics.[53] Making matters more complicated is the form's close similarity with the LRA 13, which resembles the Yassi Ada form except for its fuller body (which tends to bulge toward the middle and lacks the characteristic "cinch) and elongated handles (IMAGE 11).[54] Making this identification even more complicated is the fact that both forms were produced in the same region, Cyprus and eastern Cilicia. Like their fabrics the dimensions even of jars produced at the same production center (e.g., Elaiussa Sebaste) vary widely.[55] The heights of twenty-six LRA 1 and LRA 13 forms processed at the Anamur Archaeological Museum ranged from 37 to 55 cm with half the collection clustering at 48–51cm, and all but five clustering at 45–52 cm in height. The relatively small, "corrugated," nondescript form of these "bottle-shaped" amphorae and their widespread use appear to set the tone for the era.

A more oddly shaped amphora is the LRA 7, Carrot type (4th to 7th centuries AD),[56] a medium sized jar (approximately 78cm tall) with a tall conical rim and an equally long, narrow, tapering body (IMAGE 12). The rim is finely molded and

---

51 Tomber 2004.

52 Riley 1979, 212–216; Bass – van Doorninck 1971, 1982; van Alfen 1996; Sibella 2002, 10.

53 Zoroğlu *et al.* 2009, the more widely identified gray or light cream fabric; a "pink" fabric, a "red" fabric, and a "brown" fabric. It is, of course, recognized that the coloration may overlap and/or may be the result of differing firing conditions.

54 Also their necks tend to be shorter and their handles tend to bow out further before turning downward.

55 See Ferrazzoli – Ricci 2010b.

56 Riley 1979, LRA 7; Sibella 2002, 19b, 19; Alpözen *et al.* 1995, no. 104.

flattened on top with a slightly raised edge on the interior. Below the rim the form exhibits a round onion-shaped shoulder that tapers sharply inward to a pointed foot. Wheel ridging is visible on the neck and the handles are small and irregularly fashioned. The fabric is a gritty, hard, red clay (2.5yr 7/4). The uniqueness of this shape notwithstanding, it needs to be emphasized that the LRA 7 is one of several "types" of carrot-shaped amphorae being manufactured along the coast of Syria, Phoenicia, and Palestine at this time. A similar form that could be mentioned is the so-called "Beirut" amphora (IMAGE 13).[57] The point to be stressed here is that much like the LRA 1 "Yassi Ada" amphora the "Carrot type" amphora was produced in an array of variant forms in a broad region extending along the eastern Mediterranean coast.

The so-called "Samos Cistern" amphora[58] (4th to 7th centuries AD) exhibits a large cylindrical (slightly bag-shaped) jar with a short collar-like rim and a visible interior ledge for a stopper (IMAGE 14). The short thick neck slopes to a high shoulder; the oval body then bulges out slightly to its widest extent low on the form before sloping inward to large pointed toe. The body is wheel ridged beginning at the top of shoulder. The handles are thick, short, hastily worked, and strap like. The fabric exhibits a hard gritty brownish clay (2.5yr 6/6). At the Anamur Archaeological Museum the form survives in two sizes, a larger jar that is 75 cm tall, and four smaller jars with heights ranging from 56 to 59 cm.[59] The significance of this jar is that in some respects it sustains the morphology of Aegean produced jars (rolled rim, cylindrical neck, fashioned toe) while in others it adapts to the new "amorphous" tendencies of Late Roman times (wheel ridging, bag-shaped body, variable dimensions).

The small Palestinian bag-shaped amphora (LRA 5; Zemer 60) seems to represent everything that is new with this era (4th to 7th centuries AD). Its short vertical rim stands atop a squat, bag-shaped body that gradually curves inward to a rounded base (IMAGE 15). Thick, small lug handles are set near the turn of the shoulder. Deeply combed grooves or wheel-ridges extend from the shoulder to the base, alternately narrowly grooved or flattened into bands. The fabric exhibits a medium hard, dark red, relatively fine clay (2.5yr 6/4). The dimensions of this small round amphora are typically wider (36cm) than tall (30cm), though the form varies anywhere from 25 to 30 cm in height and in some instances is actually taller than it is wide. Although the form came into being during the Early Roman era, it became one of the most widely circulating Late Roman forms of the eastern Mediterranean. Its similarities with the taller (44cm), more elongated LRA 6 (IMAGE 16) version makes identification of this form challenging, and again points to the widely variable morphology of this "type" form throughout its production region.

57 Because of its identified production origin in modern Beirut (Reynolds 2000).

58 So named due to the discovery of a number of these jars in a cistern on the island, Sibella 2002, 14, fig 20; Zemer 1977, 42; Opaiţ 2004, 301f.

59 Zoroğlu *et al.* 2009.

When compared to the design norms of previous eras, it is safe to conclude that these forms marked an important transition in the purpose of amphora design. Late Roman amphorae typically exhibit amorphous, hastily worked walls and handles and are heavily wheel-ridged. Their dimensions vary widely. In general, the forms are smaller (typically less than 0.5 m tall) than those of the previous era, although their novel shapes possibly compensate for this in terms of volume. Assuming, for all the reasons given above, that amphora design mattered greatly in previous eras, the design of amphora forms of the Later Roman era suggests that certain principles which previously governed amphora design were no longer prevalent. Certainly, there is a visible decline in reliance on visual cues such as complexity, congruence, convergence, and completeness as defined by modern packaging design.

One argument attributes the changes that occurred in amphora design at the end of the 2nd century AD to labor shortages commensurate with the plague that occurred during the reign of M. Aurelius (161–180 AD) and to the prevailingly high levels of violence sustained in this era. These ultimately reduced the availability of labor for amphora production (and other commodities) on a mass scale.[60] According to this scenario, labor crises could have compelled amphora producers to deemphasize the importance of "finished" forms and to prioritize quantity over quality. In favor of this argument, the discovery of the kiln site at Sebaste Elaiussa with more than 750 misfired LRA 1 Yassi Ada amphorae would seem to indicate that the volume of production did not necessarily decline at this time.[61] A second explanation holds that the trend toward wheel ridging on Roman amphorae (something already visible by the late 1st century AD) imitated the aesthetic appeal of surface relief also displayed in Late Roman fine and table wares.[62] However, this returns us to our central argument that the design of amphora forms was implicitly and consciously driven by principles of "sensation transference" and "packaging design." By and large the design of Late Roman amphorae experienced a pronounced decline in "aesthetic detailing"; the widely varying dimensions of Late Roman amphorae point to a decline in uniformity, and the hastily worked features and heavy reliance on wheel ridging seems too prevalent and long lived for the explanation to be reduced to something as singular as a labor crisis.[63] In these respects the nondescript character of Late Roman amphora forms points to an implicit change in the principles and objectives that determined amphora design in the first place (van Alfen 1996, 213).

60 Ward-Perkins 2005, 88–96.

61 Ferrazzoli – Ricci 2011. 2010a; Ferrazzoli – Ricci 2010b; Ferrazzoli 2010.

62 Suggested by E. Lyding Will, who argued that this conformed to wider Roman trends in "baroque art" (personal communication with Rauh). In this regard it must be conceded that the shift toward wheel ridging extended across ceramics manufacture and appears to reflect a widespread trend.

63 It also finds its way into amphora design as explained below.

It is important to avoid the urge to exaggerate the extent of these changes. Uniformity in the production of Late Roman amphorae was sufficient to enable modern researchers to identify specific forms, for example, and even to make fine distinctions between the LRA 1 and the LRA 13, the LRA 7 Carrot form and the Beirut form, or the LRA 5 Bag-shaped Palestinian jar and the more elongated LRA 6 version. If we suspend discussion of the tendency toward varying dimensions for the moment, the uniformity of shapes within typologies, however diminished from previous eras, nonetheless indicates that the need for visual cues was not abandoned altogether. Intuitive decision-making in amphora design is potentially detectable. Modern packaging specialists argue, for example, that elongated forms like the carrot shaped amphorae and bag-shaped forms that sag at the base give the illusion of holding greater capacity than more regularly shaped forms of the same volume.[64] Smaller dimensions to packages, meanwhile, exude the impression of costlier, more valuable commodities. Amphora specialists have argued, in fact, that the general Roman-era trend toward smaller containers, much like a similar modern trend, came in response to consumer demand for fresher contents.[65] While these arguments still do not explain the corrugated forms, the widely varying dimensions, or the hastily worked components of Late Roman forms, they do at least allow for the possibility of purposefulness in amphora design.

Recently the argument that systematic principles of amphora design declined during Late Roman era has been challenged by Paul Reynolds (2005). Relying on published fabric descriptions and identified production regions for the various Late Roman amphora forms, Reynolds argues that the production areas of the various Late Roman amphora types correspond to the reorganized boundaries of smaller, more highly integrated Late Roman diocesan provinces and that the rising number of these provincial units appears to explain the bewildering variations visible in the forms of specific types. This raises the possibility that each diocesan district generated a distinct amphora form intended "visually" to represent its yield of imperial tax quotas. According to this rationale, the nondescript forms of the Late Roman era remained sufficiently uniform to be identifiable to imperial authorities who assembled taxes and requisitions in kind for the military. If true, amphora producers, nonetheless, increasingly deemphasized the amount of care they devoted to "consumer appeal," unlike production in previous eras. Smaller forms, meanwhile, possibly reflected the desire to keep commodities fresh until decanting, but they could just as easily reflect the military establishment's need to distribute commodities to smaller, more widely dispersed regiments in the field.

64 Larrabee 1935, 50; Holmberg 1975, Folkes – Matta 2004; Krishna 2008, 179–191; Greenleaf – Raghubir 2008, 120–132; Raghubir 2009, 210.

65 Moore 2010, 108; van Alfen 1996, 213. A smaller amphora presumably meant that the wine could be consumed in a single sitting. Modern packaging specialists (Larrabee 1935, 45) likewise point to the growing trend toward smaller package servings to accommodate urban-dwelling consumers who lack the storage space for large quantities of foodstuffs.

Smaller forms would also have been easier to convey across land[66] as well as by smaller cargo ships sailing to less accessible locations, particularly given a decline in reliance on large "trading hubs" at this time.

Even our concern with the varying dimensions of Late Roman amphora types is possibly misguided. F. H. Van Doorninck Jr. and P. Van Alfen's recent analyses of the volumetrics of LRA 1 amphorae from the Yassi Ada and Serçe Limanı shipwrecks shed important insight in this regard.[67] As noted earlier, van Alfen identifies more than 11 different forms within the type typically classified as LRA 1, indicating that they were manufactured by numerous artisans at a variety of different sites. This would seem to support the general assumption that uniformity had diminished in this era. However, his analysis of the volumes of these jars demonstrates the existence of far more precise volumetric control in production: volumetric variations within the 11 forms are relatively minimal and measurements themselves appear to be based on new, more precise volumetric systems of the Late Roman / early Byzantine Era (the *litra* and *daktylos*). In other words, in the Late Roman era heightened emphasis was placed on the achievement of volumetric uniformity than on the exterior design of the jars. Together with the significant scale of production, this indicates that the guiding forces at work in Late Roman amphora production were not the same as those exhibited by earlier Hellenistic forms.

Van Alfen (1996, 211) points to the heightened military considerations of the Late Roman era as playing the greatest role in this development, particularly the creation of the quaestura exercitus during the reign of the Emperor Justinian (527–565 AD). Comprising Cyprus, Caria, the Aegean islands, and the Danubian provinces of Scythia and Moesia II, this new logistical administration was organized to furnish supplies from throughout the eastern Mediterranean empire to military units situated along the devastated northern frontiers. Headquartered most likely at Samos the quaestor exercitus in charge of this administration quickly assumed authority as the quartermaster general of the army and collected supplies equally from private and church estates throughout this region. The wide variety of LRA 1 (and LRA 13) forms and dimensions possibly point to the rapid production of these amphorae at landed and church estates scattered along the eastern Mediterranean coast to meet urgent military requisitions as well as to fulfill the imperial annona. This change in logistical infrastructure possibly resulted in the piecemeal assemblages of cargoes visible in the Serçe Limanı and Yassi Ada shipwrecks, each of which were found to contain LRA 1 amphorae of widely varying dimensions, sources, and ages (van Alfen 1996, 212). In addition, Van Doorninck Jr. (1995) and van Alfen (1996, 213) pursue the logic inherent in smaller containers (equaling fresher commodities) by arguing that the various volumes of LRA 1 amphorae were intended to accommodate individualized commodities such as

66 Cf. Lund 2007.

67 Van Doorninck Jr. 1993, 1995; van Alfen 1996.

red wine, white wine, and olive oil. Since *dipinti* recorded on Late Roman amphorae indicate that commodities were increasingly exchanged by weight rather than by volume, the differing weights of these commodities possibly explain the varying LRA 1 volumes (van Alfen 1996, 205). As van Alfen notes (1996, 213), "Study of Late Roman and Byzantine metrology does indicate an overall move towards greater accuracy and efficiency which may parallel or be dependent on changes in the way amphora borne commodities were exchanged".

Since so few metrological investigations of this type have been conducted with Late Roman amphorae, it remains impossible to determine how widespread these considerations actually were. Preliminarily, the recent work of Reynolds, van Doorninck Jr., and van Alfen demonstrate the likely implementation of coherent design principles to the packaging Late Roman maritime commodities. In some respects this purposefulness in amphora design continued to rely on visual cues of the past in an effort to advertise the contents of a given package through "sensation transference". In other respects, however, the forms point to newly directed attention to the needs of smaller packaging, heightened volume control, and ruggedized exteriors to accommodate the more violent times of the Late Roman era. In this last respect, modern packaging specialists draw distinct contrasts between the design of packaging directed toward consumers and those intended for purposes of military supply (Sacharow 1982, 144–151). Sacharow (1982, 144) notes that in lieu of sales appeal or advertising, packaging for the military emphasizes product protection, identification, marking, and physical handling. "All products intended for the armed forces must be delivered in a usable condition. Since the ultimate destination of the packages cannot always be anticipated at the procurement stage, efficient packaging is the only solution, and the packaging must be of a higher quality than would be needed commercially (Sacharow 1982, 148)." Another factor to be considered in military packaging is standardization: to insure uniform and precise control of product quality; heightened specifications in size and volume become necessary (Sacharow 1982, 151).

In short, if Reynolds, Van Doorninck Jr., and van Alfen are correct, then the Late Roman military establishment imposed requirements for production, organization, and distribution of goods shipped via maritime transport at the local level. Diocesan populations were required by the state to supply specified quantities of surplus agricultural commodities such as wine, oil, garum, and other goods for redistribution to military units across the seas. The Roman military establishment increasingly assumed control over the distribution of commodities that had formerly been conducted by means of "commerce." Conceivably, the elimination of market mechanisms in the redistribution of surplus commodities reduced interest in or the need for unique and highly polished amphora designs. The Late Roman military establishment was less concerned with the distinctiveness of a given amphora (or "sensation transference") and far more concerned about the logistical process of supplying military cadres in the field. The new requirements placed greater emphasis on volumetric uniformity and ruggedized packaging of transport amphorae. Accordingly, reduced attention to amphora design would appear to reflect the Late Roman military establishment's relative indifference to marketing needs. Instead of focusing on Late Roman consumers, military authorities focused on the logistical requirements of the establishment itself.

Conclusions

The principles of modern advertising and packaging design have important things to offer to the investigation of the material remains of commerce such as ancient transport amphorae. Modern marketing researchers enjoy greater resources and more abundant means with which to investigate questions of packaging design, "sensation transference", and consumer-driven advertising than do Roman archaeologists. The former can measure reactions to and solicit responses from hundreds of living subjects to intricate design elements of packaging in ways that are not possible to those who investigate past human behavior. Even while allowing for inevitable differences in time, place, technology, and culture, the conclusions obtained through modern marketing research seem relevant to ancient commercial behavior precisely because they derive from the investigation of behavioral responses that occur subliminally within the human mind. The advantage that archaeologists bring to this discussion is the command we have of the archaeological remains of commercial artifacts whose uses extended over not merely dozens of years, but literally centuries of time. By applying modern principles of market advertising and packaging design to the study of ancient Mediterranean amphorae, we have attempted to show that the well-designed forms of the Hellenistic era functioned as advertising tools in an "economy of abundance". The aesthetically inferior but ruggedized forms of the Late Roman era, on the other hand, appear better designed for use in an era of sustained conflict. In a limited and extremely preliminary manner, we believe that we have demonstrated the advantages obtained from the application of modern marketing theory to changes in amphora morphology and by extension to the adaptations that occurred in amphora design as economic conditions in the ancient Mediterranean evolved.

Bibliography

Alpözen *et al.* 1995 = Alpözen T.O. – Özdas A.H. – Berkaya B., Commercial Amphoras of the Bodrum Museum of Underwater Archaeology. Maritime trade of the Mediterranean in ancient times. Ankara: Bodrum Museum of Underwater Archaeology.

Archibald *et al.* (eds.) = Archibald Z.H. – Davies J.K. – Gabrielsen V. (eds.), Making, Moving and Managing. The New World of Ancient Economies, 323–31 BC. Oxford: Oxbow Books.

Badoud – Dana forthcoming = Badoud N. – Dana D., L'onomastique des fabricants d'amphores rhodiennes, in: Badoud N. – Marangou A. (eds.), Analyse et exploitation des timbres amphoriques grecs. Actes du colloque international tenu à l'Ecole française d'Athènes (3–5 février 2010), forthcoming.

Badoud – Marangou forthcoming = Badoud N. – Marangou A. (eds.), Analyse et exploitation des timbres amphoriques grecs. Actes du colloque international tenu à l'Ecole française d'Athènes (3–5 février 2010), forthcoming.

Bass – van Doorninck 1971 = Bass G.F. – van Doorninck F.H., A Fourth-century Shipwreck at Yassi Ada, AJA 75, 27–37.

Bass – Van Doorninck 1982 =Bass G.F. – van Doorninck F.H., Yassi Ada: A Seventh-Century byzantine Shipwreck. College Station TX: Texas A&M University Press.

Benoit 1961 = Benoit F., L'Épave du Grand Congloué à Marseille. Gallia Suppl. 14. Paris: CNRS.

Boussac 1992 = Boussac M.-F., Les sceaux de Délos, 1. Sceaux publics, Apollon, Hélios, Artémis, Hécate. Paris: De Boccard.

Calver 2004 = Calver G., What is packaging design? Essential design handbooks, Mies, Switzerland, RotoVision.

Cheskin 1959 = Cheskin L., Why people buy? Motivation research and its successful applications. 2nd edition. NY: Liveright Publishing Co.

D'Arms 1981 = D'Arms J.H., Commerce and Social Standing in Ancient Rome. Cambridge, MA: Harvard U. Press.

Demesticha 2011 = Demesticha S., The 4th-century-B.C. Mazotos Shipwreck, Cyprus. A Preliminary Report, IntJNautA 40, 39–59.

Descat 2006 = Descat R. (ed.), Approches de l'économie hellénistique, Entretiens d'Archéologie et d'Histoire 7. Saint-Bertrand-de-Comminges: De Boccard.

Diamanti 2010 = Diamanti C., Stamped Late Roman/Proto-Byzantine Amphoras from Halasarna of Kos, ReiCretActa 41, 1–8.

Diamanti 2012 = Diamanti C., Byzantine Emperors on stamped Late Roman/Early Byzantine Amphoras, ReiCretActa 42, 1–5.

Doğer 1992 = Doğer E., Antik Cağda Amphoralar. Izmir: Sergi Yayın Evi.

Eiring – Lund (eds.) 2004 = Eiring J. – Lund J. (eds.), Transport Amphorae and Trade in the Eastern Mediterranean. Acts of the International Colloquium at the Danish Institute at Athens, Sept. 26–29, 2002. Monographs of the Danish Institute at Athens, Volume 5. Aarhus: Danish Institute at Athens.

Empereur 1982 = Empereur J.-Y., Les Anses d'Amphores Timbrées et les Amphores: Aspects Quantitatifs. BCH 106, 219–233.

Empereur - Garlan (eds.) 1986 = Empereur J.Y. - Garlan Y. (eds.), Recherches sur les amphores grecques, Actes du colloque international organisé par le centre national de la recherche scientifique, l'Université de Rennes II et l'École française d'Athènes (Athènes, 10–12 Septembre 1984), BCH Supplément 13. Athènes & Paris: De Boccard.

Ferrazzoli 2010 = Ferrazzoli A.F., Ch. IX, Instrumentum Domesticum, in E. Equini Schneider, ed., Elaiussa Sebaste III. L'agora Romana, Istanbul, Ege Yayınları, 682–687.

Ferrazzoli - Ricci 2010a = Ferrazzoli A.F. - Ricci M., Le produzione di ceramiche comuni decorate di età protobizantina di Elaiussa Sebaste in Cilicia, in: Menchelli S. *et al.* (eds.), 803–813.

Ferrazzoli - Ricci 2010b = Ferrazzoli A.F. - Ricci M., Un centro di produzione delle anfore LR 1: Eliaussa Sebaste in Cilicia. Gli impianti, le anfore, in: Menchelli S. *et al.* (eds.), 815–826.

Ferrazzoli - Ricci 2011 = Ferrazzoli A.F. - Ricci M., Un centro di produzione delle anfore LR 1. Elaiussa Sebaste in Cilicia, in: Menchelli S. *et al.* (eds.), 815–826.

Finkielsztejn 2001 = Finkielsztejn G., Chronologie détaillée et révisée des éponymes amphoriques rhodiens, de 270 à 108 av. J.-C. environ. Premier bilan. BAR International Series 990. Oxford: Archaeopress.

Finkielsztejn 2006 = Finkielsztejn G., Production et commerce des amphores hellénistiques: récipients, timbrage et métrologie, in: Descat R. (ed.),17–34.

Folkes - Matta 2004 = Folkes V.S. - Matta S., The effect of package shape on consumers' judgments of product volume: attention as a mental contaminant, Journal of Consumer Research 31, 390–401.

Gabrielsen 1997 = Gabrielsen V., The Naval Aristocracy of Hellenistic Rhodes, Aarhus, Aarhus U. Press.

Garlan 2000 = Garlan Y., Amphores et timbres amphoriques grecs: entre érudition et idéologie, Mémoires de l'Académie des Inscriptions et Belles-lettres nouvelle série XXI. Paris: De Boccard.

Garlan 2006 = Garlan Y., Des consommateurs aux producteurs: nouvelles perspectives dans l'étude des timbres amphoriques grecs, in Descat R. (ed.), 9–16.

Γιαννικουρή *et al.* 2011 = Γιαννικουρή Α.– Στεφανάκι Β.Ε. – Γεωργοπούλου Β., Σφραγίσματα αμφορέων και νομίσματα της Κω της ύστερής κλασικής και ελληνιστικής περίοδου: Συγκριτική Μελέτη, in Ζ' Επιστημονική Συνάντηση για την Ελληνιστική Κεραμεική Αίγιο 4–9 Απρίλιου 2005. Πρακτικά Κείμενα. Αθήνα, 887–906.

Grace 1934 = Grace V., The Stamped Amphora Handles Found in the American Excavations in the Athenian Agora 1931–1932. A catalogue treated as a chronological study. Cambridge MA: Harvard U. Dissertation, published in Hesperia 3 (1934), 197–310.

Grace 1949 = Grace V., Standard Pottery Containers of the Ancient Greek World, in Hesperia Suppl. VIII, Commemorative Studies in honor of Theodore Leslie Shear. Princeton Uinversity Press, 175–189.
Grace 1956 = Grace V., Stamped Wine Jar Fragments. Hesperia. Supplement X. Small Objects from the Pnyx: II. Princeton: American School of Classical Studies, 113–189.
Grace 1965 = Grace V., The Commercial Amphoras, in: Weinberg G.D. – Grace V.R. – Edwards G.R. – Robinson H.S. – Throckmorton P. – Ralph E.K., The Antikythera Shipwreck Reconsidered. Transactions of the American Philosophical Society. N.S. Vol. 55, Part 3. Philadelphia: APS.
Grace 1979 = Grace V., Amphoras and the Ancient Wine Trade. Excavations of the Athenian Agora. Picture Book No. 6. Princeton: ASCSA.
Grace – Savvatianou-Petropoulakou 1970 = Grace V. – Savvatianou-Petropoulakou M., Les timbres amphoriques grecs, in: Bruneau Ph., L'Ilot de la Maison des Comediens. EAD 27. Paris: De Boccard, 277–374.
Greenleaf – Raghubir 2008 = Greenleaf E. – Raghubir P., Geometry in the marketplace, in: Wedel M. – Pieters R. (eds.), 113–142.
Höghammar 1993 = Höghammar K., Sculpture and Society. A Study of the Connection between Free-Standing Sculpture and Society on Kos in the Hellenistic and Augustan Periods. Boreas. Uppsala Studies in Ancient Mediterranean and Near Eastern Societies 23. Uppsala.
Holmberg 1975 = Holmberg L., The influence of elongation on the perception of volume of geometrically simple objects, Psychological Research Bulletin 15.2, 1–18.
Kahn – Deng 2009 = Kahn B.E. – Deng X., Effects on Visual Weight Perceptions of Product Image Locations on Packaging, in: Krishna A. (ed.), Sensory Marketing, NY – London: Routledge, 259–317.
Koehler 1986 = Koehler C., Handling of Greek Transport Amphorae, in: Empereur J.-Y. – Garlan Y. (eds.), 49–67.
Koehler 2004 = Koehler C., Knidian Amphora Chronology, Pergamon to Corinth, in: Eiring J. – Lund J. (eds.), 163–169.
Krishna 2008: Krishna A., Spatial perception research, in: Wedel M. – Pieters R. (eds.), 167–192.
Lang 1976 = Lang M., Graffiti and dipinti, The Athenian Agora. Princeton NJ: Princeton University Press.
Larrabee 1935 = Larrabee C.B., How to package for profit; a manual of packaging, NY: Harper Bros.
Lawall 2004 = Lawall M., Nothing to do with Mendaian Amphoras? Athenaeus 11.748C, in: Egan R.B. – Joyal M., DAIMONOPYLAI: Essays in Classics and the Classical Tradition Presented to Edmund G. Berry. University of Manitoba Centre for Hellenic Civilization: Winnipeg, Manitoba, 241–249.
Lawall 2005 = Lawall M., Amphoras and Hellenistic economies: addressing the (over)-emphasis on stamped amphora handles, in: Archibald Z.H. *et al.* (eds.), 188–232.

Lawall 2011 = Lawall M., Greek Amphorae in the Archaeological Record, in: Lawall M. - Lund J. (eds.), 37–50.

Lawall - Lund (eds.) 2011 = Lawall M. - Lund J. (eds.), Pottery in the Archaeological Record: Greece and Beyond, Aarhus: Gösta Enbom Monograph 1.

Lawall - van Alfen 2010 [2011] = Lawall M. - van Alfen P., Caveat Emptor: A Collection of Papers on Imitations in Ancient Greco-Roman Commerce, MBAH 28, 1–20.

Lund 2007 = Lund J., Transport amphorae as a possible source for the land use and economic history of the Akamas Peninsula, Western Cyprus, in: Bonifay M. - Tréglia J.-C. (eds.), LRCW 2: Late Roman Coarse Wares, Cooking Wares and Amphorae in the Mediterranean. Archaeology and Archaeometry, BAR International Series 1662 (II). Oxford: Archaeopress, 781–789.

Lund 2011 = Lund J., Iconographic Evidence for the Handling and Use of Transport Amphorae in the Roman Period, in: Lawall M. - Lund J. (eds.), 51–60.

Matheson - Wallace 1981 = Matheson P.M.W. - Wallace M.B., Some Rhodian amphora capacities, Hesperia 51, 293–320.

Menchelli *et al.* (eds.) 2010 = Menchelli S. - Santoro S. - Pasquinucci M. - Guiducci M. (eds.), LRCW 3: Late Roman Coarse Wares, Cooking Wares, and Amphorae in the Mediterranean, Archaeology and archaeomoetry, Comparison between western and eastern Mediterranean, Vol. II BAR International Series 2185 (II), Oxford, Archaeopress.

Monachov 2006 = Monachov S.J., Rhodian Amphoras: Developments in Form and Measurements, in: Stolba V.F. - Hannestad L. (eds.), Chronologies of the Black Sea Area in the Period c. 400–100 BC, Black Sea Studies 3. Aarhus : Aarhus University Press, 69–95.

Moore 2010 [2011] = Moore J., When not just any wine will do? The Proliferation of Koan-type wines and amphoras in the Greco-Roman world, MBAH 28, 89–122.

Muller 2011 = Muller A., Les minerais, le marbre et le vin. Aux sources de la prospérité thasienne, REG 124, 179–192.

Opaiţ 2009 = Opaiţ A., A Weighty Matter: Pontic Fish Amphorae, in: Gabrielsen V. - Lund J. (eds.), The Black Sea in Antiquity: Regional and Interregional Economic Exchanges, Black Sea Studies 6. Aarhus: Aarhus University Press, 101–121.

Palaczyk forthcoming = Palaczyk M., Gibt es Verbreitungsmuster der rhodischen «Fabrikantenstempel»?, in: Badoud N. - Marangou A. (eds.).

Peña 2007 = Peña J.T., Roman Pottery in the Archaeological Record. Cambridge: Cambridge UP.

Pike 2011 = Pike A., Introduction: Brands and branding geographies, in: Pike A. (ed.), Brands and Branding Geographies, Cheltenham UK, Northhampton MA: Edward Elgar, 1–24.

Raghubir 2008 = Raghubir P., Are visual perceptual biases hard-wired?, in: Wedel M. - Pieters R. (eds.), 143–165.

Raghubir 2009 = Raghubir P., Visual Perception, an Overview, in: Krishna A.(ed.), Sensory Marketing, NY & London: Routledge, 201–217.

Rauh 2000 = Rauh N.K., Rhodes, Rome, and the Eastern Mediterranean Wine Trade, 166–88 BC, in: Gabrielsen V. – Bilde P. – Engberg-Pedersen T. – Hannestad L. – Zahle J. (eds.), Hellenistic Rhodes: Politics, Culture, and Society.: Aarhus: Aarhus University Press, 162–186.

Rauh 2003 = Rauh N.K., Merchants, Sailors, and Pirates in the Roman World. Stroud, Tempus Press.

Rauh 2004 = Rauh N.K., Pirated Knock-Offs. Cilician Imitations of Internationally Traded Amphoras, in: Eiring J. – Lund J. (eds.), 329–336.

Reger 2005 = Reger G., The manufacture and distribution of perfume, in: Archibald Z.H. *et al.* (eds.), Making, Moving, and Managing. The New World of Ancient Economies, 323–31 BC. Oxford: Oxford UP, 253–297.

Reger 2010 [2011] = Reger G., Formation of Taste and Fashion Perfumes and Imitations in the Hellenistic and Early Imperial World, MBAH 28, 21–44.

Reynolds 2000 = Reynolds, The Beirut amphora type, 1st century BC–7th century AD: an outline of its formal development and some preliminary observations of regional economic trends, Rei Cretariae Romanae Fautorum Acta (Ephesus, 1998). Abingdon, 387–395.

Reynolds 2005 = Reynolds P., Levantine amphorae from Cilicia to Gaza: a typology and analysis of regional production trends from the 1st to 7th centuries, in: Gurt i Esparraguerra J.M. – Buxeda i Garrigós J. – Cau Ontiveros M.A. (eds.), LRCWI. Late Roman Coarse Wares, Cooking Wares and Amphorae in the Mediterranean: Archaeology and Archaeometry (Conference papers, held at Barcelona, 14–16th March 2002), (British Archaeological Reports, International Series), Oxford: Archaeopress, 563–611.

Riley 1979 = Riley A.J., The Coarse Pottery from Benghazi, in: Lloyd A.J.(ed.), Excavations at Sidi Khrebish Benghazi (Berenice), vol. 2, Tripoli, 91–467.

Rodriguez Almeida 1985= Rodriguez Almeida E., Il Monte Testaccio, ambiente, storia, materiale. Rome: Quasar.

Rodriguez Almeida 1989 = Rodríguez Almeida E., Los tituli picti de las ánforas olearias de la Bética I. Madrid.

Sacharow 1982 = Sacharow S., The Package as a Marketing Tool. Chilton book co. Radnor Pa: Chilton.

Salviat 1986 = Salviat F., Le vin de Thasos. Amphores, vin et sources écrites, in: Empereur J.-Y. – Garlan Y. (eds.), Recherches sur les Amphores Grecques. BCH Supplément 13. Paris: De Boccard, 145–195.

Sherwin-White 1978 = Sherwin-White S., Ancient Cos. An Historical Study from the Dorian Settlement to the Imperial Period. Hypomnemata 51, Göttingen: Vandenhoeck und Ruprecht.

Sibella 2002 = Sibella P., The George McGhee Amphora Collection at the Alanya Museum, Turkey. The INA Quarterly Vol. 29 Suppl. 1. College Station: Institute of Nautical Archaeology.

Sutnar 1953 = Sutnar L., Package Design: the Force of Visual Selling Arts, New York: IMC.

Tchernia 1986 = Tchernia A., Le vin de l'Italie romaine. Essai d'histoire économique d'après les amphores, Bibliothèque des Ecoles françaises d'Athènes et de Rome 261. Rome: Ecole française de Rome.

Thomas – Tomber 2006 = Thomas R. – Tomber R., Vessel Stoppers, in: Maxfield V.A. – Peacock D.P.S. (eds.), Survey and Excavations Mons Claudianus 1987–1993 III: Ceramic Vessels & Related Objects. Le Caire 239–258.

Tomber 2004 = Tomber R., Polarising and Integrating the Late Roman Economy: the Role of Late Roman Amphorae 1–7, Ancient West & East 3.1, 155–165.

van Alfen 1996 = van Alfen P.G., New light on the 7th–c. Yassi Ada shipwreck: capacities and standard sizes of LRA 1 amphoras, JRA 9, 189–213.

van Doornick Jr. 1993 = van Doorninck Jr. F.H., Giving good weight in eleventh-century Byzantium: the metrology of the Glass Wreck amphoras, INA Quarterly 20.2, 8–12.

van Doornick Jr. 1995 = van Doorninck Jr. F.H., The piriform amphoras from the 11th–century shipwreck at Serçe Limanı: sophisticated containers for Byzantine commerce in wine, Graeco-Arabica 6, 181–189.

Wallace 2004 = Wallace M.B., Standardization in Greek amphora capacities, in: Eiring J. – Lund J. (eds.), 6, 429–431.

Wallace-Hadrill 2008 = Wallace-Hadrill A., Rome's Cultural Revolution. Cambridge – New York: Cambridge UP.

Ward-Perkins 2005 = Ward-Perkins B., The fall of Rome and the end of civilization. Oxford: Oxford UP.

Wedel & Pieters 2008 = Wedel M. – Pieters R., Introduction to visual marketing, in: Wedel M. – Pieters R. (eds.), 1–8.

Wedel & Pieters (eds.) 2008 = Wedel M. – Pieters R. (eds.), Visual Marketing: from attention to action, NY London: Lawrence Erlbaum Assocication.

Will 1979 = Will E.L., The Sestius Amphoras: A Reappraisal, Journal of Field Archaeology 6, 339–350.

Will 1983 = Will E.L., Exportation of Olive Oil from Baetica to the Eastern Mediterranean, in: Blázquez Martínez J.M. *et al.*, Producción y comercio del aceite en la antigúedad (II Congreso Internacional). Madrid: Universidad Complutense, 391–440.

Will 1987 = Will E.L., The Roman Amphoras, in: McCann A.M. *et al.*, The Roman Port and Fishery of Cosa, Princeton NJ: Princeton UP, 170–220.

Will 2001a = Will E.L., Defining the Regna vini of the Sestii, in: Goldman N.W. (ed.), New light from ancient Cosa: classical Mediterranean studies in honor of Cleo Rickman Fitch, New York: P. Lang, 35–47.

Will 2001b = Will E.L., Truth in Roman Labeling? American Journal of Archaeology 105, 263.

Zemer 1977

A. Zemer, Storage Jars in Ancient Sea Trade. Haifa: National Maritime Museum Foundation.

Zevi 1966 = Zevi F., Appunti sulle anfore romane, Archeologia Classica 18, 208–247.

Zoroğlu *et al.* 2009 = Zoroğlu L. – Dillon M. – Yakınlar D. – Rauh N., Anamur Arkeoloji Müzesindeki Amfora Araştırmaların Raporu, Araştırma Sonuçları Toplantısı (Mayis 2008). T.C. Kültür Bakanligi, Anitlar ve Müzeler Genel Müdürlügü, Ankara, 2 Cilt 2009, 33–50.

Image 1: Hellenistic Rhodian Amphora from Kelenderis
(Photograph by Matthew J. Dillon and Nicholas Rauh)

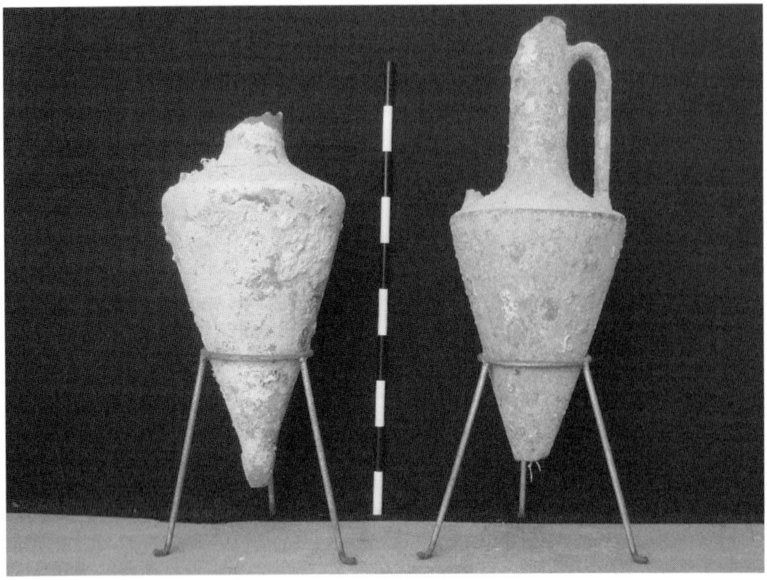

Image 2: Hellenistic Chian Amphoras at the Anamur Museum
(Photograph by Matthew J. Dillon and Nicholas Rauh)

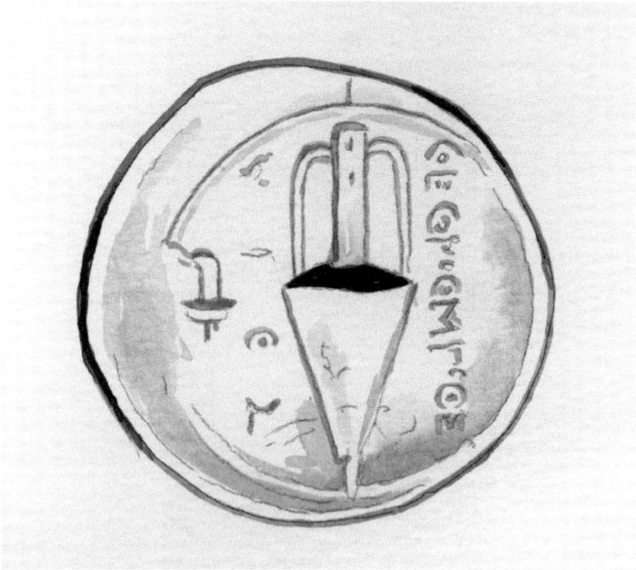

Image 3: Drawing of Chian Coin by Herb Rauh

Image 4: Hellenistic Koan Amphorae at the Anamur Museum
(Photograph by Matthew J. Dillon and Nicholas Rauh)

Image 5: Hellenistic Knidian Amphora at the Alanya Museum
(Photograph by Nicholas Rauh)

Image 6: Sekoma at Delos
(Photograph by Nicholas Rauh)

Image 7: Rhodian Amphora Stamp from Kelenderis
(Photograph by Nicholas Rauh)

Image 8: Stamped Lid on Italian Amphora at Delos
(Photograph by Nicholas Rauh)

Image 9: Tituli Picti on Italian Amphora at Delos
(Photograph by Nicholas Rauh)

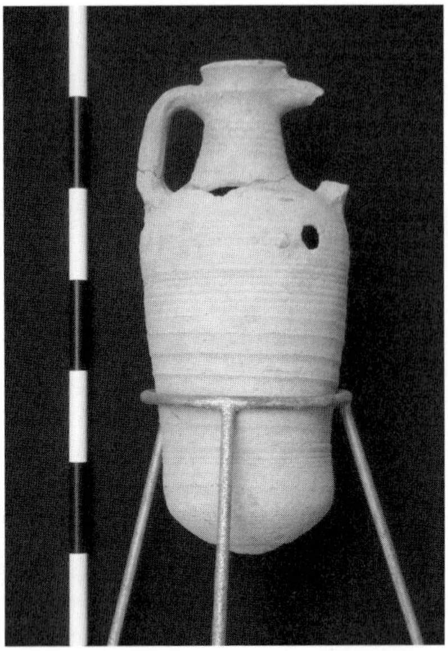

Image 10: LRA 1 Yassi Ada Amphora from Kelenderis
(Photograph by Matthew J. Dillon and Nicholas Rauh)

Image 11: LRA 1 and LRA 13 Amphorae at the Anamur Museum
(Photograph by Matthew J. Dillon and Nicholas Rauh)

Image 12: LRA 7 Carrot Shaped Amphorae at the Anamur Museum
(Photograph by Matthew J. Dillon and Nicholas Rauh)

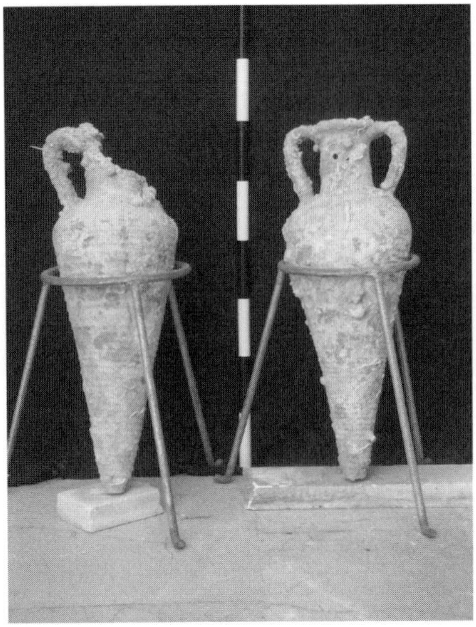

Image 13: LRA 7 Beirut Amphorae at the Anamur Museum
(Photograph by Matthew J. Dillon and Nicholas Rauh)

Image 14: Samos Cistern Amphorae at the Anamur Museum
(Photograph by Matthew J. Dillon and Nicholas Rauh)

Image 15: LRA 5 Palestinian Bag-Shaped Amphorae at the Anamur Museum
(Photograph by Matthew J. Dillon and Nicholas Rauh)

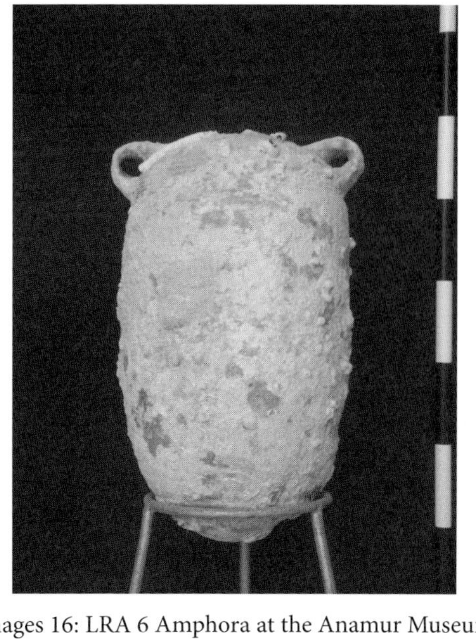

Images 16: LRA 6 Amphora at the Anamur Museum
(Photograph by Matthew J. Dillon and Nicholas Rauh)

Angebot, Nachfrage und Kaufverhalten angesichts von Naturkatastrophen des Mittelalters und der Frühen Neuzeit

Christian Rohr

Einleitung

Extreme Naturereignisse stellen besondere Herausforderungen, ja mitunter massive Einschnitte im Wirtschaftsleben einer Gesellschaft dar. Sie zeigen auch auf, wie verwundbar eine Wirtschaftsordnung im Ausnahmefall ist. Zudem haben Extremereignisse für den Historiker den „Vorteil", dass sie eher dokumentiert werden als der Normalfall.

Im folgenden Beitrag soll anhand von ausgewählten Beispielen aus dem Ostalpenraum aufgezeigt werden, wie vormoderne Gesellschaften auf solche Extreme reagierten und welche Vorkehrungsmaßnahmen getroffen wurden. Die Erkenntnisse für das Spätmittelalter sowie die Frühe Neuzeit können aber mit einer gewissen Vorsicht auch auf andere Epochen der Geschichte übertragen werden, besonders bezüglich der Frage, welche Faktoren zu einer Wahrnehmung als Katastrophe führten. Daher soll an den Beginn ein allgemeines Kapitel gestellt werden, das den Parametern gewidmet ist, die eine derartige Katastrophenwahrnehmung ausmachen bzw. warum und auf welche Weise ständig wiederkehrende extreme Naturereignisse in das Alltags- und Wirtschaftsleben integriert werden konnten. Die konkreten Fallbeispiele aus dem heutigen Österreich sollen verdeutlichen, inwiefern die Berechenbarkeit solcher Ereignisse Auswirkungen auf die lokale und überregionale Wirtschaftsstruktur hatte und damit auch Angebot, Nachfrage und Kaufverhalten der Menschen beeinflusste.

Vom Naturereignis zur Naturkatastrophe

„Naturkatastrophen kennt allein der Mensch, sofern er sie überlebt. Die Natur kennt keine Katastrophen."[1] Dieser Satz aus der Feder des Schweizer Dramatikers Max Frisch – entnommen aus dem 1979 erschienenen Spätwerk „Der Mensch erscheint im Holozän" – hat in den letzten Jahren weite Verbreitung gefunden, ja er fehlt in kaum einer Publikation zur Geschichte und zum Wesen von Naturkatastrophen. Er macht deutlich, dass eine Geschichte der Naturkatastrophen nur über eine Geschichte der Wahrnehmung, Deutung und Bewältigung derselben durch den Menschen verlaufen kann.

Die Suche nach einer allgemein anwendbaren Definition von (Natur-)Katastrophen hat in der Forschung noch zu keinem befriedigenden Ergebnis geführt

1 Frisch 1979/1986, 271.

und vermutlich lässt sich auch gar keine endgültige Definition finden.[2] Ins Leere gehen freilich Versuche, die den Aspekt der Wahrnehmung und damit einen kulturgeschichtlichen Zugang außer Acht lassen. So definiert etwa Josef Nussbaumer in seiner Chronik der Naturkatastrophen seit 1500 eine Naturkatastrophe lapidar: „Eine Naturkatastrophe ist eben eine Katastrophe, bei der – *nomen est omen* – die Natur eine für den Menschen katastrophale Situation auslöst, die im schlimmsten Fall zu Massensterben, Massenobdachlosigkeit und Vernichtung von großen materiellen Werten führt."[3] Nussbaumer, der rein sozialwissenschaftlich nach Opferzahlen klassifiziert, lässt somit einmal die Frage offen, was denn eine Katastrophe an sich sei. Weiters vermittelt er in seiner Definition das Bild, dass die Natur gleichsam über den Menschen hereinbreche. Nun ist es aber der Mensch, der sich im Laufe der Kultivierung der Natur in Bereiche vorwagt, die eben anfällig für extreme Naturgefahren sind: Wer zu nahe am Fluss siedelt, muss Überschwemmungen in Kauf nehmen, wer zu nahe am Berg wohnt, den treffen vielleicht Bergstürze oder Lawinen. Es ist somit nicht die Natur, die für die Katastrophe verantwortlich ist, sondern es ist vielmehr das Empfinden, die Wahrnehmung des Menschen.

Die folgenden Ausführungen sollen dazu dienen, das Umfeld und die Parameter für eine Katastrophenwahrnehmung bei extremen Naturereignissen modellhaft herauszuarbeiten. Sie sind so allgemein gefasst, dass sie im Prinzip genauso auch für Naturkatastrophen in der Antike und in der heutigen Zeit, ja auch für technische Katastrophen und andere einschneidende Ereignisse mit schwerwiegenden Auswirkungen für einzelne Menschen, eine Gruppe oder eine ganze Gesellschaft anwendbar sind. Im Normalfall müssen zumindest drei bis vier Kriterien in Kombination zutreffen, damit von einer Katastrophe für die betroffenen Menschen die Rede sein kann.[4]

a) Mangel an Hilfskräften

Trifft ein extremes Naturereignis mit voller Wucht auf eine Gruppe von Menschen, so ist in ganz besonderem Maße entscheidend, wie weit Hilfe von außen oder Selbsthilfe schon in der Akutphase, d. h. in den ersten sechs bis acht Stunden nach dem Ereignis, einsetzen kann. Gerade wenn viele Menschen im Unglücksgebiet selbst getötet oder verletzt werden, kommt es zu einer großen Verknappung an Hilfskräften, die etwa Evakuierungen oder andere Formen der Soforthilfe leisten können. Tritt während der Akutphase ein eklatanter Mangel an Hilfskräften auf, so hat dies auch einschneidende mittelfristige und langfristige Folgen, nicht zuletzt deswegen, weil dann für Schwerverletzte oft jede Hilfe zu spät kommt. Zu-

2 Vgl. die Definitionsversuche bei Berlioz 1998, 9–13; Berlioz – Quenet 2000; Pfister 2002; Groh – Kempe – Mauelshagen 2003, 15–19; Ossimitz – Lapp 2006; Groh 2007, 10–11; Rohr 2007, 55–62; Rohr 2008, 5–8.

3 Nussbaumer 1996, 12–13.

4 Vgl. zu den folgenden Ausführungen Rohr 2007, 55–62; Rohr 2008, 5–8.

dem kann eine hohe Zahl an Toten auch Auswirkungen auf die längerfristige ökonomische Entwicklung haben, besonders im Rahmen des Wiederaufbaus.

b) Erklärungsmuster und „soziale Gewissheit“

Der Mensch strebt als „vernunftbegabtes“ Wesen nach Erklärungen. Je nachdem, ob er schlüssige Erklärungen für ein ungewöhnliches Ereignis finden kann oder nicht, erlangt er Sicherheit oder er verfällt in Ratlosigkeit, was in der Folge zur Hinwendung zu religiösen oder sonstigen übernatürlichen Deutungsmustern führt. Auch die Schuldzuweisung an andere, vor allem an Außenseiter der Gesellschaft wie Juden, als Hexen diffamierte Frauen oder Fremde, ist Ausdruck dieser Unsicherheit, die aus dem Fehlen von Erklärungen resultiert. Umgekehrt werden extreme Naturereignisse, die sich Menschen erklären können, nur dann zur Katastrophe, wenn sie Ausmaße annehmen, in denen etwa ein Mangel an Hilfskräften eintritt. Das Wissen etwa um die Entstehungsmuster von Überschwemmungen nimmt zumindest einen Teil der Unsicherheit weg.

c) Direkte oder indirekte Betroffenheit

Ist jemand von einem extremen Naturereignis direkt betroffen, etwa wenn sein Hab und Gut vernichtet wird, wenn Personen in seinem Umkreis zu Schaden kommen, dann entsteht für die Überlebenden eine persönliche Katastrophensituation. Je mehr Menschen von einem katastrophalen Ereignis betroffen sind, desto größer ist auch die kollektive Katastrophenwahrnehmung innerhalb einer Gesellschaft. Naturkatastrophen können aber auch indirekt Menschen in große Krisen stürzen: So treffen Überschwemmungen, Hagelgewitter oder Heuschreckenplagen, die große Teile der Ernte vernichten, nicht nur die Bauern vor Ort, sondern die gesamte Gesellschaft, die auf diese Ernteerträge angewiesen ist. Somit gibt es auf die eigentliche Naturkatastrophe mit direkt Betroffenen häufig eine Folgekatastrophe, die auch Menschen miteinbezieht, die vom Naturereignis eigentlich nicht direkt betroffen waren.

d) Unerwartetheit versus Alltag

Das aus kulturgeschichtlicher Sicht vielleicht wichtigste Kriterium für die Wahrnehmung als Katastrophe ist das unerwartete Eintreten eines elementaren Ereignisses. Kommt eine Naturgewalt – etwa ein Erdbeben, ein Hagelgewitter oder ein Tsunami – so schnell, dass keine Vorwarnung und keine Flucht mehr möglich ist, dann ist der Sachschaden meist gewaltig und auch die Opferzahlen sind deutlich höher als bei einem Ereignis, für das Vorkehrungen getroffen werden können. Ein schweres Unwetter, das regional einen Gebirgsbach kurzfristig zu einem wilden Strom anschwellen lässt, der entwurzelte Bäume und Geröll mitführt, löst daher mitunter eine größere Katastrophe aus als eine großflächige Überschwemmung, bei der der Wasserspiegel durch Überregnung allmählich steigt. Häufig spielt auch Sorglosigkeit bezüglich der Siedlungsplätze und der Baumaterialien eine Rolle, dies jedoch eher in unserer Zeit als in historischen Gesellschaften.

In diesem Zusammenhang gewinnt der Aspekt der Erfahrung eine zentrale Bedeutung. Wenn Menschen auf der Basis ihrer langjährigen Erfahrungen im Umgang mit demselben Naturereignis ihre Lebensgewohnheiten darauf abstimmen, so bleibt eine Katastrophenwahrnehmung weitgehend aus. Zum einen ist die Wahrscheinlichkeit, dass große materielle Schäden und Tote zu beklagen sind, relativ gering, wenn beispielsweise von Überflutungen bedrohte Plätze nicht besiedelt werden. Zum anderen können Menschen durch Schutzbauten und andere Vorkehrungen, die während der „Ruhezeiten" getroffen werden, zumindest kleinere und mittlere Naturereignisse so weit abhalten, dass der große Schaden ausbleibt.

Auch spielte es eine Rolle, dass sich Menschen ganz bewusst am Fluss niederließen, um die Vorteile des Lebens am Fluss nutzen zu können, und sich dabei aber des Risikos sehr wohl bewusst waren. Im Normalfall passten sie die Bauweise und Raumaufteilung der Häuser auf die jeweilige Situation bestmöglich an. Nach dem Modell der „Risikospirale" werden freilich im Zuge von Innovationen nicht nur Risiken reduziert und neue Produktivität gewonnen, sondern es entstehen auch neue Unsicherheiten, die wiederum erneute Innovationen nötig machen.[5] Einzelne Gesellschaften können somit bestimmte Naturereignisse durch den repetitiven Umgang in ihren Alltag integrieren.[6] Dadurch entsteht ein „natürlicher" Umgang mit dem Naturereignis, dem zwar stets der Charakter der Bedrohung bzw. Gefahr inhärent ist, dem aber das Wissen über die Bewältigung der Gefahr entgegen gesetzt wird. Das Risiko im Umgang mit möglichen Naturereignissen ist wohl überlegt und dosiert, so dass es nur selten zur Katastrophe für die Gesellschaft kommt. Vor allem verliert das Naturereignis den Charakter des Unerwarteten, des Außergewöhnlichen. Greg Bankoff hat in diesem Zusammenhang den Begriff *cultures of disaster* geprägt,[7] der etwa auch auf den Umgang mit Überschwemmungen in Mitteleuropa adaptiert werden kann; an dieser Stelle sollte aber besser der Begriff „Risikokultur" verwendet werden.[8]

e) Häufung schwerer Naturereignisse in kurzer Zeit

Ein einzelnes extremes Naturereignis ließ sich in vormodernen Gesellschaften zumeist noch einigermaßen bewältigen, so dass es nicht sogleich zu einer Katastrophenwahrnehmung kam. Wenn aber mehrere Naturgewalten innerhalb kurzer Zeit wirksam wurden oder aufgrund des ersten Naturereignisses eine Kettenreaktion entstand, war die Gesellschaft so geschwächt, dass das nachfolgende Ereignis, obwohl es vielleicht objektiv gesehen weniger stark als das erste war, deutlich katastrophalere Auswirkungen zeigte. Dies trifft besonders bei mehreren Überschwemmungen hintereinander zu: Die Menschen sind noch mitten im Wiederaufbau, der Boden kann durch die vorangegangene Überschwemmung noch nicht viel Wasser

5 Sieferle 2006, 157–166.
6 Schmidt 1999, 7–8.
7 Bankoff 2003.
8 Vgl. dazu ausführlich Rohr 2007, 279–327.

aufnehmen, die finanziellen Ressourcen sind erschöpft. Die Folge sind oft totale Ernteausfälle, die notgedrungen auch im Folgejahr zu Engpässen bei der Nahrungsversorgung führen, weil das Saatgut fehlt. Verhängnisvoll sind daher Serien von Großüberschwemmungen im Zweijahresabstand, die in den jeweils darauf folgenden Jahren eine Hungerkrise hervorrufen.

f) Symbolische Konnotationen

Ein Naturereignis muss in der vormodernen Gesellschaft nicht unbedingt materiellen Schaden anrichten, wie dies heute für eine Katastrophe konstitutiv ist, sondern kann auch durch seinen Symbolgehalt ein Katastrophenszenario auslösen. Dies gilt vor allem für Ereignisse, die im Sinne der Bibel hinweisenden Charakter auf das Jüngste Gericht oder eine Strafe Gottes haben. Dazu zählen etwa Heuschreckenplagen, Erdbeben und vor allem auch kosmische Zeichen wie Kometenerscheinungen und Sonnenfinsternisse, die als Vorzeichen (Prodigien) gedeutet wurden.

g) Allgemeine Krisenstimmung

Die Wahrnehmung extremer Naturereignisse als Katastrophe ist schließlich auch in Zeiten intensiver, die allgemein als Krisen zu bezeichnen sind. Die so genannte „Kleine Eiszeit“[9] erreichte um 1570 ihren ersten Tiefpunkt – mitten in der konfessionellen Auseinandersetzung zwischen katholischer, protestantisch-lutherischer und reformiert-calvinistischer Kirche. Gerade für die Jahre um 1570 lesen wir von besonders vielen Naturkatastrophen. Diese Häufung mag zum einen ein Zufall sein, zum anderen auch tatsächlich klimatisch bedingt sein; in jedem Fall aber war auch die Sensibilität der Menschen für die Zeichen der Natur bzw. Gottes deutlich höher. Eine ähnliche Phase allgemeiner Krisenhaftigkeit bilden die 1330er- und 1340er-Jahre.

In den meisten jüngeren Studien zum Wesen von Katastrophen spielen die Faktoren Gefahr, Risiko und Vulnerabilität eine wichtige Rolle bei der Abwägung, ob im konkreten Fall von einer Katastrophenwahrnehmung gesprochen werden muss.[10] Dabei wird unter „Naturgefahr“ vornehmlich die unberechenbare Bedrohung durch die Natur verstanden, während das „Naturrisiko“ die bewusst eingegangene Beziehung meint, bei der der Mensch abschätzt, wie weit er sich der Naturgewalt nähert. Vulnerabilität umschreibt schließlich die potenzielle „Verletzbarkeit“ einer Gesellschaft durch ein extremes Naturereignis, bezogen auf die wirtschaftliche Basis, das soziale Gefüge, den aktuellen Deutungsdiskurs, etc. Je mehr eine Gesellschaft nun zu einer *culture of disaster* bzw. „Risikokultur“ neigt, umso obsoleter wird das Konzept der Vulnerabilität, da ja das ständig wiederkehrende Naturereignis den Alltag nicht unterbricht, sondern im Gegenteil zum Bestandteil desselben wird.[11]

9 Zum Begriff der „Kleinen Eiszeit“ (Little Ice Age) vgl. zusammenfassend Glaser 2010.

10 Vgl. Alexander 2000, 10–20; Plate – Merz – Eikenberg 2001, 14–19.

11 Bankoff 2003, 182–183.

Risikokulturen und ihr Umgang mit Überschwemmungen im Mittelalter und in der Frühen Neuzeit

Überschwemmungen haben im Alpenraum verschiedene Ursachen: Erstens führt die Schneeschmelze im Alpenraum besonders bei Warmwettereinbrüchen durch Föhn sowie im Frühjahr zu einem raschen Ansteigen der Nebenflüsse der Donau, so dass nicht nur diese, sondern vor allem auch die Donau selbst hochwassergefährdet sind.

Zweitens kommt es in den Sommermonaten (Juni bis Anfang September) durch die Überregnung weiter Teile des Ostalpenraums zu ausgedehnten Überschwemmungen sowohl im Gebirge als auch im Alpenvorland. Dabei führen in erster Linie Tiefdruckgebiete über dem nördlichen Mittelmeer, die nordwärts ziehen und am Alpenhauptkamm hängen bleiben, zu intensiven und längeren Regenfällen, weniger die Westwetterlagen vom Atlantik, die zumeist schon über Westeuropa und Deutschland an Kraft verlieren.

Schließlich spielen auch Gewitterregen, die sich vor allem in den warmen Monaten (Mai bis September) innerhalb der Alpen, aber auch im Alpenvorland bilden können, eine bedeutende Rolle für Überschwemmungen. Meist sind die extremen Regenfälle zwar auf ein kleines Gebiet begrenzt, doch führen sie durch die Plötzlichkeit zum einen dazu, dass das Wasser nicht über die üblichen Wege abrinnen bzw. versickern kann, und zum anderen verursachen sie schwere Schäden, ohne dass die ansässige Bevölkerung genug Zeit für Gegenmaßnahmen findet. Großflächigere Gewitter, vor allem nach längeren Trockenperioden, können zudem auch überregionale Überschwemmungen hervorrufen.[12]

Eisstöße sind heute im Ostalpenraum selten geworden. Dies liegt nicht nur an der allgemeinen Klimaerwärmung in der zweiten Hälfte des 20. und im beginnenden 21. Jahrhundert, sondern auch an der Fließgeschwindigkeit der Flüsse, die sich seit den Regulierungen des 19. und 20. Jahrhunderts deutlich erhöht hat. Weitere Eingriffe des Menschen wie Wasserkraftwerksketten und industrielle Nutzung erhöhen ebenfalls die Wassertemperatur. In früheren Jahrhunderten, besonders während der „Kleinen Eiszeit", waren zugefrorene Flüsse und Eisstöße hingegen häufig, ja während des 16. Jahrhunderts fast die Regel.

Geht man von der historischen Quellenlage aus, so sind die Überschwemmungen unterschiedlich gut dokumentiert: überregionale, schwere Hochwasser werden oft als einzige Ereignisse ausführlicher beschrieben, etwa die verheerenden Ereignisse von 1501, 1567, 1572 oder 1598. Auch kleinräumige Überschwemmungen, die nach schweren Gewittern entstehen und Bäche zu reißenden Flüssen machen, aber auch Eisstöße, die selbst große Flüsse innerhalb von wenigen Stunden aufstauen, werden aufgrund ihrer hohen Schadensbilanz ebenfalls in erzählenden Quellen sowie im Verwaltungsschrifttum genauer erwähnt. Hingegen finden überregionale, aber moderate Hochwasser, wie sie an vielen Flüssen fast jährlich

12 Zu den hydrographischen und klimatischen Rahmenbedingungen im heutigen Österreich vgl. ausführlich Lichtenberger 2002, besonders 114–115 und 127–130.

stattfanden, kaum Niederschlag in den Quellen. Diese „normalen Hochwasser" gehörten offensichtlich so sehr zum täglichen Leben, dass sie der betroffenen Bevölkerung kaum berichtenswert erschienen. Grundsätzlich stellt sich aber die Frage gerade nach diesem Normalfall, wenn man einschätzen will, was für Risikogesellschaften die Regel war und welche Ereignisse wirklich als Katastrophen wahrgenommen wurden.

a) Das Beispiel Wels (14.–16. Jahrhundert)

Die Stadt Wels in Oberösterreich liegt am Unterlauf der Traun, einem der wichtigsten Zuflüsse der Donau in Oberösterreich. Der Platz war schon in keltischer Zeit relativ dicht besiedelt, vielleicht auch schon früher. Die Römer errichteten am Kreuzungspunkt der West-Ost-Verbindung mit der Nord-Süd-Verbindung die Zivilstadt *Ovilavis* (*Ovilava*), die im 3. Jh. n. Chr. sogar zur Hauptstadt der Provinz *Noricum Ripense* aufstieg. Das mittelalterliche Wels lag weiterhin am nördlichsten Arm der Traun, umfasste aber nur mehr etwa ein Viertel des römischen Stadtgebiets. Im Laufe des späten Mittelalters und der Frühen Neuzeit erreichte Wels wieder die einstige Ausdehnung.

Im Gegensatz zu heute bildete die Traun in der Gegend von Wels ein weit verzweigtes Flusssystem, dessen Arme bis an die antike und mittelalterliche Südmauer der Stadt, den heutigen Mühlbach, heranreichten. Das Flussbett war hier nur wenig eingetieft und dadurch für einen Übergang gut geeignet. Allerdings kam es immer wieder zu großen Überschwemmungen, bei denen größere Schottermassen abgelagert wurden, so dass die Flussarme häufig ihren Verlauf änderten. Der Fluss spielte daher im Leben der Stadt stets eine wichtige Rolle, sowohl als Ernährer und Garant für einen wirtschaftlichen Wohlstand als auch als Zerstörer.

Auf der Basis archäologischer Untersuchungen lässt sich erschließen, dass Überschwemmungen der Traun zumindest seit der Römerzeit das Leben der Menschen in Wels bzw. *Ovilavis* maßgeblich beeinflusst haben müssen. Schon im Laufe des 2. Jh. n. Chr. hatte eine Überschwemmungskatastrophe Teile der Stadt wohl völlig zerstört. Die ältesten römischen Gräberfelder liegen daher unter einer 1,5 bis 5 Meter dicken sterilen Schotterschicht.[13]

Auch das Problem der Südmauer von *Ovilavis*, die erst durch die Grabungen bei der Renovierung des Minoritenklosters in den 1990er-Jahren erstmals archäologisch nachgewiesen werden konnte,[14] hat vermutlich eine hydrologische Dimension. Die ältere Forschung hatte sogar angenommen, dass das antike *Ovilavis* über gar keine Südmauer verfügte, eine irrige Annahme, die auch jede sonstige Befestigungsanlage ad absurdum führen würde. Allem Anschein nach reichten die nördlichen Seitenarme der Traun bis an die römische Stadtmauer, d. h. bis etwa zum Verlauf des heutigen Mühlbaches, heran und unterspülten die antike Stadtmauer bei jedem Hochwasser. Als das römische *Ovilavis* schließlich aufgegeben wurde und die Stadtmauer verfiel, dürfte der Fluss das Seine dazu beigetragen haben,

13 Vgl. im Detail Holter 1970/71.
14 Vgl. im Detail Miglbauer 1991.

dass bis heute kaum mehr als kleine Reste der Mauer ans Tageslicht gebracht werden konnten.

Die Frage nach dem Untergang des römischen *Ovilavis* selbst könnte ebenfalls mit Überschwemmungen zusammenhängen: Wie ist es zu erklären, dass *Ovilavis* im 5. Jahrhundert plötzlich von der Bildfläche verschwand? Ist es nur ein reiner Zufall, dass *Ovilavis* in der *Vita Severini* nicht erwähnt ist, in Wirklichkeit aber damals noch als Stadt existierte? Eine Zerstörung der römischen Stadtmauer durch kriegerische Ereignisse oder eine Brandkatastrophe ist an keinem der bisherigen Fundorte nachweisbar. Es stellt sich somit die Frage, ob nicht die häufigen Überschwemmungen der Stadtmauer von *Ovilavis* mehr zugesetzt hatten als feindliche Plünderungszüge. Freilich ist dieser Befund archäologisch nur in Ansätzen nachweisbar, weil sich der Verlauf der Traunarme im Lauf der Jahrhunderte mehrfach veränderte und der Fluss zudem jedes Jahr sowohl Schotter als auch Teile der römischen Stadtmauer mit sich transportierte.[15]

Die Quellen zur Geschichte von Wels im Frühmittelalter lassen keinerlei Rückschlüsse auf Überschwemmungen der Traun zu. Auffallend ist jedoch, dass auch die deutlich verkleinerte mittelalterliche Siedlung nahe am nördlichsten Seitenarm der Traun lag. Bald entwickelte sich Wels wieder zu einem Verkehrsknotenpunkt, an dem die Straße den Fluss kreuzte. Vermutlich an derselben Stelle wie in der Römerzeit wurde im wenig eingetieften und durch mehrere Inseln untergliederten Bereich zwischen Aigen (heute im Gemeindegebiet von Thalheim bei Wels) und dem späteren Trauntor eine mehrteilige, rund 600 Meter lange Holzbrücke errichtet,[16] die auf weite Strecken der Brücke ähnlich gewesen sein dürfte, wie sie noch der Merian-Stich des Jahres 1649 (Abb. 1) wiedergibt. Die Brücke dürfte zwischen dem Hochmittelalter und dem 19. Jahrhundert ihr Aussehen und ihre Lage nicht wesentlich verändert haben. Wann die mittelalterliche Brücke errichtet wurde, muss zwar unklar bleiben, doch für das 12. Jahrhundert sind insgesamt vier Nachrichten erhalten, die sich auf Brückenprivilegien beziehen. Ein eigenes Amt zur Verwaltung der Brücke wurde vermutlich zwischen 1236 und 1261 geschaffen; 1298 ist ein Bruckmeister erstmals indirekt belegt.[17]

Überschwemmungen der Traun sind für das Spätmittelalter mehrfach direkt oder indirekt durch Urkunden und anderes Verwaltungsschrifttum belegt: Im Jahr 1355 waren umfangreiche Reparaturarbeiten an der Welser Traunbrücke nötig, die in der zweitältesten der Welser Bruckamtsrechnungen ihren Niederschlag fanden; ganz offensichtlich war ein Hochwasser für die entstandenen Schäden an der Brücke verantwortlich gewesen.[18]

15 Rohr 2007, 281.
16 Vgl. Holter 1955, 124–136.
17 Vgl. Holter 1955, 139–150; Rohr 2007, 282.
18 Vgl. Aspernig 1972, 73–75.

Abb. 1: Die Traunbrücke vor den Toren der Stadt Wels von Süden aus gesehen. Kupferstich von Matthäus Merian, 1649. Im Zentrum sind die Umschlagplätze für Holz gut zu erkennen. In der Nähe des Stadttors befinden sich die Verkaufsbuden der Fleischer (*fleischpenckh*) auf der Brücke. Entlang des Flussufers wurden aus Holz Schutzbauten zur Verstärkung (*schlachten*) errichtet; im Fluss selbst (links der Brücke sowie auf der rechten Seite des Bildes nahe der Stadt) befinden sich weitere hölzerne Schutzvorrichtungen (*wuer*), die den Zweck hatten, Treibholz von den Brückenpfeilern fernzuhalten. Die letzte Holzbrücke wurde 1899 durch ein Hochwasser zerstört und danach durch eine Konstruktion aus Stein und Stahl ersetzt.

Mehrere Urkunden seit dem 14. Jahrhundert geben auch Aufschluss über den Hochwasserschutz:[19] Am 5. Juni 1352 gewährte Herzog Albrecht II. von Österreich (1330–1358) den Bürgern von Wels, auf zwei Jahre das Ungeld – eine Art Mehrwertsteuer – von Salz, Wein, Gewand und anderen Waren auf der Maut zu Wels für Bauvorhaben der Stadt, insbesondere für Wasserschutzbauten zu verwenden. Eine weitere Urkunde mit demselben Datum betrifft ebenfalls den Hochwasserschutz und wurde in die so genannte Pancharte des Jahres 1582 aufgenommen, in der die meisten der für die „Verfassung" der Stadt maßgeblichen Dokumente abschriftlich festgehalten und nochmals durch Kaiser Rudolf II. bestätigt wurden – darunter allein fünf Urkunden zum Hochwasserschutz. In der Urkunde von 1352 kommt ein offensichtlich aktuelles Problem beim Hochwasserschutz zutage: Man-

19 Vgl. zum Folgenden im Detail Rohr 2007, 283–286 mit einer Neuedition der Urkunden.

che Grundbesitzer weigerten sich, auf ihren Grundstücken öffentliche Schutzbauten errichten zu lassen, doch wurde das Gemeinwohl über den Privatbesitz gestellt, da zum Zwecke von Schutzbauten jeder Acker und jede Au offengestellt werden musste. Die beiden Urkunden Albrechts II. wurden jeweils in Wels selbst ausgestellt. Es ist daher anzunehmen, dass im Rahmen des Besuchs des Herzogs ein „Lokalaugenschein" durchgeführt wurde, der schließlich zu den Regelungen über den Hochwasserschutz führte.

Die nächste abschriftlich in der Pancharte von 1582 überlieferte Urkunde über den Hochwasserschutz stammt aus dem Jahr 1376; sie verpflichtete die in der Umgebung liegenden Klöster Lambach und Kremsmünster zur aktiven Hilfe bei der Errichtung von Wasserschutzbauten und vor allem auch beim Ausbau des Welser Stadtgrabens. Der Stadtgraben bildete indirekt einen Teil des Hochwasserschutzes, da er gleichsam ein Auffangbecken darstellte, das zumindest bei kleineren Hochwassern die Schäden für die Stadt selbst gering hielt. Allerdings dürften derart große Projekte die Möglichkeiten der Stadtbürger bei weitem überfordert haben, so dass Herzog Albrecht III. (1365–1393) auch die Äbte der benachbarten Benediktinerstifte zur Mithilfe aufrief.

Am 30. Dezember 1409 stellten die Herzöge Leopold IV. (1395–1411) und Ernst (1402–1424) als Vormünder ihres Vetters Albrecht V. (1404–1439) eine weitere Urkunde für die Bürger der Stadt Wels aus, in der Steuerschulden in der Höhe von 320 Gulden erlassen wurden, um die Wasserschutzbauten voranzutreiben. Ganz offensichtlich war die Stadt in den Jahren 1408 und 1409 so sehr in neue Schulden geraten, dass sie selbst für die wichtigsten Maßnahmen praktisch zahlungsunfähig war. Auch hier dürften Hochwasserschäden die Ursache für die finanziellen Probleme der Stadt gebildet haben.

Eine ähnliche Ausrichtung wie die Urkunde von 1376 weist das Diplom König Friedrichs IV. (1440–1493, der spätere Kaiser Friedrich III.) vom 26. Juni 1445 auf. Der König forderte darin die Grundherren aller Grundherrschaften im Raum Wels auf, dass sie ihre Grundholden beauftragen, mit Robot und Fuhren auf Verlangen der Stadt zu helfen, um die schweren Schäden nach dem letzten Hochwasser zu beheben und neuen Schäden vorzubeugen. Offensichtlich hatten erneut die Ressourcen der Stadt Wels an Menschen und finanziellen Mitteln nicht ausgereicht, die schweren Hochwasserschäden einigermaßen rasch zu beseitigen.

Am 29. März 1469 erließ Kaiser Friedrich III. eine weitere Urkunde, die sich mit der Bewältigung von Hochwasserschäden in Wels befasste: Nach dem großen Wassereinbruch in die Stadt sollten alle Grundholden und Wegleute im Umkreis von drei Meilen um die Stadt mit Wagen, Hauen und Schaufeln zu Hilfe kommen, um die Schäden zu beseitigen.

Wenn auch die erwähnten Urkunden einen ersten Einblick in den Umgang der Welser Bürgerschaft mit den Überschwemmungen geben, so bleiben diese Nachrichten doch auf einige große Hochwasser beschränkt. Vor allem der Aspekt der Solidarität auf regionaler Ebene bei größeren Überschwemmungen wurde in den

Urkunden angesprochen, offensichtlich weil diese nicht von vornherein selbstverständlich war.

Beschränkt man sich auf diesen leichter zugänglichen Quellenbestand, so bleiben freilich viele Desiderate zurück: Von wie vielen großen Hochwassern wissen wir, von wie vielen nicht? Wie oft traten kleinere Überschwemmungen auf? Welche Auswirkungen hatten sie? Lassen sich die materiellen Schäden der großen und kleineren Hochwasser einigermaßen eruieren?

Die Antwort auf derartige Fragen können Urkunden und auch erzählende Quellen nicht oder nur sehr lückenhaft geben. Im Falle von Wels freilich gewähren die Bestände der Bruckamtsrechnungen zumindest für die Zeit ab der Mitte des 15. Jahrhunderts einen lebendigen Einblick in den Umgang auch mit den kleineren Überschwemmungen. Die Welser Traunbrücke mag dabei gleichsam als Hauptindikator des Umgangs mit den Hochwassern dienen.

Die von der Stadt ernannten Bruckmeister schufen in ihrer Verwaltungstätigkeit eine umfassende Serie an Jahresabrechnungen, in denen u. a. die Ausgaben für die Instandsetzung der Brücke festgehalten wurden. Die Einträge erfolgten im Normalfall nach wöchentlich. Die Art und die Dauer der Handwerksarbeiten, für die das Bruckamt nach Überschwemmungen (*wegen der güss*) Löhne bezahlte, deuten somit präzise auf die Auswirkungen der Hochwasser hin – in den meisten Fällen kann mittels der Bruckamtsrechnungen das Naturereignis auf die Woche genau datiert werden (Abb. 2). Zudem werden in den Abrechnungen auch die Holzeinkäufe für die Brückenreparaturen festgehalten. Dabei ist es für die Auswertung von Vorteil, dass das Bruckamt tatsächlich nur für die Brücke und die in deren Umfeld befindlichen Schutzbauten zuständig war, während andere Uferbefestigungen, die Instandhaltung des Stadtgrabens und weitere dem Hochwasserschutz dienende Konstruktionen vom Stadtkammeramt durchgeführt wurden.

Einnahmen lukrierte das Welser Bruckamt seitens der nahe gelegen St.-Ägidienkirche. Einzelne Fragmente dieser Abrechnungen datieren aus den Jahren 1350, 1355, 1397/98 und 1428; ab 1441 hingegen sind die Jahrgänge mit einigen Lücken durchgehend erhalten und bilden so einen der bedeutendsten Bestände des Stadtarchivs Wels zum 15. und 16. Jahrhundert.[20] Eine quantifizierende und statistische Auswertung solcher Bruckamtsrechnungen stößt freilich auch auf Probleme, da manche Jahrgänge deutlich detaillierter gestaltet sind als andere, und zwar unabhängig von der Menge der Ausgaben.

20 Vgl. im Detail Rohr 2007, 79–82.

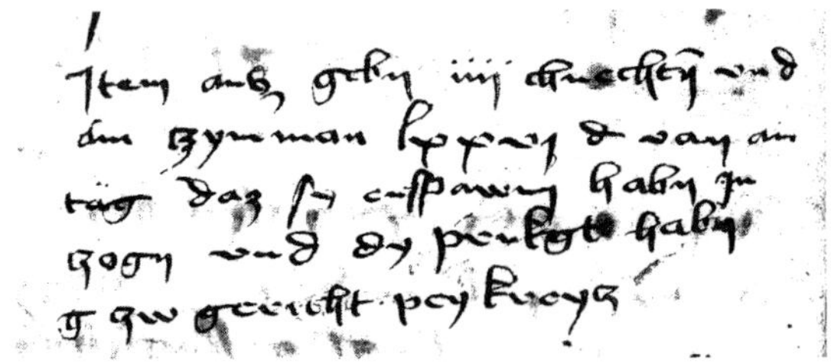

Abb. 2: Eintrag aus den Welser Bruckamtsrechnungen aus dem Jahr 1443 (Wels, Stadtarchiv, Bruckamtsrechnungen 1443, fol. 8v): *Item aus gebn iiii chnecht(e)n und dm zymman lxxvi d van ain täg daz sy enspawm haben inzogn und dy prukgt haben g zw gericht pey kreyz* („Ebenso habe ich [nach der Überschwemmung] für vier Gehilfen und für den Zimmermann 76 Pfennige für einen Tag ausgegeben, weil sie lange Holzbretter (*enspawm*) eingebaut und die Brücke beim Kreuz repariert haben.")

Allgemein sind Brücken und deren Reparatur nach Überschwemmungen als Parameter für die Intensität von Überschwemmungen besonders geeignet, da sie in jedem Fall nur wenige Meter über dem durchschnittlichen Pegelstand der Flüsse liegen, unabhängig von der Lage der Siedlungen. Außerdem ist aus einer wirtschafts- und kulturgeschichtlichen Perspektive weniger die tatsächliche Wasserdurchflussmenge, sondern das Ausmaß der Schäden maßgeblich, die in besonderem Maße durch Treibholz oder Eisgänge verursacht wurden. Die folgenden Klassifikationskriterien sind daher vornehmlich auf die Auswirkungen der Überschwemmung auf (Holz-)Brücken sowie auf die Lebenswelten der Menschen im Allgemeinen ausgerichtet.[21]

<u>Intensität 1:</u>
geringe und moderate Überschwemmungen von ufernahen Wiesen, Feldern und Siedlungen ohne nennenswerte Schäden

<u>Intensität 2:</u>
größere Überschwemmungen, die Schäden anrichten, die in vorindustriellen Gesellschaften innerhalb eines Monats völlig behoben werden können

<u>Intensität 3:</u>
sehr große Überschwemmungen, die große Schäden anrichten und Teile der (Holz-)Brücke völlig zerstören; dadurch wird ein Fährverkehr über den Fluss zumindest für einige Tage notwendig. Die Schäden können von den Menschen in vorindustrieller Zeit nur in ein bis drei Monaten völlig behoben werden.

<u>Intensität 4:</u>
extrem große Überschwemmungen, die aufgrund der enormen Schäden als Katastrophe wahrgenommen werden; die wirtschaftlichen und sozialen Strukturen

21 Rohr 2007, 206.

sind zumindest für mehrere Monate schwer gestört, die Aufräumarbeiten dauern mehr als drei Monate. Die Menschen markieren den Wasserstand zur Erinnerung an die Katastrophe mit Hochwassermarken an Kirchen, Stadttoren und anderen öffentlichen Gebäuden.

Für die historisch-hydrologische Auswertung wurden weniger die Holzeinkäufe als Parameter herangezogen, denn diese erfolgten kontinuierlich, da man in einer Risikokultur ständig damit rechnete, dass das nächste Hochwasser innerhalb weniger Jahre eintreten werde. Vielmehr sind es vor allem die Dauer der Reparaturarbeiten und die Zahl der Handwerker, die daran beteiligt waren, weiters Angaben zur Einrichtung von Fährverkehr, die die Auswirkungen der Hochwasser klassifizieren lassen. Auch wenn durch den alle fünf bis zehn Jahre stattfindenden Wechsel im Bruckmeisteramt die Daten nicht vollständig homogen sind, so lassen sich doch seriöse, langjährige Vergleiche anstellen.

An den Flüssen des Ostalpenraumes sowie des Alpenvorlandes waren großflächige Überregnungen zwischen Mitte Juni und Ende August in den meisten Fällen die Ursache für schwere Hochwasser. Die extreme Konzentration von Überschwemmungen auf die Sommermonate gehört zu den Spezifika des Ostalpenraums und lässt sich auch für die Flüsse Lech und Isar bestätigen,[22] während etwa in Mitteldeutschland eine signifikante Überschwemmungshäufung nicht im Sommer, sondern im Winter festzustellen ist.[23]

Für ein Sommerhochwasser katastrophalen Ausmaßes war im Normalfall eine Serie von Niederschlagsperioden notwendig, d. h. das erste Regenereignis führte zumeist noch nicht zu einem extremen Hochwasser, sondern verringerte zunächst nur die Aufnahmefähigkeit des Bodens. Folgte dann im Abstand von weniger als zwei Wochen erneut eine zweite, lange Überregnungsphase, so floss nun der größte Teil des Wassers oberflächlich ab. Die Bäche und Flüsse schwollen daraufhin sehr rasch zu außergewöhnlicher Höhe an. Derartige „Doppelregenphasen“, die schließlich zu extremen Überschwemmungen führten, sind etwa für die Jahre 1501 (Regen Ende Juli und Mitte August), 1572 (Regen um den 30. Juni und um den 7./8. Juli) und 1598 (Regen um den 8. und um den 16. August) belegt.

Ständig wiederkehrende Hochwasser müssen zum Alltag der Menschen dazugehört haben. Das Kriterium der Unerwartetheit kommt bei Überschwemmungen somit nicht so stark zum Tragen wie bei singulären Naturereignissen. Die aus den Welser Bruckamtsrechnungen gewonnenen Erkenntnisse zeigen deutlich, dass an den österreichischen Flüssen eine derartige Risikokultur in vorindustrieller Zeit bestanden hat. Dazu gehört erstens eine genaue Kenntnis von Ursachen und Auswirkungen der Überschwemmungen; dies beinhaltete auch, dass Vorwarnsysteme existierten, etwa durch die Salzschiffer an der Traun.[24] Zweitens stellten Gemeinschaften wie Städte ihre Vorsorge darauf ein, dass es zu einer raschen

22 Vgl. Böhm – Wetzel 2006.
23 Vgl. Mudelsee – Deutsch – Börngen – Tetzlaff 2006.
24 Rohr 2007, 371.

Abfolge von Überschwemmungen kommen kann, und versuchen auch in Normalzeiten stets sich auf kleinere und größere Hochwasser vorzubereiten, etwa durch den regelmäßigen Ankauf von Holz für Brücken und Wasserschutzbauten. Schließlich resultiert daraus, dass sich etwa einzelne Berufsgruppen auf die Vorsorge sowie die Behebung von Schäden spezialisierten, ja von derartigen Aufträgen sogar abhängig waren. Bis auf ganz wenige Ausnahmen, etwa die extremen Hochwasser von 1501, 1572 und 1598, wurden extreme Abflussereignisse somit nur selten als Katastrophe wahrgenommen und mussten daher nicht übernatürlich, etwa als Strafe Gottes, gedeutet werden – solche Deutungen fehlen in den Bruckamtsrechnungen völlig.

Jahr	**Monat**	**Überschwemmung**	**Intensität**
1497	Mai/Anfang Juni	Überschwemmung mit Schäden	Stark (2)
1498	März, August?	Zwei Überschwemmungen	Mäßig (1/1)
1499	**Ende Mai/Juni**	**Überschwemmung mit schweren Schäden**	**Sehr stark (3)**
1500	April, Mai	Zwei? Überschwemmungen mit Schäden	Mäßig/stark (1/2)
1501	**Juli?, August**	**Katastrophale Überschwemmung**	**Extrem stark (4)**
1502		Keine Überschwemmung	
1503	**September**	**Überschwemmung mit schweren Schäden**	**Sehr stark (3)**
1504	Mai	Überschwemmung	Mäßig (1)
1505	Mai/Juni, August	Zwei Überschwemmungen	Mäßig (1/1)
1506	Juli	Überschwemmung?	Gering (1)
1507	August?	Überschwemmung?	Mäßig (1)
1508	**Juli, August**	**Zwei Überschwemmungen mit Schäden**	**Sehr stark (3)**
1509	Herbst?	Überschwemmung?	Gering (1)
1510		Keine Abrechnungen	

Tabelle 1: Rekonstruktion von Überschwemmungen der Traun in Wels auf der Basis der Welser Bruckamtsrechnungen.[25] Die Aufstellung zeigt zum einen, dass zumindest kleinere oder mittlere Überschwemmungen fast jedes Jahr auftraten, und zum anderen, dass selbst extreme Ereignisse mehrfach pro Jahrzehnt vorkommen konnten. Von den vier Überschwemmungen mit schweren Schäden waren nur zwei (1501 und 1508) bisher aus erzählenden Quellen für das Einzugsgebiet der Donau bekannt.

25 Rohr 2013 (im Druck).

Der Aufbau der Brücke lässt sich aus den Bruckamtsrechnungen recht genau nachvollziehen: Die Pfähle der Brücke, die in den Fluss sowie in den Auengrund gerammt wurden, bestanden aus Eichenstämmen,[26] die vorwiegend bei Bauern aus der Umgebung angekauft wurden; ab 1471 sind diese Bauern vermehrt auch namentlich genannt. Zudem wurden Eichenstämme auch für die Joche verwendet.[27] Auf den Eichenpfählen befestigte man größere Längsbalken, die so genannten En(n)sbäume,[28] und kürzere Querbalken, Streubäume[29] genannt; das Holz kam in Flößen auf den Flüssen Traun und Ager nach Wels.[30] Zusätzlich wurde noch eine geringere Menge an nicht näher spezifiziertem Holz für die Errichtung der Geländer und Fleischbänke benötigt.

Ab den 1470er-Jahren tauchen vermehrt auch Angaben über Metallteile auf, die für die Brückenkonstruktion benötigt wurden, besonders Eisenschuhe,[31] die wohl dazu dienten, dass die zugespitzten Enden der Pfähle beim Einschlagen nicht aufsprangen, diverse Metallbänder[32] und natürlich mehrere Nagelarten. Gelegentlich wird auch Gressing[33] erwähnt, worunter junge Zweige von Nadelholz, besonders von jungen Tannen, zu verstehen sind; sie wurden vermutlich nicht nur für Fischreusen, sondern auch für Wasserwehre verwendet.

Die vergüteten Arbeitsleistungen wurden in den Bruckamtsrechnungen ausführlich dokumentiert. Die Arbeiten des Zimmermanns und der Knechte wurden jeweils wöchentlich abgerechnet; zum Teil wurden Tätigkeiten sogar Tag für Tag aufgelistet, besonders bei Spezialarbeiten wie dem Einschlagen von Pfosten mit einem großen Schlägel. Somit lässt sich aus diesen Auflistungen klar die Dauer der

26 In den Bruckamtsrechnungen meist *aichen(n)* genannt. Die Verwendung als Brückenpfähle wird mitunter explizit hervorgehoben, vgl. ebd. 1474, fol. 10v: *It(em) ich hab kauft von dem Jorg zw Perbend vii aichen zw prukstekchen je ain per iiii ß. d. ...* Der Preis der Eichenstämme, die als Brückenpfeiler verwendet wurden, lag meist deutlich über 100 d., während die übrigen Eichenstämme zwischen 35 und 70 d. kosteten. Zur Bedeutung von Eichenholz, das im Mittelalter als das beste Bauholz galt, vgl. Radkau – Schäfer 1987, 28.

27 Vgl. etwa explizit Wels, Stadtarchiv, Bruckamtsrechungen 1472, fol. 13v: *It(em) vb(er) ain aichen zu einem joch xliiii d.* Schließt man nach dem Preis, so wurden die meisten der Eichenstämme für Joche verwendet.

28 In den Bruckamtsrechnungen *enspaum*, *enspawm*, *enns paumb* oder *ennspem* genannt. Zum Begriff des En(n)sbaums vgl. Rohr 2007, 248 Anm. 151.

29 In den Bruckamtsrechnungen meist kurz *streu*, *strey* oder *strä*, ab 1475 auch *streipawm* genannt. Streubäume wurden nach dem Stich von Merian zu schließen auch für die Begrenzungen zwischen Flussbett und Inseln verwendet (vgl. Abb. 1).

30 Vgl. in diesem Sinne Holter 1955, 137. Die Herkunft des Holzes ist allerdings nur in ganz seltenen Fällen erwähnt. In Wels, Stadtarchiv, Bruckamtsrechungen 1463, fol. 8v wird für die Wehr verwendetes Holz explizit als *atergaysche holczl* (Holz aus dem Attergau) bezeichnet.

31 In den Bruckamtsrechnungen meist *eysenschuech* oder nur *schu(e)ch* genannt.

32 In den Bruckamtsrechnungen *twerichpandtn* oder *eysnes pannt* genannt, oft verbunden mit einer Angabe zum Verwendungsbereich, etwa *an ein prukhstekhen* (so Wels, Stadtarchiv, Bruckamtsrechungen 1479a, fol. 14r).

33 In den Bruckamtsrechnungen *gressing* oder *grassäng* genannt.

Reparaturen ableiten und damit auf die Intensität der Brückenschäden schließen.[34]

Interessant ist schließlich auch ein Blick auf die Holzeinkäufe, die in den Jahren nach 1501 auffallend niedrig waren. Die Überschwemmungen im ganzen Land hatten Holz zu einer begehrten Mangelware gemacht. So verwundert es kaum, dass im Jahr 1502 anstelle der Eichenstämme auch Lärchenstämme für die Pfähle angekauft wurden, um dem steigenden Bedarf gerecht zu werden. In den Jahren 1503 bis 1506 waren dann die Eichenvorräte offensichtlich endgültig erschöpft: kein einziger Eichenstamm wurde angekauft, dafür aber 1503 nicht weniger als 85 Lärchenstämme um die Summe von 4180 Pfennigen, die – wie der regelmäßige Zusatz *für stekchen* andeutet – alle dem Zweck dienten, den sonst die Eichenstämme einnahmen. Vor dieser Versorgungskrise wurden nie Lärchenstämme für die Pfähle verwendet. Bei den Ennsbäumen wiederum lässt sich eine mehr als 20-prozentige Preissteigerung pro Stück gegenüber den Vorjahren feststellen.[35] Bemerkenswert ist auch, dass der Gesamtpreis für das eingekaufte Holz in den 1510er-Jahren explodierte, etwa im Jahr 1516, als Holz für nicht weniger als 11.583 Pfennig eingekauft wurde, während noch im Jahr 1505 gerade 1.831 Pfennig aufgewendet werden mussten (Grafik 1).

Grafik 1: Ausgaben für Holz durch das Welser Bruckamt, 1471–1520. Die Grafik macht deutlich, dass die Holzeinkäufe kontinuierlich erfolgten, unabhängig davon, ob sich gerade eine Überschwemmung ereignet hatte oder nicht. Die Katastrophenflut von 1501 hatte daher zunächst keinen entscheidenden Einfluss auf das System der Holzeinkäufe und auf die Preisentwicklung. Allerdings wurden Eichenstämme nach den drei aufeinander folgenden schweren Überschwemmungen von 1499, 1501 und 1503 schließlich so knapp, dass für drei Jahre überhaupt keine Eichenstämme verfügbar waren und man danach auf Lärchenstämme auswich. Nach einer weiteren zerstörerischen Flut im Jahr 1508 begannen schließlich die Holzpreise allgemein deutlich zu steigen – bis zur doppelten Höhe durchschnittlicher Jahre.

34 Vgl. dazu ausführlich Rohr 2004, 312–315 am Beispiel der Arbeiten nach dem Hochwasser von 1443 (Wels, Stadtarchiv, Bruckamtsrechungen 1443, fol. 5r–9v und fol. 14rv).

35 Für Jahrzehnte war der Preis pro Ennsbaum bei etwa 35 bis 42 Pfennig gelegen. 1503 kosteten sie durchwegs 50 Pfennig und mehr.

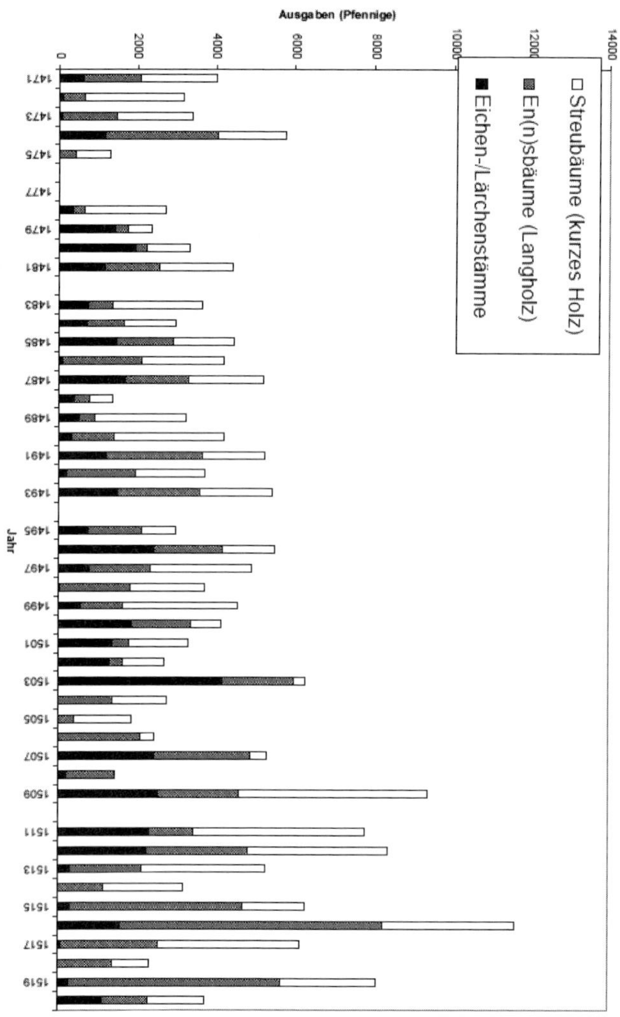

Grafik 1: Ausgaben für Holz durch das Welser Bruckamt, 1471-1520

Die Analyse der Ausgaben des Bruckamts für Bauholz und für die Reparaturen zeigt auch, dass die dafür aufgewendeten Summen enorm waren. So waren in vielen Jahren die Zimmerleute viele Wochen nur mit Arbeiten an der Brücke beschäftigt, im Durchschnitt 10–20 Prozent der Jahresarbeitszeit. Umgekehrt lässt sich daraus ableiten, dass in einer Risikokultur wie in Wels innerhalb der Zimmererzunft mehr Meister und Gehilfen nötig waren als in ähnlich großen Städten. Die Überschwemmungen wurden auf diese Weise zum Arbeitgeber.

b) Die Stadt Krems in den Jahren 1572 und 1573

Während beim Beispiel Wels die Langzeitperspektive im Vordergrund stand, soll bei den folgenden Ausführungen über die Stadt Krems an der niederösterreichischen Donau der Blick auf zwei knapp aufeinanderfolgende Ereignisse und deren ökonomische Bewältigung gerichtet werden: ein schweres Sommerhochwasser 1572, ausgelöst durch lang anhaltende Überregnung, und ein Eisstoß im Januar 1573. Die Überschwemmungen des Sommers 1572 waren die schwersten seit dem „Jahrtausendhochwasser" von 1501 und betrafen den gesamten österreichischen Donauraum und sein Einzugsgebiet von Tirol bis Ungarn.[36] Das Naturereignis wurde insbesondere auch deswegen zur Katastrophe, weil es in eine allgemeine Krisenzeit fiel: die allgemeine Klimaverschlechterung der „Kleinen Eiszeit" erreichte damals ihren ersten Höhepunkt, was zu massiven Teuerungen beim Getreide führte. Zudem waren schon 1567 und 1569 schwere Hochwasserschäden zu beklagen gewesen.

Eine sehr anschauliche Quelle zu den Auswirkungen des Hochwassers vom Juli 1572 an der Donau stellt ein Schreiben der Stadt Krems an Kaiser Maximilian II. vom 17. Februar 1573 dar.[37] Darin wird der Kaiser und Landesherr um Hilfe und Steuernachlass gebeten, da auf das zerstörerische Hochwasser ein noch schlimmerer Eisstoß im Januar 1573 gefolgt sei. Offensichtlich war das Sommerhochwasser noch einigermaßen mit den zur Verfügung stehenden Mitteln bewältigbar gewesen, die Serie zweier extremer Naturereignisse wurde hingegen endgültig für die Menschen zur Katastrophe. Zum Sommerhochwasser 1572 berichteten die Kremser und Steiner Stadtoberen zunächst, dass ein großer Teil der Stadt unter Wasser gestanden sei und die zumeist dicken Mauern völlig aufgeweicht habe. Einer der Türme von Stein war demnach so stark durch das Wasser in Mitleidenschaft gezogen worden, dass die darin aufbewahrte Urkunden und Rechnungen des Waisenhauses zumindest zum Teil zerstört worden sein dürften. Blickt man allerdings in die Bestände des heutigen Kremser Stadtarchivs, so ist ansonsten kein Bruch mit 1572/1573 feststellbar.[38] Der Bericht fährt fort, dass die Schäden an der inneren und äußeren Stadtmauer sowie an zahlreichen Häusern nicht mehr bis zum Winter behoben werden konnten, ja die Bewältigung und Reparatur der Zerstörungen noch Jahre dauern würde. Zudem sei die ökonomische Basis vieler Bürger, die Weingärten, Äcker und Wiesen, ebenfalls durch das Hochwasser völlig zerstört.

Am 9. Januar des Jahres 1573 wurden die beiden Städte Krems und Stein in der Wachau von einem gewaltigen Eisstoß heimgesucht, der nicht zuletzt wegen der noch nicht behobenen Schäden des Julihochwassers 1572 rasch zur Katastrophe

36 Zu den Auswirkungen des Hochwassers von 1572 vgl. im Detail Rohr 2007, 247–257.

37 Der Bericht ist ediert bei Kinzl 1869, 150–152, aufbauend auf Krems, Stadtarchiv, Missivprotokoll des Magistrats 1573; er ist erneut wiedergegeben bei Rohr 2007, 255–256 sowie 333–335.

38 Zu den Beständen vgl. im Überblick Lackner 1993, 82–84 (zu Krems) und 84–85 (zu Stein). Auch die Ratsprotokolle sind erst ab 1577 erhalten. Die älteren Jahrgänge könnten daher ebenfalls beim Julihochwasser 1572 oder beim Eisstoß 1573 vernichtet worden sein.

wurde. Im Schreiben an Kaiser Maximilian II. schilderten die Bürger zunächst, wie es zum Eisstoß gekommen sei, wie viele Häuser beschädigt worden seien und dass die Menschen gerade noch über die Dächer ins Freie kommen konnten. In der von Hochwassern und auch Eisstößen ständig geplagten Stadt war man es mit Sicherheit gewohnt, immer wieder Teile der Stadt evakuieren zu müssen. Dennoch kam der Eisstoß unerwartet schnell, da er sich im Gegensatz zu den meisten Donauüberschwemmungen nicht innerhalb von Tagen, sondern in wenigen Stunden aufbaute. In einem weiteren Abschnitt der Petition wird auf die Verluste von Wein und Getreide eingegangen. Zudem wird erwähnt, dass man durch die lange Dauer des Eisstoßes – immerhin zwölf Tage – nicht mit den Aufräumarbeiten habe beginnen können. Noch mehr als fünf Wochen danach lägen Berge von Eisschollen in der Stadt herum; Häuser, Türme und Stadtmauern seien schwer beschädigt:

> Die Wein und Traidt, daran dann unser aller Narung am maisten gelegen und anderes im Wasser umgeschwumben und des großen Gewässers auch Eis welches dan in die 12 Tage und Nachte Continuo an einander und noch lenger also gestandten ain solicher Jamer und nott gewest, das wir samentlich uns anders nichts zu besorgen noch zu fürchten gehabt, als es trage das Wasser und gewaltige Eiß baide Stett was doch im wasser gestanden in Grundt hinweg, so gar erschrecklich und gewaltig ist gewest wie es dann noch heuttigs tags zum thail vor Augen und das Eiß wie die großen berge daligt, das man auch zu Krembs gegen die Thunau die Maur noch thor nicht weniger aus noch ein mag, die Stadtmeur und thurn nidergerissen, vill heuser gar eingefallen auch noch vil also erwaicht, das anders nichts zu besorgen, dan das dieselben noch eingehen werden.[39]

Daraufhin folgt ein Blick in die Zukunft: Das Julihochwasser 1572 und der Eisstoß vom Januar 1573 hätten die Weingärten und anderen agrarisch genutzten Flächen an der Donau so sehr zerstört, dass an einen Ertrag für viele Jahre nicht zu denken sei. Ebenso seien die Weinvorräte in den Kellern vernichtet, so dass die Menschen vor dem Ruin stünden. Die Häuser in Krems und Stein würden aufgrund der Armut der Bevölkerung öd stehen bleiben; an die Ausübung eines Gewerbes in diesen Häusern sei nicht zu denken:

> Die Baumb und Weingartten auch Aeckher und Wisen und derglaichen gründt, so in der Nider und neben am wasser gelegen, dermassen verschut, verschwembt und verderbt, das auch in villen Jaren die nicht mögen zu Früchten gebracht werden, und da auch gleich nun die Thunau verrunnen ist doch jetzo wie das waich wetter angangen, die Krembs so gewaltig angeloffen, und weil die vor dem großen Eißstos, so die Thunau angetragen, iren rechten lauff nit gehaben khönnen, sich eingeschwellt und vom neuen die Keller mit was-

39 Kinzl 1869, 151; Rohr 2007, 334.

> ser angefüllt und durch die weingarten, Aeckher, Wißen und andern gründt auß laufft, also noch khain aufhören und in Summa solicher Jammer und nott schaden und verderben entstanden, daß zu erbarmen und alles anzuzeigen nit wol möglich, auch nit wol glaublich, dann man hett es selbs mit Augen gesehen, hierdurch um baide Stett sambt derselben armen Burgerschafft in hoches unüberwindtliches Verderben geratten, vil aus Armuet ihre Heuser Ödt und wüst werden ligen lassen, wie dan ohne das zuvor zu Stain In 40 Heußer ödt ligen, auch nit weniger zu Krembs ödt stehen, die Manschaft geschmellert wirdt. So haben beede Stett keine sondern gewerb auch gar kain einkhommen, und seit aber nun das wasser durch so vielfeltig güß sowol ob als under der Erdten seinen Lauff und Ader in die Keller und gemeur gerunnen und durchgangen, nunmer wie ein wenig das wasser sich ergießt, dann dasselbige in die Keller steht die Heußer erwaickht, und niemand wol sicherlich seine Wein darinen sich erhalten wirdt, und also alle Narung so maistentheils an dem Wein war gelegen, den Stetten wird entzogen werden, und gemainer Burgerschafft ihre Narung nit mer wirdt gehaben, als dann auch weder Steur noch anderes nit mer raichen noch erlegen khönnen.[40]

Der Bericht legt nahe, dass in den vom Weinbau lebenden Zwillingsstädten Krems und Stein das Angebot für Wein völlig zusammengebrochen sei, weil die beiden Extremereignisse insbesondere die nahe am Donauufer wohnenden Weinbauern mitsamt ihren Weingütern betroffen habe. Auch die Stadtordnung von Krems aus dem Jahr 1524 geht auf dieses offenbar häufige Szenario ein und erwähnt explizit die Weinbauern in Ufernähe, denen es bei Überschwemmungen gestattet war, die gefährdeten Weinfässer in ihren Kellern an sichere Orte zu bringen und dort ihren Wein auszuschenken, damit sie weiterhin Frau und Kind ernähren können.[41]

Der Bericht der Kremser und Steiner Bürgerschaft sollte beim Landesfürsten natürlich Solidarität wachrufen. Für eine Quellenkritik wird damit klar, dass die Schilderungen mit Sicherheit besonders drastisch ausfallen mussten. Natürlich wird es die angeführten Schäden in Teilen der Stadt gegeben haben, doch wurde offensichtlich bewusst pauschaliert, d. h. die Schäden betrafen wohl allein die Häuser und Stadtmauern in der Ebene, kaum aber die an den Abhängen gelegenen Stadtteile von Krems und Stein, von denen in dem Bericht nichts zu lesen ist.[42] Zudem fällt auf, dass von Obdachlosen oder Erfrorenen nirgendwo die Rede ist.

40 Kinzl 1869, 151–152; Rohr 2007, 334–335.

41 Stadtordnung für Krems und Stein vom 12. März 1524, erlassen von der zur Reformation des Kammerguts bestellten Kommission, Artikel 63. Vgl. zu dieser Stelle Rohr 2007, 377–378 mit Anm. 638.

42 Dass das Hochwasser allgemein an der niederösterreichischen Donau verheerend gewesen sein muss, bezeugt auch ein Nachtrag in der Kleinen Klosterneuburger Chronik zum Jahr 1572, in dem von schweren Überschwemmungen des Tullnerfelds und Marchfelds die Rede ist: *Im selben iar [1572] umb Margaretha [13. Juli] ist die Thonaw gewaltig groß gewest, daz daz gancz Thulner velt ist uberrunen; auch daz Marichvelt. Und hat grossen schaden gethon an dem getraidt, dan es hats an dem velt hinwöckhgefürt und ist gleich zur erndtezeid geschehen.*

Auch hat sich im Wiener Finanz- und Hofkammerarchiv ein Akt vom Sommer 1573 erhalten, der von einem Kredit über 5.500 Gulden handelt, den einige Bürger von Krems dem in Geldnöten steckenden Kaiser Maximilian II. gewährten.[43] Diese reichen Bürger dürften demnach das Sommerhochwasser und den Eisstoß ohne nennenswerte materielle Schäden überstanden haben. Dennoch kann davon ausgegangen werden, dass es sich damals in Krems und Stein nicht zuletzt durch die rasche Aufeinanderfolge von Sommerhochwasser und Eisstoß um eine Großkatastrophe gehandelt haben dürfte, deren Behebung sich über mehrere Jahre dahinzog und dauerhafte Folgen für die Wirtschaft des Kremser Raums mit sich brachte.

Ökonomische Auswirkungen von Heuschreckenplagen

Tierplagen haben das Leben der Menschen zu allen Zeiten wohl ebenso beeinflusst wie elementare Naturereignisse und extreme Wetterverhältnisse, nicht zuletzt deshalb, weil sie die Nahrungskette des Menschen massiv bedrohten.[44] Sie fallen daher in einem weiteren Sinne unter die Naturereignisse, die in vielen Fällen von den Menschen als Katastrophen erlebt wurden.

Wanderheuschrecken treten vor allen in warmen und trockenen Klimaten auf. Die Europäische Wanderheuschrecke (*locusta migratoria*) erreicht im Normalfall eine Größe von 2–6 cm. Ihre Fluggeschwindigkeit beträgt etwa 12–18 km/h, die Flughöhe bis zu 200 Meter. Sie ernährt sich von allen Pflanzenteilen, also auch von Rinden und holzigen Zweigen, und kann pro Tag bis zum Doppelten ihres Eigengewichts an Nahrung aufnehmen. Zu unterscheiden sind zwei Erscheinungsformen im Lebensrhythmus der Tiere, die jeweils hormonell gesteuert sind: In der Solitärphase leben die Wanderheuschrecken oft über Jahre hindurch allein und stellen damit keine Bedrohung dar. In der Gregärphase hingegen steigt zunächst die Zahl der Wanderheuschrecken sprunghaft an.[45] Sie schließen sich danach zu großen Schwärmen (bis zu zwei Milliarden Tiere) zusammen, die bis zu 12 km^2 groß werden können. Bei der Fortbewegung bilden die jüngeren Tiere die Hüpferschwärme, die älteren, geflügelten Tiere die Luftschwärme. Die Richtung der Heuschreckenschwärme wird zu einem maßgeblichen Anteil von den Winden beeinflusst. Bei heißem und nicht zu feuchtem Wetter legen die Heuschrecken ihre Eier im Boden ab; aus den Larven schlüpfen im Folgejahr wieder Heuschrecken und verlängern somit die Plage. Starker Regen und Kälte hingegen führten rasch zu einem weitgehenden Verschwinden der Heuschreckenschwärme.[46]

---

43 Wien, Finanz- und Hofkammerarchiv, Niederösterreichische Herrschaftsakten, K 57/a. In dem umfangreichen Akt ist nie von den eben vergangenen Naturkatastrophen die Rede.

44 Zur Wahrnehmung, Deutung und Bewältigung von Heuschreckenplagen im Alpenraum vgl. zuletzt ausführlich Rohr 2007; 463–492 sowie speziell zu Tirol Rohr 2009; Jäger 2010, 105–121.

45 Vgl. Delort 1987, 187–188.

46 Vgl. etwa Baron 1975, 11–16, 34 und 103–104.

Trockene Perioden begünstigten die Ausbreitung von Heuschreckenzügen in Mitteleuropa im 5., im 9. sowie vom 14. bis zum frühen 16. Jahrhundert. Eine hohe Frequenz an Invasionen ist für das 14. Jahrhundert belegt, etwa 1310, 1338–1341, 1364 und 1366. Eine zweite Invasionswelle betraf zwischen 1477 und 1480 v.a. den Ostalpenraum, während die Welle nach dem „Jahrtausendsommer" 1540 weite Teile Mitteleuropas bis hinauf nach Schlesien erfasste und bis 1547 anhielt. Nach der Mitte des 16. Jahrhunderts verschwanden die Heuschrecken in Mitteleuropa für rund 150 Jahre fast völlig und kamen praktisch nur mehr im Mittelmeerraum vor. Erst zwischen 1690 und 1694 zogen wieder nennenswerte Schwärme von Ungarn ostwärts und erreichten 1693 auch Mitteldeutschland, Schlesien, Böhmen und Mähren. Ein Großteil der Heuschreckenzüge betraf Mitteleuropa zur Zeit der Ernte im Juli oder danach im August. Je nachdem war auch die Schadhaftigkeit der Invasionen größer oder geringer.

Die Verbreitungswege lassen sich auf einige Grundmuster verallgemeinern. Im Normalfall gingen die Heuschreckenplagen von der Großen Ungarischen Tiefebene oder der Schwarzmeerregion aus. Viele Schwärme verließen diese Räume nicht, doch bei trockenem Wetter und Ostwinden erreichten sie zunächst Westungarn. Von dort führte eine erste Wanderroute nördlich der Alpen entweder durch Nieder- und Oberösterreich bis nach Bayern und mitunter bis an den Rhein oder über Mähren nach Böhmen, Schlesien, Sachsen und Meißen. Eine zweite Route verlief inneralpin durch die Steiermark, Kärnten und Krain nach Nord- und Südtirol und ins Trentino. Eine dritte Route, die auch noch während der Klimaverschlechterung im 16. und 17. Jahrhundert wichtig blieb, brachte die Heuschrecken über die Slawonische Tiefebene und die nördliche Adria nach Norditalien, wo in der Poebene die meisten Schäden zu beklagen waren; mitunter erreichten die Tiere von Süden kommend auch über das Etschtal das Trentino und Südtirol.[47]

Es soll im Folgenden nicht auf die einzelnen Wellen an Heuschreckeneinfällen eingegangen werden, sondern der Schwerpunkt auf die ökonomischen Auswirkungen gelegt werden. Vorab ist aber festzuhalten, dass die Berichte über die Heuschreckeneinfälle des ausgehenden Mittelalters und der beginnenden Neuzeit zwar durchaus zahlreich sind, doch in vielen Fällen in ihrer Wahrnehmung, Deutung und schriftlichen Verarbeitung stark durch biblische Konnotationen geprägt wurden. Heuschrecken sind in der Bibel als achte ägyptische Plage erwähnt, werden ausführlich im Buch Joel beschrieben und sind auch in der Offenbarung des Johannes Vorzeichen auf das Jüngste Gericht. Sie wurden deswegen durchgehend als Strafe und Zeichen Gottes interpretiert.[48]

Wie schwer die Verwüstungen und die wirtschaftlichen Schäden durch die Heuschreckeneinfälle tatsächlich gewesen sind, lässt sich daher nur „zwischen

47 Rohr 2011, 2–3.

48 Exodus 10, 3–19; Joel 1, 2–2, 11; Offenbarung 6, 1–8 und 9, 1–11. Vgl. zu den biblischen Mustern bei der Schilderung von Heuschreckenplagen in mittelalterlichen und frühneuzeitlichen Quellen ausführlich Rohr 2007, 456–463.

den Zeilen“ rekonstruieren.[49] Offensichtlich war der „symbolische Schaden“ aber in vielen Fällen deutlich höher als der materielle. So ist in keiner mittelalterlichen Quelle aus dem österreichischen Raum im Zusammenhang mit Heuschreckenplagen von einer Preissteigerung beim Getreide die Rede![50] Dies fällt umso mehr auf, als sich einige Quellen, wie die Mattseer Annalen oder die 1428 entstandene Kleine Klosterneuburger Chronik, ausgesprochen interessiert an Preissteigerungen zeigen; diese traten im 14. und 15. Jahrhundert allerdings nicht aufgrund von Heuschrecken – und auch nur selten aufgrund von Überschwemmungen – auf, sondern zumeist in sehr heißen, trockenen oder völlig verregneten Sommern, in denen der Weizen und andere Getreidesorten klein blieben.[51]

Erst im Zuge der Heuschreckenplage in Niederösterreich in den 1540er-Jahren sah sich der Landesfürst, Ferdinand I., gezwungen, durch einen Generalerlass die Teuerung von Getreide zu unterbinden – m. W. der erste Beleg überhaupt, dass es im Zuge von Heuschreckenschwärmen zu einem Preisanstieg beim Getreide gekommen sei. Auch in Krain entwickelte sich im Zuge der Heuschreckenplage 1543 eine große Hungersnot, die vielen Menschen das Leben kostete. Krainer Gesandte sprachen deswegen sogar auf dem Reichtag zu Augsburg 1547/48 vor.[52]

Die Beantwortung der Frage nach den tatsächlichen wirtschaftlichen Auswirkungen der Heuschreckenschwärme muss über mehrere Aspekte erfolgen: Zunächst sind drei Erscheinungsformen der Heuschrecken deutlich zu unterscheiden. Fliegende Wanderheuschrecken verursachten bei den Menschen des ausgehenden Mittelalters und der beginnenden Neuzeit zwar apokalyptische Assoziationen, nicht zuletzt, da die Schwärme oft als so dicht beschrieben wurden, dass sich die Sonne verdunkelte. Im Flug selbst richten die Heuschrecken aber keinen Schaden am Getreide und an den Wiesen an, und auch keine Vergiftung von Mensch und Vieh kann im Flug erfolgen, wie dies in einigen Quellen berichtet wird. Erst wenn sich die Heuschrecken am Boden niederließen, begann der eigentliche Schadensbefall. Die Tiere fraßen das Getreide von der Wurzel weg ab

49 Vgl. zu den folgenden Ausführungen Rohr 2007, 488–492.

50 Vgl. in diesem Sinne schon Pautsch 1953, 43, die auch darauf hinwies, dass zum Zeitpunkt der meisten Heuschreckeninvasionen rund um Maria Himmelfahrt (15. August) ein Großteil der Ernte schon eingebracht worden sein dürfte.

51 Vgl. etwa die Kleine Klosterneuburger Chronik zu den Jahren 1405, 1406, 1416, 1426 und 1427: Das Jahr 1405 war verregnet, so dass der Wein sauer und das Getreide teuer war; es musste sogar aus Böhmen importiert werden. Ein Metzen Weizen wurde um 80–90 Pfennig, ein Metzen Hafer um 40 Pfennig gehandelt. 1406 war ebenfalls ein Jahr mit wenig Getreideertrag und auch wenig Wein, so dass es erneut zu einer Teuerung kam. 1416 betraf die Teuerung beim Getreide zunächst Bayern, in der Folge aber auch Österreich. 1426 war ein derart heißer, dürrer und trockener Sommer, dass der Weizen kurz und teuer war; die Preise für Mehl stiegen vor allem auch dadurch an, dass die Bachmühlen zwanzig Wochen lang wegen des Niedrigwassers nicht mahlen konnten. Im darauf folgenden strengen Winter 1427 konnten erneut die Mühlen für mehrere Wochen nicht mahlen; die Preise für einen Metzen Weizen stiegen wieder auf 50–60 Pfennig, die für einen Metzen Hafer auf 28–32 Pfennig. Keine derartige Nachricht findet sich hingegen zu den Jahren mit Heuschreckeninvasionen.

52 Vgl. Rohr, 2007, 480–481 mit Anm. 89.

und auch die Wiesen wurden häufig schwer in Mitleidenschaft gezogen.[53] Die Heuschrecken dürften aber die Wiesen nicht völlig vernichtet haben, sondern sie einfach wie Kühe, Schafe und Ziegen gründlich „abgegrast" haben.[54] Dadurch entstand vor allem ein zeitlich begrenzter Nahrungsausfall für das Weidevieh. Dieser konnte allerdings noch deutlich erhöht werden, wenn die Heuschrecken auch die Heuschober kahl fraßen. Als dritte Erscheinungsform sind die jungen Heuschreckenlarven erwähnt, die zum Teil den Haustieren sogar als Futter dienten.[55] Da die Larven nicht fliegen konnten, versuchten die Menschen den Heuschrecken in diesem Zustand zu begegnen, indem die Larven in großen Behältern gesammelt und danach verbrannt oder vergraben wurden. Zudem machten Nässe und Kälte den Heuschreckenschwärmen oft ein rasches Ende. Somit zeigt sich, dass allein die Gegenden wirklich großen wirtschaftlichen Schaden erlitten, in denen sich die Heuschrecken tatsächlich zu Boden ließen und mit dem Fressen begannen.

Einen weiteren wichtigen Aspekt bei der Einschätzung der wirtschaftlichen Auswirkungen bilden die topographischen Gegebenheiten. Es entsteht in den Quellen der Eindruck, dass die Heuschrecken im Flachland, etwa im nieder- und oberösterreichischen sowie im bayerischen Alpenvorland, im Normalfall eine Schneise der Verwüstung durch die Landschaft zogen, die vermutlich eine Breite von einigen Kilometern aufwies.[56] Die Gebiete abseits dieser Schneise dürften offensichtlich weitgehend unversehrt geblieben sein.

In inneralpinen Tal- und Beckenlandschaften wie in der Steiermark, in Kärnten, in Krain sowie in Nord- und Südtirol konnten sich die Heuschrecken hingegen nur in den vorgegebenen Tälern ausbreiten. Dies lässt sich beispielhaft an den Schilderungen von Jakob Unrest zur Heuschreckenplage 1477 nachvollziehen: Über das Mur- und das Drautal drangen die Heuschrecken aus der Pannonischen Tiefebene in die inneralpinen Regionen vor und befielen danach ein Tal Kärntens und Südtirols nach dem anderen: das Lavanttal, die Wörtherseeregion, das Rosental, das Gailtal, das Kanaltal, das Pustertal und schließlich das Eisacktal.[57] Diese

53 Vgl. dazu die Bemerkung bei Johann von Viktring, Liber certarum historiarum 6, 7 ad a. 1338: *Semen in sulcis terre et cespitibus reliquerunt, sed non disparuerunt donec brumalis temporis strictitudinem persenserunt.* Demnach hätten die Heuschrecken das Getreide und die Grasnarbe nicht so weit zerstört, dass es auch für die Zukunft zerstört worden wäre.

54 Vgl. etwa in diesem Sinne Anonymus, Anmerkungen zum Jahr 1350: *Und wo es sich auf dy wis legt, daz fras ez ab, daz man want, es hiet das viech abgefressen ...*

55 Vgl. Rurscheyt 1542, 3–4.

56 Zum Jahr 1475 wird berichtet, dass der Heuschreckenschwarm eine Länge von drei Meilen und eine Breite von eineinhalb Meilen gehabt hätte. Vgl. dazu Pilgram 1788, 314 unter Berufung auf die Fortsetzung der Chronik von Ursperg (Schwaben), verfasst im 16. Jahrhundert durch Abt Conrad von Lichtenau. Die autobiographische Vita Caroli Quarti (p. 142 Hillenbrand) berichtet zu den Ereignissen von 1338, dass der Schwarm sieben Meilen lang und in der Breite nicht überschaubar war: ... *ubi finis earum erat per septem miliaria in longitudine; latitudinem vero earum minime potuimus considerare.*

57 Jakob Unrest, Österreichische Chronik 10, 84 zum Jahr 1477: *Anno Domini 1477 des nagsten tag vor Vnnser Frawen Schidung [15. August] kamen die haberschreckh gen Kerndten von Ungern durch die Steyrmarckh nach der Muer und nach der Tra und kamen in das Lauental, zwm Werdtsee,*

Täler und Becken wiederum waren genau die für den Getreideanbau und die Weidewirtschaft genutzten Gebiete, so dass in diesen Regionen von einem deutlich höheren Prozentsatz an vernichteten Kulturflächen ausgegangen werden muss.

Auch der Zeitraum, in dem die Heuschreckenschwärme auftraten, deutet eher darauf hin, dass die Schäden nicht die gesamte Ernte betrafen. Die meisten Heuschreckenzüge fielen in die zweite Augusthälfte: sehr häufig ist von Datierungen ab Laurentius (10. August), ab Maria Himmelfahrt (15. August) oder ab Bartholomäus (24. August) zu lesen. Die Heuschreckeninvasion 1340 in Südtirol fand überhaupt erst im September statt. Die Erntezeit wiederum ist mit Ende Juli bzw. Anfang August anzusetzen; manche Berichte über Heuschreckenplagen in der Mitte des Augusts sind mit dem Vermerk *tempore messis* versehen.[58] Es war daher für die Menschen wichtig, die Ernte noch vor dem Eintreffen der Heuschrecken abzuschließen, um den Schaden in Grenzen zu halten. Problematisch wurde es dann, wenn die Heuschrecken schon sehr früh einfielen, wie beispielsweise 1341 in Südtirol schon im Juni[59] oder 1547 im mittleren Inntal gar schon ab 26. Mai.[60] Dadurch kam es nicht nur zu Versorgungsengpässen bei Getreide in den jeweiligen Jahren, sondern die Not wurde auch in das darauf folgende Jahr prolongiert, da etwa ein Viertel des Ertrags in Normaljahren für die Aussaat benötigt wurde.

Schließlich ist noch der klimageschichtliche Aspekt bei der Einschätzung der wirtschaftlichen Schäden bzw. bei der Frage nach der Verwundbarkeit der damaligen Gesellschaft zu beachten. Im 14. Jahrhundert setzte die Abkühlung hin zur „Kleinen Eiszeit" zwar schon ein, doch brachten die Anbauflächen für Getreide in Normaljahren immer noch einen gewissen Überschuss, so dass die Ausfälle in den von den Heuschreckeninvasionen betroffenen Gebieten ohne deutliche Preissteigerungen wettgemacht werden konnten. Es ist anzunehmen, dass gerade die regional begrenzten Schäden durch Heuschreckenbefall insgesamt nicht mehr Einbußen bei der Getreideernte brachten als Zerstörungen durch Starkregen und Hagel.

Im Vergleich dazu fiel die Heuschreckenplage der 1540er-Jahre schon in eine Zeit permanenter Versorgungsengpässe, da die Winter tendenziell länger dauerten und die Sommer feuchter und kühler wurden. Dazu kam für den Ostalpenraum noch die ständige Bedrohung durch die Einfälle der Osmanen, die bei ihren

Reyffnitz und in [das] Rostal; do haben sy hyerss und hayden und hew vast verderbt. Sy kamen auch an die Geyl, in das Kanall, auf gegen Luentz und gar auf geyn Stertzing, Potzen und gar an den Gardtsee. Mann hat sich auch uber Venedig fliegen sehen. Sy belyben auch an etlichen enndten untz auf den wintte, das sich vor kelten muesten sterben. Sy haben auch an vill enndten den gesetzten wintterrockhen aus der erden geessen. Sy flugen an vill enndten so dickh, als wie grosser rauch und, wo sy nidervielen, do verderbten sy alle frucht.

58 Vgl. zu dieser Beobachtung schon Pautsch 1953, 43.

59 Bozner Chronik zum Jahr 1341. Neben dem raschen Abmähen der Felder und Weiden versuchte man mit Lärmschlagen die Heuschrecken zu vertreiben. Interessant ist auch, dass hier m. W. das einzige Mal sechs verschiedene Getreidesorten angeführt sind, die von den Heuschreckenplagen betroffen waren, und auch die materiellen Verluste mit vielen Tausend Mark angegeben werden.

60 Franz Schweyger, Chronik der Stadt Hall zum Jahr 1547. Zur Textstelle vgl. ausführlich Rohr 2007, 482–483; Rohr 2009, 21–23.

Kriegszügen – wie damals allgemein im Krieg üblich – wohl auch durch Plünderungen die Versorgung ihres Heeres sicherstellten. Die großen Versorgungskrisen im Zuge der Heuschreckenplagen in den 1540er-Jahren und die daraus resultierende „Politisierung" des Problems sind daher in erster Linie vor dem Hintergrund der allgemein schlechter werdenden Getreideversorgung – und damit stark schwankender Getreidepreise – sowie der Kriegssituation zu sehen. Der Erlass Ferdinands I. und das Vorsprechen der Krainer Gesandten auf dem Augsburger Reichstag von 1547/1548 hatten daher viele Ursachen; die wirtschaftlichen Schäden durch die Heuschrecken waren nur eine davon.

Zusammenfassung

Der Blick auf den Umgang mit Überschwemmungen hat gezeigt, dass sich Risikokulturen ökonomisch auf ständig wiederkehrende Hochwasserereignisse einstellten, indem sie etwa kontinuierlich Holz für Brücken ankauften und über eine entsprechende Anzahl an Zimmerleuten verfügten. Die Kremser Stadtordnung von 1524 sah für Weinbauern, die vom Hochwasser betroffen waren, Sonderregelungen vor, die ansonsten unvorstellbar gewesen wären. Somit hatten nur Serien von Extremereignissen signifikante ökonomische Auswirkungen, wie das Beispiel Wels im ersten Jahrzehnt des 16. Jahrhunderts zeigt.

Bei Heuschreckenplagen, die im Gegensatz zu Überschwemmungen weitgehend singulär auftraten, kommt zum einen das Element der Unerwartetheit dazu, zum anderen biblische Deutungsmuster, die in jedem Fall, unabhängig vom tatsächlichen ökonomischen Schaden, eine Katastrophenwahrnehmung verursachten. In Wirklichkeit war der wirtschaftliche Schaden wohl nicht größer als jährliche Hagelschäden. Landesfürstliche Schutzmaßnahmen für den Getreidemarkt sind erstmals in den 1540er-Jahren festzustellen, als die allgemeine Versorgungslage durch die geringeren Getreideernten während der „Kleinen Eiszeit" schlechter wurde.

Literatur

Alexander D., Confronting catastrophe. New perspectives on natural disasters, Oxford 2000.

Aspernig W., Quellen und Erläuterungen zur Geschichte von Wels, 1. Teil (1350–1355), Jahrbuch des Musealvereines Wels 18, 1972, 49–77.

Bankoff G., Cultures of Disaster. Society and Natural Hazard in the Philippines, London – New York 2003.

Baron S., Die achte Plage. Die Wüstenheuschrecke – der Welt größter Schädling, Hamburg – Berlin 1975.

Berlioz J., Catastrophes naturelles et calamités au Moyen Age, Turnhout 1998 (Micrologus' Library 1).

Berlioz J. – Quenet G., Les catastrophes: définitions, documentation, in: Favier R. – Granet-Abisset A.M. (Hg.), Histoire et Mémoire des risques naturels. Actes du séminaire international Histoire et Mémoire des risques naturels en région de montagne, 25–26 Novembre 1999, Grenoble 2000, 19–38.

Böhm O. – Wetzel K.-F., Flood history of the Danube tributaries Lech and Isar in the Alpine foreland of Germany, Hydrological Sciences Journal 51, 5, 2006, 784–798.

Delort R., Der Bär, die Biene und der heilige Wolf. Die wahre Geschichte der Tiere, München – Wien 1987.

Frisch M., Der Mensch erscheint im Holozän. Eine Erzählung, in: Frisch M., Gesammelte Werke in zeitlicher Reihenfolge 7, Frankfurt am Main 1986, 205–300 [erstmals erschienen als Einzeltitel Frankfurt 1979, zitiert wird nach der Ausgabe 1986].

Glaser R., Kleine Eiszeit, in: Enzyklopädie der Neuzeit 6, Stuttgart – Weimar 2007, 767–771.

Groh D., Zur Anthropologie von Naturkatastrophen, in: Schläder J. – Wohlfarth R. (Hg.): AngstBilderSchauLust. Katastrophenerfahrungen in Kunst, Musik und Theater, Berlin 2007, 9–26.

Groh D. – Kempe M. – Mauelshagen F., Einleitung. Naturkatastrophen – wahrgenommen, gedeutet, dargestellt, in: dies. (Hg.), Naturkatastrophen. Beiträge zu ihrer Deutung, Wahrnehmung und Darstellung in Text und Bild von der Antike bis ins 20. Jahrhundert (Literatur und Anthropologie 13), Tübingen 2003, 11–33.

Holter K., Die römische Traunbrücke und die Anfänge des Welser Bruckamtes, Jahrbuch des Musealvereines Wels 2, 1955, 124–151.

Holter K., Beobachtungen über römerzeitliche Funde auf dem Gelände des ehemaligen Friedhofes in Wels (Baustelle Gerngroß-Markthalle), Jahrbuch des Musealvereines Wels 17, 1970/71, 24–42.

Jäger G., Schwarzer Himmel – kalte Erde – weißer Tod. Wanderheuschrecken, Hagelschläge, Kältewellen und Lawinenkatastrophen im „Land im Gebirge". Eine kleine Agrar- und Klimageschichte von Tirol, Innsbruck 2010.

Kinzl J., Chronik der Städte Krems, Stein und deren nächster Umgebung. Mit den Freiheitsbriefen beider Städte und den Schriftstücken ihrer gewerblichen Innungen vom Jahre 985–1869, Krems 1869.

Lackner H., Dokumentation ungedruckter Quellen zur Geschichte der Städte Österreichs (Mit Ausnahme der Stadt Wien), Linz 1993 (Arbeitsbehelf 6).

Lichtenberger E., Österreich, 2. Aufl., Darmstadt 2002 (Wissenschaftliche Länderkunden).

Miglbauer R., Ausgrabungen im ehemaligen Minoritenkloster von Wels, OÖ, Beiträge zur Mittelalterarchäologie in Österreich 7, 1991, 93–113.

Mudelsee M. – Deutsch M. – Börngen M. – Tetzlaff G., Trends in flood risk of the River Werra (Germany) over the past 500 years, Hydrological Sciences Journal 51, 5, 2006, 818–833.

Nussbaumer J., Die Gewalt der Natur. Eine Chronik der Naturkatastrophen von 1500 bis heute, Grünbach 1996.

Ossimitz G. – Lapp Ch., Katastrophen – systemisch betrachtet, in: Katastrophen in Natur und Umwelt (Wissenschaft und Umwelt interdisziplinär 10), Wien 2006, 55–66.

Pautsch E., Elementarereignisse in den erzählenden österreichischen Geschichtsquellen des 14. und 15. Jahrhunderts, Wien 1953 (ungedr. phil. Dissertation Wien).

Pfister Ch., Naturkatastrophen und Naturgefahren in geschichtlicher Perspektive, in: ders. (Hg.), Am Tag danach. Zur Bewältigung von Naturkatastrophen in der Schweiz 1500–2000, Bern – Stuttgart – Wien 2002, 11–25.

Pilgram A., Untersuchungen über das Wahrscheinliche der Wetterkunde, durch vieljährige Beobachtungen, Wien 1788.

Plate E. J. – Merz B. – Eikenberg Ch., Naturkatastrophen: Herausforderung an Wissenschaft und Gesellschaft, in: Plate E. J. – Merz B. (Hg.), Naturkatastrophen. Ursachen – Auswirkungen – Vorsorge, Stuttgart 2001, 1–45.

Radkau J. – Schäfer I., Holz. Ein Naturstoff in der Technikgeschichte, Reinbek bei Hamburg 1987.

Rohr Ch., Überschwemmungen an der Traun zwischen Alltag und Katastrophe. Die Welser Traunbrücke im Spiegel der Bruckamtsrechnungen des 15. und 16. Jahrhunderts, in: Festschrift 50 Jahre Musealverein Wels (Jahrbuch des Musealvereins Wels 33, 2001/02/03), Wels 2004, 281–328.

Rohr Ch., Extreme Naturereignisse im Ostalpenraum. Naturerfahrung im Spätmittelalter und am Beginn der Neuzeit, Köln – Weimar – Wien 2007 (Umwelthistorische Forschungen 4).

Rohr Ch., Naturkatastrophen als Gegenstand einer kulturgeschichtlich orientierten Umweltgeschichte, in: ders. (Hg.), Naturkatastrophen in der Geschichte. Wahrnehmung, Deutung und Bewältigung von extremen Naturereignissen in Risikokulturen (Historische Sozialkunde 2008/2), Wien 2008, 2–13.

Rohr Ch., Sie seind krochen wie ain kriegsordnung. Heuschreckenplagen im Land Tirol im Spätmittelalter und in der Frühen Neuzeit, Tiroler Heimatblätter 84, 1, 2009, 20–25.

Rohr Ch., Zur Wahrnehmung, Deutung und Bewältigung von Heuschreckenplagen in Mitteleuropa im Spätmittelalter und in der Frühen Neuzeit, in: Klein Th. – Prass R. – Rau S. – Schladitz L. (Hg.), Umweltgeschichte in globaler Perspektive. Vortragsreihe des Historischen Seminars der Universität Erfurt im Sommersemester 2010, Erfurt 2011, 34 S. (online unter http://www.db-thueringen.de/servlets/Derivate-Servlet/Derivate-23892/Rohr_Heuschreckenplagen.pdf).

Rohr Ch., Floods of the Upper Danube River and Its Tributaries and Their Impact on Urban Economies (c. 1350–1600), Environment and History 19, 2, 2013 (im Druck).

Rurscheyt A., Warhafftige und erschrockenliche Newe Zeyttung inn Schlessien geschehen inn disem XXXXII. Jar Am tag der Hym(m)elfart Marie. Von unerhörten hewschrecken Wie vil der gewesen unnd was sie schaden gethan haben. Werdt ihr hyerinn warhafftig begriffen finden, o. O. 1542.

Schmidt A., „Wolken krachen, Berge zittern, und die ganze Erde weint ...“: Zur kulturellen Vermittlung von Naturkatastrophen in Deutschland 1755 bis 1855, Münster – New York – München – Berlin 1999.

Sieferle R.P., Die Risikospirale, in: Katastrophen in Natur und Umwelt (Wissenschaft und Umwelt interdisziplinär 10), Wien 2006, 157–166.

Auctions and Markets in the Roman Empire

KAI RUFFING

Introduction

In 1953 HERBERT BLOCH published the following inscription discovered in Ostia in 1938: "*To the genius of the most splendid guild of those importing and selling wine Caius Septimius Quietus, auctioneer of wines, has given (this statue) as a gift.*"[1] The base on which the text was engraved was found in a building located on the *via del Tempio d'Ercole* in the vicinity of the *Terme di Mitra*.[2] The monument was erected in the 2nd century AD, sometime between 131 and 170 AD.[3] The short, but remarkable, text was not of particular interest to modern research. For FILIPPO COARELLI the place where the inscription was found is one main argument for locating the *forum vinarium* of Ostia there.[4] Furthermore it was taken by RUSSEL MEIGGS in his groundbreaking study of Roman Ostia as evidence for the commercial activities of the *negotiatores vinarii* in the town,[5] cautiously concluding: "...we may infer regular auctions in the wine market."[6] But the fact that an auctioneer of wines is dedicating something to the *corpus* wine sellers and importers is in terms of economic history a very interesting one and gives every reason to have a closer look at auctions and markets in the Roman Empire.

This is to an greater extent true, if one takes into consideration that, although economic history recently has drawn much attention in the actual research, scholars have been less interested in the market itself and its conceptualisation.[7] One exception to this rule is an article written by HERBERT GRASSL, which *inter alia* is dedicated to the question of the formation of prices on the market.[8] What has been said is true not only for historians, but also for economists. As underlined in an article published some weeks ago by RUDOLF RICHTER a reason for that can be seen in the fact that in a neoclassical view there is no need for a specific market system, because it is a world without transaction costs, with perfect foresight and

1 AE 1955, 165 = Cébeillac-Gervasoni, Caldelli, Zevi 2010, Nr. 80: Genio corporis | splendidissimi | inportantium | et negotiantium | vinariorum | C(aius) Septimius Quietus | praeco vinorum | d(onum) d(edit).

2 Cf. Coarelli 1996, 111.

3 Cf. EDR074037: http://www.edr-edr.it/edr_programmi/res_complex_new.php?Bibliografia=HD019431 [30.08.11].

4 Cf. Coarelli 1996. See also DeLaine 2005, 43 and García Morcillo 2005, 210.

5 Cf. Meiggs 1973, 275–276.

6 Cf. Meiggs 1973, 275.

7 One main interest in the actual research was the question of the existence of an integrated market in the Roman empire and the question whether the Roman economy can be described as a market economy. See on these themes for example Temin 2001; Bang 2008, 131–201. Furthermore Bang characterized the Roman market as a bazaar, particularly defined as a social network: see Bang 2008, 239–289.

8 See Graßl 2004.

perfect rationality used by every individual acting on the market. In this neoclassical world there is no place for the use of different market systems, because it is a world of a general equilibrium. This means that everyone is trading with everybody else whatever and wherever he wants. Consequently institutions do not matter. Thus this neoclassical model can be applied for example to a capitalist as well as to a socialist economy.[9] This neoclassical position may have contributed to the fact that the market in the actual research on the ancient economy is more or less conceived as a homogeneous phenomenon, which is defined by offer and demand, the formation of prices being just a simple function of the latter.[10] This model of a market seems indeed not very much grounded in the real world. Thus for example Herbert Grassl in his above mentioned article demonstrated convincingly that bargaining was an integral part of every day market life in the Roman Empire and in other ancient economies.[11] A telling example for that is a dialogue in the Corpus Glossariorum Latinorum: "*I walk to the seller of clothes. How much the cloak? 100 denarii. How much the raincoat? 200 denarii. That's too much. Take 100 denarii. This cannot be the price that costs as much as I pay to the supplier. How much should I give? As much as you think. Give him 125 denarii.*"[12] The example shows, that the formation of prices is not only defined by offer and demand, but also by social forms of behaviour such as bargaining. This mode of formation of prices works only in a particular market situation, that is offering goods during a direct contact between seller and customer, the latter being able to view and to check the quality of the good he is interested in. As a consequence both had to make a specific choice in which market situation they wanted to act before selling or acquiring goods. This choice is an institutional one. Thus in the given context a permanent offer is imagined, that means we are dealing with a permanent market.

In the view of Neo Institutional Economics (NIE) this is a specific form of a market system or better a specific market organization.[13] Using the NIE concept of different forms of market organization, which is defined by specific institutions, one moves on solid ground in discerning different market systems in the Roman Empire as well: permanent markets, periodical markets, fairs and producer markets.[14]

9 Cf. Richter 2011, 35.

10 Cf. Richter 2011, 43, who qualifies this rule as a neoclassical mantra.

11 Cf. Graßl 2004, 356.

12 Corp. Gloss. Lat. III 657 c. 13: *Ἐγὼ πορεύομαι πρὸς ἱματιοπώλην. Πόσου ἡ ζυγή; Ἑκατὸν δηναρίων. Πόσου ἡ φελόνη; Διακοσίων δηναρίων. Πολὺ λέγεις. λάβε ρ´ δηνάρια. Οὐ δύναται τοσούτου. τοσούτου καθέστηκεν παρὰ τῶν προαγοραστῶν. [...] Τί δώσω; Ὃ ἂν κελεύῃς. Δὸς αὐτῷ ⟨ρ⟩κε´ δηνάρια.* – Ego duco me ad vestiarium. Quanti pareclum? Centum denariis. Quanti paenula? Ducentis denariis. Multum dicis. accipe centum denarios. Non potest tanti. tanti constat de infertoribus [...]. Quid dabo? Quod iusseris. Da illi <C>XXV denarios.

13 See Richter 2011, 36.

14 See e.g. de Ligt 1993 on periodical markets. See also Andreau 1991 (1997), 312–313 on the different types of markets.

From the NIE perspective, establishing these markets is a collective action between a multiplicity of suppliers and demanders guided either by an invisible or by a visible hand with the aim of economizing on the costs of transactions, incomplete foresight and bounded rationality.[15] To make market organizations work there have to be aids of trade, that means for example common timing, common measures, common locations of trade, common usage of money and other things. Such an aid of trade of particular importance and – as observed by GRASSL – until now not sufficiently analysed by actual research is the organization of price formation. The auction is one possible form of it.[16] On the other hand this specific institutional choice regarding price formations brings a particular market organization with it, that is the auction market which for example is to be distinguished from customer markets.[17]

The scope of the present paper is to analyse the case of the Ostian wine auctions making a first step in analysing the role of auctions in the economy of the Roman Empire by using the theoretical framework of NIE. Thus firstly some observations regarding auctions in the Roman world are to be made. Secondly a more specific case, that is the said auctions of wines, will be treated in more detail.

Auctions in the Roman Economy

Auctions in the Roman world are well studied in modern research from different point of views. In 1961 GEORG THIELMANN published his PhD thesis on private auctions in Roman law, in which he paid special attention to Roman banking law.[18] Focusing on the *societates publicanorum* ULRIKE MALMENDIER further discussed state auctions in the context of awarding contracts to the publicans. In so doing, she gave an overview of modern economic theories of auctions as well.[19] Recently the auctions were put in a more historical context by MARTA GARCÍA MORCILLO.[20] Furthermore the one-percent-tax on auctions (*centesima rerum venalium*) was of special interest for scholars of the history of the Roman Empire.[21] In addition auctions were studied in connection with the affairs of the Pompeian banking house of L. Caecilius Iucundus and the bank of the Sulpicii in ancient Puteoli,[22] both well documented thanks to the eruption of the Vesuvius in AD 69. Last but not least MONIKA FRASS paid some attention to the vending of gardens by means of auctions.[23] Thanks to these studies and to a sometimes sketchy, but nevertheless rather

15 Cf. Richter 2011, 36–37.
16 Cf. Richter 2011, 37–38.
17 Cf. Richter, Furubotn 2003, 346.
18 See Thielmann 1961.
19 Cf. Malmendier 2002, esp.144–222.
20 See García Morcillo 2005 and García Morcillo 2008.
21 See lastly Günther 2008, 127–147 on this tax. See also García Morcillo 2008, 265–274.
22 See Andreau 1974, 73–116; Petrucci 2008. For the banking house of the Sulpicii see also Gröschler 1997.
23 See Frass 2006, 47–55 and 58–59.

broad, corpus of sources the functioning and the details of auctions in the Roman world can be reconstructed in a fairly reliable way.

Auctions were evidently used to sell goods by a wide range of social stratums of the Roman society. In the light of the literary tradition auctions were not an unusual choice for Roman emperors to sell goods and generate money in cash in case of pressing needs.[24] But combining all the evidence one gets the impression that at least in Rome if not in the whole empire auctions were part of everyday life in society. They were not only utilized to monetize agricultural crops, slaves, cattle and landed property but served also to get money for rummage.[25] In the Pompeian tablets illustrating the affairs of Jucundus slaves, wood and linen are mentioned as objects of auctions.[26] The tablets of the Sulpicii from Puteoli mention purple clothes (*purpurae laconicae*),[27] landed property[28] and slaves.[29]

Different persons were involved in executing an auction. First of all the *praeco*,[30] who in ancient times evidently announced the time and place of an auction and afterwards acted during the transaction as auctioneer. The *praecones* are prominent literary characters, which are described as persons disposing of a certain wealth. Their social reputation on the contrary was rather low, at least in republican times. This becomes clear in the *lex Iulia municipalis*, where those making the *praeconium* are excluded from municipal *magistrates*.[31] But during the empire the wealth generated by auctioneers gave them the possibility of social advancement. Thus Flavius Iosephus speaks for example of a certain Arruntius Euarestus, who „...accumulated money till he had as much as the wealthiest of the Romans...." in this way becoming an important political person in Rome in the time of Gaius.[32] Although Iosephus chose this person to characterize Gaius as a bad emperor one may conclude that by means of wealth vertical mobility was possible also for auctioneers. If we take all the available evidence for *praecones* together, we can see the everyday occurrence and the economic importance of auctions in the Roman economy.

In selling the goods during the auction the *praeco* acted for the seller of goods – in the juristic literature normally specified as the *dominus auctionis* – and had to be paid by the latter for his services. The *dominus auctionis* was either the proprietor of the goods or for example in the case of legacies the possessor or a legal

24 Cf. García Morcillo 2005, 283–303.

25 Cf. Thielmann 1961, 47–48, Malmendier 2002, 101; García Morcillo 2005, 207–233.

26 Cf. Andreau 1974, 104.

27 TPN 70 = TPSulp. 83 (51 n. Chr.); TPN 71 = TPSulp 84.

28 TPN 72 = TPSulp. 88 (53 n. Chr.).

29 TPN 73 = TPSulp. 90 (61 n. Chr.); TPN 74 = TPSulp. 91 (61 n. Chr.); TPN 75 = TPSulp. 92 (61 n. Chr.); TPN 76 = TPSulp. 85 (51 n. Chr.); TPN 78 = TPSulp. 87a (51 n. Chr.).

30 On the *praecones* see Thielmann 1961, 53–54; Malmendier 2002, 102–104; García Morcillo 2005, 137–156.

31 ILS 6085 (89).

32 Ioseph. ant. Iud. 19, 145. The English version is taken from Feldman 1965, 283. On the person of Arruntius Euarestus see Mratschek-Halfmann 1993, 94 and 296.

guardian acting in the name of a minor or a pupil. He also could be a creditor, who sold by the way of the auction goods used as security in giving credits or someone who sold pledges. As it seems the *dominus auctionis* was not present or rather had not to be present during the auction of his goods.[33] Now the *dominus auctionis* used the services of an *argentarius*, a *coactor* or a *coactor argentarius* like the Pompeian Iucundus for the execution of the auction paying one percent of the purchasing prices for them.[34] Obviously a *coactor argentarius* had the possibilty to announce the time and location for an auction. There were particular places for auctions called *atria auctionaria*,[35] but they were executed also in other places, as in *macella* and *fora*.[36] From an archaeological point of view also *horrea* and a market bulding in Ostia were facilitated for auctions.[37] It is interesting to see how the procedure worked in this respect in Puteoli. The surviving announcements for auctions do not mention in every case the place where they were executed. Only the date is regularly mentioned.[38] This means, that the place for auctions – in Puteoli the *Chalcidicum Caesonianum* – was known at least to the urban community.[39] The customer after having bought the goods he was interested in had to pay the purchasing price(s) to the *coactor argentarius*, who in the following step transferred the money gained in the purchases to the *dominus auctionis*. In the Roman world the English type of auction was in use, a successive raising of the price until one bidder remains. Thus at any given point all bidders are informed about the level of the best bid.[40] As in modern auctions the *praeco* started with a minimum price, raising it after bidders had signalled their bid by nodding in agreement (in Latin *adnuere*) or by raising the hand (*digitum tollere*). At the end the *praeco* awarded the goods to the highest bidder (*addictio*).[41]

What emerges here is a complex market organzation with its own set of rules, that is institutions and different players using these institutions. Without going here into too much detail we should highlight the role of law. All subjects were acting on clear and solid ground given by the rules of Roman law. By means of the *addictio* through the *praeco* an act of sale was concluded between the *dominus auctionis* and the purchaser. According to Roman law such an auction concluded

33 Cf. Petrucci 2008, 281.

34 On *argentarii* and *coactores argentarii* respectively and their role in auctions see Thielmann 1961, 49; Andreau 1987, 61–167; Rauh 1989, 60; Malmendier 2002, 104–105; García Morcillo 2005, 107–136; García Morcillo 2008, 260–263; Petrucci 2008, 278–280. The example of L. Caecilius Iucundus and his business in auctions is studied comprehensively by Andreau 1974, 73–116. esp. 80–95 regarding the payment of gains of the auctions to a *dominus auctionis* and 95–103 regarding credits given by Iucundus.

35 Cf. García Morcillo 2005, 190–194.

36 Cf. García Morcillo 2005, 194–219.

37 Cf. DeLaine 2005, 43–44.

38 TPN 70–76.

39 Cf. TPSulp. p. 185; see also Jaschke 2010, 185.

40 Cf. McAfee, McMillan 1987, 702; Krishna 2002, 2.

41 Cf. Thielmann 1961, 85–86, Malmendier 2002, 118–119.

Scheme of Persons Involved in an Auction

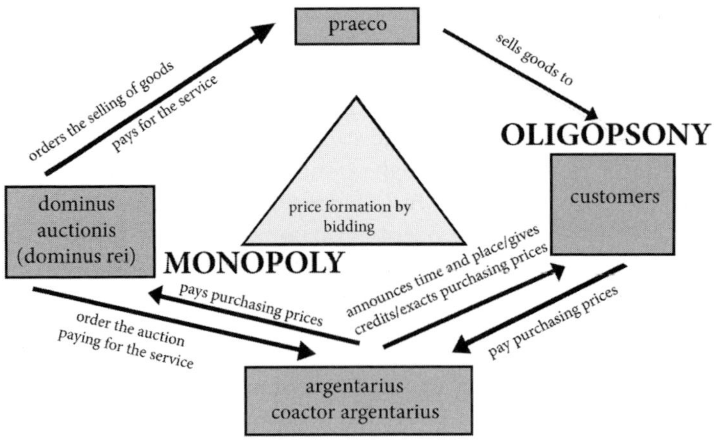

an *emptio venditio* the two parties agreed upon.[42] Customarily the *argentarius* paid the prices immediately to the *dominus auctionis* accepting the *sponsio* of the purchaser to pay later.[43] The relationship between the *dominus auctionis* and the *coactor argentarius* was also clearly defined by Roman law.[44]

Scheme of Persons Involved in a Transaction on a Permanent Market

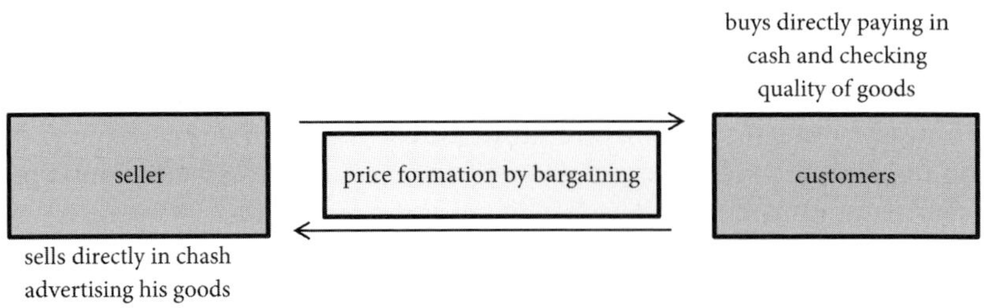

Noteworthy is that in most cases the main part of the risk lays with the *argentarius*.[45] Thus the auction market is a system very different from the market system briefly sketched at the beginning of the paper and had a very different form of price formation.

The choice for the auction market as a particular market system to sell one's goods bears several advantages for sellers and purchasers as well regarding the lowering of transaction costs. These transaction costs normally are divided into

42 Cf. Jakab 2009, 54 with note 46 against Thielmann 1961, 84–131.
43 Cf. Jakab 2009, 54.
44 Cf. Thielmann 1961, 200–221.
45 Cf. Thielmann 1961, 216–217.

four main categories, namely information, negotiation and monitoring/enforcement costs as well as those of investment in social capital.[46] Information costs are clearly reduced by using an auction market. Given the problem of gathering information in any premodern society, the existence of a system which is known by sellers and possible purchasers reduces these costs by a considerable amount.[47] The place and rules of the system are known,[48] participants as well, and the time of auctions was announced in known places to the public with a suitable distance of time before enacting it. As proven by the evidence of the *Tabulae Pompeianae Sulpiciorum* goods and their proprietors were also publicized.[49] In this way all persons acting during an auction were provided with ample information. Last but not least the auction market did not have to be a permanent market. This was a great advantage for a possible seller of goods, because it was his initiative to put an auction into effect.[50] In terms of the Roman system it means that a *dominus auctionis* exactly in the moment in which he disposed of goods could order an *argentarius* to sell them. In a world in which production mainly is based on agriculture, this is of the greatest importance, because production and monetization of crops to a high degree are governed by the rhythms of the agricultural calendar.[51]

Certainly, according to auction theory some asymmetry of information remains. This is especially true for the fact that the seller does not know the valuation that bidders will attribute to the goods to be sold on auction. This means that the seller's ability to extract a surplus is limited. But here the situation of the auction matters. Normally at least an monopoly-oligopsony relation in auctions is to be expected. That means that competition between bidders will raise the price for the auctioned goods.[52] Furthermore the number of bidders matters for price-formation, which is a consequence of the second-best-bit model. The more bidders present at an auction the higher is the chance that the bidder with the greatest willingness to pay is constricted to bid high amounts of money for the items he wants to purchase. Supposing that the one with the strongest willingness to pay, tries to act in a way that he has not to pay the full amount of cash he is willing to spend, and supposing furthermore that he will raise his bid only slightly to the second best bid, competition between the bidders, which is growing by number of present bidders, will raise the probability of an higher second-best-bid. That me-

46 Cf. Richter, Furubotn 2003, 58–61 on transaction costs on the market; Hobbs 1997, 1083–1090 on the different kinds of transaction costs in connection with auctions regarding the example of cattle auctions in the UK.

47 Cf. Malmendier 2002, 145–146.

48 See McAfee, McMillan 1987, 703 on the ability of the seller(s) to make commitments, by which the bidders know that the seller cannot change his procedures after observing the bids.

49 Cf. García Marcillo 2005, 83–85.

50 The question of initiative is treated by Malmendier 2002, 146–147.

51 See on this e.g. Ruffing 1993, 18–21: The transport activities documented by the ostraka of the Nikanor-archive are clearly related to the harvest times of specific products.

52 Cf. McAfee, McMillan 1987, 704.

ans that he will pay in effect a higher price the more bidders are present.[53] This is the reason why the ability of the *praeco* to assemble as many people as possible is highlightened in ancient literary sources.[54]

Negotiation costs are considerably lowered as well by chosing an auction market system for selling goods. Under the condition of Roman law the bid and the *addictio* by the *praeco* constituted an oral act of sale, which was liable for trial in a court of justice.[55] That means that negotiation costs regarding the conclusion of contracts in an auction market for the *dominus auctionis* tended to be zero. He only had to pay a modest rate of the purchase prices for the services of the auctioneer and the *argentarius*, as already mentioned above. Because the sales in auctions through the *addictio* of items to a bidder become an oral act of sale, they are final and thus monitoring costs tend to be zero.[56]

This is also true for the investment in social capital. Participants on the market are embedded in a complex social network, which helps them to bear the threat of uncertainty, to process complex information and to take decisions under the condition of limited rationality. A new participant in a market system has to establish new social relations.[57] This is clearly the reason why merchants in the Roman empire normally followed the same trade routes for a considerable amount of time, as in the case of a certain Flavius Zeuxis of Hierapolis in Phrygia, who travelled 72 times to Italy.[58] Using an auction market these costs can be reduced, because a given new participant has to invest only in social relations with an *argentarius*, who supposedly is already well established in a network. Taking all this evidence together it becomes clear, that a market system using auctions as an institution as well as a mechanism for the formation of prices lowers transaction costs for all participants.

Auctions of wine in Roman Ostia

Having briefly considered the auction market in the Roman empire in general it remains to consider the auctions of wine in Roman Ostia. Firstly some general observations on the trade in wine in Ostia will be made. The huge population of Rome necessitated not only the importation of grain but also of huge quantities of wine. According to the calculations of André Tchernia, each year between 1,000,000 hl and 1,800,000 hl were consumed by the Roman population,[59] giving us an idea of the dimension of the wine trade in the high empire. Using the evidence of amphoras excavated in Ostia one gets an impression of the origin of the wines traded in Ostia, which then were shipped upstream on the Tiber and were unloaded in

53 Cf. McAfee, McMillan 1987, 711; Malmendier 2002, 148–149.

54 Cf. Thielmann 1961, 54; Malmendier 2002, 103; García Morcillo 2005, 147–154.

55 Cf. Thielmann 1961, 84–93.

56 Cf. Hobbs 1997, 1088.

57 Cf. Richter, Furubotn 2003, 61.

58 CIG 3920 = I. Hierapolis Judeich 51 = Syll.^{3} 1229.

59 Cf. Tchernia 1987, 26–27. See Ruffing 1997, 121 regarding older calculations.

the river port of Rome situated south of the Tiber Island on both banks and having an extension of nearly 2 km.[60] In the High Empire – i.e. the period from 50–150 AD – wines came mainly from Italy, Southern Gaul, Hispania and the Eastern Mediterranean.[61] However, there were certainly imports of wines from the areas to the north of Rome, which were unloaded north of the *isola Tiberiana*.[62] After it's completion Portus and as a consequence Ostia became the main point of arrival for imported goods in general and for wines in particular. The importance of the Roman wine trade is reflected in the existence of a *forum vinarium* and a *portus vinarius* in Rome and – as already mentioned – in Ostia.[63] Interestingly the *portus vinarius* of Rome itself is known thanks to two inscriptions, in which *coactores a (de) portu vinario* are mentioned.[64] Likewise we find *argentarii de foro vinario* and a *coactor vinarius de foro vinario* in two other inscriptions from Rome.[65]

The four Roman and the Ostian inscriptions mentioning the *praeco vinorum* indicate a close connection between the wine trade and auctions. Indeed already the elder Cato in his *de agricultura* advised to sell wine produced on an estate using an auction market.[66] The evidence of the Roman and Ostian inscriptions demonstrates that this practice lived on in the times of the empire. Very interesting in this context is how the risk in sales and purchases of wine is regulated in Roman law with regard to possible dangers for the product. Wine is a particular commodity that had for sellers and purchasers its own risks in trading it. These risks are basically connected to the point of time in which wines are sold, and consequently to the taste as well as to the quantity of wine. A good starting point to illustrate these risks and problems is the so-called *lex vini* of the elder Cato.[67] The following reconstruction based on the research done by Éva Jakab concerning the management of risk in sales of wine is a very likely scenario: the wine sold in the auction was neither displayed in the auction nor after the auction given immediately to the purchaser; hence the latter had to make taste test (*degustatio*) to check the quality of the items sold to him. In the next step the wine had to be measured before the 1st of January to the purchaser, who had to make another taste test in order to exclude that the wine had become neither sour nor musty. The measurement itself was a control of the quantity sold in the previous auction. Until this point of time the risk laid with the seller, as this was the ultimate check of quality before the wine became the property of the purchaser, and only now the latter had to bear the risk for possible dangers for his wares. That did not include the physical movement of

60 On the river port of Rome see Castagnoli 1980; Colini 1980; Colini 1986; Le Gall 1953; Rodríguez Almeida 1998. For wines imported to Rome from the north see Tchernia 1986, 154-155.

61 Martin 2008, 107–108.

62 On the importance of the Tiber for imports to Rome from the north see Quilici 1986.

63 On the *forum vinarium* in Rome see Platner, Ashby 1929, 245; Kolb 1995, 419; Coarelli 1996, 106.

64 CIL VI 9189 = ILS 7929; CIL VI 9190. See also CIL VI 37807 = ILS 2429 = AE 1910, 74.

65 CIL VI 9181; CIL VI 9182 = ILS 7502.

66 Cato agr. 2,7. Cf. Thielmann 1965, 45; Malmendier 2002, 98–101. On Cato's *lex* for selling wine in an auction see Jakab 2009, 50–54.

67 Cato agr. 148.

the wine to a place owned by the purchaser, as can be seen in the following quotation: The wine has to be transported away before the 1st of October of the following year.[68] All other available evidence points in the direction that these specific regulations for the sale of wine were implemented also in the time of the empire. That is a kind of risk management between purchaser and seller of wine inherent in every act of sale, which is described by taste tests (risk of quality) and measurements (risk of quantity).[69] Since the sale in an auction constituted an oral act of sale, these here only briefly mentioned rules for the sale of wine were applicable to auctions as well.

To sum up: with the auction market we have a specific market system. In the case of wine there were particular institutions, which without doubt were known to participants in this market. Dennis Kehoe comments: Roman law and the actions of the Roman emperors as well as those of the Roman administration provided a fair playing ground for participants in the economic system of the Roman Empire.[70] In the case of the selling of wine this 'fair playing ground' is provided by the management of risk for sellers as well as for purchasers.

Having these contextualizations in mind we are now in a position to have a closer look at the auctions of wine in Roman Ostia. As already mentioned the location of the dedication of the *praeco vinorum* Caius Septimius Quietus was the main argument for Filippo Coarelli to locate the *forum vinarium* of Ostia in the *regio I* between the *via degli Horrea Epagathiana* and the *via del Tempio d'Ercole*. One further argument to locate it here was a more general deduction: Due to the presence of three horrea in the vicinity and its neighborhood to the Tiber the whole area seemed to be a business district.[71] Furthermore the position of the Ostian *macellum* on the *via del Pomerio* – the southern extension of the *via degli Horrea Epagathiana* – shows[72] that both streets were an important commercial axis in the town.[73] However, the location of the *dolia defossa* excavated in Ostia shows that these deposits were used as wholesale stores for bars, inns and retailers in Ostia itself.[74] Thus they are not to be seen in a context with ongoing business on the *forum vinarium*. The position and extent of the area are clear indications of the importance of this presumed commercial space, which Coarelli compared with the situation of the *Piazzale dei Corporazioni* before the reconstruction of the latter in Claudian times.[75] The *forum vinarium* has never been excavated. But thanks to a couple of inscriptions something can be said about the monumental appear-

68 Cf. Jakab 2009, 71–72.
69 Cf. Jakab 2009, 203–242.
70 Cf. Kehoe 2007, 193–199.
71 On the *horrea Epagathiana* in the neighbourhood of the presumed *forum vinarium* see Cébeillac-Gervasoni, Caldelli, Zevi 2010, 154–155.
72 On the *macellum* of Ostia see Cébeillac-Gervasoni, Caldelli, Zevi 2010, 156–157.
73 Cf. Coarelli 1996, 109–111.
74 Cf. Meiggs 1973, 274–275.
75 Cf. Coarelli 1996, 109. On the commercial function of the *Piazzale dei Corporazioni* see Rohde 2009; see also Cébeillac-Gervasoni, Caldelli, Zevi 2010, 251–259.

ance of the Ostian *forum vinarium*.[76] Parts of the forum were a quadriga,[77] a temple (may be of the *genius fori vinari*)[78] and measures built there by one of the most prominent men of Ostia named Publius Lucilius Gamala.[79]

Having a look at the dedication of Septimius Quietus to the *genius corporis* it is more than a fair assumption that auctions of wine took place in the *forum vinarium* or in one of the buildings surrounding the place, since the inscription supposingly was found *in situ*.[80] The fact that auctioneers in the Roman Empire were specialized is very interesting itself, because in this case it is a further hint for the huge extent and importance of the wine trade in Rome and Ostia. But that he has made a dedication to the *collegium* of those importing and selling wine seems to be a hint of a closer connection between the wine merchants of Ostia and this auctioneer. At least the dedication is an investment made by Septimius Quietus in social capital, if it is not a clear hint for an economic action by a collegium. Supposedly the dedication could be the result of an economic cooperation between auctioneer and collegium in the sense that Septimius Quietus normally acted in auctioning for *collegiati* of the *corpus splendidissimum inportantium et negotiantium vinariorum*. If this is true, the relationship between Septimius Quietus and the collegium is one of vertical desintegration, that is the services of the *praeco* were acquired by the *collegiati* by means of the market.[81] This gives some reason to believe that the collegium mentioned in the dedication of Septimius Quietus gave assistance to the *collegiati* to sell their imports in Ostia.[82] This however means nothing else than a lowering of transaction costs for participants coming from outside Ostia and Rome to the auction market of Ostia by using a socio-economic network, which was established around this specific auction market.

Perhaps we can go even further guessing that this network was more complex. As already mentioned the collegium of wine importers and merchants was centered in the *forum vinarium* of Ostia and had its own temple with a Genius worshipped by a particular *corpus* and another collegium those of the temple. The inscription of the famous Cnaeus Sentius Felix shows,[83] that there was a collegium of shippers from the Adriatic and other shippers *ad quadrigam fori vinari*, if here not the same collegium is intended.[84] In any case the shippers from the Adriatic sea

76 See on the following Corelli 1996, 106.
77 CIL XIV 409 = ILS 6146.
78 AE 1940, 64; AE 1940, 65.
79 CIL XIV 376.
80 Cf. Coarelli 1996.
81 On vertical integration and disintegration see Silver 2009.
82 This fits very well with the concept of economic functions of the collegia put forward by Brokaert forthcoming.
83 On his person see Meiggs 1973, 200–201; Tran 2006, 68–70, 77–78 and 80–81, where Tran assumes, that the wealth of Cnaeus Sentius Felix had its origins in the trade of wine from the northern Adriatic to Ostia; Cébeillac-Gervasoni, Caldelli, Zevi 2010, 276–279.
84 CIL XIV 409 = ILS 6146: „...gratis adlect(o) | inter naviculari(os) maris Hadriatici et ad quadrigam | fori vinari...“.

clearly had a close connection to the wine trade in Rome and Ostia.[85] Interestingly Sentius Felix had also a close connection to the wine trade of Rome being patron of the *praecones et argentarii et negotiatores vinarii ab urbe*.[86] The latter are known from another Ostian inscription, where they are mentioned together with wine merchants from Ostia.[87] It seems that this collegium provided a social and certainly also an economic connection between the wine merchants of Ostia and Rome. On the other hand it was also part of the socio-economic network around the *forum vinarium*. The dedication of Septimius Quietus reveals a network with the *forum vinarium* and its auction market as a center that provided connections for import, transportation and sale of wine in Ostia with further connections to Rome itself in a specific manner.[88]

The socio-economic network of the forum vinarium in Ostia

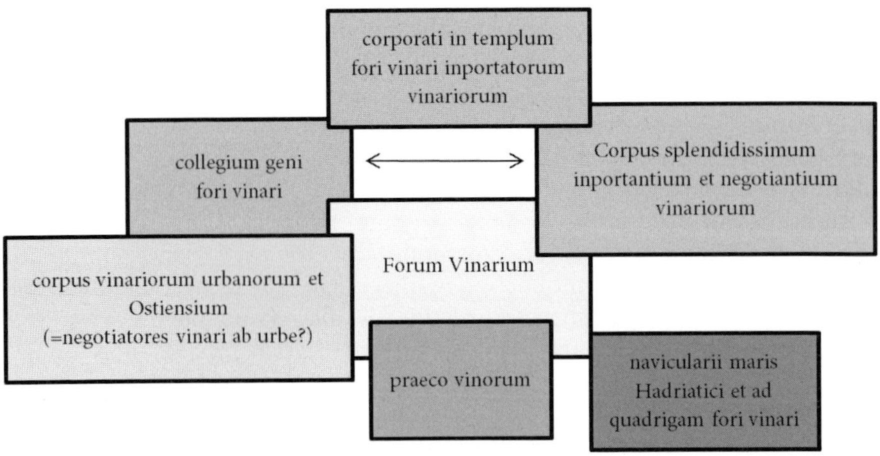

We can go even a step further in underlining the importance of this socio-economic network for traders of wine. Assuming – as Nicolas Tran did –, that the wealth of the already mentioned Cnaeus Sentius Felix had its origins in the trade

85 The close connection of the *navicularii maris Hadriatici* to the wine trade is confirmed by an inscription from Rome mentioning the wine merchant Lucius Scribonius Ianuarius, who was at the same time *curator corporis maris Hadriatici*: CIL VI 9682. See also AE 1988, 178 and AE 1987, 191–192. Cf. De Salvo 1992, 432–436, who underlines the connection of these *navicularii* with the wine trade. On the *corpus* see also Pellegrino 1987.

86 CIL XIV 409 = ILS 6146: „...item (sc. patrono) praeconum et | et argentarior(um) et negotiator(um) vinarior(um) ab urbe...".

87 CIL XIV 318 = ILS 6162.

88 It is remarkable, that *argentarii* or *coactores argentarii* are absent in the epigraphic records regarding the *forum vinarium*; but they are present in Ostian inscriptions: AE 1988, 189; AE 1988, 204; cf. Cébeillac-Gervasoni, Caldelli, Zevi 2010, 279–280. See also CIL XIV 405 = ILS 7512 mentioning a *stipulator argentarius*.

of wine between the northern Adriatic and Rome,[89] this person is to be seen as an incarnation of this network, since he was an *adlectus* of all important *collegia* regarding the wine trade of Ostia.[90]

Conclusion

What has been said about auctions and markets up this point can be summarized as follows: Using the concepts of NIE in analysing the economies of the ancient world in general and the economy of the Roman Empire in particular the existence of different market systems becomes visible.[91] Further research is needed to discuss and analyze the different market systems and their institutions in more detail. By looking at the Ostian auction market for wine it becomes clear that even in different market systems diverging subsystems using particular institutions existed. Although the wine market was an auction market, Roman law provided a particular set of rules for selling and purchasing wine, i.e. the *degustatio* and *mensura*. Thus a kind of risk management came into being which lowered the transaction costs for all participants within this specific market system. As it seems, the example of the Ostian wine trade gives reason to think the same regarding the social capital or the socio-economic networks woven around this market system. Here too supposedly market systems and subsystems generated particular networks, which are connected with other ones.

All in all this means that regarding the market as a mere function of offer and demand and considering the economy as an optimization of production and allocation is a theoretical framework for economic history that has too many shortcomings. The same goes for the idea that the institutions involved can be seen as neutral. On the contrary, the market systems are to be seen and analyzed as parts of complex institutional frameworks shaping the economy, which is on the other hand – to use a concept of Jacob Burckhardt – only one potency of a given historical society like the Roman one.[92] The advantage of using such a theoretical framework lies in the possibility to compare the economies of historical societies without transferring concepts of specific institutions for one particular society to another society.

---

89 Cf. Tran 2006, 80–81.

90 CIL XIV 409 = ILS 6146.

91 Cf. Andreau 1991 (1997), 322, who already spoke about a series of markets, which existed in the Roman Empire.

92 On Jacob Burckhardt's concept of potencies and its development after Burckhardt see Schulin 1991, 152–154 regarding the economy. See in general Hatscher 2003, 46–49. As far as I see it was only Kloft 1992, 4–5, who used this concept as part of a theoretical framework for economic history. For future research a connection of the concept of potencies and that of institutions is promising in the sense that these potencies shape the institutions used in economy on the one hand and on the other hand become institutions in the economy. A good example in this sense is the oath: cf. Silver 2011..

Bibliography

Andreau 1974= Andreau J., Les affairs de monsieur Jucundus, Roma 1974 (CEFR 19).

Andreau 1987 = Andreau J., La vie financière dans le monde romain. Les metiers de manieurs d'argent (IVe siècle av. J.-C. – IIIe siècle ap. J.-C.), Roma 1987 (BEFAR 265).

Andreau 1991 (1997) = Andreau J., Mercati e mercato, in: ders. (ed.), Patrimoines, échanges et prêts d'argent: l'économie romaine, Roma 1997, 311–334 (= Storia di Roma 2.2. L'impero mediterraneo, i principi e il mondo, Turin 1991, 367–385).

Bang 2008 = Bang P.F., The Roman Bazaar. A Comparative Study of Trade and Markets in a Tributary Empire, Cambridge 2008.

Brokaert forthcoming = Brokaert W., Partners in Business. Roman Merchants and the potential advantages of being a collegiatus, Anc. Soc. forthcoming.

Castagnoli 1980 = Castagnoli F., Installazioni portuali a Roma, in: D'Arms J.H. – Kopff E.C. (eds.), The Seaborne Commerce of Ancient Rome: Studies in Archaeology and History, Rom 1980 (Memoirs of the American Academy in Rome XXXVI), 35–42.

Cébeillac-Gervasoni – Caldelli – Zevi 2010 = Cébeillac-Gervasoni M. – Caldelli M.L. – Zevi F., Epigrafia Latina. Ostia: cento iscrizioni in contesto, Roma 2010.

Coarelli 1996 = Coarelli F., Il forum vinarium di Ostia: un'ipotesi di localizzazione, in: Zevi A.G. – Claridge A. (eds.), 'Roman Ostia' Revisited. Archaeological and Historical Papers in Memory of Russel Meiggs, Roma 1996, 105–113.

Colini 1980 = Colini A.M., Il porto fluviale del foro boario a Roma, in: D'Arms J.H. – Kopff E.C. (eds.), The Seaborne Commerce of Ancient Rome: Studies in Archaeology and History, Rom 1980 (Memoirs of the American Academy in Rome XXXVI), 43–53.

Colini 1986 = Colini A.M., Portus Tiberinus, Archeologia Laziale VII, 2, 1986, 157–197.

DeLaine 2005 = DeLaine J., The Commercial Landscape of Ostia, in: Mac Mahon A.– Price J. (eds.), Roman Working Lives and Urban Living, Oxford 2005, 29–47.

de Ligt 1993 = de Ligt L., Fairs and Markets in the Roman Empire. Economic and Social Aspects of Periodic Trade in a Pre-Industrial Society, Amsterdam 1993.

de Salvo 1992 = de Salvo L., I corpora naviculariorum. Economia privata e pubblici servizi nell'impero romano, Messina 1992 (Kleio 5).

Frass 2006 = Frass M., Antike römische Gärten. Soziale und wirtschaftliche Funktionen der Horti Romani, Wien 2006 (Grazer Beiträge Suppl. 10).

García Morcillo 2005 = García Morcillo M., Las ventas por subasta en el mundo romano: la esfera privada, Barcelona 2005 (Instrumenta 20).

García Morcillo 2008 = García Morcillo M., Auctions, Bankers and Public Finances in the Roman World, in: Verboven K. – Vandorpe K. – Chankowski V. (eds.), Pistoi dia tèn technèn. Bankers, Loans and Archives in the Ancient World. Studies in Honour of Raymond Bogaert, Löwen 2008 (Studia Hellenistica 44), 256–275.

Graßl 2004 = Graßl H., Marktorganisation und Preisbildung in der römischen Kaiserzeit, in: Rollinger R. – Ulf Ch. (eds.), Commerce and Monetary Systems in the Ancient World: Means of Transmission and Cultural Interaction. Proceedings of the Fifth Annual Symposium of the Assyrian and Babylonian Intellectual Heritage Project held in Innsbruck, Austria, October 3rd–8th 2002, Stuttgart 2004 (Melammu Symposia V), 352–365.

Gröschler 1997 = Gröschler P., Die tabellae-Urkunden aus den pompejanischen und herkulanensischen Urkundenfunden, Berlin 1997 (Freiburger rechtsgeschichtliche Abhandlungen 26).

Günther 2008 = Günther S., »Vectigalia nervos esse rei publicae«. Die indirekten Steuern in der Römischen Kaiserzeit von Augustus bis Diokletian, Wiesbaden 2008 (Philippika 26).

Hatscher 2003 = Hatscher Ch.R., Alte Geschichte und Universalgeschichte. Weltgeschichtliche Perspektiven aus althistorischer Sicht, Stuttgart 2003 (Hist.-E. 169).

Hobbs 1997 = Hobbs J.E., Measuring the Importance of Transaction costs in Cattle Marketing, American Journal of Agricultural Economics 79, 1997, 1083–1095.

Jaschke 2010 = Jaschke K., Die Wirtschafts- und Sozialgeschichte des antiken Puteoli, Rahden/Westf. 2010 (Pharos 26).

Kehoe 2007 = Kehoe D.P., Law and Rural Economy in the Roman Empire, Ann Arbor 2007.

Kolb 1995 =Kolb F., Rom. Die Geschichte der Stadt in der Antike, München 1995.

Kloft 1992 = Kloft H., Die Wirtschaft der griechisch-römischen Welt. Eine Einführung, Darmstadt 1992.

Krishna 2002 = Krishna V., Auction Theory, San Diego-London 2002.

Le Gall = Le Gall J., Le Tibre. Fleuve de Rome dans l'antiquité, Paris 1953.

Malmendier 2002 = Malmendier U., Societas Publicanorum. Staatliche Wirtschaftsaktivitäten in den Händen privater Unternehmer, Köln – Weimar – Wien 2002 (Forschungen zum römischen Recht 49).

Martin 2008 = Martin A., Imports at Ostia in the Imperial Period and Late Antiquity: The Amphora Evidence from the DAI-AAR Excavations, in: Hohlfelder R.L. (ed.), The Maritime World of Ancient Rome. Proceedings of the Maritime World of Ancient Rome Conference held at the Amercian Academy in Rome 27–29 March 2003, Ann Arbor 2008 (MAAR Suppl. VI), 105–118.

McAfee – McMillan 1987 = McAfee R.P. – McMillan J., Auctions and Bidding, Journal of Economic Literature 25, 1987, 699–738.

Meiggs 1973 = Meiggs R., Roman Ostia, Oxford ²1973.

Mratschek-Halfmann 1993 = Mratschek Halfmann S., Divites et praepotentes. Reichtum und soziale Stellung in der Literatur der Prinzipatszeit, Stuttgart 1993 (Hist.-E. 70).

Pellegrino 1987 = Pellegrino A., I navicularii maris Hadriatici ad Ostia, MGR 11 (1987), 229–236.

Petrucci 2008 = Petrucci A., Riesame del ruolo dei banchieri nelle auctiones private nel diritto classico romano, in: Verboven K. – Vandorpe K. – Chankowski V. (eds.),

Pistoi dia tèn technèn. Bankers, Loans and Archives in the Ancient World. Studies in Honour of Raymond Bogaert, Löwen 2008 (Studia Hellenistica 44), 277–300.

Platner - Ashby 1929 = Plattner S.B. - Ashby T., A Topographical Dictionary of Ancient Rome, Oxford 1929.

Quilici 1986 = Quilici L., Il Tevere e l'Aniene come vie d'acqua a monte di Roma in età imperiale, Archeologia Laziale VII, 2, 1986, 198–217.

Richter 2011 = Richter R., Institutional Economics of the "Market Itself". An Attempted Answer to a Complaint by Ronald Coase, HSR 36.3 (2011), 34–57.

Richter - Furubotn 2003 = Richter R. - Furubotn E.G., Neue Institutionenökonomik. Eine Einführung und kritische Würdigung, Tübingen [3]2003.

Rodríguez Almeida 1998 = Rodríguez Almeida E., Il porto fluviale di Roma, paradigma e eccezione, in: Ballester J.P. (ed.), Puertos antiguos y comercio marítimo. III Jornadas de Arqueología Subacuática, Facultat de Geografia i Història Valencia, 13, 14 y 15 de Noviembre de 1997, Valencia 1998, 23–38.

Rohde 2009 = Rohde D., Der Piazzale dei Corporazioni in Ostia: wirtschaftliche Funktion und soziale Bedeutung, MBAH 27, 2009, 31–61.

Ruffing 1993 = Ruffing K., Das Nikanor-Archiv und der römische Süd- und Osthandel, MBAH XII 2, 1993, 1–26.

Ruffing 1997 = Ruffing K., ...qui emere vina et vendere solet... Zum Berufsbild des Weinhändlers nebst einigen Bemerkungen zur Terminologie, in: Ruffing K. - Tenger B. (eds.), Miscellanea oeconomica. Studien zur antiken Wirtschaftsgeschichte. Harald Winkel zum 65. Geburtstag, St. Katharinen 1997 (Pharos IX), 116–134.

Schulin 1991 = Schulin E., Kulturgeschichte und die Lehre von den Potenzen. Bemerkungen zu zwei Konzepten Burckhardts und ihrer Weiterentwicklung im 20. Jahrhundert, in: Boockmann H. - Jürgensen K. (eds.), Nachdenken über Geschichte. Beiträge aus der Ökumene der Historiker in memoriam Karl Dietrich Erdmann, Neumünster 1991, 145–156.

Silver 2009 = Silver M., Glimpses of Vertical Integration/Disintegration in Ancient Rome, Anc. Soc. 39, 2009, 171–184.

Silver 2011 = Silver M., Transaction/Administrative Costs in Graeco-Roman Antiquity. With Special Reference to the Implications of Atheism/Naturalism in Classical Athens, MBAH 29, 2011, 49-94.

Tchernia 1986 = Tchernia A., Le vin de l'Italie romaine. Essai d'histoire économique d'après les amphores, Roma 1986 (BEFAR 261).

Temin 2001 = Temin P., A Market Economy in the Early Roman Empire, JRS 91, 2001, 169–181.

Thielmann 1961 = Thielmann G., Die römische Privatauktion zugleich ein Beitrag zum römischen Bankenrecht, Berlin 1961 (Berliner juristische Abhandlungen Bd. 4).

Tran 2006 = Tran N., Les membres des associations romaines. Le rang socal des collegiati en Italie et en Gaules sous le Haut-Empire, Roma 2006 (CEFR 367).

Die „Ware Mensch" in der Antike und in der Neuzeit*

Ingomar Weiler

Auf einige Beispiele, die im ersten Teil die Aktualität des Themas unter dem Motto *Slavery proper still exists today*[1] dokumentieren sollen, folgen ein wissenschaftsgeschichtlicher Abschnitt über die Erforschung der antiken Sklaverei und des Menschenhandels und Überlegungen zur komparativen Betrachtung des Sklavenhandels von einst und jetzt. Angeschlossen daran sind Themen, die sich mit der „Ware" Mensch auf den antiken Märkten befassen und sich dabei auf das Marktgeschehen, auf Probleme beim Kauf und Verkauf der Sklaven und auf die Preisgestaltung konzentrieren; ein Seitenblick auf die moderne „Bepreisung" von Menschen soll dabei nicht fehlen.

I. Zur Aktualität der Thematik

Seit Jahren berichten die Medien über aktuelle Vorkommnisse im Zusammenhang mit Menschenhandel. Sie informieren über verschiedene Details und Praktiken des heutigen Menschen-, insbesondere des Frauen- und Kinderhandels, und sie provozieren den Althistoriker geradezu, über Analogien, Parallelen, konstante und variable Verhaltensmuster und Singularitäten nachzudenken. Einige Beispiele aus den letzten sieben Jahren mögen das exemplifizieren.

Nach einer Veröffentlichung der Staatsanwältin Annette von Schmiedeberg, Mitglied des Runden Tisches zur *Bekämpfung des Menschenhandels in Hessen*, gehört „Menschen- bzw. Frauenhandel zu den ertragreichsten Geschäften des organisierten Verbrechens".[2] Er wird nach einigen ökonomischen Expertisen, was den Kapitalertrag betrifft, gleichrangig mit oder als „drittwichtigste Einnahmequelle" unmittelbar nach dem Waffen- und Drogenhandel eingestuft. Dazu kommt noch, dass er, so die Staatsanwältin, „mit ungleich geringerem Risiko" verbunden ist und „Strafverfahren [...] schwieriger und zeitaufwendiger" durchzuführen sind.[3] Im gleichen Jahr, in welchem von Schmiedeberg ihre Ergebnisse publiziert, werden bei der vom 13. bis 15. Februar 2008 im *Austria Center Vienna* veranstalteten ersten UNO-Konferenz gegen Menschenhandel den 1.300 Delegierten aus 100 Staaten Unterlagen vorgelegt, in denen von weltweit 2.500.000 verkauften Männern, Frauen und Kindern die Rede ist und davon, dass nach UNO-Schätzungen jährlich 31 Milliarden Dollar in die Hände der Menschenhändler gelangen.

---

* Der Beitrag enthält Wiederholungen von zwei Arbeiten, die ich 2007 und 2009 veröffentlicht habe (vgl. die Bibliographie im Anhang). Es war der Wunsch der Veranstalter, denen ich für die Einladung herzlich danke, über dieses Thema zu referieren.

1 Phillips 1985, 3.

2 Von Schmiedeberg 2008, 2; vgl. auch Cacho 2011, 19–21.

3 Von Schmiedeberg 2008, 12. Tageszeitung *Standard* (25. April 2007): „Der Menschenhandel bildet mittlerweile die drittwichtigste Einnahmequelle für das organisierte Verbrechen."

Was Europa betrifft, so sind es vor allem junge Frauen und Mädchen, die aus dem Osten und den Balkanstaaten sowie aus Afrika in die westlichen Länder gelangen und hier zumeist als Prostituierte arbeiten.[4] Langfristige historische Perspektiven spielten in der Wiener Tagung bestenfalls eine marginale Rolle. Erwartungsgemäß stehen dabei tagespolitische Fragen im Vordergrund. Anders haben bei der UNO-Weltkonferenz gegen Rassismus in Durban (2001) afrikanische Staaten auf ihre eigene leidvolle Geschichte verwiesen, auf den Sklavenhandel, wie er von Kolonialmächten ab dem 16. Jh. in großem Stil betrieben wurde.[5] Eine damals in Südafrika verabschiedete Deklaration bezeichnet den „transatlantischen Sklavenhandel [...] als eine schreckliche historische Tragödie und eine Quelle für Rassismus und Intoleranz". Im Schlussprotokoll wird in genereller Form festgehalten, dass Sklavenhandel „ein Verbrechen gegen die Menschlichkeit ist – und immer schon war", und nicht nur Afrikaner, sondern auch Asiaten und indigene Völker als Opfer des diskriminierenden Menschenhandels zu betrachten seien.[6] Geschichte wird hier zum Argument für die Forderung um finanzielle Entschädigung. Unter dem Titel *Sklaverei. Im Inneren des Milliardengeschäfts Menschenhandel* (2011) hat die mexikanische Journalistin Lydia Cacho die Ergebnisse ihrer Recherchen über die internationalen Netzwerke des Handels mit sehr jungen Mädchen in Zentralamerika und in Ostasien insbesondere im Kontext der an und unter der Armutsgrenze lebenden Familien veröffentlicht. Ausgehend vom Begriff „Menschenhandel", wie er in einem Protokoll der Vereinten Nationen am 15. November 2000 definiert wurde, schreibt die Autorin:

> „Der Menschenhandel, der in 175 Ländern der Erde dokumentiert ist, legt die Schwächen des globalisierten Kapitalismus genauso bloß wie die Ungleichheiten, die durch die wirtschaftlichen Spielregeln der Mächtigen entstehen. Vor allem aber zeigt er eindrucksvoll, inwieweit sich die menschliche Grausamkeit inzwischen in der Kultur festgesetzt hat und als normal angesehen wird. Jedes Jahr werden weltweit rund 1,4 Millionen Menschen, überwiegend Frauen und Mädchen, in die Sexsklaverei gezwungen. Sie werden gekauft, verkauft und weiterverkauft wie Rohstoffe der Industrie, wie Trophäen, wie Opfergaben oder wie gesellschaftlicher Müll."[7]

Die deutschsprachige Altertums- und Geschichtswissenschaft hat in den letzten Jahren diesem Gegenstand mit Blickrichtung auf die antike Sklaverei besondere Aufmerksamkeit gezollt und dabei universalhistorische Vergleiche und Gegenwartsbezüge berücksichtigt. Drei Beispiele seien exemplarisch angeführt. Im Jahr 2005 hat Elisabeth Herrmann-Otto nach Abschluss eines Graduiertenseminars in

4 *Die Presse* (29./30. Jänner 2008). Vgl. auch Bales 2001/1999, 332.

5 Claudia Kaufmann: Nach der UNO-Weltkonferenz gegen Rassismus vom September 2001 in Durban, Südafrika. Erwartungen und Möglichkeiten. Nationale Tagung der EKR, 20. März 2002. Schatten der Vergangenheit und die Last der Bilder. Rassismus gegen Schwarze in der Schweiz.

6 Haedrich 2005, 294.

7 Cacho 2011, 19f. und 335.

Trier über *Sklaverei, Knechtschaft, Zwangsarbeit* (2003/2004) einen Sammelband herausgegeben. Darin werden auf interdisziplinärer Ebene Fragen des Sklaven- und Menschenhandels, der Zwangsarbeit und „Entwurzelung des Menschen“ teilweise komparatistisch analysiert. Neben den Bezügen zur Antike, die dabei den Schwerpunkt bilden, behandeln die Autoren dieser Publikation in materialreichen Recherchen den Mittelmeerraum als „Handelsdrehscheibe“ in der Welt des Mittelalters und der frühen Neuzeit sowie die modernen Formen des Menschenhandels mit den diversen Versuchen, diesen zu unterbinden.[8] Der Bogen dieser Einzelstudien reicht dabei vom Ägypten der Pharaos bis zur Gegenwart. Ein Jahr später (2006) veranstaltete die *Kommission für Geschichte des Altertums der Akademie der Wissenschaften und der Literatur* in Mainz unter der Ägide von Heinz Heinen eine Konferenz über *Menschenraub, Menschenhandel und Sklaverei in antiker und moderner Perspektive.* Den Eröffnungsvortrag hielt die bereits oben zitierte Staatsanwältin Annette von Schmiedeberg. Die Vorträge darüber liegen gedruckt vor.[9] In chronologischer Hinsicht beginnen die Untersuchungen mit den Deportationen in Altmesopotamien und thematisieren sodann den Menschenhandel von der mykenischen Zeit bis in die Spätantike. In einer sowohl kunst- wie auch rezeptionshistorisch aufschlussreichen Analyse berühmter historisierender Gemälde von Jean León Gérôme (*Achat d'une esclave*, 1857; *Marché d'esclaves*, 1866; *Esclave grecque*, 1870; *Vente d'esclaves à Rome*, 1884 und 1886) kommt Johannes Deißler zu der Erkenntnis, dass der französische Maler der Belle Epoque mit „austauschbaren gestischen Mustern und zeitlosen Stereotypen“ arbeitete, was „alleine deshalb möglich [war], weil der Menschenhandel in der Antike wie zu Zeiten Gérômes wohl nach gleichen oder zumindest ähnlichen Mechanismen funktionierte.“[10]

Im Jahr 2007 wurde an der Innsbrucker Universität am *Institut für Wirtschaftstheorie, -politik und -geschichte* ein wirtschaftshistorisches Symposion abgehalten mit dem Titel *Von Menschenhandel und Menschenpreisen. Wert und Bewertung von Menschen im Spiegel der Zeit* (2006). Die Beiträge behandeln den Kauf und Verkauf von Menschen vor allem in Verbindung mit der Frage, welchen „Marktwert“ orientalische oder antike Sklaven, Muslime und Christen, Malteserritter, Afrikaner, Asoziale, Juden, Roma und Sinti bei Händlern, Piraten und in verschiedenen politischen Systemen erzielen konnten. Der Organisator der Tagung, Josef Nussbaumer, hatte sich vorgenommen, Fragen des „Handels mit Menschen in seinen vielfältigen Formen und auch [der] ‚Bepreisung‘ von Menschen“ vom Altertum bis zur Gegenwart zu erörtern. Nussbaumer bezeichnet die Thematik als „so-

8 Herrmann-Otto 2005, XIVf. Speziell zum Frauenhandel in der Antike vgl. Binsfeld 2008, 85–98.
9 Heinen 2008, 1–7.
10 Deißler 2008, 192.

zialhistorischen Dauerbrenner, eine traurige ökonomische und soziale Realität".[11] Die Publikation der Ergebnisse liegt seit 2007 vor.[12]

II. Wissenschaftsgeschichtliche Anmerkung[13]

Wie viele andere altertumswissenschaftliche Arbeitsfelder so nimmt auch die Beschäftigung mit der antiken Sklaverei ihren Anfang im Zeitalter des Humanismus. Die Liste rezeptions- und wissenschaftsgeschichtlicher Studien, die in der letzten Auflage der Mainzer *Bibliographie zur antiken Sklaverei* (2003) mit 10.415 Titeln unter dem Lemma *Sklaverei als Forschungsproblem* erfasst sind, zählt 1.564 Titel, nur rund ein Dutzend davon betrifft schwerpunktmäßig Fragen des Sklavenhandels. In Relation zur Gesamtzahl nimmt sich der Anteil der Forschungen zum Sklavenhandel somit eher bescheiden aus. Während im mittelalterlichen Schrifttum antike Sklavenfragen (abgesehen von der aristotelischen Sklaventheorie) kaum beachtet wurden, zählen die humanistischen Werke des friesischen Philologen Titus Popma, *De operis servorum* (1608) und des italienischen Antiquarius Lorenzo Pignoria, *De servis et eorum apud veteres ministeriis commentarius* (1613) zu den frühesten Monographien über antike Sklaverei.[14] Beide Abhandlungen lassen sich jener historiographischen Tradition zuordnen, die Arnaldo Momigliano unter dem Begriff Antiquarianismus subsumiert. Auf sie greift mehr als hundert Jahre später Johann Friedrich Jugler in der ersten Einzeldarstellung des Sklavenhandels zurück: *ANDRAPODOKAPHLEION sive de nundinatione servorum apud veteres liber singularis historico-iuridicus, ex quo lucem capere possunt auctorum loca complura* (1741).

Juglers „Standardwerk zum Sklavenhandel"[15] dient als eine der quellenkundlichen Grundlagen für Johann Friedrich Reitemeiers (1755–1839) *Geschichte und Zustand der Sklaverey und Leibeigenschaft in Griechenland* (1789), ein Werk, von dem Moses I. Finley sagt, dass es wegen „der Abkehr Reitemeiers sowohl von der rein antiquarischen als auch von der eng moralischen Ansicht der antiken Sklaverei [...] kaum hoch genug eingeschätzt werden" könne.[16] Diese Wertschätzung teilt Finley mit Karl Marx und Karl Christ, der der „verdienstvollen Monographie" bescheinigt, sie gehe „ohne jede Beschönigung auf die fundamentale wirtschaftliche und gesellschaftliche Bedeutung der Sklaverei ein".[17] Die Bedeutung, die Reitemeier dem Sklavenhandel beimisst, lässt sich an seiner Aussage ablesen, dass zwei

11 Nussbaumer 2007, 9.

12 Eine Notiz in der Zeitschrift *Das Ausland - Monthly* 1869, 136–138 über den „letzten nordamerikanischen Sklavenhändler" mag angesichts der heutigen Situation naiv wirken.

13 Eine reichhaltige Bibliographie zur Rezeptions- und Wissenschaftsgeschichte bieten Bellen – Heinen 2003, Band 1, 3–101. Vgl. auch Deißler 2003, 47–59.

14 Deißler 2000, 10 und 222.

15 Deißler 2000, 222.

16 Finley 1981, 44. Vgl. auch Deißler 2000, 441.

17 Deißler 2000, 443; Christ 1999, 10f.

Drittel des Nachschubs über den Handel nach Griechenland gelangt seien.[18] Einen frühen moralischen Protest gegen den Menschenhandel hat übrigens Friedrich Schiller in der Kammerdienerszene in *Kabale und Liebe* (1783) formuliert, indem er just in jenem Jahr, als Reitemeier sein Buch abschließt, den herzoglichen Verkauf von 7.000 Soldaten nach Amerika anprangert und auf protestierend zurückbleibende Mütter, Kinder und Bräute verweist. Reitemeiers Werk steht an einem Wendepunkt der Historiographie. An die Stelle des bloßen Sammelns und Systematisierens der *antiquitates* tritt in der zweiten Hälfte des 18. Jh. allmählich eine entwicklungsgeschichtlich konzipierte Altertumswissenschaft. Ihr fühlt sich Reitemeier verpflichtet. In der Gründung des Göttinger *Historischen Instituts* (1766) und in dem dortigen Wirken von Christian Gottlob Heyne (1729–1812), einem der Lehrer Reitemeiers, findet dieser für die Geschichtswissenschaft bemerkenswerte Wandel vom Antiquarianismus zur Historisierung der Altertumswissenschaft in der deutschsprachigen Historiographie seinen Ausdruck.[19] Die beiden Autoren begegnen sich auch dort, wo der Gegenwartsbezug der antiken Sklaverei im transatlantischen Menschenhandel hergestellt wird und an Querverbindungen zum Londoner Abolitionismus und zu den Debatten in der französischen Nationalversammlung, schließlich auch zur Deportation Straffälliger nach Australien erinnert wird.[20] Eine Monographie von W.O. Blake, *The History of Slavery and the Slave Trade, Ancient and Modern* (1857) hat unter komparativem Aspekt die Aufmerksamkeit auf den Sklavenhandel gelenkt.

Reitemeier wiederum empfängt für seine Sklavenforschung wichtige Impulse aus dem angelsächsischen Raum. Vor allem John Millars keineswegs bloß deskriptiv konzipierten *Observations Concerning the Distinction of Ranks in Society* (1771) und dessen unmissverständlich pragmatischer Ansatz, auf den sich „die Abolitionisten bald berufen sollten“, weisen in eine Richtung, die in der historischen Dimension der Sklaverei auch politische Argumente für die Abschaffung dieser Institution sieht. Zum Ausdruck kommt dieses Engagement auch darin, dass Millar in seiner Funktionsperiode als Chairman der Universität in Glasgow im Jahr 1791 an William Wilberforce (1759–1833), den wohl prominentesten der britischen Protagonisten im Kampf gegen den Sklavenhandel, ein Ehrendoktorat verleiht.[21] Es ist nicht zu übersehen, dass in den Staaten, in denen vor allem der Transatlantikhandel einen wesentlichen Wirtschaftsfaktor darstellt, antike Quellen eine nicht unwesentliche Rolle spielen. Die naturrechtlichen Argumente, insbesondere jene des Aristoteles und der römische Juristen, aber auch Belege aus dem Alten und

18 Deißler 2000, 226.

19 Momigliano 1955/1991, 95. Christ 1999, 9. Zur wechselseitigen Beeinflussung zwischen Heyne und Reitemeier, die über das Lehrer-Schülerverhältnis hinausweist, siehe auch Deißler 2000, 56 und 312–323.

20 Deißler 2000, 314f. – Zur Abschaffung des Sklavenhandels, für die sich Abolitionisten ohne Berufung auf Humanisten oder antike Autoren engagierten, s. Vogt 1972, 124.

21 Delacampagne 2004, 205; Lehmann 1967, 50. Zur Diskussion der Sklavenfrage in der schottischen Aufklärung vgl. auch Webster 2003, 481–489.

Neuen Testament und der Scholastik, dienen der Legitimierung der Sklaverei und des Sklavenhandels. Seit der bekannten *Disputation von Valladolid* (1552) zwischen Las Casas und Sepúlveda verstummt dieser teilweise mit aristotelischen Argumenten geführte Diskurs über die Rechtmäßigkeit der Sklaverei nicht mehr.[22]

Was die Erforschung des antiken Sklavenhandels in den letzten Jahrzehnten betrifft, so kann man zunächst einmal auf die Arbeiten zur griechischen Geschichte von Moses I. Finley, vor allem auf *Die Sklaverei in der Antike. Geschichte und Probleme* (1980/1981) und auf Hans Volkmanns *Die Massenversklavungen der Einwohner eroberter Städte in der hellenistisch-römischen Zeit* (1961/1990) sowie auf die Sklavenstudien von Paul Cartledge verweisen. Cartledge beklagt trotz der beiden erwähnten Monographien und zahlreicher spezieller Untersuchungen von Walter Scheidel, William V. Harris, Keith Bradley, Joachim Szidat und der etwas weiter zurückliegenden von Keith Hopkins und für Byzanz von Helga Köpstein noch im Jahr 2001 den defizitären Kenntnisstand über den Sklavenhandel im griechisch-römischen Altertum und betont zugleich, wie wichtig die vorhandenen Quellen für das Verständnis des antiken Wirtschaftslebens sind, und das nicht nur für die zentralen Bereiche der „Versorgung der Landwirtschaft und des Handwerks". Im letzten Dezennium (2001–2011) wurde eine Reihe kompetenter Arbeiten zur Behebung der von Cartledge registrierten Defizite vorgelegt. Dazu gehört der von Heinz Heinen herausgegebene Band *Menschenraub, Menschenhandel und Sklaverei* (2008). Ein Sammelband über die antiken Transportrouten und Marktplätze für Sklaven wurde von Girea (*Groupe International de Recherches sur l'Esclavage dans l'Antiquité,* Besançon) vor wenigen Jahren publiziert.[23] Neuere Studien bietet der von K. Bradley und P. Cartledge edierte erste Band der *Cambridge World History of Slavery. Vol. 1: The Ancient Mediterranean World* (2011).[24] Sehr informative Aspekte und Gesamtübersichten über den Handel mit Sklaven bieten auch der von Elisabeth Herrmann-Otto herausgegebene Sammelband *Freie Arbeits- und Lebensverhältnisse von der Antike bis zur Gegenwart* (2005) und Leonhard Schumachers *Sklaverei in der Antike* (2001).[25] Wie Herrmann-Otto und

22 Siehe etwa Deißler 2000, 55–57; zum Vorschlag von Las Casas, die Indios freizulassen und Negersklaven nach Amerika zu holen, vgl. Delgado 2002, 319f. und 2011; Isaac 2004, 172–175. Bitterli 1991,176 nennt als Vorläufer von Las Casas den Dominikanermönch Antonio de Montesinos und zitiert sein bemerkenswertes Dokument gegen die Versklavung der Indianer.

23 Garrido-Hory 2002.

24 Cartledge – Bradley 2011; zum Sklavenhandel hier vor allem die Beiträge Braund 2011, 112–133 (zu Griechenland), Bradley 2011, 241–264 (römische Republik), Scheidel 2011, 287–310 (Roman Slave Supply) und Grey 2011, 482–509 (Spätantike). – Zur älteren Forschung: Scheidel 1998, 830f.; Herrmann-Otto 2002, 113–126; Hopkins 1978; Bradley 1986, 49–58; Harris 1980, 117–140; Szidat 1985, 360–371; Köpstein 1966, 487–493. – Vgl. auch das unter dem Stichwort „Handel mit Sklaven" erfasste Schrifttum im Registerteil bei Bellen – Heinen 2003, Band 2, 737.

25 Auf die deutschsprachigen Beiträge sei hier mit besonderem Nachdruck verwiesen, weil die angloamerikanische Forschung nur selten davon Notiz nimmt. Herrmann-Otto (Hg.) 2005, 141–144, 155–158, 237–240, 281–284, 292–296; für Schumacher 2001, 3–19 steht außer Streit, „dass das Phänomen des Menschenhandels keineswegs der Vergangenheit angehört" (14).

Schumacher so hat sich auch der Althistoriker Egon Flaig in seiner *Weltgeschichte der Sklaverei* (2009) bei seiner Analyse des Sklavenhandels keineswegs auf die Antike beschränkt und die Rolle des Islam in den afrikanischen „Lieferzonen“, die „Fangapparate“, die „afrikanischen Menschenverkäufer“ und die „europäischen Menschenkäufer“ im Rahmen des transatlantischen Sklavenhandels zum Gegenstand seiner Untersuchung gemacht.[26]

Zum neuzeitlichen Menschen- und Sklavenhandel liegen zahlreiche zeitgenössische Publikationen vor. Sie lenken die Aufmerksamkeit insbesondere auf das Handelsdreieck Afrika-Europa-Amerika und begnügen sich dabei mit gelegentlichen Seitenblicken auf die Antike. Dazu kommt ein umfangreiches Schrifttum mit solide recherchierten Beiträgen zur aktuellen Situation der „Ware Mensch“, über Anwerbung und Transport, über Arbeitslager, Zwangs- und Kinderarbeit bis hin zu Themen wie Prostitution und illegale „Entnahme von Körperorganen“ – eine Maßnahme, die der Antike aus technisch-medizinischen Gründen unbekannt geblieben ist.[27] Auch Babyhandel wäre hier ergänzend zu nennen.[28] Vergleichende Betrachtungen zum antiken Sklavenhandel spielen dabei, soweit ich die Literatur überblicke, kaum noch eine Rolle. Dafür ist der moderne Menschenhandel ein nicht selten behandelter Gegenstand der Boulevardpresse mit reißerischer Aufmachung, wie etwa „Kolumbianische Prostituierte in Frankfurt“ oder „Frischfleisch“ für österreichische Bordelle.[29]

III. Sklavenforschung und vergleichende Betrachtung

Es fällt auf, dass der antike Sklavenhandel selten als Gegenstand komparativer Forschung thematisiert wird, obwohl erst jüngst wieder festgestellt wurde: *The slave trade was everywhere.*[30] Dort, wo Vergleiche angestellt werden, geschieht das zumeist, ohne auf irgendwelche Methoden- und Terminologieprobleme oder die Analyse behaupteter Parallelen und Divergenzen näher einzugehen. Auf dieses Manko kann hier nur hingewiesen werden. Es muss genügen, einige Thesen zur Theorie und Praxis vorzutragen, selbst auf die Gefahr hin, dass man mich mit Georg von Belows zynischem Verdikt konfrontiert: „Wer nichts von der Sache versteht, schreibt über die Methode“.[31] An Einwänden zum Vergleichen fehlt es nicht. Drei kritische Stimmen seien genannt. Schon der schottische Aufklärer William Blair hat es in seiner Abhandlung *An Inquiry into the State of Slavery amongst*

---

26 Flaig 2009, 99–112, 171–178.

27 Schmiedeberg 2008, 9. Siehe auch die Monographien von Bales 2001, Delacampagne 2004 und Cacho 2011.

28 Schumacher 2001, 15.

29 Gesetzestexte zum Menschenhandel, zum Menschenrechtsschutz und zu Forschungsvorhaben bieten Haedrich 2005, 281–297, Heinz 2005, 298–314, Von Schmiedeberg 2008, 9–19; Bales 1999/2001, 354–364; Cacho 2011, 333–346. – Bernhard Torsch: Interventionsstelle für Betroffene des Frauenhandels (Wien).

30 Braund 2011, 112.

31 Von Below 1898, 271.

the Romans (1833) strikt abgelehnt, Vergleiche zwischen antiker und moderner Sklaverei anzustellen, mit der Begründung, „the two systems differ so widely, that they could serve but little to illustrate each other".[32] Ähnliche Vorbehalte sind in der Altertumswissenschaft nicht unbekannt. In genereller Form hat sie Hermann Strasburger in seiner Studie *Zum antiken Gesellschaftsideal* (1976), in der die unterschiedlichsten Sklavenfragen angesprochen werden, auf den Punkt gebracht: „Ich beschränke meinen [...] Beitrag [...] auf dieses mein Fachgebiet und werde weder aus zweiter Hand vom Gruppenverhalten der Affen noch von Mittelalter und Neuzeit, geschweige denn außereuropäischen Kulturen reden".[33] Und Strasburger begründet seine Haltung mit der Feststellung: „Vorstellungen, die sich vom abolitionistischen Klischee der Negersklaverei in Amerika oder gar von Konzentrationslagern herleiten, können nur zu einer völligen Fehleinschätzung der antiken Sklaverei führen".[34] Zum Sklavenhandel selbst hat der Autor sich in diesem Kontext nicht näher geäußert.

In grundsätzlicher Form hat im Hinblick auf die dürftige Quellenlage des Altertums Wilfried Nippel vor den Versuchen gewarnt, das Fehlen statistischer Data mit einem vergleichenden Blick auf spätere Geschichtsepochen kompensieren zu wollen. Dieses methodische Bedenken, das Nippel in einer Rezension zum demographischen Konzept von Scheidel ausspricht, findet sich, so der Kritiker, bereits bei David Hume.[35] Dass dieser Methodendiskurs immer schon, auch in der Frage der Sklaverei kontrovers geführt wurde, zeigt die Rezeptionsgeschichte zur *Querelle des Anciens et Modernes* (1687) von Charles Perrault ebenso wie die Beobachtung von Johannes Deißler, „dass es ein in der Aufklärung immanentes Bestreben war, Parallelen und Analogien zwischen Antike und Gegenwart aufzuzeigen".[36]

Gegen die rigorose Ablehnung der vergleichenden Betrachtung lassen sich heute andere Forschungspositionen, die teils in schroffem Widerspruch dazu stehen, anführen. Zum Grundsätzlichen: Mit verschiedenen Vorbehalten wird der komparativen Methode in der Geschichtswissenschaft eine wichtige Aufgabe zugewiesen. Theodor Schieder hat beispielsweise in seiner Kritik am Historismus und dessen Bemühen, das historisch Singuläre, die Individualität, zum zentralen Gegenstand historischer Erkenntnis zu machen und den Vergleich als Domäne der deskriptiven Naturwissenschaften aufzufassen, die Anwendung komparativer Methoden mit Nachdruck empfohlen und dafür „einige Grundregeln" aufgestellt.[37] Schieder beruft sich dabei unter anderem auf Marc Bloch, dessen programmatisches Plädoyer *Pour une histoire comparée des sociétés européennes* (1927/1994)

32 Blair 1833, IX.

33 Strasburger 1976, 13f.

34 Strasburger 1976, 59 (mit Literaturangaben); vgl. auch 71 (zur Unmöglichkeit, „eine faire vergleichende Statistik der einst und jetzt Menschen von Menschen zugefügten Leiden" vorzulegen).

35 Nippel 2005 (Scheidel-Rezension).

36 Deißler 2000, 271–273, 440 und 442. Zur Sklavenliteratur der amerikanischen Aufklärung vgl. Morrow 1985/1986, 236–255.

37 Schieder 1968, 204. Vgl. dazu allerdings die kritischen Einwände von Welskopp 2010.

als eine der Pionierarbeiten anzusprechen ist. Hier werden unter Berücksichtigung freier und unfreier Menschen die Möglichkeiten und Grenzen der komparativen Methoden gezeigt. Im Zentrum stehen dabei Versuche, Analogien, Ähnlichkeiten und Unterschiede, Singularitäten sowie konstante und variable Verhaltensmuster in zwei oder mehreren sozialen Milieus festzustellen. Neue Impulse erhält die vergleichende Sklavenforschung von den systematischen Sozialwissenschaften. Der Soziologe George Murdock hat mit seinem *Ethnographic Atlas* (1967) dafür einen Grundstein gelegt. Hier werden 186 Gesellschaften aus Geschichte und Gegenwart aufgelistet, in denen Sklaverei eine erwähnenswerte Rolle spielt. In 66 dieser Fälle wird ihnen der Status von *slaveholding societies* eingeräumt.[38] Bei seinem Versuch, eine gemeinsame *typology of social structures* zu definieren, hat sich Murdock einer komparatistischen und statistischen Arbeitsweise bedient. Orlando Patterson hat in seinem berühmten Buch *Slavery and Social Death* (1982), das, wie schon der Untertitel *A Comparative Study* ankündigt, auf den Resultaten Murdocks aufbaut, dem Vergleich sowie der Frage des Sklavennachschubs einen hohen Stellenwert eingeräumt. In seinem Einleitungskapitel *The Constituent Elements of Slavery* legt der Autor einige seiner Leitlinien für eine komparative Betrachtung dar, im Kapitel *The Acquisition of Slaves* wird sodann die Rolle des Sklavenhandels in allen Geschichtsepochen und auf allen Kontinenten ausführlich dargelegt.[39] Für Patterson, der auch die Preispolitik im Sklavenhandel anspricht (s. unten IV. Abschnitt), gilt als prominenter Gewährsmann hinsichtlich der antiken Sklaverei Moses I. Finley. Im Gegensatz zu William Blair und in Übereinstimmung mit einem der meistzitierten amerikanischen Sklavenforscher, David Brian Davis, befürwortet Finley die komparative Betrachtungsweise. Immer wieder benutzt der Althistoriker die Neue Welt als Folie für seine Analysen. Im Unterschied zu den zuvor angeführten Versuchen einer vergleichenden Betrachtung der amerikanischen und antiken Sklavenfrage, die rechtliche und/oder moralische Kriterien in den Vordergrund rückt, dominieren bei Finley ökonomische Aspekte.[40] Nippel hat in seiner Analyse von Finleys komparativem Ansatz hervorgehoben, dass dieser „den Vergleich mit Sklavengesellschaften in der Moderne“ gesucht habe, „um Grundannahmen der Forschung zu kontrollieren, nicht um Lücken unseres Wissens zu schließen“.[41]

Von Patterson ausgehend, sieht auch Magnus Mörner die Chancen für einen Erkenntnisfortschritt; er unterscheidet dabei *diachronic* und *synchronic compari-*

---

38 Murdock 1967, 109–263. Dazu vgl. Patterson 1982, 345–364.

39 Patterson 1982, 1–14 und 148–171. In einer früheren Studie benennt Patterson 1977, 430 „Key issues in the Comparative Study of Slavery: (a) The problem of the nature of slavery; (b) the problem of the evolutionary origins of slavery; (c) the problem of the structural causes of slavery; and (d) the problem of the structure and dynamics of slave society proper, i.e. that special category of societies in which slavery is the dominant mode of production“.

40 Finley 1980/1981, 154. Zu seiner Beurteilung der Sklavenpreise und der Preisschwankungen im Altertum vgl. unten den IV. Abschnitt: Die „Ware“ Mensch auf antiken Märkten.

41 Nippel 2006, 68.

son und ist überzeugt, für Fragen der demographischen Bedingungen, der humanen und inhumanen Behandlung von Sklaven, der Möglichkeiten, ein quasi-familiäres Leben zu führen und der Häufigkeit von Freilassungen sei der Vergleich ein "necessary tool to clarify these intricate issues".[42] Ähnliche Überlegungen zu den Vergleichsmöglichkeiten mit dem transatlantischen Sklavenhandel finden sich auch in Henry W. Plekets Beitrag *Slavernij in de Oudheid: 'Voer' voor oudhistorici en comparatisten* (1982). Dabei bemüht sich der niederländische Autor, psychologische Aspekte, die Praktiken des Umgangs mit Kriegsgefangenen und die Versorgungsprobleme beim Sklavennachschub (*shortage of slaves*) vor allem im Kontext des kaiserzeitlichen Handels zu diskutieren und die Ergebnisse von David Brian Davis und C.N. Degler zu den amerikanischen Verhältnissen in seine Studie zu integrieren.[43] In letzter Zeit haben Leonhard Schumacher und Egon Flaig von sehr unterschiedlichen Zugängen aus in ihren Beiträgen zur Sklavenforschung auch vergleichende Perspektiven eingebaut. „In bezug auf die amerikanische 'Negersklaverei'" drängen sich dem Mainzer Althistoriker „Parallelen zur antiken Sklaverei" geradezu auf. Andererseits wird einschränkend auch auf „erhebliche Unterschiede" beim Einsatz der importierten Sklaven als Produktionsmittel und bei den Assimilierungsschwierigkeiten der im „Atlantischen Dreieckshandel" nach Amerika gelangenden Neger hingewiesen.[44] Fragen zur Theorie des Vergleichens werden dabei nicht erörtert.[45] Das geschieht in der Untersuchung *Den Untermenschen konstruieren* (2001) von Flaig, die wie Schumachers *Sklaverei in der Antike* im gleichen Jahr erscheint. Flaig bietet ein Plädoyer für den „interkulturellen Vergleich" und begründet ihn mit dem Fehlen der Selbstzeugnisse der antiken Sklaven. Für den Autor bietet die vergleichende Betrachtung einen „durchaus akzeptablen methodischen Ansatz". Flaig rät den Altertumswissenschaftlern zum „systematischen und kontrollierten Vergleich [...] mit der brasilianischen, der karibischen und der südstaatlichen Sklaverei sowie mit den nachträglich niedergeschriebenen Erfahrungen im Gulag und in den NS-Konzentrationslagern".[46] Und nach der Betonung der Wichtigkeit „des interkulturellen Vergleichs als einer legitimen Methode" in der Sklavenforschung fährt er in einer etwas soziologisch abgehobenen Sprache fort:

> „Doch nur mit vergleichenden Verfahren ist es möglich, ein konzeptualisierbares Inventar von sozialen Differenzen menschlicher Unfreiheit zu erstellen,

42 Mörner 2002, 59–67; Zitat: 67.

43 Pleket 1982, 1–30.

44 Schumacher 2001, 12 und 14. Ähnlich Deißler 2000, 445: „Die Erkenntnis, dass antike Sklaverei und moderne Formen der Unfreiheit auf unterschiedlichen Voraussetzungen beruhen, dringt erst mit der Zeit durch."

45 Auf Methodenfragen und „strukturelle Überlegungen zum Phänomen der Unfreiheit" in der antiken und modernen Sklaverei geht Schumacher 1998, 15–26 näher ein.

46 Flaig 2001, 31f. Der Autor zitiert auch Th. Mommsen, der „gewiß unter dem Eindruck abolitionistischer Untersuchungen" schreibt: „Es ist leicht möglich, dass mit denen der römischen Sklavenschaft verglichen die Summe aller Negerleiden ein Tropfen ist".

> welches einer theoretisch informierten Historischen Anthropologie ermöglicht, schärfere Fragen zu stellen, ohne dass ihr Blick sich in einer apologetischen oder in einer moralisierenden Perspektive verfängt.“[47]

Schließlich seien nochmals Paul Cartledge und sein Verhältnis zur Komparatistik hier zitiert. Der Autor zahlreicher Sklavenstudien und Mitherausgeber der *The Cambridge World History of Slavery* (2011) definiert gleichsam unter dem Motto *Comparison, like charity, should begin at home*[48] – gemeint ist für den Althistoriker die griechisch-römische Welt – sein Arbeitsziel wie folgt: „to establish a model of ancient slavery and then employing comparative details to put flesh on the model's skeleton“.[49] Cartledge, der vermeiden möchte, dass die komparative Geschichte den Amateuren überlassen wird, bekennt sich darin geradezu kompromisslos zur Adaption einer vergleichenden Vorgangsweise. Er ist überzeugt davon, dass trotz aller Grenzen und Gefahren, die die vergleichende Methode in sich birgt ("it is fiendishly difficult of achievement"), die Vorteile überwiegen. Auf andere Weise würde es dem Historiker nicht gelingen, "to move beyond descriptive antiquarianism". Das gelte vor allem dann, wenn man konsequent auf das methodische Prinzip achten wollte, dass der Vergleich die fehlenden Primärquellen nicht ersetzen kann, „but rather can only serve to provoke hypotheses to explain the evidence we have“. Der Mangel an antiken Quellen macht es unmöglich, Statistiken über den antiken Sklavenhandel aufzustellen. Ausdrücklich bezeichnet Paul Cartledge den heutigen Kenntnisstand über den Sklavenhandel im griechisch-römischen Altertum als „vage und hypothetisch“.[50] Um dieses ungenaue und verschwommene Bild ein wenig schärfer konturieren zu können, erscheint es hilfreich, über den Zaun der Alten Geschichte hinauszublicken. Der Umstand, dass offizielle Dokumente über Handelsaktivitäten und Nachrichten über die Lage am Arbeitsmarkt im Altertum weitgehend fehlen oder nur in Fragmenten vorliegen, sollte davon nicht abhalten.[51]

Im Jahr 2001 veröffentlichte Robert Harms, Historiker an der Yale University, einen voluminösen Band über die Geschichte eines Sklavenschiffes, *The Diligent: A Voyage through the Worlds of the Slave Trade* (2002), das in den Jahren 1731/1732 von Guinea nach Amerika unterwegs war. In dem preisgekrönten Buch berichtet Harms vor allem auf der Grundlage des 1984 entdeckten Bordbuches eines Seemanns über den Transport von 256 Sklaven, die im Unterdeck „wie Kornsäcke zusammengepfercht“[52] wurden. Der Leser bekommt eine detailreiche Schilderung über die gesamten Aktivitäten dieses kommerziellen Unternehmens vorgesetzt. Er wird informiert über die Herkunft der anonymen Westafrikaner, die Abwicklung

47 Flaig 2001, 33.
48 Cartledge 1985, 21.
49 Cartledge 1985, 20f.
50 Cartledge 2001, 621.
51 Garnsey – Saller 1989, 65.
52 Rezension von R. Habermas in der „Frankfurter Rundschau“ (24.03.2004).

des Kaufgeschäfts, über Versorgung, Krankheit und Tod auf der Überfahrt, über die Bewachung der Sklaven und schließlich ihren Einsatz auf den amerikanischen Plantagen. Hier werden Themen und Probleme behandelt, die auch für den antiken Sklavenhandel und -transport relevant sein können oder sind.

IV. Die „Ware" Mensch auf antiken Märkten nebst einem Seitenblick auf die neuzeitliche Entwicklung

Freie und Sklaven kommen als „Ware" (*merx*) auf die antiken Sklavenmärkte.[53] Woher kommt die „Ware"? In der Regel gelten als Lieferanten professionelle Sklavenhändler (*andrapodokapeloi, somatemporoi, andrapodistai, mercatores venalicii* bzw. *mangones*). Sie agieren teilweise im Zwischenhandel, indem sie von Piraten, die mit Lösegelderpressungen arbeiten, und von siegreichen Feldherren beliefert werden.[54] Ohne auf die schwer zu beantwortenden logistischen Fragen des Transports hier näher einzugehen, erweist sich m. E. als unbestreitbar, dass die „Ware" in die großen Handelszentren gelangt, sofern die Sklaven am Leben bleiben. Hier werden sie in der Regel auf einem Verkaufsstein (*prater lithos, trapeza* oder *katastasis; catasta*) ausgestellt; zuweilen hat man ihre Beine mit billiger Krei-

53 Große Märkte etablierten sich an der Seite von Delos, wo angeblich bis zu 10.000 Sklaven täglich verkauft wurden (Strabon 14.5.2): Athen, Chios, Ephesos, Kythera, Thyatira in Kleinasien, Syrakus, Rom, Brundisium, Capua, Puteoli und Aquileia. In der Spätantike und in byzantinischer Zeit kommen weitere Zentren hinzu: die Hafenstädte in Kilikien, auf Kreta und der Krim, Massilia und vor allem Byzanz/Konstantinopel. – Auch im Altertum werden bekanntlich nicht nur Sklaven verkauft: Freie Männer und Frauen, Kinder; Brautraub und Kinderaussetzung sind Themen, von denen schon die Mythen erzählen; *plagium*, das Verbrechen, Freie und Sklaven zu rauben; d.h. ungenaue Umschreibung mit den Begriffen „Menschenraub" und „Menschenhandel"; in der Spätantike Kolonen, Selbstverkauf. – Dass Menschen, insbesondere Sklaven und Sklavinnen, als „Ware", als Handelsgut verstanden werden, geht beispielsweise aus Polybios 4.38 hervor. Er beschreibt Byzantion als idealen Handelsplatz zum Pontosgebiet für die von „Großkaufleuten" (*emporoi*) besorgten Güter, die im alltäglichen Leben nützlich sind; Polybios nennt dabei konkret neben Honig, Wachs und Salzfisch „das Vieh und die große Menge in die Sklaverei geführter Menschen, beides bekanntlich in unerschöpflicher Fülle und von bester Qualität" (Üs. H. Drexler). Strabon 5.1.8: Die italischen Kaufleute bekommen im *emporion* Aquileia für Erzeugnisse des Meeres, Wein und Öl im Tauschwege Sklaven, Schlachtvieh und Häute (*andrapoda kai boskemata kai dermata*); vgl. auch 11.2.3. Finley 1960, 74–75. – Bei Xenenophon, *anabasis* 6.6.38 heißt es, dass die Soldaten bei einem Streifzug viele Sklaven und Schafe (*polla kai andrapoda kai probata*) erbeuteten und diese dann verkauften. Dazu auch Braund 2011, 215, 218 und 220: "Slaves were a routine part of the booty of warfare. They are often listed with lifestock and other goods seized from the enemy." – Der „Warencharakter" von Sklaven findet sich auf zwei Papyri, die außer „Säcken mit Safran im Wert von 10 Minen" oder Weihrauch, Rosenparfüm und Panzer auch Sklaven in den Warenlisten anführen; vgl. Scholl 1990 Nr.44 (S.170) und Nr.223 (S.899). – Zum Sklaven als Objekt des Rechtsverkehrs s. Rainer und Herrmann-Otto 1999, 45–48. – Zum römischen Marktgeschehen vgl. Gellius, *Noctes Atticae* 4.2.1.

54 Zur moralischen Einschätzung der Sklavenhändler siehe Cartledge 2001, 620 und unten Anm. 86; zu dem bekannten Sklavenhändler Aulus Kapreilius Timotheus s. Finley 1986, 162–176; Fischer 2008. Vgl.auch Xenophon, *memorabilia* 1.2.62.

de bestrichen,[55] vermutlich um dem Käufer zu signalisieren, dass die „Ware“ per Schiff transportiert wurde, oder die „Ware“ wurde anders markiert.[56] Besondere Agenten, die Auktionäre (*praecones*), preisen ihre „Ware“ (*merx*) an; ein Werbeslogan ist überliefert: *Sardi venales* (Keith Bradley: *Sardinians for sale!*).[57]

Sowohl bei Griechen als auch bei Römern scheint es beim Verkauf von Sklaven an neue Eigentümer erhebliche Probleme gegeben zu haben. Man hat deshalb Vorsorge dafür getroffen, dass ein betrügerisches Kaufgeschäft auf dem Markt mit Sklaven (und Tieren) rückgängig gemacht werden konnte und der bezahlte Preis zu refundieren war, wenn sich bei der „Ware“ verheimlichte Mängel herausstellten. Auf das bei A. Gellius in den *Noctes Atticae* (4.2.1) überlieferte Edikt, das sich mit der *actio rehibitoria* beim Sklavenkauf befasst, wurde schon hingewiesen. Schon Platon hatte in den *Nomoi* die Frage des Rückgängigmachens von Geschäften angesprochen und zur Kaufsklaverei gemeint:[58]

> „Wer bei einem Verkauf einen Preis von mindestens fünfzig Drachmen erhalten hat, ist verpflichtet, wenigstens zehn Tage in der Stadt zu bleiben; der Käufer aber soll die Wohnung des Verkäufers kennen wegen der Beschwerden, die in solchen Fällen vorzukommen pflegen, und wegen der gesetzlich zulässigen Rückgabe (*kata nomous anagoge*). Für die gesetzmäßige Rückgabe oder deren Verweigerung gelten folgende Bedingungen. Wenn jemand einen Sklaven verkauft, der an Schwindsucht oder Steinbeschwerden oder Harnzwang oder an der so genannten heiligen Krankheit leidet oder auch an sonst einer langwierigen und schwer heilbaren Krankheit des Leibes oder des Geistes, die für die meisten nicht zu erkennen ist, so soll, falls der Verkauf an einen Arzt oder einen Gymnastiklehrer erfolgte, dieser kein Recht auf Rückgabe an den Verkäufer haben, ebenso wenig wenn ein Verkäufer einem Käufer vorher die Wahrheit gesagt hat. Falls aber ein Sachverständiger einem Nichtfachmann einen solchen Sklaven verkauft, so soll der Käufer ihn binnen sechs Monaten zurückgeben außer bei der heiligen Krankheit; bei dieser soll die Rückgabe innerhalb eines Jahres gestattet sein. Entschieden werden soll die Sache vor drei Ärzten, die beide Parteien durch gemeinsamen Vorschlag wählen; wer aber in diesem Verfahren schuldig gesprochen wird, soll das Doppelte des Kaufpreises bezahlen. Falls ihn aber ein Nichtfachmann einem anderen Nichtfachmann verkauft, so soll zwar eine Rückgabe in der vorgenannten Weise erfolgen, ebenso wie die ärztliche Entscheidung, doch soll der schuldig Befundene nur den einfachen Preis bezahlen.“

55 Plinius, *naturalis historia* 35.199f.

56 Thompson 2011,207: “moles or marks (*phakoi*)”.

57 Festus, *de verborum significatu* 472 S. 428f.: *Sardi venales (alius alio neq)uior*; vgl. auch Cicero, *ad familiares* 7.24.7: *Sardos venalis alium alio nequiorem* (Die Sarden sind käuflich, einer nichtsnutziger als der andre. Üs. M. Fuhrmann); Bradley 1994, 56; Welwei 2000, 12; hier wird auch auf den Verkauf von Kriegsgefangenen als Sklaven mit der Formel *sub corona vendere* verwiesen.

58 Platon, *Nomoi* 915d–916c (Üs. K. Schöpsdau – H. Müller). Dazu die Interpretation von Jakab 1997, 59–70.

In Rom hat ein Erlass aus dem Jahr 214 n. Chr., der offensichtlich auf das schon genannte Ädilenedikt zu beziehen ist, versucht, die betrügerischen Methoden beim Geschäft mit den Sklaven zu unterbinden:[59]

> „Wenn jemand nicht aufrichtig, sondern in der Absicht des Betrugs (*consilio fraudis*) dir ohne dein Wissen einen entflohenen oder sonst mit irgendeinem Mangel behafteten Sklaven verkauft hat und derselbe wieder geflohen und abwesend ist, so wird der zuständige Richter nach längst angenommenen Rechtsgrundsätzen den Verkäufer des Sklaven nicht nur auf den Kaufpreis zu belangen gestatten, sondern auch die Vergütung des Schadens anordnen, den du durch ihn erlitten hast."

Ein Sklave durfte auch nicht mit der Auflage verkauft werden, dass er freizulassen sei. Dennoch scheint dies vorgekommen zu sein, wie ein Dekret des Jahres 240 n. Chr. *expressis verbis* betont:[60]

> „Sklaven, die unter der Bedingung verkauft worden sind, dass sie nicht freigelassen werden sollten, können auch durch Freilassung die Freiheit nicht erlangen. Denn die auf der Person haftende Bedingung kann durch den, der dieselbe beim Kauf eingegangen ist, nicht geändert werden [...]."

Schriftlich abgefasste Kaufverträge, die *bona fide* abgeschlossen wurden, informieren über Manipulationen (*dolus malus, consilium fraudis*) und Rückgaberecht (*causa redhibitionis*) und andere unerfreuliche Begleiterscheinungen beim Geschäft mit den Menschen.[61] In schematisierter Form sei hier ein Beispiel angeführt, das die schon erwähnten Sicherheitsklauseln wiedergibt:[62] Kauf einer etwa 12-jährigen phrygischen Sklavin (151 n. Chr.): Datums- und Ortsangabe. Der Käufer X aus Alexandria kauft auf dem Markt von Y ein Mädchen für 350 Silberdenare. Dabei bestätigt Z in eigener Verantwortlichkeit, dass das Mädchen gesund ist, weder Neigung zum Herumtreiben noch zum Entlaufen hat und frei von Epilepsie ist. Sollte jemand Ansprüche auf die Sklavin oder einen Teil von ihr erheben, dann hat Y den doppelten Kaufpreis einschließlich der Vorladung des Klägers zu bezahlen. Mehrere Unterschriften bestätigen den Kaufvertrag.

---

59 *Codex Iustinianus* 4.58.1 (Üs. G. Härtel). Dazu Jakab 1997, 218f.

60 Über Sklaven, die unter der Bedingung verkauft wurden, dass sie freigelassen werden: *Codex Iustinianus* 4.57.5 pr. (Üs. G. Härtel).

61 Zu den Kaufverträgen siehe Söllner 2000, 1–24 und ders. 2001, 83–96. Dazu kommen noch die so genannten Siebenbürgischen Kaufurkunden (2. Jahrhundert n. Chr.) und Papyrusverträge (z.B. POxy. 95, 129 n. Chr.). Eine kommentierte Auswahl dazu bietet Thierfelder 1963, 121–128. Vgl. Schumacher 2001, 62–64, wo auch ein Kaufvertrag über 625 Denare zwischen einem Sklavenhändler aus Milet und einem Flottensoldaten über eine *puella veterana* wiedergegeben und kommentiert wird.

62 *Berliner Griechische Urkunden* III 887; übersetzt von Thierfelder 1963, 126. – Zum Kauf der Sklaven in literarischen Texten und Urkunden siehe zusammenfassend Jakab 1997, 195f. und 219–221.

Kai Ruffing und Hans-Joachim Drexhage haben sich in mehreren Untersuchungen, so auch im Jahr 2008, gründlich mit den Sklavenpreisen befasst und dabei die Preisentwicklung von der klassischen Periode Griechenlands bis zur Spätantike verfolgt. Als Quellengrundlage dienen dabei Papyri, Inschriften, literarische Notizen und Rechtstexte.[63] Unter Außerachtlassung von Angaben über spektakuläre Höchstpreise wird gezeigt, dass Sklaven im klassischen Griechenland durchschnittlich 300–600 Drachmen, als Bergwerkssklaven von Laureion 125–200 Drachmen kosten;[64] im Hellenismus (im ptolemäischen Ägypten) zahlt man 100–300 Drachmen.[65] In der römischen Republik kostet ein ungelernter Sklave etwa 1.000 HS und in der Kaiserzeit zwischen 820–4.000 HS.[66] Die von A.H.M. Jones vertretene These,[67] die Sklavenpreise hätten sich zwischen dem 4. Jahrhundert v. Chr. und dem 2. Jahrhundert n. Chr. um das Achtfache erhöht, mit der Begründung, dass es mit dem Ende der römischen Expansionskriege zum Versiegen des Sklavennachschubs gekommen sei, wird von M.I. Finley als „pseudo-statistische Erörterung“ bezeichnet.[68] Fehlende Quellenangaben für eine statistische Auswertung, große Preisschwankungen und die Ablehnung des Arguments, dass ein kausaler Zusammenhang zwischen Preisanstieg und Nachschubproblemen existiere, werden gegen die Interpretation von Jones ins Treffen geführt. Dabei bedient sich Finley auch eines komparatistischen Arguments, wenn er auf die US-amerikanische Preisentwicklung rekurriert: „In den Vereinigten Staaten wiesen die Preise ganz allgemein von der Einführung der Sklaverei bis zu ihrem Ende eine stetig steigende Tendenz auf, wobei in den 1850er Jahren ein besonders auffallender Preissprung festzustellen ist.“[69]

Für eine realistische Einschätzung dieser Marktpreise in der antiken Ökonomie ist es gewiss hilfreich, dass die beiden Autoren die Durchschnittspreise in Relation zu den Tageslöhnen setzen.[70] Ausschlaggebend für die Preisgestaltung sind dabei neben dem wohl zeitlosen ökonomischen Prinzip von Angebot und Nach-

63 Ruffing – Drexhage 2008, 320–351. Zur Bedeutung des Sklavenhandels im klassischen Griechenland vgl. Klees 1998, 52–56.

64 Ruffing – Drexhage 2008, 337, 339.

65 Zu hellenistischen Sklavenpreisen vgl. Scholl 1990, Nr.37–52, Preistabelle 213 und Register 1108; zu Sklavenhändlern Thompson 2011, 206–208.

66 S. außer Ruffing – Drexhage 2008 auch Szaivert – Wolters 2005, 113–116. – Ausführlich nunmehr Scheidel 2011, 300–304.

67 Jones 1956, 191–194.

68 Finley 1981, 157.

69 Finley 1981, 157. Im Anschluss an diese Feststellung zitiert Finley zur Unterstützung seiner Kritik an der These von Jones noch Štaerman und Trofimova 1975, 27 sowie Štaerman 1969, 25f., 55f.: „Es ist keine Gewissheit darüber zu erlangen, ob die Sklaven sich zahlenmäßig verringert haben. Die Theorie, dass sie im Preis gestiegen sind, hat sich nicht bestätigt.“

70 Ruffing – Drexhage 2008, 337; 339; 347 für die klassische griechische Periode: 150–200 Tageslöhne; Hellenismus: 240–3.000; Republik: 333, Prinzipat: 200–2.800; Spätantike: 66–1.500. – Eine Tabelle mit Sklavenpreisen auf ptolemäischen Papyri bietet Scholl 1990, 213f.

frage[71] in erster Linie berufliche Fähigkeiten, Bildungsniveau, Charakter, Aussehen, Geschlecht, Alter, Herkunft/Ethnizität, wie die *titulus*-Angaben zeigen.[72] Nur teilweise evident (Geschlecht und Alter) wird dies im *edictum de pretiis rerum venalium* aus dem Jahr 301 (n. Chr.), das folgende Maximaltarife anordnet (hier liegt ein Schematismus zugrunde, der zehn Tarifkategorien nennt, die von Walter Scheidel zusammengefasst wurden):[73]

Alter	Sklaven	Sklavinnen
0 bis 8 Jahre	15.000 Denare	10.000 Denare
8 bis 16	20.000 Denare	20.000 Denare
16 bis 40	30.000 Denare	25.000 Denare
40 bis 60	25.000 Denare	20.000 Denare
über 60 Jahre	15.000 Denare	10.000 Denare

Aus dem Jahr 530 n. Chr. stammt ein kaiserliches Dekret,[74] das ein klares Preisschema vorgibt: Sklaven und Sklavinnen ohne besondere Ausbildung kosten 20 *solidi*, sind sie jünger als 10 Jahre die Hälfte; für qualifizierte, gebildete Sklaven sind 30 bis 70 *solidi* zu bezahlen, kastrierte Knaben und ungelernte Eunuchen kosten 30 bzw. 50 *solidi*.

Gibt es bei den Sklavenpreisen einen Unterschied zwischen der Antike und

71 Dazu Volkmann 1990, 117: „Daß von den Massenversklavungen die sonst für Sklaven üblichen Preise beeinflußt wurden, versteht sich zwar von selbst, wird aber in den Quellen verhältnismäßig wenig betont." Der Autor führt einige deutliche Belege für die Korrelation von Angebot und Nachfrage an; so Plutarchs Anspielung (Aem. 29.5f.) auf die „Schleuderpreise" bei der Versklavung von 150.000 Molossern nach der Schlacht von Pydna; Orosius 7.37.16 (nach dem römischen Sieg über Radagais): „Es soll aber eine so gewaltige Menge gefangener Goten gegeben haben, dass nach der Art billigsten Viehs für einzelne Goldstücke allenthalben Herden von Menschen zum Verkauf angeboten wurden" (Üs. A. Lippold); vgl. auch Demandt 1989, 290.

72 Zu den Qualitäten der Sklaven und Sklavinnen Braund 2011, 123–129. – Zu anderen Preisangaben kommt Brockmeyer 1979, 159, 181, 193 und 321f. Republikanische Periode: etwa 200–500, Prinzipatszeit: 200 bis 625 Denare. Verwiesen wird auch auf die Talmud-Angaben über jüdische und nicht-jüdische Sklaven, und zwar zahlte man für Juden 1–10, für Nicht-Juden bis zu 100 Minen, d.h. etwa 100–1.000 respektive bis zu 10.000 Denare (vorausgesetzt Drachme und Denare lassen sich hier gleichsetzen). Vgl. auch die Preise bei Fischer 2011. – Zu den Kriterien für Sklavenpreise auf Papyrus vgl. die Tabelle bei Scholl 1990, Band 1, 213; zu den Kirchenvätern vgl. Milewski 2000, 56f.; Preisangaben auf Papyrus bei Ruffing 2002, 34; Kudlien 1986, 247–252; inflationäre Preise siehe Demandt 1989, 290f. und Scheidel 1996, 67.

73 Scheidel 1996, 67; Ruffing – Drexhage 2008, 344–346; Fischer HAS. Vgl. auch Demandt 1989, 291.

74 *Codex Iustinianus* 7.7.1.5: *Ne autem quantitas servilis pretii sit incerta, sed manifesta, sancimus servi pretium sive ancillae, si nulla arte sunt imbuti, viginti solidis taxari, his videlicet, qui usque ad decimum annum suae venerunt aetatis, in decem tantummodo solidis ponendis: sin autem aliqua arte praediti sunt exceptis notariis et medicis, usque ad triginta solidos pretium eorum redigi sive in masculis sive in feminis.* Vgl. dazu Demandt 1989, 291. Zur spätantiken Sklaverei jetzt Grey 2011, 482–509; zu den Preisangaben 489, 492 und 494.

späteren Geschichtsepochen einschließlich der Gegenwart? Generelle Aussagen über die Preisgestaltung beim Sklavenkauf wie jene von Kevin Bales lassen sich wohl kaum verifizieren. Der Autor, Mitglied des Komitees von *Anti-Slavery International*, spricht in seiner Analyse der „Hauptunterschiede zwischen der alten und der neuen Sklaverei“ von einem gegenwärtig „äußerst geringen Kaufpreis“ und einem „sehr hohen Profit“ im Gegensatz zu früheren Zeiten, in denen ein „hoher Kaufpreis“ mit „niedrigem Profit“ korreliert habe.[75] Diese Annahme ist m. E. nicht verifizierbar. Die überlieferten neuzeitlichen Sklavenpreise liefern dennoch für den Vergleich mit der Antike und die Bewertung der „Ware Mensch“ wertvolle Einsichten. Orlando Patterson berichtet über Preisschwankungen im transatlantischen Sklavenhandel je nach Zeit zwischen 3 und 4 Pfund Sterling (in der 2. Hälfte des 17. Jahrhunderts) bis zu 18 Pfund (um 1740)[76], und wenn in Westafrika ein einzelner Sklave zwischen 3 und 6 Kühe wert war (was um 1890 etwa 3 Pfund Sterling entsprochen haben soll)[77], so erinnert das an antike Verhältnisse. In der *Ilias* 23.705 wird eine Frau als zweiter Wettkampfpreis im Wert von vier Rindern erwähnt, und Plutarch (*Lukullus* 14) berichtet vom beutereichen Feldzug, bei dem ein Rind nicht mehr als eine Drachme, ein Sklave nur vier Drachmen wert war. Sein argumentativer Kommentar zu diesem Preisverfall:[78] „Denn man konnte nichts an irgend jemand verkaufen, weil alle mehr als genug hatten“ (Üs. K. Ziegler). Bales vergleicht den Kauf eines Sklaven in unseren Tagen mit dem eines „einfachen Fahrrades oder eines billigen Computers“.[79] In Indien kostet ein Landarbeiter heute zwischen 500 und 1.000 Rupien (ungefähr $ 12 bis 23), ein 12- bis 15-jähriges Mädchen für den Bordellbetrieb $ 800 bis 2.000.[80] In Mauretanien erhält man für einen „jungen männlichen Sklaven [...] vielleicht $ 500 bis 700, für eine reife Sklavin zwischen $ 700 und 1.000, für eine junge sogar noch mehr“.[81] Nicht uninteressant ist es zu erfahren, dass der Befehlshaber der US-amerikanischen Armee beim Vormarsch mit Hunderten von LKWs in Nordafrika während des Zweiten Weltkriegs mit den einheimischen arabisch-berberisch-islamischen Bürgermeistern bei Schadenersatzverhandlungen folgende Tarife vereinbarte: Die Amerikaner zahlten für den von ihnen verursachten Tod eines Kamels 25.000 Francs ($ 500), eines Knaben 15.000 Francs, eines Esels 10.000 Francs und eines Mädchens 500 Francs.[82] Dass der heutige Transfermarkt im Spitzensport, beispielsweise der Kauf junger Fußballtalente in Brasilien oder Afrika, ihre Ausbildung und der Weiter-

75 Bales 1999/2001, 26 und 127. – Zu neuzeitlichen Sklavenpreisen Priesching – Steinke 2007, 41–55; Exenberger 2007, 66–77; Schreiber 2007, 83–107.

76 Patterson 1982, 163f.

77 Patterson 1982, 168.

78 Vgl. Volkmann 1990, 188. Erinnert sei hier auch an den Beitrag von Bellen 2001, 3–29, wo im Anschluss an die *Odyssee* 17.322f. gezeigt wird, dass mit der Versklavung eines Menschen dieser die Hälfte seines Wertes verliert.

79 Bales 1999/2001, 25; vgl. dazu auch Heinz 2005, 300.

80 Bales 1999/2001, 27, 30, 60.

81 Bales 1999/2001, 117.

82 Atkinson 2003, 168 (freundlicher Hinweis von E. Kastrun, Graz).

verkauf (in Millionenbeträgen) an Großclubs, Assoziationen zur Sklaverei auslöst, ist verständlich und wird daher von den Medien auch immer wieder zur Diskussion gestellt.[83] Und wenn ein englischer Fußballverein für einen Portugiesen, der von einem spanischen Club um 94 Millionen Euro gekauft wurde, eine Ablösesumme von 180 Millionen zu zahlen bereit ist und die Spanier dafür aber eine Milliarde Euro fordern, so mag das hier als ein zweifellos extremes Beispiel aus dieser Geschäftswelt des Menschenhandels erwähnt werden.[84]

Die offenbar großen Gewinnspannen stimulierten die Sklavenhändler zu allerlei Manipulationen, die zu moralischer Kritik, rechtlichen Sanktionen und zum Teil auch zur sozialen Stigmatisierung dieser Menschenverkäufer führten. Seneca Minor findet dafür deutliche Worte. Er vergleicht sie mit Rosstäuschern:

> „Willst du ein Pferd kaufen, lässt du die Decke abnehmen, du nimmst die Kleidung ab zum Verkaufe stehender Sklaven, damit keine körperlichen Fehler verborgen bleiben: einen Menschen schätzt du in seiner Umhüllung ein? Die Sklavenhändler verbergen, was immer es ist, das missfallen könnte, durch irgendeinen Trick, daher ist den Käufern gerade der Zierrat verdächtig: wenn du ein Bein verbunden sähest oder einen Arm, entblößen ließest du ihn und dir den Körper selbst zeigen."[85]

In den Schriften vor allem des Augustinus und der kappadokischen Bischöfe mangelt es nicht an Verurteilungen der brutalen und inhumanen Kaufs- und Verkaufspraktiken von Sklavenhändlern, die auch „von mächtigen *patroni* unterstützt wurden", wie ein neueres Briefdokument des Augustinus kritisch anmerkt.[86]

83 Vgl. dazu Schumacher 2001, 11–16.

84 http://de.wikipedia.org/wiki/Cristiano_Ronaldo.

85 Seneca, *epistula* 80.9: *Equum empturus solvi iubes stratum, detrahis vestimenta venalibus ne qua vitia corporis lateant: hominem involutum aestimas? Mangones quidquid est quod displiceat, id aliquo lenocinio abscondunt, itaque ementibus ornamenta ipsa suspecta sunt: sive crus alligatum sive brachium aspiceres, nudari iuberes et ipsum tibi corpus ostendi.* – Von ganz anderen betrügerischen Methoden beim Sklavenkauf berichtet Diodor 5.26.3: Danach sollen in Gallien geldgierige italische Kaufleute in Kenntnis der gallischen Trunksucht billig Sklaven erworben haben. – Zur moralischen Bewertung des Sklavenhandels in Antike und Gegenwart vgl. Orth 2007 (sehepunkte) über die Genese der Menschenrechte und die Sklavenfrage. Allgemein zu Stigmatisierung, Infamie und *capitis deminutio* sowie zum „sozialen Tod" des Sklaven Herrmann-Otto 2002, 20–29; Demandt 1989, 290. – Ein extremes Beispiel aus England (1783) führt Delacampagne 2004, 214 an: In einer Gerichtsverhandlung musste der Kapitän eines Sklavenschiffes zugeben, dass er „132 kranke Sklaven über Bord hatte werfen lassen, angeblich um Trinkwasserreserven zu sparen, in Wirklichkeit aber, um die Versicherungssumme zu kassieren (auf die er keinen Anspruch gehabt hätte, wenn sie verdurstet oder an einer Krankheit gestorben wären)."

86 Klein 1988, 138 und ders. 2000, 208 und 210f.

Literatur

Atkinson R.. An Army at Dawn. The War in North Africa. An Abacus Book, New York 2003.

Atlantic Monthly. Der letzte nordamerikanische Sklavenhändler, in: Das Ausland [...] 42. Jg. Nr.6, 1869, 136–138.

Bales K., Die neue Sklaverei (1999), München 2001.

Bellen H. – Heinen H. (Hg.), Bibliographie zur antiken Sklaverei. Im Auftrag der Kommission für Geschichte des Altertums der Akademie der Wissenschaften und Literatur (Mainz). Neu bearbeitet von D. Schäfer und J. Deißler auf der Grundlage der von E. Herrmann in Verbindung mit N. Brockmeyer erstellten Ausgabe (Bochum 1983). Stuttgart 2003 (FAS Beiheft 4), 2 Teile. – s.v. Handel mit Sklaven (46 Titel). Literatur zur vergleichenden Sklavenforschung bzw. komparatistische Untersuchungen zur antiken Sklaverei ebd. 96–101, Nr. 1495–1564.

Bellen H., Vom halben zum ganzen Menschen. Der Übergang aus der Sklaverei in die Freiheit im Spiegel des antiken und frühchristlichen Freilassungsbrauchtums, in: Bellen H. – Heinen H.(Hg.), Fünfzig Jahre Forschungen zur antiken Sklaverei an der Mainzer Akademie 1950–2000. Wiesbaden 2001, 3–29 (FAS Bd. 35).

Below G. von, Die neue historische Methode, HZ 81, 1898, 193–273.

Binsfeld A., Menschenhandel – Frauenhandel, in: Heinen H. (Hg.) – Deißler J. (Redaktion), Menschenraub, Menschenhandel und Sklaverei in antiker und moderner Perspektive. Ergebnisse des Mitarbeitertreffens des Akademievorhabens Forschungen zur antiken Sklaverei (Mainz, 10. Oktober 2006), Stuttgart 2008, 85–98 (FAS Bd.37).

Bitterli U., Die „Wilden“ und die „Zivilisierten“. Grundzüge einer Geistes- und Kulturgeschichte der europäisch-überseeischen Begegnung, München 2. Auflage 1991.

Blair W., An Inquiry into the State of Slavery amongst the Romans from the Earliest Period till the Establishment of the Lombards in Italy, Edinburgh 1833.

Blake W.O., The History of Slavery and the Slave Trade, Ancient and Modern. The Forms of Slavery that Prevailed in Ancient Nations, Particularly in Greece and Rome. The African Slave Trade and the Political History of Slavery in the United States, Columbus/Ohio 1857 [ND 1969 und 1971].

Bloch M., Pour une histoire comparée des sociétés européennes (1927) / Für eine vergleichende Geschichtsbetrachtung der europäischen Gesellschaften, in: Middell M. – Sammler S. (Hg.), Alles Gewordene hat Geschichte. Die Schule der Annales in ihren Texten 1929–1992. Mit einem Essay von P. Schöttler, Leipzig 1994, 121–167.

Bradley K., Social Aspects of the Slave Trade in the Roman World, MBAH 5.1, 1986 49–58.

Bradley K., Slavery and Society at Rome, Cambridge 1994.

Bradley K., Slavery in the Roman Republic, in: Cartledge P. – Bradley K. (Hg.), The Cambridge World History of Slavery. Vol. 1. The Ancient Mediterranean World. Cambridge 2011, 241–264.

Bradley K. s. auch Cartledge.

Braund D., The Slave Supply in Classical Greece, in: Cartledge P. – Bradley K. (Hg.), The Cambridge World History of Slavery. Vol. 1. The Ancient Mediterranean World, Cambridge 2011, 112–133.

Brockmeyer N., Antike Sklaverei, Darmstadt 1979.

Cacho L., Sklaverei. Im Inneren des Milliardengeschäfts Menschenhandel (2010), Frankfurt am Main 2011.

Cartledge P.A., Sklavenhandel, in: Der Neue Pauly 11 (2001), 619–621.

Cartledge P.A. – Bradley K. (Hg.), The Cambridge World History of Slavery. Vol. 1.The Ancient Mediterranean World, Cambridge 2011.

Christ K., Hellas. Griechische Geschichte und deutsche Geschichtswissenschaft, München 1999.

Davis D.B., Slavery and Human Progress, New York – Oxford 1984.

Deißler J., Antike Sklaverei und Deutsche Aufklärung im Spiegel von Johann Friedrich Reitemeiers „Geschichte und Zustand der Sklaverey und Leibeigenschaft in Griechenland" (1789), Wiesbaden 2000 (FAS Bd.33).

Deißler J., Sklaverei, in: Der Neue Pauly 15/3 (2003), 47–59.

Deißler J., Realitätsgetreues Abbild oder künstlerische Interpretation eines römischen Sklavenverkaufs? Zu Jean-Léon Gérômes Vente d'esclaves à Rome, in: Heinen H. (Hg.) – Deißler J. (Redaktion), Menschenraub, Menschenhandel und Sklaverei in antiker und moderner Perspektive. Ergebnisse des Mitarbeitertreffens des Akademievorhabens Forschungen zur antiken Sklaverei (Mainz, 10. Oktober 2006), Stuttgart 2008, 183–194 (FAS Bd.37).

Delacampagne Chr., Die Geschichte der Sklaverei, Düsseldorf – Zürich 2004.

Delgado M., Las Casas vor Karl V. oder Prophetie und Politik in der Konquistadorenzeit, in: Archiv für Kulturgeschichte 84.2, 2002, 313–346.

Delgado M., Las Casas, in: Heinen H. (Hg.), Handwörterbuch der antiken Sklaverei. CD-ROM. Lieferungen I–IV, Stuttgart 2011.

Delgado M., Sepúlveda, in: Heinen H. (Hg.), Handwörterbuch der antiken Sklaverei. CD-ROM. Lieferungen I–IV, Stuttgart 2011.

Demandt A., Die Spätantike. Römische Geschichte von Diocletian bis Justinian. 284–565 n. Chr., München 1989 (Handbuch der Altertumswissenschaft III 6).

Exenberger A. – Nussbaumer J. (Hg.), Von Menschenhandel und Menschenpreisen. Wert und Bewertung von Menschen im Spiegel der Zeit, Innsbruck 2007.

Exenberger A., Der lange Schatten der Globalisierung: Der Kostenfaktor Mensch im weltweiten Warenkreiskauf, in: Exenberger A. – Nussbaumer J. (Hg.), Von Menschenhandel und Menschenpreisen. Wert und Bewertung von Menschen im Spiegel der Zeit, Innsbruck 2007, 57–81.

Finley M.I., The Black Sea and Danubian Regions and the Slave Trade in Antiquity, in: Comité international des sciences historiques. XIe congrès international des sciences historiques (Stockholm 21–28 août 1960). Résumés des Communications, Göteborg – Stockholm – Uppsala 1960, 74–75.

Finley M.I., Aulus Kapreilius Timotheus, Slave Trader, in: ders., Aspects of Antiquity. Discoveries and Controversies, London 1968, 2. Auflage 1986, 162–176.

Finley M.I., Die Sklaverei in der Antike. Geschichte und Probleme (engl. 1980), München 1981.

Fischer J., Sklavenhandel, in: Heinen H. (Hg.), Handwörterbuch der antiken Sklaverei. CD-ROM. Lieferungen I–IV, Stuttgart 2011.

Flaig E., Den Untermenschen konstruieren. Wie die griechische Klassik den Sklaven von Natur erfand, in: von den Hoff R. – Schmidt S. (Hg.), Konstruktionen von Wirklichkeit. Bilder im Griechenland des 5. und 4. Jahrhunderts v. Chr, Stuttgart 2001, 27–49.

Flaig E., Weltgeschichte der Sklaverei, München 2009.

Garnsey P. – Saller R., Das römische Kaiserreich. Wirtschaft, Gesellschaft, Kultur (engl.1987), Reinbek bei Hamburg 1989.

Garrido-Hory M. (Hg.), Routes et marchés d'esclaves. 26e colloque du GIREA. Besançon, 27–29 septembre 2001, Paris 2002.

Grey C., Slavery in the Late Roman World, in: Cartledge P. – Bradley K. (Hg.), The Cambridge World History of Slavery. Vol. 1. The Ancient Mediterranean World, Cambridge 2011, 482–509.

Haedrich M., Formen von Sklaverei, Leibeigenschaft, Zwangsarbeit und Menschenhandel und der internationale Menschenrechtsschutz, in: Herrmann-Otto E. (Hg.), Unfreie Arbeits- und Lebensverhältnisse von der Antike bis in die Gegenwart. Eine Einführung, Hildesheim – Zürich – New York 2005, 281–297 (Sklaverei. Knechtschaft. Zwangsarbeit. Untersuchungen zur Sozial-, Rechts- und Kulturgeschichte. Bd.1).

Harms R., The Diligent: A Voyage through the Worlds of the Slave Trade, New York 2002.

Harris W.V., Towards a Study of the Roman Slave Trade, in: D'Arms J.D. – Kopff E.C. (Hg.), The Seaborne Commerce of Ancient Rome: Studies in Archaeology and History, Rom 1980, 117–140 (Memoirs of the American Academy in Rome. Bd.36).

Heinen H., Rez. Patterson O., Slavery and Social Death. A Comparative Study, Cambridge Mass., London 1982, in: European Sociological Review 4.3, 1988, 263–268.

Heinen H., Sklaverei im nördlichen Schwarzmeerraum: Zum Stand der Forschung, in: Bellen H. – Heinen H. (Hg.), Fünfzig Jahre Forschungen zur antiken Sklaverei an der Mainzer Akademie 1950–2000. Miscellanea zum Jubiläum, Wiesbaden 2001, 487–503 (FAS Bd.35).

Heinen H. (Hg.), Handwörterbuch der antiken Sklaverei. CD-ROM. Lieferungen I–IV, Stuttgart 2011.

Heinen H., Einführung, in: Heinen H. (Hg.), Menschenraub, Menschenhandel und Sklaverei in antiker und moderner Perspektive. Vorträge beim Mitarbeitertreffen des Akademievorhabens Forschungen zur antiken Sklaverei (Mainz, 10. Oktober 2006), Stuttgart 2008, 1–7 (FAS Bd.37).

Heinz W.S., Von der Sklaverei zum Menschenhandel, in: Herrmann-Otto E. (Hg.), Unfreie Arbeits- und Lebensverhältnisse von der Antike bis in die Gegenwart. Eine

Einführung, Hildesheim - Zürich - New York 2005, 298–314 (Sklaverei. Knechtschaft. Zwangsarbeit. Untersuchungen zur Sozial-, Rechts- und Kulturgeschichte. Bd.1).

Herrmann-Otto E., Modes d'acquisition des esclaves dans l'empire romain. Aspects juridiques et socio-économiques, in: Garido-Hory M. (Hg.), Routes et marchés d'esclaves. 26e colloque du GIREA. Besançon, 27–29 septembre 2001, Paris 2002, 113–126.

Herrmann-Otto E., Einführung, in: Herrmann-Otto E. (Hg.), Unfreie Arbeits- und Lebensverhältnisse von der Antike bis in die Gegenwart. Eine Einführung, Hildesheim - Zürich - New York 2005, IX–XVII (Sklaverei. Knechtschaft. Zwangsarbeit. Untersuchungen zur Sozial-, Rechts- und Kulturgeschichte. Bd.1).

Herrmann-Otto E., Sklaverei und Freilassung in der griechisch-römischen Welt, Hildesheim 2009.

Hopkins K., Conquerors and Slaves: Sociological Studies in Roman History, Cambridge 1978, Bd.1.

Hopkins K., Economic Growth and Towns in Classical Antiquity, in: Abrams Ph. - Wrigley E.A. (Hg.), Towns in Society. Essays in Economic History and Historical Sociology, Cambridge 1978, 35–77.

Isaac B., The Invention of Racism in Classical Antiquity, Princeton 2004.

Jakab É., Praedicere und Cavere beim Marktkauf. Sachmängel im griechischen und römischen Recht, München 1997 (Münchener Beiträge zur Papyrusforschung und antiken Rechtsgeschichte. Heft 87).

Jones A.H.M., Slavery in the Ancient World, Economic History Review 9, 1956, 185–199.

Jugler J.F., ΑΝΔΡΑΠΟΔΟΚΑΠΗΛΕΙΟΝ sive de nundinatione servorum apud veteres liber singularis historico-iuridicus, ex quo lucem capere possunt auctorum loca complura, Leipzig 1741.

Klees H., Sklavenleben im klassischen Griechenland, Stuttgart 1998 (FAS Bd.30).

Klein R., Die Sklaverei in der Sicht der Bischöfe Ambrosius und Augustinus, Stuttgart 1988 (FAS Bd.20).

Klein R., Die Haltung der kappadokischen Bischöfe Basilius von Caesarea, Gregor von Nazianz und Gregor von Nyssa zur Sklaverei, Stuttgart 2000 (FAS Bd. 32).

Köpstein H., Zum byzantinischen Sklavenhandel, Wissenschaftliche Zeitschrift der Karl-Marx-Universität Leipzig. Gesellschafts- und Sprachwissenschaftliche Reihe 15. Jg. Heft 3, 1966, 487–493.

Kudlien F., Empticius servus. Bemerkungen zum antiken Sklavenmarkt, Historia 35, 1986, 240–56.

Lehmann W.C., Einleitung, in: John Millar: Vom Ursprung des Unterschieds in den Rangordnungen und Ständen der Gesellschaft. Übersetzt von Zirker H., mit einer Einleitung von Lehmann W.C., Frankfurt am Main 1967, 7–57.

Milewski I., Löhne und Preise bei den Kappadokischen Kirchenvätern und bei Johannes Chrysostomos, MBAH 19.1, 2000, 48–58.

Millar J., The Origin of the Distinction of Ranks or: An Inquiry into the Circumstances Which Give Rise to Influence and Authority in the Different Members of Society, London 1779.

Miller J.C., Slave Trade: An Overview, in: Finkelman P. – Miller J.C. (Hg.), MacMillan Encyclopedia of World Slavery. Bd.2, London – New York 1998, 827–830.

Momigliano A., Alte Geschichte und antiquarische Forschung (1955), in: A. Momigliano: Wege in die Alte Welt. Mit einer Einführung von Karl Christ, Berlin 1991, 79–107.

Mörner M., Comparing Slavery in History, in: Hernaes P. – Iversen T. (Hg.), Slavery across time and space. Studies in slavery in medieval Europe and Africa, Trondheim 2002, 59–67 (Trondheim Studies in History. No. 38).

Morrow N.V., The Problem of Slavery in the Polemic Literature of the American Enlightenment, Early American Literature 20, 1985/1986, 236–255.

Murdock G.P., Ethnographic Atlas: A Summary, Ethnology 6, 1967, 109–263.

Nippel W., Rez.: Scheidel, Debating Roman Demography (2001), The Classical Review 55.1, 2005, o.S.

Nippel W., Moses I. Finley (1912–1986), in: Raphael L. (Hg.), Klassiker der Geschichtswissenschaft. Bd.2. Von Fernand Braudel bis Natalie Z. Davis, München 2006, 63–76.

Nussbaumer J., Vorwort. Einleitende Anmerkungen zum vorliegenden Band, in: Exenberger A. – Nussbaumer J. (Hg.), Von Menschenhandel und Menschenpreisen. Wert und Bewertung von Menschen im Spiegel der Zeit, Innsbruck 2007, 9–14.

Orth W., Rez.: Girardet K.M. – Nortmann U. (Hg.), Menschenrechte und europäische Identität. Die antiken Grundlagen, Stuttgart 2005, in: sehepunkte 7 (2007).

Patterson O., Slavery, Annual Review of Sociology 3, 1977, 407–449.

Patterson O., Slavery and Social Death. A Comparative Study, Cambridge Mass. – London 1982.

Phillips W.D. Jr., Slavery from Roman Times to the Early Transatlantic Trade, Minnesota – Manchester 1985.

Pleket H.W., Slavernij in de Oudheid: ‘Voer’ voor oudhistorici en comparatisten, Tijdschrift voor Geschiedenis 95, 1982, 1–30.

Priesching N. – Steinke M., Menschen als Ware: Sklaverei in der Frühen Neuzeit im Mittelmeerraum, in: Exenberger A. – Nussbaumer J. (Hg.), Von Menschenhandel und Menschenpreisen. Wert und Bewertung von Menschen im Spiegel der Zeit, Innsbruck 2007, 41–55.

Prinzing G., Sklaverei (Byzanz), in: Der Neue Pauly 11 (2001), 630–632.

Rainer J.M. – Herrmann-Otto E., Corpus der römischen Rechtsquellen zur antiken Sklaverei. Prolegomena, Stuttgart 1999 (FAS Beiheft 3).

Ruffing K., Preise und Wertangaben aus Dura Europos und Umgebung, Laverna 13, 2002, 24–44.

Ruffing K. – Drexhage H.-J., Antike Sklavenpreise, in: Mauritsch P. – Petermandl W. – Rollinger R. – Chr. Ulf unter Mitarbeit von I. Huber (Hg.), Antike Lebenswelten.

Konstanz – Wandel – Wirkungsmacht. Wiesbaden 2008, 321–351 (Philippika. Marburger altertumskundliche Abhandlungen. Bd.25).

Scheidel W., Reflections in the Differential Valuation of Slaves in Diocletian's Price Edict and in the United States, MBAH 15.1, 1996, 67–79.

Scheidel W., Slave Trade: Ancient Mediterranean, in: Finkelmann P. – Miller J.C. (Hg.), MacMillan Encyclopedia of World Slavery, London – New York 1998, Bd.2, 830f.

Scheidel W., Slave Systems: Ancient and Modern. Abstracts, Discourses in Economic History 14.04., 2005, 1–14.

Scheidel W., The Roman Slave Supply, in: Cartledge P. – Bradley K. (Hg.), The Cambridge World History of Slavery. Vol. 1. The Ancient Mediterranean World, Cambridge 2011, 287–310.

Schmiedeberg A. von, Menschenhandel – ein Bericht aus der staatsanwaltlichen Praxis, in: Heinen H. (Hg.) – Deißler J. (Redaktion), Menschenraub, Menschenhandel und Sklaverei in antiker und moderner Perspektive. Ergebnisse des Mitarbeitertreffens des Akademievorhabens Forschungen zur antiken Sklaverei (Mainz, 10. Oktober 2006), Stuttgart 2008, 9–19 (FAS Bd.37).

Scholl R., Corpus der Ptolemäischen Sklaventexte, Stuttgart 1990, 3 Teile (FAS Beiheft 1).

Schreiber H., Der Wert des Menschen im Nationalsozialismus, in: Exenberger A. Nussbaumer J. (Hg.), Von Menschenhandel und Menschenpreisen. Wert und Bewertung von Menschen im Spiegel der Zeit, Innsbruck 2007, 83–107.

Schumacher L., Sklaverei in der Antike. Alltag und Schicksal der Unfreien, München 2001.

Štaerman E.M., Die Blütezeit der Sklavenwirtschaft in der römischen Republik, Wiesbaden 1969.

Štaerman E.M. – Trofimova M.K., La schiavitù nell'Italia imperiale. I–III secolo, Rom 1975.

Siegel B.J., Some Methodological Considerations for a Comparative Study of Slavery, American Anthropologist N.S. 47.3, 1945, 357–392.

Strasburger H., Zum antiken Gesellschaftsideal, Heidelberg 1976 (4. Abhandlung der Heidelberger Akademie der Wissenschaften, philos.-hist. Klasse).

Szaivert W. – Wolters R., Löhne, Preis, Werte. Quellen zur römischen Geldwirtschaft, Darmstadt 2005, 113–116.

Szidat J., Zum Sklavenhandel in der Spätantike (Aug. epist. 10), Historia 34, 1985, 360–371

Thompson D.J., Slavery in the Hellenistic World, in: Cartledge P. – Bradley K. (Hg.), The Cambridge World History of Slavery. Vol. 1. The Ancient Mediterranean World. Cambridge 2011, 194–213.

Volkmann H., Die Massenversklavungen der Einwohner eroberter Städte in der hellenistisch-römischen Zeit. Durchgesehene und erweiterte Auflage von G. Horsmann, Stuttgart 2. Auflage 1990 (FAS Bd.22).

Webster A., The Contribution of the Scottish Enlightenment to the Abandonment of the Institution of Slavery, The European Legacy 8–4, 2003, 481–489.

Weiler I., Die Beendigung des Sklavenstatus im Altertum. Ein Beitrag zur vergleichenden Sozialgeschichte, Stuttgart 2003 (FAS Bd.36).

Weiler I., Über Sklavenhandel und Sklavenpreise in der Antike, in: Exenberger A. – Nussbaumer J. (Hg.), Von Menschenhandel und Menschenpreisen. Wert und Bewertung von Menschen im Spiegel der Zeit, Innsbruck 2007, 15–39.

Weiler I., Moderner Menschenhandel und antiker Sklavenhandel. Eine vergleichende Betrachtung, in: Losemann V. unter Mitarbeit von Droß K. und Velte S. (Hg.), Alte Geschichte zwischen Wissenschaft und Politik. Gedenkschrift Karl Christ, Wiesbaden 2009, 241–267.

Welskopp, Th., Vergleichende Geschichte, Europäische Geschichte Online (EGO), hg. vom Institut für Europäische Geschichte (IEG), Mainz European History Online (EGO), published by the Institute of European History (IEG), Mainz 2010-12-03. URL: http://www.ieg-ego.eu/welskoppt.

Welwei K.-W., Sub corona vendere. Quellenkritische Studien zu Kriegsgefangenschaft und Sklaverei in Rom bis zum Ende des Hannibalkrieges unter Berücksichtigung des Nachlasses von G. Prachner, Stuttgart 2000 (FAS Bd.34).

Welwei K.-W.: Piraterie und Sklavenhandel in der frühen römischen Republik, in: Bellen H. – Heinen H. (Hg.), Fünfzig Jahre Forschungen zur antiken Sklaverei an der Mainzer Akademie 1950–2000. Miscellanea zum Jubiläum, Wiesbaden 2001, 73–81 (FAS Bd.35)

Welwei K.-W., Menschenraub und Deportation in frühen Kulturen, in: Heinen H. (Hg.), Menschenraub, Menschenhandel und Sklaverei in antiker und moderner Perspektive. Vorträge beim Mitarbeitertreffen des Akademievorhabens Forschungen zur antiken Sklaverei (Mainz, 10. Oktober 2006), Stuttgart 2008, 21–43 (FAS Bd.37).